UK income tax rates (England, Wales and Nor[thern Ireland])

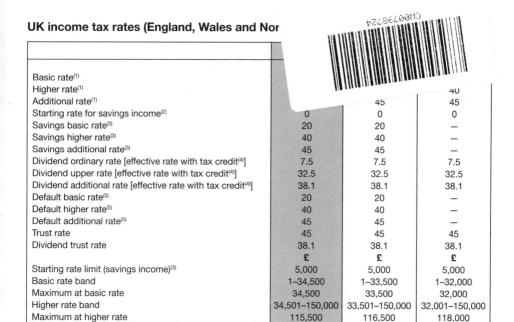

Basic rate(1)			
Higher rate(1)			
Additional rate(1)	45	45	40
Starting rate for savings income(2)	0	0	0
Savings basic rate(3)	20	20	—
Savings higher rate(3)	40	40	—
Savings additional rate(3)	45	45	—
Dividend ordinary rate [effective rate with tax credit(4)]	7.5	7.5	7.5
Dividend upper rate [effective rate with tax credit(4)]	32.5	32.5	32.5
Dividend additional rate [effective rate with tax credit(4)]	38.1	38.1	38.1
Default basic rate(5)	20	20	—
Default higher rate(5)	40	40	—
Default additional rate(5)	45	45	—
Trust rate	45	45	45
Dividend trust rate	38.1	38.1	38.1
	£	£	£
Starting rate limit (savings income)(3)	5,000	5,000	5,000
Basic rate band	1–34,500	1–33,500	1–32,000
Maximum at basic rate	34,500	33,500	32,000
Higher rate band	34,501–150,000	33,501–150,000	32,001–150,000
Maximum at higher rate	115,500	116,500	118,000

Notes

(1) From 2017–18, the main rates are separated into the main rates, the savings rates and the default rates with the main rates continuing to apply to non-savings, non-dividend income only (income to which the main rates apply includes income from employment, property or pensions not subject to the Scottish rate of income tax). Prior to 6 April 2017, main rates applied to all non-dividend income, including income from savings, employment, property or pensions.

(2) The starting rate is available for savings income only. If an individual's taxable non-savings income (i.e. after deduction of their personal allowance) exceeds the starting rate limit, then the starting rate is not available.

(3) From 6 April 2017, savings rates apply to savings income. Prior to 6 April 2017, basic rate, higher rate or additional rate applied.

(4) From April 2016, the dividend tax credit is abolished and replaced with a £5,000 tax-free dividend allowance.

(5) From 6 April 2017, the default rates apply to non-savings and non-dividend income of any taxpayer that is not subject to either the main rates or the Scottish rates of income tax.

Scottish income tax rates

	2017–18	2016–17
	%	%
Basic rate(2)	20	20(1)
Higher rate(2)	40	40(1)
Additional rate(2)	45	45(1)
	£	£
Basic rate band	1–31,500	1–32,000(3)
Maximum at basic rate	31,500	32,000(3)
Higher rate band	31,501–150,000	32,001–150,000(3)
Maximum at higher rate	118,500	118,000(3)

Notes

(1) For the 2016–17 tax year, the Scottish rate of income tax was 10% and was added to the UK basic rate, higher rate or additional rate minus ten percentage points; the rates shown in the table above are the resultant effective rates. See ¶1-100 for full table of rates.

(2) For the tax year 2017–18 and subsequent tax years, separate rates of income tax apply to certain non-savings and non-dividend income of a Scottish taxpayer (ITA 2007, s. 11A).

(3) UK income tax bands applied for the tax year 2016–17.

Income tax reliefs

	2018–19 £	2017–18 £	2016–17 £
Personal allowance	11,850	11,500	11,000
Income limit for personal allowance	100,000	100,000	100,000
Marriage allowance	1,190	1,150	1,100
Married couple's allowance			
– entitlement partner born before 6 April 1935	8,695	8,445	8,355
Minimum amount of allowance	3,360	3,260	3,220
Income limit for MCA (reliefs for older taxpayers)	28,900	28,000	27,700
Abatement income ceilings			
Personal allowance (basic)	123,700	123,000	122,000
Married couples allowance	39,570	38,370	37,970
Blind person's allowance	2,390	2,320	2,290
Dividend allowance	2,000	5,000	5,000
Personal savings allowance			
– basic rate taxpayers	1,000	1,000	1,000
– higher rate taxpayers	500	500	500
'Rent-a-room' limit	[7,500]	7,500	7,500

National Insurance contributions

Class 1 primary (employee) contributions	2018–19	2017–18	2016–17
Lower earnings limit (LEL)	£116 weekly	£113 weekly	£112 weekly
Primary threshold	£162 weekly	£157 weekly	£155 weekly
Upper earnings limit (UEL)	£892 weekly	£866 weekly	£827 weekly
Rate on earnings up to primary threshold	0%	0%	0%
Rate above primary threshold	12% on £162.01 to £892 weekly; 2% above £892	12% on £157.01 to £866 weekly; 2% above £866	12% on £155.01 to £827 weekly; 2% above £827
Reduced rate	5.85% on £162.01 to £892 weekly; 2% above £892	5.85% on £157.01 to £866 weekly; 2% above £866	5.85% on £155.01 to £827 weekly; 2% above £827

Class 1 secondary (employer) contributions	2018–19	2017–18	2016–17
Secondary earnings threshold (ST)	£162 weekly £702 monthly £8,424 yearly	£157 weekly £680 monthly £8,164 yearly	£156 weekly £676 monthly £8,112 yearly
Upper secondary threshold for U21s (UST)	£892 weekly £3,863 monthly £46,350 yearly	£866 weekly £3,750 monthly £45,000 yearly	£827 weekly £3,583 monthly £43,000 yearly
Apprentice upper secondary threshold for U25s (AUST)	£892 weekly £3,863 monthly £46,350 yearly	£866 weekly £3,750 monthly £45,000 yearly	£827 weekly £3,583 monthly £43,000 yearly

Class 1 secondary (employer) contributions	2018–19	2017–18	2016–17
Rate	13.8% on earnings above the ST/UST/ AUST	13.8% on earnings above the ST/UST/AUST	13.8% on earnings above the ST/UST/AUST
Employment allowance (per year, per employer)	£3,000	£3,000	£3,000

Class 2 – Self-employed	2018–19	2017–18	2016–17
	£	£	£
Small earnings exemption limit (annual)	6,205	6,025	5,965
Weekly rate	2.95	2.85	2.80
Class 3 – Voluntary contributions	2018–19	2017–18	2016–17
	£	£	£
Weekly rate	14.65	14.25	14.10
Class 4 – Self-employed	2018–19	2017–18	2016–17
	£	£	£
Annual earnings limit – upper	46,350	45,000	43,000
– lower	8,424	8,164	8,060
Rate	9% (£8,424–£46,350); 2% above £46,350	9% (£8,164–£45,000); 2% above £45,000	9% (£8,060–£43,000); 2% above £43,000

Taxation of capital gains

	Individuals %	Trustees and PRs %
2016–17 to 2018–19		
– Gains eligible for entrepreneurs' relief	10	10
– Standard rate (within income tax basic rate band)	10	28
– Higher rate (above income tax basic rate band)	20	
– Gains on residential property not eligible for private residence relief and carried interest gains	18/28	28
2011–12 to 2015–16		
– Gains eligible for entrepreneurs' relief	10	10
– Standard rate (within income tax basic rate band)	18	28
– Higher rate (above income tax basic rate band)	28	

Exemptions and reliefs	2018–19	2017–18	2016–17
	£	£	£
Annual exempt amount	11,700	11,300	11,100
Chattel exemption (max. sale proceeds)	6,000	6,000	6,000

Inheritance tax

Gross cumulative transfer (on or after 6 April 2017)		Gross rate of tax	
		Transfers on death	Lifetime transfers
		%	%
£1–£325,000		Nil	Nil
Above £325,000	Rate	40	20
	Reduced rate for estates leaving 10% or more to charity	36	—

Note
Estate on death taxed as top slice of cumulative transfers in the seven years before death. Most lifetime transfers (other than to discretionary trusts) are potentially exempt, only becoming chargeable where death occurs within seven years.

Residence nil-rate band		Tapered withdrawal	
Year of death	Additional nil-rate band £	Net estate value £	Withdrawal rate
2018–19	125,000	> £2m	£1 for £2

Annual exemption	£3,000
Small gift exemption (to the same person)	£250

Taxation of companies

Financial year	2018	2017	2016
Main rate[1]	19%	19%	20%
Intellectual property rate	10%	10%	10%

Note
[1] Main rate on ring fence profits (CTA 2010, s. 276) is 30%, small profits rate is 19% and the marginal relief ring fenced fraction is 11/400ths.

VAT

Standard rate	
From 4 January 2011	20%
1 January 2010 – 3 January 2011	17.5%
1 December 2008 – 31 December 2009	15%
1 April 1991 – 30 November 2008	17.5%
Annual registration limit – taxable supplies (from 1 April 2017)	85,000
Deregistration limit – taxable supplies (from 1 April 2017)	83,000
VAT fraction	
For standard rate of 20%	1/6
For standard rate of 17.5%	7/47
For standard rate of 15%	3/23

Bank base rates

Date effective		Rate %	Date effective		Rate %
2017	2 November	0.50	**2006**	9 November	5.00
2016	4 August	0.25		3 August	4.75
2009	5 March	0.50	**2005**	4 August	4.50
	5 February	1.00	**2004**	5 August	4.75
	8 January	1.50		10 June	4.50
2008	4 December	2.00		6 May	4.25
	6 November	3.00		5 February	4.00
	8 October	4.50	**2003**	6 November	3.75
	10 April	5.00		10 July	3.50
	7 February	5.25		6 February	3.75
2007	6 December	5.50	**2001**	8 November	4.00
	5 July	5.75		4 October	4.50
	10 May	5.50			
	11 January	5.25			

PREFACE

Now in its 52nd edition, *Hardman's Tax Rates & Tables* contains the numerical and factual data in everyday use by the tax practitioner. The material is conveniently arranged in 23 chapters:

- Principles of income tax
- Taxation of business profits
- Taxation of investment income
- Taxation of earnings
- Taxation of capital gains
- Inheritance tax
- Taxation of companies
- Capital allowances
- National Insurance contributions
- Tax credits
- State benefits and statutory payments
- General
- Stamp taxes
- Value added tax
- Insurance premium tax
- Landfill tax
- Aggregates levy
- Climate change levy
- Air passenger duty
- Vehicle excise duty
- Scottish taxes
- Welsh taxes
- Northern Irish taxes

This edition takes full account of Autumn Budget 2017. Where available, 2018–19 rates and allowances are included. The 2018–19 Second Edition will contain full coverage of 2018–19.

Cross-references to CCH's *Tax Reporter, Indirect Tax Reporter* and *SDLT Reporter* are included.

The data in this book is maintained by Sarah Arnold of Elucidate Tax Limited and CCH's team of tax writers: Mark Cawthron, Julie Clift, Paul Davies, Stanley Dencher, Stephen Relf and Meg Wilson.

Every effort has been taken to include, within the constraints of available space, the information of greatest use to the practitioner. A number of changes have been made in the light of suggestions received from users of previous years' editions. CCH welcomes further suggestions as to material which might be inserted in future editions.

Paul Robbins

December 2017

Note: the late Philip Hardman was the original editor of *Hardman's Tax Rates & Tables*. CCH gratefully acknowledges the considerable help and guidance that he provided.

Disclaimer

This publication is sold with the understanding that neither the publisher nor the authors, with regard to this publication, are engaged in rendering legal or professional services. The material contained in this publication neither purports, nor is intended to be, advice on any particular matter.

Although this publication incorporates a considerable degree of standardisation, subjective judgment by the user, based on individual circumstances, is indispensable. This publication is an 'aid' and cannot be expected to replace such judgment.

Neither the publisher nor the authors can accept any responsibility or liability to any person, whether a purchaser of this publication or not, in respect of anything done or omitted to be done by any such person in reliance, whether sole or partial, upon the whole or any part of the contents of this publication.

Legislative and other material

While copyright in all statutory and other materials resides in the Crown or other relevant body, copyright in the remaining material in this publication is vested in the publisher.

The publisher advises that any statutory or other materials issued by the Crown or other relevant bodies and reproduced and quoted in this publication are not the authorised official versions of those statutory or other materials. In the preparation, however, the greatest care has been taken to ensure exact conformity with the law as enacted or other material as issued.

Crown copyright legislation is reproduced under the terms of Crown Copyright Policy Guidance issued by HMSO. Other Crown copyright material is reproduced with the permission of the controller of HMSO. European Communities Copyright material is reproduced with permission.

ISBN: 978-1-78887-051-1
CCH Code: UP/TRT-BI18001

© 2017 Croner-i Ltd

Previously published by Wolters Kluwer (UK) Ltd

British Library Cataloguing-in-Publication Data.

A catalogue record for this book is available from the British Library.

Typeset by Innodata Inc., India

Printed and bound in the UK by Hobbs the Printers Ltd

About the Publisher

Croner-i Ltd is part of the international The Peninsula Group. Croner-i Ltd is the leading publisher specialising in tax, business and law publishing throughout Europe, the US and the Asia Pacific region. The group produces a wide range of information services in different media for the accounting and legal professions and for business.

All Croner-i Ltd publications are designed to be practical and authoritative reference works and guides and are written by our own highly qualified and experienced editorial team and specialist outside authors.

Croner-i Ltd publishes information packages including electronic products, loose-leaf reporting services, newsletters and books on UK and European legal topics for distribution world-wide.

Croner-i Ltd
145 London Road
Kingston upon Thames KT2 6SR
United Kingdom
Telephone: 0844 561 8166
E-mail: customer.services@croneri.co.uk
Website: croneri.co.uk

Acknowledgements

Certain material in this publication is Crown Copyright and is reproduced with the kind permission of the Controller of Her Majesty's Stationery Office.

CCH acknowledges the endorsement of this publication by the Chartered Institute of Taxation and the Tax Faculty of the Institute of Chartered Accountants in England and Wales.

THE
CHARTERED
INSTITUTE OF
TAXATION

The Association of Taxation Technicians

PRINCIPLES OF INCOME TAX

INCOME TAX RATES

Note: See also ¶26-100 for rates applicable in Scotland from April 2016.

[¶1-000]   Structure of income tax rates: 2018–19

(ITA 2007, s. 9A, 10–15; FA 2016, s. 6)

Finance Act 2016 included legislation to separate the income tax rates that apply to savings (the savings rates), from those that apply to non-savings, non-dividends income (the main rates), with effect for the tax year 2017–18 (as the first tax year for which the Scottish Government can set Scottish rates of income tax (SI 2016/1161, reg. 3)) and subsequent tax years, in order to facilitate the devolution of income tax rates to Scotland (for Scottish taxpayers) and, in due course, to Wales (for Welsh taxpayers).

The savings and dividend rates are not being devolved and apply across the UK whereas the main rates were devolved to Scotland from April 2017 (for Scottish taxpayers) and will be devolved, in due course, to Wales (for Welsh taxpayers).

Finance Act 2016 also created a default rate of income tax on non-savings, non-dividends income that will apply to, but is not limited to, trustees and non-residents.

The general effect of ITA 2007, s. 10–15 is outlined in the following table:

Type of taxpayer	Rates payable on savings income	Rates payable on most dividend income	Rates payable on other income
UK resident individual who is neither a Scottish taxpayer nor a Welsh taxpayer	Savings rates	Dividend rates	Main rates
Scottish taxpayer	Savings rates	Dividend rates	Scottish rates
Welsh taxpayer	Savings rates	Dividend rates	Main rates while ITA 2007, s. 11B is not in force; Welsh rates once in force
Non-UK resident individual	Savings rates	Dividend rates	Default rates
Non-individual, except some trustees subject to trust rate or dividend trust rate in certain circumstances	Default basic rate	Dividend ordinary rate	Default basic rate

Note
(1) The table does not address the effect of some exceptions referred to in ITA 2007, s. 10–15.

[¶1-002]   Income tax rates: 2018–19

(Autumn Budget 2017)

	Rate	Taxable income band	Tax on band
	%	£	£
Main rates			
Basic rate	20	1–34,500	6,900
Higher rate	40	34,501–150,000	46,200
Additional rate	45	Over 150,000	
Default rates			
Default basic rate	20	1–34,500	6,900
Default higher rate	40	34-501–150,000	46,200
Default additional rate	45	Over 150,000	
Scottish rates			
Scottish basic rate			
Scottish higher rate			
Scottish additional rate			

Other rates	Rate	Taxable income
	%	
Savings rates		
Starting rate for savings	0	£1–£5,000
Savings nil rate	0	First £1,000 or £500
Savings basic rate	20	Savings income otherwise chargeable at basic rate or default basic rate
Savings higher rate	40	Savings income otherwise chargeable at higher rate or default higher rate
Savings additional rate	45	Savings income otherwise chargeable at additional rate or default additional rate
Dividend rates		
Dividend nil rate	0	First £2,000
Dividend ordinary rate	7.5	Dividend income otherwise chargeable at basic rate or Scottish basic rate
Dividend upper rate	32.5	Dividend income otherwise chargeable at higher rate or Scottish higher rate
Dividend additional rate	38.1	Dividend income otherwise chargeable at additional rate or Scottish additional rate
Special rates for trustees' income		
Trust rate	45	Trustees accumulated or discretionary income and other amounts under
Dividend trust rate	38.1	ITA 2007, Pt. 9, Ch. 3–6

[¶1-003] Income tax rates: 2017–18
(ITA 2007, s. 6–9; FA 2016, s. 6)
(Tax Reporter: ¶148-075ff.)

	Rate	Taxable income band	Tax on band
	%	£	£
Main rates[1][2]			
Basic rate	20	1–33,500[3]	6,700
Higher rate	40	33,501–150,000	46,600
Additional rate	45	Over 150,000	
Default rates[4]			
Default basic rate	20	1–33,500[3]	6,700
Default higher rate	40	33,501–150,000	46,600
Default additional rate	45	Over 150,000	
Scottish rates			
Scottish basic rate	20	1–31,500	6,300
Scottish higher rate	40	31,501–150,000	47,400
Scottish additional rate	45	Over 150,000	

Other rates	Rate	Taxable income
	%	
Savings rates		
Starting rate for savings[5]	0	£1–£5,000
Savings nil rate[6]	0	First £1,000 or £500
Savings basic rate	20	Savings income otherwise chargeable at basic rate or default basic rate
Savings higher rate	40	Savings income otherwise chargeable at higher rate or default higher rate
Savings additional rate	45	Savings income otherwise chargeable at additional rate or default additional rate
Dividend rates		
Dividend nil rate[7]	0	First £5,000
Dividend ordinary rate	7.5	Dividend income otherwise chargeable at basic rate or Scottish basic rate
Dividend upper rate	32.5	Dividend income otherwise chargeable at higher rate or Scottish higher rate
Dividend additional rate	38.1	Dividend income otherwise chargeable at additional rate or Scottish additional rate

Other rates	Rate %	Taxable income
Special rates for trustees' income[8]		
Trust rate	45	Trustees accumulated or discretionary income and other amounts under
Dividend trust rate	38.1	ITA 2007, Pt. 9, Ch. 3–6

Notes

[1] Income tax lock: F(No. 2)A 2015, s. 1 set a ceiling for the main rates of income tax at 20%, 40% and 45% respectively for tax years beginning on or after 18 November 2015 (Royal Assent) but before the date of the first parliamentary general election after that day.

[2] From 2017–18, the main rates are separated into the main rates, the savings rates and the default rates. From 6 April 2017, the main rates apply to non-savings, non-dividend income (income to which the main rates apply includes income from employment, property or pensions not subject to the Scottish rate of income tax). Prior to 6 April 2017, the main rates applied to all non-dividend income, including income from savings, employment, property or pensions.

[3] Autumn Statement 2016 confirmed the Government's commitment to raise the income tax personal allowance to £12,500 and the higher rate threshold to £50,000, by the end of this Parliament, on which figures the basic rate limit will increase to £37,500.

[4] Default rates apply from 6 April 2017 to non-savings and non-dividend income of any taxpayer that is not subject to either the main rates or the Scottish rates of income tax.

[5] The 'starting rate for savings' is available for savings income only. If an individual's taxable non-savings income (i.e. after deduction of their personal allowance) exceeds the starting rate, then the starting rate is not available and an individual's savings income is chargeable at the nil rate (to the extent available), the basic, higher or additional rate (as would otherwise apply).

[6] The savings allowance (the savings nil rate) is available to individuals with savings income. The savings allowance is £1,000 for basic rate taxpayers, £500 for higher rate taxpayers and nil for additional rate taxpayers. Savings income within the savings allowance is chargeable at the savings nil rate 0% (ITA 2007, s. 12A and 12B). The 'savings nil rate' is available in addition to the 'starting rate for savings' (where this is available) on savings income above the starting rate limit.

[7] The tax-free dividend allowance operates as a 0% tax rate substituted for the dividend ordinary rate, dividend upper rate or dividend additional rate as would otherwise apply on the first £5,000 of an individual's dividend income (ITA 2007, s. 13A). From 2018–19, the dividend allowance will be reduced to £2,000 (F(No. 2)A 2017, s. 8).

[8] The special trust rates do not apply to the first £1,000 slice of the 'trust rate income'. Instead, the normal income tax rates (currently the basic rate and dividend ordinary rate) apply as appropriate (ITA 2007, s. 491(1)–(3)).

[¶1-004]   Income tax rates: 2016–17

(ITA 2007, s. 6–15; FA 2015, s. 4; FA 2016, s. 1)

(Tax Reporter: ¶148-075ff.)

UK rates (England, Wales and Northern Ireland)

	Taxable income band £	Tax rate[1] %	Tax on band £
Basic rate	1–32,000	20	6,400
Higher rate	32,001–150,000	40	47,200
Additional rate	Over 150,000	45	
Starting rate for savings income	1–5,000	0	

Principles of Income Tax

Scottish rates

UK rate for England, Wales and Northern Ireland	Taxable income band £	UK rate paid in Scotland %	Scottish rate %	Total rate for Scottish taxpayers %
Basic rate 20%	1–32,000	10	10	20
Higher rate 40%	32,001–150,000	30	10	40
Additional rate 45%	Over £150,000	35	10	45

Savings, dividends and special trust rates

Starting rate for savings income[2]	0% up to starting rate limit
Rate on non-dividend savings income	0% on savings income charged at the savings nil rate[3] 20% up to basic rate limit 40% up to higher rate limit 45% thereafter
Dividend nil rate[5]	0% on first £5,000 dividends
Dividend ordinary rate	7.5%[5] up to basic rate limit
Dividend upper rate	32.5%[5] up to higher rate limit
Dividend additional rate	38.1%[5] above higher rate limit
Trust rate	45%[4]
Dividend trust rate	38.1%[4]

Notes

[1] Income tax lock: F(No. 2)A 2015, s. 1 set a ceiling for the main rates of income tax at 20%, 40% and 45% respectively for tax years beginning on or after 18 November 2015 (Royal Assent) but before the date of the first parliamentary general election after that day.

[2] The 'starting rate for savings' is available for savings income only. If an individual's taxable non-savings income (i.e. after deduction of their personal allowance) exceeds the starting rate limit, then the starting rate is not available and an individual's savings income is chargeable at the basic, higher or additional rate (as would otherwise apply). From 6 April 2016, a new savings allowance is available to individuals with savings income, 'the savings nil rate'.

[3] The savings allowance is £1,000 for basic rate taxpayers, £500 for higher rate taxpayers and nil for additional rate taxpayers. Savings income within the savings allowance is chargeable at the savings nil rate 0% (ITA 2007, s. 12A and 12B). The 'savings nil rate' is available in addition to the 'starting rate for savings' (where this is available) on savings income above the starting rate limit.

[4] The special trust rates do not apply to the first £1,000 slice of the 'trust rate income'. Instead, the normal income tax rates (currently the basic rate and dividend ordinary rate) apply as appropriate (ITA 2007, s. 491(1)–(3)).

[5] From April 2016, the dividend tax credit was abolished and replaced with a £5,000 tax-free dividend allowance. The allowance operates as a 0% tax rate substituted for the dividend ordinary rate, dividend upper rate or dividend additional rate as would otherwise apply on the first £5,000 of an individual's dividend income (ITA 2007, s. 13A).

[¶1-005]   Income tax rates: 2015–16

(ITA 2007, s. 6–15; FA 2014, s. 2)

(Tax Reporter: ¶148-075ff.)

2015–16

	Taxable income band £	Tax rate %	Tax on band £
Basic rate	1–31,785	20	6,357
Higher rate	31,786–150,000	40	47,286
Additional rate	Over 150,000	45	

Rate on non-dividend savings income	0% up to £5,000[(1)] 20% up to basic rate limit 40% up to higher rate limit 45% thereafter
Dividend ordinary rate (effective rate with tax credit)	10% up to basic rate limit 0%
Dividend upper rate (effective rate with tax credit)	32.5% up to higher rate limit 25%
Dividend additional rate (effective rate with tax credit)	37.5% above higher rate limit 30.6%
Trust rate	45%[(2)]
Dividend trust rate	37.5%[(2)]

Notes

[(1)] The starting rate is available for savings income only. If an individual's taxable non-savings income (i.e. after deduction of their personal allowance) exceeds the starting rate limit, then the starting rate is not be available.

[(2)] The special trust rates do not apply to the first £1,000 slice of the 'trust rate income'. Instead, the normal income tax rates (currently the basic rate and dividend ordinary rate) apply as appropriate (ITA 2007, s. 491(1)–(3)).

[¶1-006]   Income tax rates: 2014–15

(ITA 2007, s. 6–15; FA 2014, s. 1)

(Tax Reporter: ¶148-075ff.)

2014–15

	Taxable income band £	Tax rate %	Tax on band £
Basic rate	1–31,865	20	6,373
Higher rate	31,866–150,000	40	47,254
Additional rate	Over 150,000	45	

Rate on non-dividend savings income	10% up to £2,880[1] 20% up to basic rate limit 40% up to higher rate limit 45% thereafter
Dividend ordinary rate (effective rate with tax credit)	10% up to basic rate limit 0%
Dividend upper rate (effective rate with tax credit)	32.5% up to higher rate limit 25%
Dividend additional rate (effective rate with tax credit)	37.5% above higher rate limit 30.6%
Trust rate	45%[2]
Dividend trust rate	37.5%[2]

Notes

[1] A 10% starting rate applies to the first £2,880 of non-dividend savings income. The starting rate does not apply if non-savings income exceeds the personal allowance plus £2,880.

[2] The special trust rates do not apply to the first £1,000 slice of the 'trust rate income'. Instead, the normal income tax rates (currently the basic rate and dividend ordinary rate) apply as appropriate (ITA 2007, s. 491(1)–(3)).

[¶1-008]   Income tax rates: 2013–14

(ITA 2007, s. 6–15; FA 2013, s. 3)

(Tax Reporter: ¶148-075ff.)

2013–14

	Taxable income band £	Tax rate %	Tax on band £
Basic rate	1–32,010	20	6,402
Higher rate	32,011–150,000	40	47,196
Additional rate	Over 150,000	45	

Rate on non-dividend savings income	10% up to £2,790[1] 20% up to basic rate limit 40% up to higher rate limit 45% thereafter
Dividend ordinary rate (effective rate with tax credit)	10% up to basic rate limit 0%
Dividend upper rate (effective rate with tax credit)	32.5% up to higher rate limit 25%
Dividend additional rate (effective rate with tax credit)	37.5% above higher rate limit 30.6%
Trust rate	45%[2]
Dividend trust rate	37.5%[2]

Notes

[1] A 10% starting rate applies to the first £2,790 of non-dividend savings income. The starting rate does not apply if non-savings income exceeds the personal allowance plus £2,790.

[2] The special trust rates do not apply to the first £1,000 slice of the 'trust rate income'. Instead, the normal income tax rates (currently the basic rate and dividend ordinary rate) apply as appropriate (ITA 2007, s. 491(1)–(3)).

Principles of Income Tax

[¶1-100]   Personal allowances and reliefs

(ITA 2007, s. 35–46)

(Tax Reporter: ¶155-000ff.)

From 2016–17 onwards, there is one income tax personal allowance regardless of an individual's date of birth.

The Government has committed to raising the personal allowance to £12,500 by the end of its Parliamentary term (first announced at Summer Budget 2015, reconfirmed at Autumn Statement 2016).

For tax years up to 2012–13, higher (age-related) allowances were available for individuals attaining 'age 65–74' or age '75 and over' in the tax year. These allowances were frozen at 2012–13 rates and phased out between 2013–14 and 2015–16 as the basic personal allowance caught up with the frozen amounts of the former allowances.

Transferable tax allowances for married couples

(ITA 2007, Pt. 3, Ch. 3A)

(Tax Reporter: ¶156-725)

From the 2015–16 tax year, a spouse or civil partner who is not liable to income tax because their income is below their personal allowance or who is liable to income tax at the basic rate, dividend ordinary rate or the starting rate for savings has been able to elect to transfer a portion (set at 10%) of their personal allowance to their spouse or civil partner, with a corresponding reduction to the transferring spouse's personal allowance. Only a spouse or civil partner who is liable to income tax at the basic rate, dividend ordinary rate or the starting rate for savings can receive the transferred personal allowance. The transferred allowance is given effect as a reduction to the recipient's income tax liability at the basic rate of tax. Married couples or civil partners entitled to claim the married couple's allowance are not entitled to make a transfer.

At Autumn Budget 2017, it was announced that amending legislation will be introduced in Finance Bill 2017–18, effective from 29 November 2017, to enable an individual whose spouse or civil partner is deceased to make an application for the marriage allowance, and for the claim to be backdated for up to four years where the entitlement conditions are met.

Specific income allowances

From 6 April 2016, two 'allowances' were introduced for savings income and dividend income. Both 'allowances' operate as 0% rates of tax substituted for the rates that would otherwise apply. The savings allowance is available for up to £1,000 of a basic rate taxpayer's savings income and up to £500 of a higher rate taxpayer's savings income each year. The savings allowance is not available to additional rate taxpayers. The dividend allowance is available to all taxpayers on up to £5,000 of dividend income.

From 6 April 2017, two further £1,000 allowances each for property and trading income were introduced (amendments by *Finance (No. 2) Act* 2017). The new allowances mean that individuals with property income below £1,000 or trading income below £1,000 do not need to declare or pay tax on that income. The trading income allowance also applies to certain miscellaneous income from providing assets or services. Those with income above the allowance may calculate their taxable profit either by deducting their expenses in the normal way or by electing for partial relief and simply deducting the relevant allowance from their gross income (instead of deducting expenses).

Type of relief[1]	2018–19[9] £	2017–18 £	2016–17 £	2015–16 £	2014–15 £	2013–14 £
Personal allowance[2]						
All ages	11,850	11,500	11,000	—	—	—
– born after 5 April 1948	—	—	—	—	10,000	9,440
– born after 5 April 1938	—	—	—	10,600	—	—
– born after 5 April 1938 but before 6 April 1948	—	—	—	—	10,500	10,500
– born before 6 April 1938	—	—	—	10,660	10,660	10,660
Marriage allowance[3]	1,190	1,150	1,100	1,060	—	—
Married couple's allowance[4]						
– born before 6 April 1935 and age 75 and over	8,695	8,445	8,355	8,355	8,165	7,915
– minimum amount of allowance	3,360	3,260	3,220	3,220	3,140	3,040
Maximum income before abatement of:						
– personal allowance[2]						100,000
– married couples allowance [reliefs for older taxpayers]	100,000 28,900	100,000 28,000	100,000 27,700	100,000 27,700	100,000 27,000	26,100
Abatement income ceiling						
Personal allowance (basic)	123,700	123,000	122,000	121,200	120,000	118,880
Single (age personal allowance)						
– born after 5 April 1938 but before 6 April 1948	—	—	—	—	28,000	28,220
– born before 6 April 1938	—	—	—	27,820	28,320	28,540
Married couple's allowance (only)	39,570	38,370	37,970	37,970	37,050	35,850
Married (age personal allowance and MCA)						
– relevant partner born after 5 April 1938 but before 6 April 1948	—	—	—	—	38,050	37,970
– relevant partner born before 6 April 1938	—	—	—	38,090	38,370	38,290
Blind person's allowance	2,390	2,320	2,290	2,290	2,230	2,160
Dividend allowance[5]	2,000	5,000	5,000	—	—	—
Personal savings allowance[6]						
Basic rate taxpayers	1,000	1,000	1,000	—	—	—
Higher rate taxpayers	500	500	500	—	—	—
Life assurance relief (policies issued before 14 March 1984)[7]	—	—	—	—	12.5% of premiums	12.5% of premiums
'Rent-a-room' limit	[7,500]	7,500	7,500	4,250	4,250	4,250
Trading allowance[8]	[1,000]	1,000	—	—	—	—
Property allowance[8]	[1,000]	1,000	—	—	—	—

Notes

[1] The personal allowance, blind persons allowance, married couples allowance (MCA), income limit for MCA abatement (but not the £100,000 income limit for personal allowance abatement) are indexed by the annual percentage increase in CPI (RPI until 2014–15) for the year to September preceding the new tax year. Amounts determined by the annual indexation order may be overridden by provision in a Finance Act. Existing legislation further provides that once the personal allowance has reached £12,500, it will be uprated in line with the national minimum wage (NMW) (and CPI based provisions would no longer apply). However, at Autumn Statement 2016, it was announced that once the personal allowance reaches £12,500, it will continue to be uprated in line with CPI rather than NMW.

[2] From April 2010, the personal allowance is gradually withdrawn for income over £100,000 at a rate of £1 of allowance lost for every £2 over £100,000 until it is completely removed (ITA 2007, s. 35).

[3] Legislation will be introduced in Finance Bill 2017–18 to amend ITA 2007, s. 55B–55D, with effect from 29 November 2017, so as to enable an individual whose spouse or civil partner is deceased to make an application for the marriage allowance, and for the claim to be backdated for up to four years where the entitlement conditions are met (Autumn Budget 2017).

⁽⁴⁾ The married couple's allowance is available only where at least one partner was born before 6 April 1935. Relief is given as a tax reduction at a rate of 10%.

⁽⁵⁾ From 6 April 2016, a 0% rate of tax (the dividend nil rate) applies to the first £5,000 of dividend income received (ITA 2007, s. 13A). The dividend allowance will be reduced to £2,000 from April 2018–19 (F(No. 2)A 2017, s. 8).

⁽⁶⁾ From 6 April 2016, a 0% rate of tax applies to an individual's savings income (the savings nil rate or savings allowance). The savings nil rate applies to the first £1,000 of a basic rate taxpayer's savings income, or the first £500 of a higher rate taxpayer's savings income. The savings nil rate is not available to additional rate taxpayers (ITA 2007, s. 12A and 12B).

⁽⁷⁾ By relief at source. Abolished for payments becoming due and payable on or after 6 April 2015, and payments becoming due and payable before 6 April 2015 but actually paid on or after 6 July 2015 (FA 2012, s. 227 and Sch. 39, para. 23).

⁽⁸⁾ Trading and property allowances introduced with effect from 6 April 2017. The allowances provide for full relief on trading and property income of up to each allowance of £1,000 (the trading allowance applies to miscellaneous income also). Individuals with gross income of up to the allowance do not have to declare or pay tax on this income. Where gross income is above the level of the allowance, individuals can either elect for partial relief and deduct the allowance from gross receipts instead of deducting actual expenses, or calculate profits applying normal rules. (ITTOIA 2005, Pt. 6A, as inserted by F(No. 2)A 2017, Sch. 3)

⁽⁹⁾ Rates announced at Autumn Budget 2017. Amounts shown in square brackets are amounts prescribed in current legislation and in respect of which no announcement was made at Autumn Budget 2017.

[¶1-110]   High income child benefit charge

(ITEPA 2003, s. 681B–681H)

(Tax Reporter: ¶490-075)

The high income child benefit charge applies to individuals whose income exceeds £50,000 who are themselves, or whose partner is, in receipt of child benefit. The charge is levied on the partner with the highest income, irrespective of which partner claims the child benefit. The charge is calculated as the 'appropriate percentage' of child benefit payments received during the tax year which equates to 1% of the amount of child benefit received for every £100 of income over £50,000.

Adjusted Net Income	Appropriate percentage
£60,000 and over	100%
£50,001–£59,999	$\dfrac{ANI - L}{X}$ %
Up to £50,000	Nil

Where:

ANI = Adjusted Net Income
L = £50,000
X = £100

Adjusted Net Income is calculated as:

- net income (total income charged to income tax less income tax reliefs);
- less grossed up (at basic rate) gift aid donations;
- less gross pension contributions (before deduction of basic rate tax);
- add back any relief for payments to trade unions or police organisations (ITEPA 2003, s. 457 or 458) deducted in calculating net income.

	2018–19[2]	2017–18	2016–17	2015–16	2014–15	2013–14
Child benefit[1]	£/week	£/week	£/week	£/week	£/week	£/week
Eldest qualifying child	20.70	20.70	20.70	20.70	20.50	20.30
Each other child	13.70	13.70	13.70	13.70	13.55	13.40

Note
[1] Individuals who elected not to continue to receive child benefit by 28 March 2013 were not liable for the charge for 2013–14. From 2014–15 onwards, individuals who opt out and whose payments stopped before the beginning of the tax year will not be liable for the charge and will otherwise be liable only for the period until payments stop.
[2] Rates per Autumn Budget 2017.

[¶1-120]   Cap on income tax relief

(ITA 2007, s. 24A)

(Tax Reporter: ¶148-450)

From 6 April 2013, a limit applies to the amount of certain income tax reliefs that may be deducted from income under the *Income Tax Act* 2007, s. 24. The limit does not apply to charitable reliefs.

From	Amount of cap
6 April 2013[1]	greater of: – £50,000; or – 25% of adjusted total income

Note
[1] The limit applies for the tax year 2013–14 and subsequent tax years, and additionally, where loss relief is claimed for a tax year before 2013–14 in relation to losses made in 2013–14 or a later year. However, the limit does not apply in relation to property loss relief arising from a loss made in 2012–13 where the loss is claimed for relief against general income in the tax year 2013–14.

Limited reliefs	Legislation
Trade loss relief against general income (excluding relief for losses attributable to overlap relief and business premises renovation allowances (BPRA)) [and excluding deductions so far as made from profits of the trade or business to which the relief relates – see next table]	ITA 2007, s. 64
Early trade loss relief (first four years of trade, profession or vocation; excluding relief for losses attributable to overlap relief and BPRA) [and excluding deductions so far as made from profits of the trade or business to which the relief relates – see table below]	ITA 2007, s. 72
Post-cessation trade relief (qualifying payments or qualifying events within seven years of the permanent cessation of the trade) [and excluding deductions so far as made from profits of the trade or business to which the relief relates – see table below]	ITA 2007, s. 96
Property loss relief against general income (property business losses arising from capital allowances or agricultural expenses; excluding relief for losses attributable to BPRA) [and excluding deductions so far as made from profits of the trade or business to which the relief relates – see table below]	ITA 2007, s. 120

Limited reliefs	Legislation
Post-cessation property relief (qualifying payments or qualifying events within seven years of the permanent cessation of the UK property business) [and excluding deductions so far as made from profits of the trade or business to which the relief relates – see table below]	ITA 2007, s. 125
Employment loss relief against general income (certain circumstances where losses or liabilities arise from employment)	ITA 2007, s. 128
Former employees' deductions for liabilities (payment made by former employees for which they are entitled to claim a deduction from their general income in the year in which the payment is made)	ITEPA 2003, s. 555
Share loss relief on non-EIS/SEIS/SI shares (capital losses on the disposal, or deemed disposal, of certain qualifying shares)	ITA 2007, Pt. 4, Ch. 6
Losses on deeply discounted securities (losses on gilt strips and on listed securities held since at least 26 March 2003)	ITTOIA 2005, s. 446, 454(4)
Qualifying loan interest (interest paid on certain loans including loans to buy an interest in certain types of company or to invest in a partnership)	ITA 2007, Pt. 8, Ch. 1

Excluded reliefs	Legislation
Deductions attributable to business premises renovation allowances	CAA 2001, Pt. 3A
Deductions so far as made from profits of the trade or business to which the relief relates in respect of: • trade loss relief; • early trade loss relief; • post-cessation trade relief; • property loss relief; • post-cessation property relief.	ITA 2007, s. 64, 72, 96, 120 and 125
Deductions so far as attributable to a deduction for overlap relief profit in final tax year or on change of accounting date (allowed under ITTOIA 2005, s. 205 or 220) in respect of: • trade loss relief; • early trade loss relief.	ITA 2007, s. 64 and 72
Deductions for amounts of relief for share losses: • where the shares in question are qualifying shares to which EIS relief is attributable; • where SEIS relief is attributable to the shares in question; • where SI tax relief is attributable to the shares in question.	ITA 2007, Pt. 4, Ch. 6 ITA 2007, s. 131(2)(a) ITA 2007, Pt. 5A ITA 2007, Pt. 5B

[¶1-150]   Gifts of assets

Nature of asset	Legislation	Effect of relief
Stock manufactured or sold by trader that is given to charity, etc. (Tax Reporter: ¶226-650)	CTA 2009, s. 105; ITTOIA 2005, s. 108	No amount is brought into account as trading receipt as result of the donation
Plant and machinery used by trader given to a charity, etc. (Tax Reporter: ¶238-235)	CAA 2001, s. 63	Disposal value is nil for capital allowances purposes

Nature of asset	Legislation	Effect of relief
Stock manufactured or sold by trader that is given to a designated educational establishment and qualifies as plant or machinery in the donee's hands (Tax Reporter: ¶226-650)	CTA 2009, s. 105; ITTOIA 2005, s. 108	No amount is brought into account as a trading receipt as result of the donation
Plant or machinery used by trader that is given to a designated educational establishment and qualifies as plant and machinery in the donee's hands (Tax Reporter: ¶238-235)	CAA 2001, s. 63	Disposal value is nil for capital allowances purposes
Listed shares and securities and securities dealt with on a recognised stock exchange, units in unit trusts, etc. interests in land, that are given to a charity (Tax Reporter: ¶115-575; ¶716-640)	CTA 2010, s. 203; ITA 2007, s. 431	Full value of gift is deductible in calculating profits for IT or CT purposes
Property settled by gift on a UK trust which has a charity as a beneficiary and the settlor retains an interest (Tax Reporter: ¶356-450)	ITTOIA 2005, s. 628	The trust income allocated to the settlor is reduced by an amount equal to the income paid to the charity in the year

[¶1-200] Gifts to the nation

(FA 2012, Sch. 14)

For the tax year 2012–13 and subsequent tax years, a reduction in income tax and/or capital gains tax is available where an individual makes a gift of pre-eminent property to be held for the benefit of the public or the nation. The tax reduction is 30% of the value of the gift. A gift offer must be made and registered in accordance with the scheme and relief is available against the individual's liability for the year in which the gift offer is registered and/or any of the succeeding four tax years.

Pre-eminent property includes any picture, print, book, manuscript, work of art, scientific object or other thing that is pre-eminent for its national, scientific, historic or artistic interest, collections of such items and any object kept in a significant building where it is desirable that it remain associated with the building.

ADMINISTRATION

[¶1-250] Submission dates for 2017–18 personal tax returns

(TMA 1970, s. 8)

(Tax Reporter: ¶180-125)

The *Taxes Management Act* 1970, s. 8 contains provisions concerning submission dates for returns issued on or after 6 April 2018 which relate to 2017–18, as follows:

- paper returns (whether or not HMRC are to calculate the tax liability) must be filed by 31 October 2018; and
- online returns must be filed by 31 January 2019.

There are the following exceptions:

Circumstances	Filing date[1]
Return issued after 31 July 2018 but before 31 October 2018	Three months from the date of issue (paper returns); 31 January 2019 (online returns)
Return issued after 31 October 2018	Three months from date of issue
Taxpayer wishes underpayment (below £3,000) to be coded out under PAYE in a subsequent year (paper returns)	31 October 2018
Taxpayer wishes underpayment (below £3,000) to be coded out under PAYE in a subsequent year (online returns)	30 December 2018

Note
[1] The time allowed for making a self-assessment when HMRC have served a notice to file a return is four years after the end of the tax year to which it relates (TMA 1970, s. 34A, as inserted by FA 2016, s. 168, with effect from 15 September 2016).

Withdrawing a notice to file a self-assessment return

(TMA 1970, s. 8B and 12AAA)

With effect in respect of returns for the tax year 2012–13 and subsequent tax years, HMRC will withdraw a notice to file a return, on request or otherwise, where they agree a self-assessment return is not required and cancel any late filing penalty already issued in respect of the outstanding return. A notice may only be withdrawn within the period of two years beginning with the end of the relevant year of assessment or period in respect of which the return is required or, in exceptional circumstances, such extended period as HMRC may agree.

Simple assessment

Simple assessment is a new HMRC assessment procedure which will remove the need for some customers to complete a tax return. From September 2017, HMRC will introduce simple assessments starting with two groups:

- new state pensioners with income more than the personal tax allowance in the tax year 2016–17;
- PAYE customers who have underpaid tax and who cannot have that tax collected through their tax code.

All existing state pensioners who receive state pension over their personal allowance will be taken out of self-assessment for the tax year 2017–18, and will receive a simple assessment notification instead (TMA 1970, s. 28H–28J and 59BA, as inserted by FA 2016, s. 167 and Sch. 23).

[¶1-260] Digital reporting and record-keeping (Making Tax Digital)

(TMA 1970, s. 12C and Sch. A1)

Finance (No. 2) Act 2017 provides powers to make regulations about digital record-keeping and reporting requirements for businesses within the charge to income tax. The measures will have effect from a day to be appointed by Treasury Order (TMA 1970, s. 12C and Sch. A1, as inserted by F(No. 2)A 2017, s. 60).

Businesses (including self-employed and landlords) will be able to keep records of their income and expenditure digitally, and send summary updates quarterly to HMRC from their software (or app).

[¶1-300] Payment dates 2017–18

(TMA 1970, s. 59A, 59B; SI 1996/1954)

(Tax Reporter: ¶182-725ff.)

Tax is paid on 31 January next following the year of assessment as a single sum covering capital gains tax[4] and income tax on all sources. Interim payments on account may be required. For 2017–18. the following due dates apply:

Type of assessment	Payment date
Self-assessment	
First interim payment[1]	31 January 2018
Second interim payment[1]	31 July 2018
Balancing payment	31 January 2019[2]
Simple assessment	31 January 2019[3]

Notes

[1] No interim payments are required if the tax paid in the preceding tax year was less than £1,000; or more than 80% of the tax due in the preceding year was collected at source. Otherwise, interim payments are calculated as 50% each of the net tax due for the preceding tax year (even if it is already clear that the actual liability for the year of assessment will exceed that for the preceding year). Where it is believed that the net tax due for the year of assessment will be less than the amount for the preceding year, a claim to reduce each payment on account accordingly can be made. Net tax is the excess of assessed tax over tax deducted at source (incl. tax credits on dividends before 6 April 2016) (TMA 1970, s. 59A).

[2] If a return is not issued until after 31 October 2018 and the taxpayer has notified chargeability by 5 October 2018, the due date for the final payment becomes three months from the issue of the return (TMA 1970, s. 59B).

[3] The due date for income tax and capital gains tax payable under a 'simple assessment' is three months after the day on which the simple assessment notice was given if given after 31 October following the year of assessment (TMA 1970, s. 59BA).

[4] From April 2020, a payment on account of any CGT due on the disposal of residential property will be required to be made within 30 days of the completion of the disposal. This will not affect gains on properties which are not liable for CGT due to private residence relief (PRR) (Autumn Budget 2017).

[¶1-325] Direct recovery of debts

(F(No. 2)A 2015, s. 51 and Sch. 8)

HMRC have the power to recover debts due (including tax and tax credit debts) directly from the bank and building society accounts (including individual savings accounts) of debtors. This is also known as the direct recovery of debts (DRD). The power can only be used to recover debts of more than £1,000, and is subject to a number of statutory safeguards, including a 30-day right of objection and a limit of £5,000 as the minimum amount HMRC must always leave across a debtor's accounts above the amount that has been held.

[¶1-350]   Main penalty provisions 2017–18

Offence[(4)(5)]	Penalty[(1)(2)]
Late return for 2010–11 and later years (FA 2009, Sch. 55; Tax Reporter: ¶181-500) Failure to submit by the filing date (by 31 October for paper return; by 31 January for online return)	£100
Failure continues three months after the filing date by HMRC notice	£10 per day for a period up to 90 days beginning with the date specified in the notice (maximum £900)
Failure still continues six months after the filing date)	The greater of £300 or 5% of the liability to tax shown by the return
Failure still continues after 12 months	The greater of relevant percentage of liability shown by the return and £300

Relevant percentage

	Category 1[(3)]	Category 2	Category 3
• withholding information deliberate and concealed	100%	150%	200%
• withholding information deliberate but not concealed	70%	105%	140%
• any other case	5%	5%	5%

Reductions for disclosure: maximum reduction weighted according to quality of disclosure determined as:

Disclosure of relevant information relating to domestic matter
- 30% for telling HMRC
- 40% for helping to quantify
- 30% for giving access to records

Discloses relevant information that relates to an offshore matter or offshore transfer
- telling HMRC
- helping to quantify
- giving access to records
- providing additional information

Tax years commencing on or after 6 April 2016

Domestic matters

Standard penalty	Prompted disclosure minimum	Unprompted disclosure minimum
70%	35%	20%
100%	50%	30%

Offshore matters and offshore transfers

Standard penalty	Prompted disclosure minimum	Unprompted disclosure minimum
70%	45%	30%
87.50%	53.75%	35%
100%	60%	40%
105%	62.50%	40%
125%	72.50%	50%
140%	80%	50%
150%	85%	55%
200%	110%	70%

No reduction below £300

Tax years prior to 6 April 2016

Standard penalty	Prompted disclosure minimum	Unprompted disclosure minimum
70%	35%	20%
105%	52.5%	30%
140%	70%	40%
100%	50%	30%
150%	75%	45%
200%	100%	60%

Offence[4][5]	Penalty[1][2]
Failure to notify chargeability For failures after 1 April 2010 (FA 2008, Sch. 41; Tax Reporter: ¶181-350):	

Percentage of potential lost revenue

	Category 1[3]	Category 2	Category 3
• failure deliberate and concealed	100%	150%	200%
• failure deliberate but not concealed	70%	105%	140%
• any other case	30%	45%	60%

Reductions for disclosure: maximum reduction weighted according to quality of disclosure determined as:

Failures involving domestic matters and non-deliberate failures involving offshore matters
• 30% for telling HMRC
• 40% for helping to quantify
• 30% for giving access to records

Deliberate failures involving offshore matters and failures involving offshore transfers
• telling HMRC
• helping to quantify
• giving access to records
• providing additional information

[Note: The case A minimum applies if HMRC become aware of the failure less than 12 months after the time when the tax first becomes unpaid by reason of the failure, otherwise the case B minimum applies.]

Tax years commencing on or after 6 April 2016

Domestic matters

Standard penalty	Prompted disclosure minimum		Unprompted disclosure minimum	
	Case A	Case B	Case A	Case B
30%	10%	20%	0%	10%
70%	35%		20%	
100%	50%		30%	

Offshore matters and offshore transfers

Standard penalty	Prompted disclosure minimum		Unprompted disclosure minimum	
	Case A	Case B	Case A	Case B
30%	10%	20%	0%	10%
37.5%	12.5%	25%	0%	12.5%
45%	15%	30%	0%	15%
60%	20%	40%	0%	20%
70%	45%		30%	
87.5%	53.75%		35%	
100%	60%		40%	
105%	62.5%		40%	
125%	72.5%		50%	
140%	80%		50%	
150%	85%		55%	
200%	110%		70%	

Tax years prior to 6 April 2016

Standard penalty	Prompted disclosure minimum		Unprompted disclosure minimum	
	Case A	Case B	Case A	Case B
30%	10%	20%	0%	10%
45%	15%	30%	0%	15%
60%	20%	40%	0%	20%
70%	35%		20%	
105%	52.5%		30%	
140%	70%		40%	
100%	50%		30%	
150%	75%		45%	
200%	100%		60%	

Offence[4][5]	Penalty[1][2]
Failure to keep and retain tax records (TMA 1970, s. 12B; Tax Reporter: ¶181-900)	Up to £3,000 per year of assessment
False statements to reduce interim payments (TMA 1970, s. 59A(6); Tax Reporter: ¶182-725)	Up to the difference between the amount correctly due and the amount paid
Failure to comply with an information notice (FA 2008, Sch. 36, para. 39 and 40; Tax Reporter: ¶186-550ff.)	
• standard amount	£300
• continued failure	Daily penalty of £60
Tax-related penalty where significant tax is at risk (FA 2008, Sch. 36, para. 50)	Tax geared amount decided by Upper Tribunal
Inaccurate information/documents in complying with an information notice (FA 2008, Sch. 36) Inaccuracy careless or deliberate	Up to £3,000 for each inaccuracy

Errors in returns
Errors in returns for periods starting 1 April 2008 where return is filed on or after 1 April 2009 (FA 2007, Sch. 24; Tax Reporter: ¶184-850)
• careless action
• deliberate but not concealed action
• deliberate and concealed action

[Note: No penalty for inaccuracies that occur despite taking reasonable care.]

Percentage of potential lost revenue

Category 1[3]	Category 2	Category 3
30%	45%	60%
70%	105%	140%
100%	150%	200%

Reductions for disclosure: maximum reduction weighted according to quality of disclosure determined as:

Domestic matters and careless inaccuracies involving offshore matters

• 30% for telling HMRC
• 40% for helping to quantify
• 30% for giving access to records

Tax years commencing on or after 6 April 2016

Domestic matters

Standard penalty	Prompted disclosure minimum	Unprompted disclosure minimum
30%	15%	0%
70%	35%	20%
100%	50%	30%

Deliberate inaccuracies involving offshore matters and inaccuracies involving offshore transfers
• telling HMRC
• helping to quantify
• allowing access to records
• providing additional information

Offshore matters and offshore transfers

Standard penalty	Prompted disclosure minimum	Unprompted disclosure minimum
30%	15%	0%
37.5%	18.75%	0%
45%	22.5%	0%
60%	30%	0%
70%	45%	30%
87.5%	53.75%	35%
100%	60%	40%
105%	62.5%	40%
125%	72.5%	50%
140%	80%	50%
150%	85%	55%
200%	110%	70%

Offence[4][5]	Penalty[1][2]		
Errors in returns: reductions for disclosure contd.	**Tax years prior to 6 April 2016** **Percentage of potential lost revenue**		
	Standard penalty	**Prompted disclosure minimum**	**Unprompted disclosure minimum**
	30%	15%	0%
	45%	22.5%	0%
	60%	30%	0%
	70%	35%	20%
	105%	52.5%	30%
	140%	70%	40%
	100%	50%	30%
	150%	75%	45%
	200%	100%	60%
Offshore asset moves (FA 2015, Sch. 21) Additional penalty for offshore asset moves from specified territory to non-specified territory on or after 26 March 2015 following an original deliberate failure penalty under: FA 2007, Sch. 24, para. 1; FA 2008, Sch. 41, para. 1; or FA 2009, Sch. 55, para. 6. See ¶1-370 for table of specified territories.	50% of original penalty		
General anti-abuse rule penalty (FA 2013, s. 212A and Sch. 43C) from 15 September 2016 Penalty where counteraction notice given under FA 2013, Sch. 43, para. 12, Sch. 43A, para. 8 or 9, or Sch. 43B, para. 8	60% of the value of the counteracted advantage		
Enabling offshore tax evasion or non-compliance (FA 2016, Sch. 20) from 1 January 2017 Penalty for engaging in offshore tax evasion or non-compliance where the tax at stake is income tax, capital gains tax or inheritance tax. Standard penalty: Where a penalty under FA 2015, Sch. 21, para. 1 arises:	The higher of: 100% of the potential lost revenue; or £3,000 The higher of: 50% of the potential lost revenue; or £3,000		
Asset based penalty for offshore inaccuracies and failures (FA 2016, Sch. 22) for tax years commencing on or after 6 April 2016 Additional penalty where one or more standard offshore penalties and the offshore potential lost revenue in relation to a tax year exceeds £25,000. Standard offshore penalties means penalties under: FA 2007, Sch. 24, para. 1; FA 2008, Sch. 41, para. 1; or FA 2009, Sch. 55, para. 6 imposed involving offshore matters or offshore transfers and deliberate behaviour.	Lower of 10% of value of asset and offshore PLR x 10.		

Principles of Income Tax

Offence[4][5]	Penalty[1][2]	
Reductions for: • disclosing to HMRC • providing a reasonable value • providing information or access to records to assist HMRC value the asset • special circumstances	**Reduction factors**	
	Unprompted disclosure 50%	**Prompted disclosure** 20%

Notes

[1] Interest is charged on penalties not paid when due. The due date is 30 days after the notice of determination of the penalty is issued.

[2] Defences of 'reasonable excuse' or 'special circumstances' may be available.

[3] FA 2015, s. 120 and Sch. 20 introduce a new category of penalty, category 0 from a date to be appointed. The new category of penalty will carry the lowest level of penalty equivalent to those currently in category 1 (i.e. 30%, 70% and 100%) and the penalty percentages for category 1 penalties will be increased to 37.5%, 87.5% and 125% respectively. New tables as follows:

Late return	Relevant percentage			
	Category 0	Category 1	Category 2	Category 3
• withholding information deliberate and concealed	100%	125%	150%	200%
• withholding information deliberate but not concealed	70%	87.5%	105%	140%
• any other case	5%	5%	5%	5%

Failure to notify chargeability	Percentage of potential lost revenue			
	Category 0	Category 1	Category 2	Category 3
• failure deliberate and concealed	100%	125%	150%	200%
• failure deliberate but not concealed	70%	87.5%	105%	140%
• any other case	30%	37.5%	45%	60%

Errors in returns	Percentage of potential lost revenue			
	Category 0	Category 1	Category 2	Category 3
• careless action	30%	37.50%	45%	60%
• deliberate but not concealed action	70.0%	87.50%	105%	140%
• deliberate and concealed action	100%	125%	150%	200%

[4] *Finance Act* 2016 contains the following changes:
- a new criminal offence that removes the need to prove intent for the most serious cases of failing to declare offshore income and gains (TMA 1970, s. 106B–106H, as inserted by FA 2016, s. 166, with effect from the tax year commencing on 6 April 2017 and subsequent tax years (SI 2017/970);
- increased public naming of tax evaders (FA 2009, s. 94, as amended by FA 2016, s. 164, with effect from 1 April 2017 (SI 2017/261)); and
- a new regime of warnings and escalating sanctions for those who persistently engage in tax avoidance schemes which HMRC defeats. Following the first defeat of a tax avoidance scheme, HMRC will place the taxpayer on a warning for five years. If the taxpayer uses any further schemes while under warning which HMRC defeats, the rate of penalty will be 20% for the first defeat, 40% for the second defeat and 60% for the third defeat. If HMRC defeat three tax avoidance schemes while the taxpayer is on warning, the taxpayer's details can be published. If three avoidance schemes which exploit reliefs are used while under warning and HMRC defeat them, the taxpayer will be denied further benefit of reliefs until the warning period expires. The regime comes into effect on 6 April 2017 (FA 2016, s. 159 and Sch. 18).

[5] *Finance (No. 2) Act* 2017 introduces a new penalty for any person who has enabled another person or business to use a tax avoidance arrangement that is later defeated by HMRC, with effect in relation to arrangements entered into on or after Royal Assent (F(No. 2)A 2017, s. 65 and Sch. 16).

[¶1-360]   Offshore penalties – territory categories

The table below shows which territories are classified in 'category 1' and 'category 3' for the purposes of penalties for offshore non-compliance. Territories not listed here (other than the UK) are in 'category 2'. Penalties for domestic (UK) matters fall into category 1.

Territories are allocated into one of the categories depending upon the level of information exchange arrangements with the UK, with category 1 territories having the highest level of information sharing arrangements so penalties are the same as for penalties involving domestic matters, whereas territories in categories 2 and 3 have correspondingly poorer information exchange arrangements.

A new category of territory, category 0, is prospectively introduced by FA 2015, s. 120 and Sch. 20, with effect from a date to be appointed. The new category of penalty will apply to overseas territories making information exchange arrangements with the UK that meet the new Common Reporting Standard. It is envisaged that most or all territories currently in category 1 will, over time, make arrangements so as to fall within category 0 (FA 2015, Sch. 20).

Category 1	Category 3[(1)]
Anguilla	Albania
Aruba	Algeria
Australia	Andorra
Belgium	Bonaire, Sint Eustatius and Saba
Bulgaria	Brazil
Canada	Cameroon
Cayman Islands	Cape Verde
Cyprus	Colombia
Czech Republic	Congo, Republic of the
Denmark (not including Faroe Islands and Greenland which are in category 2)	Cook Islands
	Costa Rica
Estonia	Curacao
Finland	Cuba
France	Democratic People's Republic of Korea
Germany	Dominican Republic
Greece	Ecuador
Guernsey (includes Alderney and Sark)	El Salvador
Hungary	Gabon
Ireland	Guatemala
Isle of Man	
Italy	Honduras
Japan	Iran
Korea, South	Iraq
Latvia	Jamaica
Lithuania	Kyrgyzstan
Malta	Lebanon
Montserrat	Macau (China and Hong Kong are in category 2)
Netherlands (not including Bonaire, Sint Eustatius and Saba)	Marshall Islands
	Micronesia, Federated States of
New Zealand (not including Tokelau)	Monaco
Norway	Nauru

Category 1	Category 3[1]
Poland	Nicaragua
Portugal (includes Madeira and the Azores)	Niue
Romania	Palau
Slovakia	Panama
Slovenia	Paraguay
Spain (includes the Canary Islands and other overseas territories of Spain)	Peru
	Seychelles
Sweden	Sint Maarten
Switzerland (from 24 July 2013)	Suriname
United States of America (not including overseas territories and possessions of the United States of America which are in category 2)	Syria
	Tokelau
	Tonga
	Trinidad and Tobago
	United Arab Emiratess
	Uruguay

Note

[1] Before 24 July 2013, category 3 territories included additionally:
- Antigua and Barbuda;
- Armenia;
- Bahrain;
- Barbados;
- Belize;
- Dominica;
- Grenada;
- Mauritius;
- Saint Kitts and Nevis;
- Saint Lucia;
- Saint Vincent and the Grenadines;
- San Marino.

[¶1-370]   Offshore asset moves penalties: specified territories
(SI 2015/866)

Andorra	Anguilla	Antigua and Barbuda	Argentina
Aruba	Australia	Austria	The Bahamas
Bahrain[1]	Barbados	Belgium	Belize
Bermuda	Brazil	British Virgin Islands	Brunei Darussalam
Bulgaria	Canada	Cayman Islands	Chile
China	Colombia	Cook Islands[1]	Costa Rica
Croatia	Curaçao	Cyprus	Czech Republic
Denmark	Dominica	Estonia	Faroe Islands
Finland	France	Germany	Ghana[1]
Gibraltar	Greece	Greenland	Grenada
Guernsey	Hong Kong	Hungary	Iceland
India	Indonesia	Ireland	Isle of Man
Israel	Italy	Japan	Jersey
Korea (South)	Kuwait[1]	Latvia	Lebanon[1]

Liechtenstein	Lithuania	Luxembourg	Macau
Malaysia	Malta	Marshall Islands	Mauritius
Mexico	Monaco	Montserrat	Nauru[1]
Netherlands (including Bonaire, Sint Eustatius and Saba)	New Zealand (not including Tokelau)	Niue	Norway
Panama[1]	Poland	Portugal	Qatar
Romania	Russia	Saint Kitts and Nevis	Saint Lucia
Saint Vincent and the Grenadines	Samoa	San Marino	Saudi Arabia
Seychelles	Singapore	Sint Maarten	Slovak Republic
Slovenia	South Africa	Spain	Sweden
Switzerland	Trinidad and Tobago	Turkey	Turks and Caicos Islands
United Arab Emirates	Uruguay	Vanuatu[1]	

Note

[1] New entries added, and previous entries 'Albania' and 'United States of America (not including overseas territories and possessions)' omitted, by SI 2017/989, with effect from 3 November 2017.

[¶1-400]   Penalties for late payment of tax 2017–18

(FA 2009, Sch. 56)

(Tax Reporter: ¶182-875)

The current penalty regime for late payments under income tax self-assessment was introduced by FA 2009, Sch. 56 and applies from 6 April 2011 to payments for the tax year 2010–11 and later years.

Tax overdue	Penalty
30 days	5% of tax overdue
6 months	further 5% of tax overdue
12 months	further 5% of tax overdue

These penalties will be issued automatically and are in addition to the interest that will be charges on all outstanding amounts, including unpaid penalties, until payment is received.

Penalties apply to:

- final tax payments on self-assessments (this includes any amounts due as interim payments which remain unpaid);

- tax on inspector's amendments to a self-assessment made during or as a result of an audit; and

- discovery assessments.

Principles of Income Tax

[¶1-450]   Interest 2017–18

(FA 2009, s. 101–105 and Sch. 53 and 54)

(Tax Reporter: ¶182-925; ¶182-975)

The current regime for interest on overdue and overpaid tax was introduced by FA 2009, s. 101–105 and Sch. 53 and 54, with effect in relation to any self-assessment amount payable or repayable on or after 31 October 2011.

Late payment interest: is payable from the 'late payment interest start date':

Payment	Late payment interest start date
First interim payment(1)	31 January 2018
Second interim payment	31 July 2018
Final payment(2)	31 January 2019
Tax due on an amendment to a return	31 January 2019
Tax due on determination of appeal	31 January 2019

Notes

(1) Where the taxpayer has provided HMRC in good time with the information required to issue a statement of account ahead of the payment date of 31 January, but no statement is received before 1 January, interest on the tax to be paid will run from 30 days after the taxpayer is actually notified rather than from 31 January.

(2) Where notice to make a return is issued after 31 October following the end of the tax year, provided there has been no failure to notify chargeability under TMA 1970, s. 7, the date from which interest is payable becomes the last day in the period of three months beginning with the day notice to make a return was given.

Repayment interest: runs from the date of payment (deemed to be 31 January following the tax year in respect of tax deducted at source) to the date on which the order for the repayment is issued.

[¶1-500]   Rates of interest

(FA 2009, s. 101–102; SI 2011/2446)

(Tax Reporter: ¶182-925; ¶182-975)

The following table gives the rates of interest applicable in recent years.

From	Late payment %	Repayment %
23 August 2016	2.75	0.50
29 September 2009 to 22 August 2016	3.00	0.50

Notes

SI 2011/2446 sets the interest rates for the purposes of s. 101 and 102 at the Bank of England base rate plus 2.5% and minus 1% respectively. Changes in interest rates announced in Bank of England Monetary Policy Committee meetings take effect from the 13th working day following the meeting and apply in respect of interest running from before that date as well as interest running from on or after that date.

(1) Tax-related judgment debts: the Government will set the rate of interest which applies on taxation-related debts payable under a court judgment or order by HMRC to a rate equal to the Bank of England base rate plus 2%. The Government will also apply the late payment interest rate to taxation-related debts owed to HMRC under a court judgment or order. These changes will apply to new and pre-existing judgments and orders in respect of interest accruing on and after 8 July 2015 (F(No. 2)A 2015, s. 52).

[¶1-600] Interest rates on certificates of tax deposit (CTD)

As of 23 November 2017, the CTD scheme has been closed for new purchases, but existing certificates will continue to be honoured until 23 November 2023. Any certificates remaining after this date should be promptly submitted to HMRC for a refund. Thereafter, any balances HMRC are unable to repay will be forfeited.

CTDs can be applied to settle most tax liabilities, except PAYE, VAT and corporation tax falling due under Pay and File.

Rates of interest vary according to the period for which the deposit is held and whether or not the CTD is used in payment of tax. The rates in force at issue apply for one year; thereafter, the rate applicable is that on the most recent anniversary of the date of issue.

Rates applicable over recent years have been as follows:

Deposits on or after	Deposits under £100,000		Deposits of £100,000 or more									
			Deposits held for under 1 month		Deposits held for 1 to under 3 months		Deposits held for 3 to under 6 months		Deposits held for 6 to under 9 months		Deposits held for 9–12 months	
	Applied in payment of tax %	Cash value %	Applied in payment of tax %	Cash value %	Applied in payment of tax %	Cash value %	Applied in payment of tax %	Cash value %	Applied in payment of tax %	Cash value %	Applied in payment of tax %	Cash value %
7 May 1997	2.75	1.50	2.75	1.50	5.50	2.75	5.25	2.75	5.50	2.75	5.25	2.75
9 June 1997	3.00	1.50	3.00	1.50	5.50	2.75	5.50	2.75	5.50	2.75	5.50	2.75
11 July 1997	3.25	1.75	3.25	1.75	6.00	3.00	5.75	3.00	5.75	3.00	6.00	3.00
8 Aug. 1997	4.50	2.25	4.50	2.25	6.00	3.00	6.00	3.00	6.00	3.00	5.75	3.00
7 Nov. 1997	4.00	2.00	4.00	2.00	6.50	3.25	6.50	3.25	6.25	3.25	6.25	3.25
5 June 1998	4.00	2.00	4.00	2.00	6.50	3.25	6.25	3.25	6.25	3.25	6.00	3.00
9 Oct. 1998	3.75	2.00	3.75	2.00	6.25	3.25	5.75	3.00	5.50	2.75	5.25	2.75
6 Nov. 1998	3.25	1.75	3.25	1.75	5.75	3.00	5.25	2.75	5.00	2.50	4.75	2.50
11 Dec. 1998	3.00	1.50	3.00	1.50	5.25	2.75	4.75	2.50	4.50	2.25	4.25	2.25
8 Jan. 1999	2.50	1.25	2.50	1.25	5.00	2.50	4.50	2.25	4.00	2.00	4.00	2.00
5 Feb. 1999	1.75	1.00	1.75	1.00	4.50	2.25	4.00	2.00	3.75	2.00	3.75	2.00
9 Apr. 1999	1.75	1.00	1.75	1.00	4.25	2.25	4.00	2.00	3.75	2.00	3.75	2.00
11 June 1999	1.50	0.75	1.50	0.75	4.00	2.00	4.00	2.00	4.00	2.00	4.00	2.00
9 Sept. 1999	1.75	1.00	1.75	1.00	4.50	2.25	4.50	2.25	4.50	2.25	4.50	2.25
4 Nov. 1999	2.00	1.00	2.00	1.00	5.00	2.50	4.75	2.50	4.75	2.50	4.75	2.50
14 Jan. 2000	2.25	1.25	2.25	1.25	5.00	2.50	5.00	2.50	5.00	2.50	5.25	2.75
11 Feb. 2000	2.50	1.25	2.50	1.25	5.25	2.75	5.00	2.50	5.25	2.75	5.25	2.75
9 Feb. 2001	2.25	1.25	2.25	1.25	4.75	2.50	4.25	2.25	4.25	2.25	4.00	2.00
6 Apr. 2001	2.00	1.00	2.00	1.00	4.25	2.25	4.00	2.00	3.75	2.00	3.50	1.75
11 May 2001	2.00	1.00	2.00	1.00	4.00	2.00	4.00	2.00	3.75	2.00	3.75	2.00
3 Aug. 2001	1.50	0.75	1.50	0.75	3.50	1.75	3.75	2.00	3.25	1.75	3.75	2.00
19 Sept. 2001	1.25	0.75	1.25	0.75	3.25	1.75	3.25	1.75	3.00	1.50	3.00	1.50
5 Oct. 2001	1.00	0.50	1.00	0.50	2.75	1.50	3.00	1.50	2.25	1.25	3.00	1.50
9 Nov. 2001	0.50	0.25	0.50	0.25	2.75	1.50	2.50	1.25	2.25	1.25	2.25	1.25
7 Feb. 2003	0.25	Nil	0.25	Nil	2.50	1.25	2.25	1.00	2.00	1.00	2.00	1.00
11 July 2003	Nil	Nil	Nil	Nil	2.50	1.25	2.25	1.00	2.00	1.00	2.00	1.00
7 Nov. 2003	0.25	Nil	0.25	Nil	3.00	1.50	3.00	1.50	3.00	1.50	3.00	1.50
6 Feb. 2004	0.50	0.25	0.50	0.25	3.00	1.50	3.00	1.50	3.00	1.50	3.00	1.50

| Deposits on or after | Deposits under £100,000 | | Deposits of £100,000 or more | | | | | | | | | | | |
| | | | Deposits held for under 1 month | | Deposits held for 1 to under 3 months | | Deposits held for 3 to under six months | | Deposits held for 6 to under 9 months | | Deposits held for 9-12 months | |
	Applied in payment of tax %	Cash value %	Applied in payment of tax %	Cash value %	Applied in payment of tax %	Cash value %	Applied in payment of tax %	Cash value %	Applied in payment of tax %	Cash value %	Applied in payment of tax %	Cash value %
7 May 2004	0.75	0.25	0.75	0.25	3.25	1.50	3.25	1.50	3.25	1.50	3.25	1.50
11 June 2004	1.00	0.50	1.00	0.50	3.75	1.75	3.50	1.75	3.75	1.75	3.75	1.75
6 Aug. 2004	1.25	0.50	1.25	0.50	3.75	1.75	3.75	1.75	3.75	1.75	3.75	1.75
5 Aug. 2005	1.00	0.50	1.00	0.50	3.50	1.75	3.25	1.50	3.00	1.50	3.00	1.50
4 Aug. 2006	1.75	0.75	1.75	0.75	4.25	2.00	4.25	2.00	4.00	2.00	4.00	2.00
10 Nov. 2006	1.50	0.75	1.50	0.75	4.00	2.00	4.00	2.00	3.75	1.75	3.75	1.75
12 Jan. 2007	1.50	0.75	1.50	0.75	4.25	2.00	4.00	2.00	4.00	2.00	4.00	2.00
11 May 2007	2.00	1.00	2.00	1.00	4.75	2.25	4.50	2.25	4.50	2.25	4.50	2.25
6 July 2007	2.25	1.10	2.25	1.10	5.00	2.50	4.75	2.25	4.75	2.25	4.75	2.25
7 Dec. 2007	3.00	1.50	3.00	1.50	5.50	2.75	5.00	2.50	4.75	2.25	4.50	2.25
8 Feb. 2008	2.00	1.00	2.00	1.00	4.50	2.25	4.25	2.25	4.00	2.00	3.75	1.50
11 Apr. 2008	2.00	1.00	2.00	1.00	4.75	2.25	4.50	2.25	4.25	2.00	4.25	2.00
9 Oct. 2008	2.50	1.25	2.50	1.25	5.25	2.50	5.00	2.50	5.00	2.50	4.75	2.25
7 Nov. 2008	1.75	0.75	1.75	0.75	4.50	2.25	4.25	2.00	4.25	2.00	4.00	2.00
5 Dec. 2008	0.00	0.00	0.00	0.00	2.50	1.25	2.50	1.25	2.50	1.25	2.25	1.00
9 Jan. 2009	0.00	0.00	0.00	0.00	1.50	0.75	1.25	0.50	1.25	0.50	1.25	0.50
6 Feb. 2009	0.00	0.00	0.00	0.00	1.00	0.50	1.00	0.50	1.00	0.50	0.75	0.25
6 Mar. 2009	0.00	0.00	0.00	0.00	0.75	0.25	0.75	0.25	0.75	0.25	0.75	0.25

[¶1-650] Remission of tax for official error
(ESC A19)

Arrears of income tax and capital gains tax may be given up if they result from HMRC's failure to make proper and timely use of information supplied by the taxpayer, or in certain circumstances by the taxpayer's employer or the Department for Work and Pensions.

The taxpayer must have reasonably believed that his or her affairs were in order. Tax will normally only be given up where there was a gap of 12 months or more between HMRC receiving the information that tax was due, and notifying the taxpayer of the arrears.

TAXATION OF BUSINESS PROFITS

[¶2-000]   Relief for fluctuating profits (farming and market gardening; creative artists): from 2016–17
(ITTOIA 2005, s. 221ff.)

(Tax Reporter: ¶272-300ff.; ¶268-300)

Two-year averaging

From 2016–17, marginal relief is removed and full two-year averaging relief is be availabe where the profits of one year are 75% or less of the profits of the other year (FA 2016, s. 25).

Five-year averaging

For 2016–17 and subsequent years, individuals are able to claim to average trading profits for income tax purposes over five consecutive tax years where the 'volatility' condition is met.

The volatility condition is that:

(a)   one of the following is less than 75% of the other:

   (i)   the average of the relevant profits of the first four tax years to which the claim relates;

   (ii) the relevant profits of the last of the tax years to which the claim relates; or

(b)   the relevant profits of one or more (but not all) of the five tax years to which the claim relates are nil.

(ITTOIA 2005, s. 222A, as inserted by *Finance Act* 2016, with effect from the tax year 2016–17 (meaning that a five-year averaging claim with 2016–17 as the final year would involve averaging the profits of the years 2012–13 to 2016–17).)

[¶2-005]   Relief for fluctuating profits (farming and market gardening; creative artists): up to 2015–16
(ITTOIA 2005, s. 221ff.)

(Tax Reporter: ¶272-300ff.; ¶268-300)

Full averaging

Full averaging applied where profits of one of the tax years were less than 70% of profits for the other year or where profits of one (but not both) of the tax years were nil.

Marginal averaging

The amount of the adjustment to the profits of each relevant tax year, where lower profits are between 70% and 75% of higher profits, was computed as follows:

$$(D \times 3) - (P \times 0.75)$$

Where:

D   is the difference between the relevant profits of the two years; and

P   is the relevant profits of the tax year of which those profits are higher.

Marginal relief was removed by FA 2016, s. 25, with effect where the latest year is 2016–17 (and subsequent tax years).

[¶2-010]   Cash basis for small businesses

(ITTOIA 2005, Pt. 2, Ch. 3A)

(Tax Reporter: ¶206-481ff.)

From April 2013 eligible businesses may elect to calculate their profits on the cash basis instead of in accordance with generally accepted accountancy principles. The cash basis is optional but circumstances under which a business can leave the scheme are limited (businesses must continue to use the scheme until their circumstances change so that the cash basis is no longer suitable for them). Under the scheme, businesses calculate their taxable income by taking business income received in a year and deducting business expenses paid in a year. This means they do not need to adjust for debtors, creditors and stock, and generally do not have to distinguish between revenue and capital expenditure. Capital allowances remain available for expenditure on cars only. Businesses using the cash basis do not have to use the simplified flat rate expenses for their cars.

Eligible barristers are able to choose either to use the cash basis and simplified expenses or the accruals basis. The former cash basis for barristers (also known as the alternative basis) under ITTOIA 2005, s. 160 (which was available in the seven years following their first holding themselves out for work) was repealed by *Finance Act* 2013 but barristers who were using the alternative basis for the tax year 2012–13 could continue to do so.

	Relevant max. Joining[2] £	Leaving threshold[2] £
From 6 April 2017		
Standard	150,000	300,000
Recipients of universal credit[1]	300,000	
2016–17		
Standard	83,000	166,000
Recipients of universal credit[1]	166,000	
2015–16		
Standard	82,000	164,000
Recipients of universal credit[1]	164,000	
2014–15		
Standard	81,000	162,000
Recipients of universal credit[1]	162,000	
2013–14		
Standard	79,000	158,000
Recipients of universal credit[1]	158,000	

Notes
[1] Recipients of universal credit must use the cash basis for income assessment for UC purposes.
[2] Joining and leaving thresholds are prescribed by ITTOIA 2005, s. 31B (as amended by SI 2017/293, for tax the tax year 2017–18 and subsequent tax years).

Excluded businesses:
- companies;
- limited liability partnerships;
- partnerships with a non-individual partner during the basis period;
- lloyds underwriters;
- farming businesses with a herd basis election in effect for the tax year;
- farming and creative businesses with a profits averaging election in effect for the tax year;
- businesses that have claimed business premises renovation allowances within the previous seven years (ending immediately before the basis period);
- businesses that carry on a mineral extraction trade during the basis period for the tax year;
- businesses that still own an asset in respect of which research and development allowances have been claimed (at any time).

Simplified cash basis for unincorporated businesses

(F(No. 2)A 2017, Sch. 2)

Finance (No. 2) Act 2017 introduces new rules relating to the calculation of the taxable profits of unincorporated businesses. This includes a simplified treatment of capital expenditure under the cash basis for trades, professions and vocations and the introduction of the cash basis for the calculation of taxable profits of property businesses. These changes will have effect for tax years from 2017–18 onwards, though for the 2017–18 tax year trading profits can be calculated using either the new rules or the existing rules.

[¶2-020]   Trade profits: deductions allowable at a fixed rate

(ITTOIA 2005, Pt. 2, Ch. 5A)

(Tax Reporter: ¶208-380)

From the tax year 2013–14, unincorporated businesses are entitled to use flat rates to calculate certain types of expenses rather than having to calculate actual amounts.

Taxation of Business Profits

Expense	From 6 April 2013
Expenditure on vehicles Car or goods vehicle – first 10,000 miles – above 10,000 miles Motorcycle	£0.45/mile £0.25/mile £0.24/mile
	Rate per Month £
Use of home for business[(1)(3)] 25–50 hours per month 51–100 hours per month 101 hours or more per month Or claim allowable portion of actual costs	10.00 18.00 26.00
Premises used both as home and business premises[(2)(3)] Disallowance (for personal element of expenses) one occupant using premises as a home two occupants using premises as a home three or more occupants using premises as a home Or identify allowable portion of actual costs	350.00 500.00 650.00

Notes

[(1)] Deduction is given for each month or part of a month in relation to the number of hours spent wholly and exclusively on work done by the person in their home wholly and exclusively for the purposes of the trade (ITTOIA 2005, s. 94H).

[(2)] Available for premises which are mainly used for the purposes of carrying on the trade but also used by the person as a home. Instead of apportioning expenses between business and personal use, a deduction may be claimed for the full expense minus the relevant flat rate non-business use amount (ITTOIA 2005, s. 94I).

[(3)] *Finance Act* 2016 amends the simplified expenses regime, with effect for the tax year 2016–17 and subsequent tax years, to ensure that partnerships can fully access the provisions in respect of the use of a home and where business premises are also a home.

[¶2-030]   Limited liability partnerships: salaried members

(ITTOIA 2005, s. 863A–863G)

(Tax Reporter: ¶292-650)

From 6 April 2014, an individual member (M) of an LLP is treated as an employee for tax purposes (subject to PAYE and to tax on any benefits in kind) if all of the three conditions set out below are met. The rules apply only to LLPs formed under the *Limited Liability Partnership Act* 2000, not to general partnerships or limited partnerships that are formed under the *Partnership Act* 1890 and the *Limited Partnership Act* 1907, respectively.

Condition	Requirements for condition to be satisfied
Condition A: Disguised salary	Arrangements are in place under which: • M is to perform services for the LLP; and • it is reasonable to expect that at least 80% of the total amount payable by the LLP in respect of M's performance of those services will be 'disguised salary' (i.e. fixed, or variable but without reference to the overall amount of the profits or losses of the LLP; or not in practice affected by the overall profits or losses of the LLP).
Condition B: Significant influence	If the mutual rights and duties of the members and the LLP do not give M significant influence over the affairs of the partnership.
Condition C: Capital contribution	M's contribution to the LLP is less than 25% of the disguised salary which it is reasonable to expect will be payable in a relevant tax year in respect of M's performance of services for the partnership.

[¶2-050]   Car hire: leases starting from 6 April 2009
(ITTOIA 2005, s. 48ff.)

(Tax Reporter: ¶212-025)

Leased cars, where the lease begins from 6 April 2009 (for income tax purposes), suffer a 15% disallowance of relevant payments if CO_2 emissions exceed the limits set out below, otherwise no disallowance. This applies to all cars (not just those costing more than £12,000).

	CO_2 emissions
On or after 6 April 2018	Over 110g/km
6 April 2013 to 5 April 2018	Over 130g/km
6 April 2009 to 5 April 2013	Over 160g/km

[¶2-060]   Car hire: leases starting before 6 April 2009
(ITTOIA 2005, s. 48ff.)

(Tax Reporter: ¶212-050)

For leased cars where the lease began before 6 April 2009, the restricted deduction for hire charges of motor cars with a retail price greater than £12,000 is calculated as follows:

$$\text{Allowable amount} = \frac{£12,000 + \frac{1}{2}(\text{retail price} - £12,000)}{\text{retail price}} \times \text{hire charge}$$

[¶2-100]   Time limits for elections and claims
(TMA 1970, s. 43(1))

(Tax Reporter: ¶191-635)

In the absence of any provision to the contrary, under self-assessment for the purposes of income tax, the normal rule is that claims are to be made within four years from the end of the tax year to which they relate.

Other specific income tax provisions are as below.

Provision	Time limit	Statutory reference
Averaging of profits of farmers or creative artists	first anniversary of the normal self-assessment filing date for the second tax year	ITTOIA 2005, s. 222
Stock transferred to a connected party on cessation of trade (or, from April 2009, profession or vocation) to be valued at higher of cost or sale price	first anniversary of the normal self-assessment filing date for the tax year of cessation	ITTOIA 2005, s. 178
Post-cessation expenses relieved against income and chargeable gains	first anniversary of the normal self-assessment filing date for the tax year	ITTOIA 2005, s. 257(4); ITA 2007, s. 96
Current and preceding year set-off of trading losses	first anniversary of the normal self-assessment filing date for the loss-making year	ITA 2007, s. 64
Three-year carry-back of trading losses in first four years of trade	first anniversary of the normal self-assessment filing date for the tax year in which the loss is made	ITA 2007, s. 72
Carry-forward of trading losses	normal rules apply (see above)	ITA 2007, s. 83ff.
Carry-back of terminal losses	normal rules apply (see above)	ITA 2007, s. 89

TAXATION OF INVESTMENT INCOME

[¶3-000]   Registered pension schemes

(FA 2004, Pt. 4, Ch. 1–7 and Sch. 28–36; SI 2014/1843)

From 6 April 2006, ('A' day) a revised set of rules applies to all forms of pension provision.

Age restrictions

Normal minimum pension age is 55 from 6 April 2010 (previously 50) except for retirement on ill-health grounds and some preserved lower retirement ages – see below.

From 2010–11 onwards, there is no minimum benefit age. Previously, benefits had to be taken by the age of 77 at the latest (age 75 before 22 June 2010).

Recent changes

- From 2017–18:
    - the Money Purchase Annual Allowance is reduced to £4,000 (F(No. 2)A 2017, s. 7);
    - alignment of the UK tax treatment of payments out of 'foreign pension schemes' with the UK's domestic tax regime and pension schemes used for those employed abroad; in particular:
        - funds in a registered pension scheme based outside the UK are subject to UK taxation consistent with the tax treatment of a UK based registered pension scheme;
        - tax the full foreign pension of UK residents, instead of 90%;
        - close specialist 'section 615 schemes' to new pension saving if individuals wish to continue to be able to receive relief from tax in respect of annuity payments from those schemes; and
        - tax foreign pension lump sums paid to UK residents that are not already liable to UK tax.

        (FA 2017, Sch. 3).
    - introduce a new tax on transfers of pension savings to qualifying recognised overseas pension schemes (QROPS). The tax applies to transfers requested on or after 9 March 2017 (FA 2017, Sch. 4) (see ¶3-100);
- *Finance Act* 2016 legislated for a number of minor changes to the pensions tax rules to ensure that they operate as intended following the introduction of pension flexibility in April 2015, with effect from 15 September 2016, that:
    - remove the requirement that a serious ill-health lump sum can only be paid from an arrangement that has never been accessed;
    - replace the 45% tax charge on serious ill-health lump sums paid to individuals who have reached age 75 with tax at the individual's marginal rate;

- enable dependants with drawdown or flexi-access drawdown pension who would currently have to use all of this fund before age 23 or pay tax charges of up to 70% on any lump sum payment, to continue to access their funds as they wish after their 23rd birthday;

- remove the rule on paying a charity lump sum death benefit out of drawdown pension funds and flexi-access drawdown funds where the member dies under the age of 75 because the equivalent tax-free payment may be made as another type of lump sum death benefit;

- enable money purchase pensions in payment to be paid as a trivial commutation lump sum;

- enable the full amount of dependants benefits to be paid as authorised payments where there are insufficient funds in a cash balance arrangement when the member dies.

Tax relief on contributions

(ITEPA 2003, s. 308; FA 2004, Pt. 4, Ch. 4)

(Tax Reporter: ¶376-000ff.; ¶376-500ff.)

Type of contribution	Tax relief
Individual	the greater of £3,600 and the amount of the member's relevant UK earnings, subject to the annual allowance
Employer	No income tax for employee (not a taxable BIK) No NIC liability Tax deductible for employer[1]

Note

[1] Where contributions in a chargeable period exceed 210% of the contributions made in the immediately preceding chargeable period, relief for the excess of the current period contributions over 110% of the previous period's contributions (where that excess amounts to £500,000 or more) is to be spread forward into future chargeable periods. A fraction of the excess is to be treated as being paid in the current and subsequent periods (as below) with any remainder of the excess being relieved in the current period:

- excess £500,000 or more but less than £1m: one-half of excess allowed in current period and the next succeeding periods;
- excess £1m or more but less than £2m: one-third of excess allowed in the current period and the two following periods;
- excess £2m or more: one quarter of excess allowed in current period and the three following periods (FA 2004, s. 197).

[¶3-050]   Authorised payments limits

(ITEPA 2003, s. 636A; FA 2004, s. 164ff., Sch. 28 and 29)

(Tax Reporter: ¶378-000ff.)

Payments	Limits
Pension commencement	25% tax free lump sum (75% as pension income at marginal rate)
Capped drawdown	No new capped drawdowns from 6 April 2015 (previously, 150% on or after 27 March 2014 and 120% before)
Flexible drawdown[(1)]	No limit from 6 April 2015 (£12,000 minimum income requirement on or after 27 March 2014; previously £20,000)
Trivial commutation lump sum[(2)]	£30,000 on or after 27 March 2014 (previously £18,000)
Small pension pot[(2)]	£10,000; three lump sums on or after 27 March 2014 (previously £2,000; two lump sums)
Dependants' trivial commutation lump sum death benefit[(3)]	£30,000 from 6 April 2015 (previously, £18,000) all at dependant's marginal rate
Uncrystallised funds pension lump sum[(4)]	25% tax free 75% at marginal rate

Notes

[(1)] From 6 April 2015, there is no limit on how much can be taken from a flexi-access drawdown fund, but when benefits are first accessed from that fund, the money purchase annual allowance rules described in Pt. 4 are triggered in respect of that member.

[(2)] Apart from flexible drawdown, the only circumstances where an individual can normally take all of their pension pot as a single one-off payment is where their total pension savings in all funds are less than £30,000 (the trivial commutation limit for commutation periods beginning on or after 27 March 2014, previously, the limit was £18,000) or in certain circumstances where the value of a small pension pot is less than £10,000 (for payments made on or after 27 March 2014, previously the limit was £2,000). From 6 April 2015, a trivial commutation lump sum can be paid only in respect of a defined benefits arrangement. Those with relatively small amounts of money purchase savings will be able to take an UFPLS from this date, so there is no longer a need for trivial commutation lump sum rules for money purchase arrangements. To qualify for these payments, the individual must have reached normal minimum pension age (normally age 55) or satisfy the ill-health condition in FA 2004, Sch. 28, para. 1 (from 6 April 2015; previously, individuals had to have reached age 60). From 15 September 2016, a trivial commutation lump sum may be paid out of a money purchase scheme pension that is already in payment (FA 2004, Sch. 29, para. 7 and ITEPA 2003, s. 636B, as amended by FA 2016, s. 22 and Sch. 5).

[(3)] A trivial commutation lump sum death benefit can be paid to a dependant and, from 6 April 2015, to an individual in respect of any entitlement they had to receive any guaranteed pension payments of a lifetime annuity or scheme pension payable after the member's death. The whole lump sum will be taxable at the dependant's marginal rate.

[(4)] A new type of authorised lump sum payment (UFPLS) can be paid on or after 6 April 2015 directly from pension savings under a money purchase arrangement to certain individuals aged 55 or over. Individuals who meet the conditions to have an UFPLS can, therefore, if they wish, access as much of their money purchase pension savings as they want, without having first to designate the funds as available for drawdown. Where an UFPLS is paid, then this is flexible access and the money purchase annual allowance rules are triggered in respect of that member (FA 2004, s. 166(1) and Sch. 29, para. 4A).

Taxation of Investment Income

[¶3-075]   Annual and lifetime allowances

(FA 2004, s. 214ff. and 227ff.)

(Tax Reporter: ¶386-000 and ¶384-000)

Since A-day, there have been no limits on the amount of pension savings an individual can have, but there are limits on the amount of tax relief that is available. These are the lifetime allowance and the annual allowance.

Year	Annual allowance limit[(1)(2)(3)]	Annual allowance income limit[(4)]	Money purchase annual allowance[(5)]	Lifetime allowance[(6)(8)(9)(10)]	Lifetime allowance charge[(7)]
2018–19[(11)]	£40,000	£150,000	£4,000	£1,030,000	25% as pension; 55% as lump sum
2017–18	£40,000	£150,000	£4,000	£1m	25% as pension; 55% as lump sum
2016–17	£40,000	£150,000	£10,000	£1m	25% as pension; 55% as lump sum
2015–16[(3)] 9 July 2015 – 5 April 2016 ('post-alignment tax year')	£40,000	—	£10,000	£1.25m	25% as pension; 55% as lump sum
2015–16[(3)] 6 April 2015 – 8 July 2015 ('pre-alignment tax year')	£80,000	—			
2014–15	£40,000	—	—	£1.25m	25% as pension; 55% as lump sum
2013–14 and 2012–13	£50,000	—	—	£1.5m	25% as pension; 55% as lump sum
2011–12	£50,000	—	—	£1.80m	25% as pension; 55% as lump sum

Notes
Annual allowance

(1) An individual's annual allowance (AA) applies to all of that individual's pension arrangements for a year. It measures the 'pension input amount' for a tax year. That is the increase in the pension savings in that tax year (including contributions made by the individual and employer); and/or the increase in the value of the individual's pension rights (depending on the type of scheme, i.e. money purchase, defined benefit, etc.). If the 'pension input amount' for a year exceeds the AA for that year, the excess is subject to the charge. For future years the AA will be fixed by Treasury Order. Where for 2011–12 onwards, an annual allowance charge arises the annual allowance for that year may be increased by the unused annual allowance of the three immediately preceding years, except where the charge arises in 2015–16 or later and in a preceding year, the member or a dependant elected for flexible drawdown (in which case, no carry forward of unused annual allowance from that preceding year is possible) (FA 2004, s. 228A).

(2) An AA charge is the liability of the individual member of the scheme (or schemes where an individual is a member of more than one scheme), but provisions introduced from 6 April 2011 enable the member to transfer that liability onto the scheme administrator in certain circumstances (Tax Reporter: ¶386-010; FA 2004, s. 227–238). From 2011–12 onwards, the rate of tax to be charged on the excess is to be the 'appropriate rate'; that is, the rate or rates which would be charged on the excess if it was to be added to the individual's 'reduced net income' for the tax year concerned. That figure is the sum calculated at Step 3 of the prescribed method of calculating income tax liabilities. Any increase in the basic rate or higher rate bands due to pension contributions made under deduction of tax or gift aid payments is also taken into account for this purpose.

(3) From 6 April 2016, pension input periods are aligned with the tax year.

(4) From 6 April 2016, the existing £40,000 annual allowance is gradually reduced to £10,000 for those with incomes, including the amount of any pension savings, above £150,000. For each £2 of income above £150,000, an individual's annual allowance will reduce by £1 until the individual's income reaches £210,000 or over, when their annual allowance will be £10,000 (FA 2004, s. 228ZA and 228ZB).

(5) Where an individual has flexibly accessed their pension savings on or after 6 April 2015, an annual allowance will immediately apply to their future money purchase pension savings: the money purchase annual allowance rules. However, those individuals will retain an annual allowance for defined benefits pension savings, depending on the value of new money purchase pension savings. Unused annual allowance brought forward from earlier tax years will not be available to increase the money purchase annual allowance (FA 2004, s. 227ZA–227G).

Lifetime allowance

(6) An individual's lifetime allowance (LTA) is a measure of the total value of an individual's pension savings at the time that pension benefits begin to be taken. For future years the LTA will be fixed by Treasury Order.

(7) An LTA charge (55% on any excess over the LTA constituting a lump sum payment; and 25% on any excess over the LTA not used to pay a lump sum but to fund pension payments) is the joint and several liability of the individual and the pension scheme administrator (Tax Reporter: ¶384-050; FA 2004, s. 214–226).

(8) *Finance Act* 2013, Sch. 22 provided a transitional protection regime (fixed protection 2014) for individuals with UK tax relieved pension rights (or anticipated rights) of more than £1.25m who notified HMRC by 5 April 2014.

(9) *Finance Act* 2014 introduced a further transitional protection regime, individual protection 2014 (IP14) which entitled individuals with pension savings on 5 April 2014 of greater than £1.25m but who did not have primary protection to a lifetime allowance equal to the value of those savings, subject to an overall limit of £1.5m. SI 2014/1842 sets out relevant notice requirements.

(10) *Finance Act* 2016 reduced the lifetime allowance for pension contributions to £1m for the tax years 2016–17 and 2017–18. *Finance Act* 2016 also provides a requirement for the Treasury to make regulations before the start of tax year 2018–19 and each subsequent tax year, specifying the amount of the standard lifetime allowance for the year. The allowance will be increased by CPI (rounded up to the nearest £100) where the CPI for the year to the previous September is higher than it was 12 months earlier, otherwise, the allowance will remain the same as for the previous tax year (FA 2004, s. 218, as amended by FA 2016, s. 19). Transitional protection for pension rights already over £1m was introduced by way of two new transitional protections 'fixed protection 2016' and 'individual protection 2016', also from 6 April 2016 (FA 2016, Sch. 4).

(11) Rates per Autumn Budget 2017.

Taxation of Investment Income

[¶3-100]   Pension schemes: tax charges

Authorised payment charges

(FA 2004, s. 204–207)

(Tax Reporter: ¶383-000ff.)

Tax charges	Pre-6 April 2015	From 6 April 2015
Short service refund lump sum charge[1] (FA 2004, s. 205; Tax Reporter: ¶383-100)	20% up to £20,000; 50% on excess	20% up to £20,000; 50% on excess
Serious ill health lump sum charge[2] (FA 2004, s. 205A; Tax Reporter: ¶383-120)	55%	45% until 15 September 2016
Special lump sum death benefits charge[3] (FA 2004, s. 206; Tax Reporter: ¶383-150)	55%	45%
Authorised surplus payments charge (FA 2004, s. 207; Tax Reporter: ¶383-200)	35%	35%

Notes

[1] A tax charge arises where a registered pension scheme repays tax-relieved pension contributions to a member who has completed less than two years service ('short service refund lump sums'). The rate is 20% on the first £20,000 and 50% thereafter.

[2] There is no charge to income tax either on the individual or the scheme administrator on payment of a serious ill-health lump sum to a member who has not reached the age of 75 (unless the lifetime allowance is an issue). A serious ill-health lump sum paid to a member who has reached the age of 75 is taxed as pension income (at marginal rates) of the recipient member. However, before 16 September 2016, such payments were subject to the serious ill-health lump sum charge, which was an income tax charge on the scheme administrator at the rate of 45% (55% where paid before 6 April 2015).

[3] Where a taxable lump sum death benefit listed below is paid on or after 6 April 2016 and directly from the pension scheme to an individual, it is usually treated as the recipient's pension income and tax deducted under PAYE by way of the RTI process. The taxable lump sum death benefits this tax treatment relates to are:

— defined benefits lump sum death benefit;

— uncrystallised funds lump sum death benefit;

— pension protection lump sum death benefit;

— annuity protection lump sum death benefit;

— drawdown pension fund lump sum death benefit;

— flexi-access drawdown fund lump sum death benefit.

But where the payment is to an individual who is receiving the payment in their capacity as:

— a trustee (but not a bare trustee);

— a personal representative;

— a director of a company;

— a partner in a firm; or

— a member of a limited liability partnership,

the payment is not treated as their income for tax purposes and instead, the scheme administrator is liable to the special lump sum death benefits charge on the amount paid.

Other charges

(FA 2004, s. 208–213, 242)

(Tax Reporter: ¶383-500ff.; ¶388-500)

Charge	Rate
Unauthorised payments charge (FA 2004, s. 208; Tax Reporter: ¶383-550)	40%
Unauthorised payments surcharge[1] (FA 2004, s. 209; Tax Reporter: ¶383-600)	15%
Scheme sanction charge[2] (FA 2004, s. 239; Tax Reporter: ¶383-700)	40%
Deregistration charge[3] (FA 2004, s. 242; Tax Reporter: ¶388-500)	40%
Overseas transfer charge[4] (from 9 March 2017 on certain transfers to and from a QROPS)	25%

Notes

[1] A surcharge may be added to the unauthorised payment charge if a scheme pays out more than 25% of the scheme's fund in unauthorised payments.

[2] The scheme sanction charge is imposed at the rate of 40% of the aggregate of the 'scheme chargeable payments' (as defined by FA 2004, s. 241). The person liable to the scheme sanction charge is the scheme administrator. Where the scheme chargeable payment is also an unauthorised payment which has given rise to an unauthorised payments charge, the tax due under the scheme sanction charge is effectively reduced by the amount of tax actually paid (rather than charged) under the unauthorised payments charge.

[3] Where a registered scheme loses its registered status, a 'deregistration charge' of 40% of the aggregate value of the pension scheme's assets is levied on an payable by the scheme administrator.

[4] *Finance Act* 2017 introduces a 25% tax charge to pension transfers made to QROPS. Exceptions apply allowing transfers to be made tax free where people have a genuine need to transfer their pension, where:
* both the individual and the pension scheme are in countries within the European Economic Area (EEA);
* if outside the EEA, both the individual and the pension scheme are in the same country; or
* the QROPS is an occupational pension scheme provided by the individual's employer.

If the individual's circumstances change within five tax years of the transfer, the tax treatment of the transfer will be reconsidered. The changes will take effect for transfers requested on or after 9 March 2017 (FA 2004, s. 244A–244N, as inserted by *Finance Act* 2017, Sch. 4, Pt. 2).

[¶3-150]   Early retirement ages: retirement annuity contracts and personal pension schemes

From 6 April 2006

(FA 2004, Sch. 36, para. 23)

(Tax Reporter: ¶390-450)

Generally, if individuals take benefits from a registered pension scheme before age 55, they will be liable to a tax charge unless they are retiring due to ill-health. However, some individuals had unqualified rights on 5 April 2006 to take benefits before the normal minimum pension age. Where certain conditions are met, these individuals may take their benefits earlier than age 55 without a tax charge. This is known as the individual's protected pension age. If an individual has a protected pension age, the tax rules provide that it replaces the prevailing normal minimum pension age for all purposes of the pensions tax legislation except for the lifetime allowance reduction that may apply where the protected pension age is less than 50 and benefits are taken before normal minimum pension age.

In order to exercise the right to a lower than normal pension age, the member must:

- be or have been in one of the occupations prescribed in the list at the *Registered Pension Schemes (Prescribed Schemes and Occupations) Regulations* 2005 (SI 2005/3451), Sch. 2, prior to 6 April 2006; and

- have had an 'unqualified right' to take a pension before the age of 50, prior to 6 April 2006 (an 'unqualified right' is when the individual needs no other party to consent to their request to take an early pension before it becomes binding upon the scheme or contract holder).

The list below will continue to apply to pension scheme members who are able to meet the conditions for a protected pension age lower than 50, as at 6 April 2006. All of the professions noted in the list below that have a retirement age of less than 50 are included in the list at SI 2005/3451, Sch. 2.

Profession or occupation
Athletes (appearance and prize money)
Badminton players
Boxers
Cricketers
Cyclists
Dancers
Divers (saturation, deep sea and free swimming)
Footballers
Golfers (tournament earnings)
Ice hockey players
Jockeys
– flat racing
– national hunt
Members of the reserve forces
Models
Motorcycle riders (motorcross or road racing)
Motor racing drivers
Rugby league players
Rugby union players
Skiers (downhill)
Snooker or billiards players
Speedway riders
Squash players
Table tennis players
Tennis players (including real tennis)
Trapeze artistes
Wrestlers

[¶3-175]   Equalisation of and increase in pensionable ages for both men and women

For the purposes of social security legislation, an individual's pensionable age is determined by the following rules and tables. These gradually increase the pensionable age for women from the traditional age of 60 to bring it into line with that for men, while also increasing the ages for both sexes. Dates in the table below are grouped in one-month periods. A person born towards the end of one of these periods would have a slightly younger pension age than someone born at the beginning.

A man born before 6 December 1953 still attains pensionable age at age 65, while a woman born before 6 April 1950 attained pensionable age at age 60. The date the pensionable age is attained by individuals born after those dates is set out in the tables below. Table 1 relates to women born before 6 December 1953, while Table 2 relates to someone of either sex born on or after that date.

Under current law, the state pension age is due to increase to 68 between 2044 and 2046. However, the Government has announced plans to bring this timetable forward so that the state pension age will increase to 68 between 2037 and 2039. This change has yet to be enacted in legislation.

Table 1: Women

Date of birth (by month)	State pension age y.m	Pensionable age attained
06/04/50 to 05/05/50	60.1–60.0	06/05/2010
06/05/50 to 05/06/50	60.2–60.1	06/07/2010
06/06/50 to 05/07/50	60.3–60.2	06/09/2010
06/07/50 to 05/08/50	60.4–60.3	06/11/2010
06/08/50 to 05/09/50	60.5–60.4	06/01/2011
06/09/50 to 05/10/50	60.6–60.5	06/03/2011
06/10/50 to 05/11/50	60.7–60.6	06/05/2011
06/11/50 to 05/12/50	60.8–60.7	06/07/2011
06/12/50 to 05/01/51	60.9–60.8	06/09/2011
06/01/51 to 05/02/51	60.10–60.9	06/11/2011
06/02/51 to 05/03/51	60.11–60.10	06/01/2012
06/03/51 to 05/04/51	61.0–60.11	06/03/2012
06/04/51 to 05/05/51	61.1–61.0	06/05/2012
06/05/51 to 05/06/51	61.2–61.1	06/07/2012
06/06/51 to 05/07/51	61.3–61.2	06/09/2012
06/07/51 to 05/08/51	61.4–61.3	06/11/2012
06/08/51 to 05/09/51	61.5–61.4	06/01/2013
06/09/51 to 05/10/51	61.6–61.5	06/03/2013
06/10/51 to 05/11/51	61.7–61.6	06/05/2013
06/11/51 to 05/12/51	61.8–61.7	06/07/2013
06/12/51 to 05/01/52	61.9–61.8	06/09/2013
06/01/52 to 05/02/52	61.10–61.9	06/11/2013

Taxation of Investment Income

Date of birth (by month)	State pension age y.m	Pensionable age attained
06/02/52 to 05/03/52	61.11–61.10	06/01/2014
06/03/52 to 05/04/52	62.0–61.11	06/03/2014
06/04/52 to 05/05/52	62.1–62.0	06/05/2014
06/05/52 to 05/06/52	62.2–62.1	06/07/2014
06/06/52 to 05/07/52	62.3–62.2	06/09/2014
06/07/52 to 05/08/52	62.4–62.3	06/11/2014
06/08/52 to 05/09/52	62.5–62.4	06/01/2015
06/09/52 to 05/10/52	62.6–62.5	06/03/2015
06/10/52 to 05/11/52	62.7–62.6	06/05/2015
06/11/52 to 05/12/52	62.8–62.7	06/07/2015
06/12/52 to 05/01/53	62.9–62.8	06/09/2015
06/01/53 to 05/02/53	62.10–62.9	06/11/2015
06/02/53 to 05/03/53	62.11–62.10	06/01/2016
06/03/53 to 05/04/53	63.0–62.11	06/03/2016
06/04/53 to 05/05/53	63.3–63.2	06/07/2016
06/05/53 to 05/06/53	63.6–63.5	06/11/2016
06/06/53 to 05/07/53	63.9–63.8	06/03/2017
06/07/53 to 05/08/53	64.0–63.11	06/07/2017
06/08/53 to 05/09/53	64.3–64.2	06/11/2017
06/09/53 to 05/10/53	64.6–64.5	06/03/2018
06/10/53 to 05/11/53	64.9–64.8	06/07/2018
06/11/53 to 05/12/53	65.0–64.11	06/11/2018

Table 2: Men and Women

Date of birth (by month)	State pension age[1] y.m	Pensionable age attained[1]
06/12/53 to 05/01/54	65.3–65.2	06/03/2019
06/01/54 to 05/02/54	65.4–65.3	06/05/2019
06/02/54 to 05/03/54	65.5–65.4	06/07/2019
06/03/54 to 05/04/54	65.6–65.5	06/09/2019
06/04/54 to 05/05/54	65.7–65.6	06/11/2019
06/05/54 to 05/06/54	65.8–65.7	06/01/2020
06/06/54 to 05/07/54	65.9–65.8	06/03/2020
06/07/54 to 05/08/54	65.10–65.9	06/05/2020
06/08/54 to 05/09/54	65.11–65.10	06/07/2020
06/09/54 to 05/10/54	66.0–65.11	06/09/2020
06/10/54 to 05/04/60	Age 66	[06/10/2020–05/04/2026]
06/04/60 to 05/05/60	Age 66 years and 1 month	[06/05/2026–05/06/2026]
06/05/60 to 05/06/60	Age 66 years and 2 months	[06/07/2026–05/08/2026]
06/06/60 to 05/07/60	Age 66 years and 3 months	[06/09/2026–05/10/2026]

Date of birth (by month)	State pension age[1] y.m	Pensionable age attained[1]
06/07/60[2] to 05/08/60	Age 66 years and 4 months	[06/11/2026–05/12/2026]
06/08/60 to 05/09/60	Age 66 years and 5 months	[06/01/2027–05/02/2027]
06/09/60 to 05/10/60	Age 66 years and 6 months	[06/03/2027–05/04/2027]
06/10/60 to 05/11/60	Age 66 years and 7 months	[06/05/2027–05/06/2027]
06/11/60 to 05/12/60	Age 66 years and 8 months	[06/07/2027–05/08/2027]
06/12/60[3] to 05/01/61	Age 66 years and 9 months	[06/09/2027–05/10/2027]
06/01/61[4] to 05/02/61	Age 66 years and 10 months	[06/11/2027–05/12/2027]
06/02/61 to 05/03/61	Age 66 years and 11 months	[06/01/2028–05/02/2028]
06/03/61 to 06/04/77	Age 67	[06/03/2028–06/04/2044]
06/04/77 to 05/05/77	67.1–67.0	06/05/2044
06/05/77 to 05/06/77	67.2–67.1	06/07/2044
06/06/77 to 05/07/77	67.3–67.2	06/09/2044
06/07/77 to 05/08/77	67.4–67.3	06/11/2044
06/08/77 to 05/09/77	67.5–67.4	06/01/2045
06/09/77 to 05/10/77	67.6–67.5	06/03/2045
06/10/77 to 05/11/77	67.7–67.6	06/05/2045
06/11/77 to 05/12/77	67.8–67.7	06/07/2045
06/12/77 to 05/01/78	67.9–67.8	06/09/2045
06/01/78 to 05/02/78	67.10–67.9	06/11/2045
06/02/78 to 05/03/78	67.11–67.10	06/01/2046
06/03/78 to 05/04/78	68.00–67.11	06/03/2046
On or after 06/04/78	Age 68	[On or after 06/04/2046]

Notes

[1] Individuals born between 6 April 1954 and 6 April 1977 and those born on or after 6 April 1978 attain state pension age at the age shown in column 2 (with figures in square brackets in column 3 being calculated date ranges). Otherwise, individuals attain state pension age at the date shown in column 3.

[2] A person born on 31 July 1960 is to be taken to attain the age of 66 years and four months at the commencement of 30 November 2026.

[3] A person born on 31 December 1960 is to be taken to attain the age of 66 years and nine months at the commencement of 30 September 2027.

[4] A person born on 31 January 1961 is to be taken to attain the age of 66 years and ten months at the commencement of 30 November 2027.

Taxation of Investment Income

[¶3-200]   State retirement pensions

	Weekly rates			
	Full rate of state pension[1] £	Single person £	Married couple wife not a contributor £	Age addition (over 80) each £
From 6 April 2017	159.55	122.30	195.60	0.25
6/4/16 to 5/4/17	155.65	119.30	190.80	0.25
6/4/15 to 5/4/16	–	115.95	185.45	0.25
7/4/14 to 5/4/15	–	113.10	180.90	0.25
8/4/13 to 6/4/14	–	110.15	176.15	0.25
9/4/12 to 7/4/13	–	107.45	171.85	0.25
11/4/11 to 8/4/12	–	102.15	163.35	0.25

Note

[1] The *Pensions Act* 2014 introduced a new single tier pension from 6 April 2016. Individuals reaching pensionable age after that date are no longer entitled to the two-component state pension (the basic state pension and additional state pension based on amounts of National Insurance contributions (NICs) paid) but are instead entitled to a single-component flat-rate pension. Basic conditions of entitlement at the full rate include having attained pensionable age and having 35 or more 'qualifying years' of NICs (based on the individuals earnings factor reaching the qualifying amount for the tax year). Entitlement is subject to a minimum number of qualifying years (no more than ten) and pro-rated for individuals with fewer than 35 years. Transitional provisions apply for individuals who have paid, or are treated as having paid, NICs in respect of tax years before the introduction of the new state pension; for inheriting entitlement from a late spouse or civil partner who had made contributions prior to the introduction of the new state pension; for women who before 1977 elected to pay a reduced rate of NICs, and for sharing a pension with a former spouse or civil partner upon divorce.

[¶3-300]   Gilt-edged securities held by non-residents

(ITTOIA 2005, s. 713; ITA 2007, s. 893–897, 1024)

(Tax Reporter: ¶120-800)

Interest on all gilt-edged securities is payable gross. Interest may be paid net, if the holder wishes, by notice to the Registrar of Government Stock. Payment gross does not of itself imply that the interest is exempt from tax.

All gilt-edged securities are automatically given FOTRA status (Free Of Tax for Residents Abroad), thereby guaranteeing exemption from tax for holders not resident in the UK. Account holders receive interest on registered holdings of FOTRA securities without deduction of tax, unless they have asked for tax to be deducted.

[¶3-350]   Individual savings accounts (ISAs)

(ITTOIA 2005, s. 694–701; SI 1998/1870; SI 2004/1450)
(Tax Reporter: ¶315-000)

	2018–19[12]	2017–18	2016–17[8][10]	2015–16	2014–15[7] 1 July 2014 – 5 April 2015	6 April 2014 – 30 June 2014	2013–14
	£	£	£	£	£	£	£
'Adult' ISAs							
Maximum subscription limit	20,000	20,000	15,240	15,240	15,000	11,880	11,520
Cash limit	—[4]	—[4]	—[4]	—[4]	—[4]	5,940	5,760
Junior ISAs/Child Trust Funds[5][6]							
Maximum subscription limit	4,260	4,128	4,080	4,080	4,000	3,840	3,720
Lifetime ISA[11]							
Maximum subscription limit	[4,000]	4,000	—	—	—	—	—
Government contribution	[25%]	25%	—	—	—	—	—
Help to buy ISA[9]							
Maximum savings per month	[200]	200	200	200	—	—	—
Government contribution	[25%]	25%	25%	25%	—	—	—

Notes

[1] To open an ISA, an individual has to be aged 18 or over (or over the age of 16 for cash ISAs) and resident in the UK for tax purposes.

[2] All income and gains derived from investments within the account are tax free and withdrawals from the account will not attract any tax charge.

[3] From 6 April 2011, the ISA subscription limits have been increased in line with inflation. From 2012–13 onwards, the index used is the consumer prices index (CPI) (previously RPI).

[4] From 1 July 2014, the restriction that only 50% of the overall subscription limit may be invested in a cash ISA was removed. SI 1998/1870 was also amended to allow transfers to be made from a stocks and shares account to a cash account (SI 2014/1450).

[5] Children born between 1 September 2002 and 2 January 2011, living in the UK and in receipt of child benefit were eligible for a Child Trust Fund account. Child Trust Funds are now closed to new accounts but subscriptions can still be paid into existing accounts. Withdrawals are not permitted until the child has reached the age of 18, except in cases of terminal illness.

[6] Junior ISAs became available form 1 November 2011 to any child under 18, living in the UK, who is not eligible for a Child Trust Fund account. Withdrawals are not permitted until the child has reached the age of 18, except in cases of terminal illness.

[7] From 3 December 2014, if an ISA saver in a marriage or civil partnership dies, their spouse or civil partner will inherit their ISA tax advantages. From 6 April 2015, surviving spouses will be able to invest as much into their own ISA as their spouse used to have, on top of their usual allowance.

[8] From 6 April 2016, ISA savers can withdraw and replace money from their cash ISA without it counting towards their annual ISA subscription limit for that year (SI 1998/1870, as amended by SI 2016/16).

Taxation of Investment Income

⁽⁹⁾ From 1 December 2015, the 'Help to buy ISA' was launched for individuals saving for their first home. Government contributions are limited with a minimum contribution of £400 (so closing balance must be £1,600 before the bonus can be claimed) and a maximum of £3,000 for £12,000 savings. The accounts are only available for first time buyers and can be opened with an additional one off deposit of £1,000 (see www.helptobuy.gov.uk/help-to-buy-isa/how-does-it-work/).

⁽¹⁰⁾ *Finance Act* 2016 introduces legislation to allow the ISA savings of a deceased person to continue to benefit from tax advantages during the administration of their estate (ITTOIA 2005, s. 694A, as inserted by FA 2016, s. 27).

⁽¹¹⁾ The Lifetime ISA is available from 6 April 2017, can be opened by adults younger than 40 years old and allows adults to save up to £4,000 each year that they are younger than 50 years old and receive a government bonus of 25% (up to £1,000 a year), which can be withdrawn tax-free to buy a first home or when the individual turns 60.

⁽¹²⁾ Rates per Autumn Budget 2017, except those shown in square brackets which reflect current rates as no changes have been announced.

[¶3-400]   Enterprise investment scheme (EIS)

(ITA 2007, Pt. 5)

(Tax Reporter: ¶323-000ff.; ¶565-400ff.)

EIS relief is available for qualifying individuals who subscribe cash for the issue of qualifying shares issued by non-quoted trading companies (except those carrying on prohibited trades).

Qualifying EIS shares issued:⁽²⁾⁽³⁾⁽⁴⁾	Maximum individual investment⁽¹⁾⁽⁵⁾	Rate of IT relief on investment	Disposal of qualifying EIS shares	Carry back of EIS relief to previous tax year
On or after 6 April 2012 but before 6 April 2025	£1,000,000 per annum	30%	Capital gains not chargeable, losses allowable	Entire investment (subject to not exceeding £1,000,000 for the earlier year).
2011–12	£500,000 per annum	30%	Capital gains not chargeable, losses allowable	Entire investment (subject to not exceeding £500,000 for the earlier year).

Notes

⁽¹⁾ For an investment to qualify under EIS, the company must have raised no more than £5m (from 6 April 2012) under any or all risk capital schemes (VCT, EIS, SEIS and any other investment which is a state aid approved by the European Commission in accordance with the community guidelines on risk capital investments in SMEs) in the 12 months ending on the date of the relevant investment. From 18 November 2015, investments under the SITR will also count towards the company's annual maximum amount as will any 'relevant investments' the company's subsidiaries have received or used in the year and investments in any trade transferred from another company. From 6 April 2018, this limit will be increased to £10m by legislation in Finance Bill 2017–18 (Autumn Budget 2017).

⁽²⁾ EIS will cease to apply to new investments from 6 April 2025, unless the legislation is renewed. The date may be changed by Treasury Order and is set to be no later than ten years after the date of the European Commission's letter approving the EIS as compatible with state aids rules, following the formal notification of the scheme in June 2015 (ITA 2007, s. 157(1)(aa)).

⁽³⁾ *Finance (No. 2) Act* 2017 amends the EIS and SEIS rules to allow companies that issue shares with rights to a future conversion into shares of another class in that company to qualify for relief, with effect for shares issued on or after 5 December 2016.

⁽⁴⁾ Legislation will be included in Finance Bill 2017–18 (with effect for investments made on or after Royal Assent) to ensure the Venture Capital Schemes (EIS/SEIS/VCT) are targeted at growth investments with relief under the schemes focused on companies where there is a real risk to the capital being invested, and to exclude companies and arrangements intended to provide 'capital preservation' (Autumn Budget 2017).

⁽⁵⁾ Limit on the amount an individual may invest under the EIS in a tax year will be increased to £2m from 6 April 2018, provided any amount over £1m is invested in one or more knowledge-intensive companies, by legislation in Finance Bill 2017–18 (Autumn Budget 2017).

[¶3-420]   Seed enterprise investment scheme (SEIS)

(TCGA 1992, Sch. 5BB; ITA 2007, Pt. 5A)

(Tax Reporter: ¶319-000ff.; ¶568-500ff.)

SEIS relief is available to qualifying individuals who subscribe cash for the issue of qualifying shares in unquoted trading companies with fewer than 25 employees and assets of up to £200,000, carrying on or preparing to carry on new business.

Qualifying SEIS shares issued:[2][3]	Maximum individual investment[1]	Rate of IT relief on investment	Disposal of qualifying SEIS shares	Carry back of SEIS relief to previous year	Capital gains reinvestment limit[3]
2017–18 (from 2013–14)	£100,000 per annum	50%	Capital gains not chargeable, losses allowable	Entire investment (subject to not exceeding £100,000 for the earlier year)	50% of qualifying SEIS expenditure
2012–13	£100,000 per annum	50%	Capital gains not chargeable, losses allowable	N/A	100% of qualifying SEIS expenditure

Notes

[1] For an investment to qualify under SEIS, the company must have raised no more than £150,000 and must not have raised any capital under EIS or VCT.

[2] *Finance (No. 2) Act* 2017 amends the EIS and SEIS rules to allow companies that issue shares with rights to a future conversion into shares of another class in that company to qualify for relief, with effect for shares issued on or after 5 December 2016.

[3] Legislation will be included in Finance Bill 2017–18 (with effect for investments made on or after Royal Assent) to ensure the Venture Capital Schemes (EIS/SEIS/VCT) are targeted at growth investments with relief under the schemes focused on companies where there is a real risk to the capital being invested, and to exclude companies and arrangements intended to provide 'capital preservation' (Autumn Budget 2017).

[¶3-430]   Social investment tax relief (SITR)

(TCGA 1992, s. 255A–255E, Sch. 8B; ITA 2007, Pt. 5B)

(Tax Reporter: ¶322-000ff.; ¶569-300ff.)

SITR is available to individual investors who invest in cash in new shares or new qualifying debt investments in qualifying social enterprises (an unquoted community interest company, community benefit society or charity with fewer than 250[6] full-time equivalent employees).

Relief is not available on any investment in respect of which the investor has obtained relief under the EIS, the SEIS or the CITRS.

Taxation of Investment Income

Qualifying investment made[5]	Maximum individual investment[3]	Rate of IT on investment	Disposal of qualifying investment[1]	Carry back of SI relief to previous tax year
On or after 6 April 2015 and before 6 April 2019	£1m[4] per annum	30%	Capital gains not chargeable, losses allowable	From 2015–16, entire investment (subject to not exceeding £1m for the earlier year)
On or after 6 April 2014	£1m per annum	30%	Capital gains not chargeable, losses allowable[2]	—

Notes

[1] The exemption from capital gains applies where an investment on which income tax relief has been received (and not subsequently withdrawn) is disposed of after it has been held for at least three years. If no claim to income tax relief is made, the investment will not qualify for exemption from capital gains tax. Losses are eligible for relief in the normal way but the base cost is treated as reduced by the amount of the SI relief attributable to the asset.

[2] A capital gains tax deferral relief enables a capital gain arising from the disposal of an asset in the period from 6 April 2014 to 5 April 2019 to be deferred where the gain is reinvested (within the period one year before to three years after the gain arising) in shares or debt investments which also qualify for SITR income tax relief. It is not, however, necessary for the investor to have made a claim for SITR income tax relief.

[3] For an investment to qualify under SI, the social enterprise must (including its subsidiaries if a parent company) have no more than £15m in gross assets immediately before the investment and £16m immediately after the investment. Additionally, the social enterprise is restricted as to the amount of money it may raise under SITR, as determined by the formula:

$$\left(\frac{€200,000 - M}{RCG + RSI} \right) - T$$

Where: T is the total of any earlier SITR investments made in the previous three years;
M is the total of any other de minimis aid received in the previous three years by the social enterprise, or by a qualifying subsidiary;
RCG is the highest rate of capital gains tax in the previous three years; and
RSI is the highest rate of SITR income tax relief in the previous three years.

[4] At Spring Budget 2017, it was confirmed that, as announced at Autumn Statement 2016, the amount of investment social enterprises aged up to seven years old can raise through SITR will increase to £1.5m, with effect for investments made on or after 6 April 2017. However, the current limit will continue to apply to older social enterprises.

[5] From 6 April 2016, all remaining energy generation activities are excluded from the venture capital schemes, as well as from the enlarged SITR (amendments by FA 2016, s. 28).

[6] Limit on number of full-time equivalent employees reduced to below 250 employees (previously 500 employees) with effect for investments made on or after 6 April 2017 (amendments by F(No. 2)A 2017, Sch. 1). *Finance (No. 2) Act* 2017 also makes further amendments to the requirements for the SITR, with effect for investments made on or after 6 April 2017, including an increase in the amount of money newer social enterprises may raise from individual investors under the scheme.

[¶3-450]   Venture capital trusts (VCTs)

(TCGA 1992, s. 151A, 151B; ITTOIA 2005, s. 709; ITA 2007, Pt. 6)

(Tax Reporter: ¶326-000ff.)

A VCT is a specialised form of investment trust, which has been approved by the Board of HMRC. Certain tax advantages are obtained by individuals who subscribe for eligible shares issued by a qualifying VCT for the purposes of raising money.

Qualifying VCT Shares issued:[1][2][3][4][5]	Maximum individual investment	Rate of IT relief on investment	Dividends paid by VCT	Disposal of shares in VCT	Minimum holding period
On or after 6 April 2006 but before 6 April 2025	£200,000 per annum	30%	Exempt from IT in hands of investor	Exempt from CGT	5 years
2005–06 and 2004–05	£200,000 per annum	40%	Exempt from IT in hands of investor	Exempt from CGT	3 years
2000–01 to 2003–04	£100,000 per annum	20%	Exempt from IT in hands of investor	Exempt from CGT	3 years

Notes

[1] To obtain and retain HMRC's approval, a VCT must satisfy a number of detailed conditions. The main ones are as follows: it must be a non-close company whose shares are quoted on the stock exchange; its income must be wholly or mainly derived from investments in shares or securities; at least 70% (by value) of its total investments must comprise of 'qualifying holdings' (broadly, shares and securities in unquoted trading companies except those carrying on prohibited trades; no holding in any company (other than a VCT or a company that would qualify as a VCT but for the listing condition) can represent more than 15% of the value of the VCT's investments; the gross assets of the companies in which the VCT has invested may not exceed £15m immediately before the issue of shares to the VCT and £16m immediately afterwards.

[2] For an investment to qualify under VCT, the company must have raised no more than £5m (from 6 April 2012) through risk capital measures (VCT, EIS, SEIS or any other investment which is a state aid approved by the European Commission in accordance with the community guidelines on risk capital investments in SMEs) in the 12 months ending on the date of the relevant investment (ITA 2007, s. 292A). From 18 November 2015, investments under the SITR will also count towards the company's annual maximum amount as will any 'relevant investments' the company or group has received or used in the year and imported investments (in any trade transferred from another company). From 6 April 2018, this limit will be increased to £10m by legislation in Finance Bill 2017–18 (Autumn Budget 2017).

[3] VCTs will no longer qualify for relief from 6 April 2025, unless the legislation is renewed. The date may be changed by Treasury Order and is set to be no later than ten years after the date of the European Commission's letter approving the VCT rules as compatible with state aids rules, following the formal notification of the scheme in June 2015.

[4] *Finance (No. 2) Act* 2017 amends the VCT rules to enable a new parent company, which has acquired an old company through a certain type of share for share exchange, to receive follow-on funding from a VCT on the basis of the old company's funding history, with effect for investments made, and relevant holdings issued, on or after 6 April 2017. *Finance (No. 2) Act* 2017 also provides a power for HM Treasury to make regulations on the exchange of non-qualifying investments held by a VCT for new shares or securities in the course of a share reorganisation or company reconstruction. This power has effect from Royal Assent.

[5] Legislation will be included in Finance Bill 2017–18 (with effect for investments made on or after Royal Assent) to ensure the Venture Capital Schemes (EIS/SEIS/VCT) are targeted at growth investments with relief under the schemes focused on companies where there is a real risk to the capital being invested, and to exclude companies and arrangements intended to provide 'capital preservation' (Autumn Budget 2017).

Social venture capital trusts

Social venture capital trusts, a new scheme based on the existing VCT scheme, were announced at Autumn Statement 2014 and again at March Budget 2015. The scheme has yet to be legislated for.

[¶3-465] Community investment tax relief

(ITA 2007, Pt. 7; CTA 2010, Pt. 7)

(Tax Reporter: ¶325-000ff.)

Tax relief is claimed on an annual basis at the rate of 5% of the 'invested amount' for the tax year (or accounting period for a corporate investor) in which the investment date falls and the four subsequent tax years (or accounting periods). If the investment is by way of a loan, the 'invested amount' is not necessarily the amount of the loan made available at the beginning of the five-year investment period. The tax relief cannot reduce the taxpayer's tax liability below zero for any single tax year (or accounting period).

[¶3-500]   Lease premiums

(ITTOIA 2005, s. 277; CTA 2009, s. 217)

(Tax Reporter: ¶300-110; ¶711-375)

Where a short-term lease (i.e. one not exceeding 50 years in duration) is granted, a proportion of any premium charged on the grant is assessable as property business profits. The amount of the premium to be treated as rental income, received at the time of the grant, is given by a formula:

$$P \times \frac{50 - Y}{50} = TP$$

Where:

- 'P' is total premium paid;
- 'Y' is duration of lease in complete years (ignoring the first year). Only whole years are counted, part years are ignored; and
- 'TP' is the amount of the premium taxed on the landlord as if it were rent.

Amount taken into account in calculating a chargeable gain will be the balance of the premium (TCGA 1992, s. 240 and Sch. 8, para. 5 and 7) for which the restriction of allowable expenditure is applicable:

Length of lease in complete years	Premium % chargeable as gain	Premium % chargeable as rent
Over 50	100	0
50	98	2
49	96	4
48	94	6
47	92	8
46	90	10
45	88	12
44	86	14
43	84	16
42	82	18
41	80	20
40	78	22
39	76	24
38	74	26
37	72	28
36	70	30
35	68	32
34	66	34
33	64	36
32	62	38
31	60	40
30	58	42

Length of lease in complete years	Premium % chargeable as gain	Premium % chargeable as rent
29	56	44
28	54	46
27	52	48
26	50	50
25	48	52
24	46	54
23	44	56
22	42	58
21	40	60
20	38	62
19	36	64
18	34	66
17	32	68
16	30	70
15	28	72
14	26	74
13	24	76
12	22	78
11	20	80
10	18	82
9	16	84
8	14	86
7	12	88
6	10	90
5	8	92
4	6	94
3	4	96
2	2	98
1 or less	0	100

The following arrangements relating to short leases may also cause amounts to be treated as rent paid to the landlord:

- the tenant carrying out work on the rented premises;
- the commutation of rent for some other type of payment;
- the payment of a lump sum from the surrender of a lease;
- the payment of a lump sum for the variation or waiver of a lease's terms; and
- the assignment of a lease which has been previously granted at undervalue.

Premiums paid by instalment

Where an amount of a premium is received by instalments any income tax or corporation tax due on the amount may be paid by instalments, at the taxpayer's request and by agreement with HMRC. The tax instalment period may not exceed eight years and must end on or before the time that the final instalment of the premium is due (ITTOIA 2005, s. 299 for income tax; and CTA 2009, s. 236(1)–(3) for corporation tax).

Relief for premiums paid

Where a tenant occupies land, under a short lease, for the purposes of a trade, profession or vocation and has paid a premium in respect of the lease; an amount of lease premium paid is allowed as a deduction in computing the business profits (ITTOIA 2005, s. 60 for income tax; and CTA 2009, s. 62 for corporation tax). The amount of the premium taxed as rent in the hands of the landlord (see above) is treated as if it were daily rent paid by the tenant over the course of the lease. The effective deduction for an accounting or basis period is therefore:

$$\frac{TP}{\text{Lease duration in days}} \times \text{No. of days in accounting or basis period} = DRP$$

Where:

- 'TP' is the amount of the premium taxed on the landlord as if it were rent; and

- 'DRP' is the amount of the deemed rent paid by the tenant.

Relief is also available, in respect of premiums paid, for the computation of property business profits where an intermediate landlord has paid a premium to the superior landlord for premises that are in turn sub-let to a tenant.

[¶3-525] Restricted deductions for finance costs related to residential property

(ITTOIA 2005, s. 272A–272B, 274A–274B; ITA 2007, s. 399A–399B)

(Tax Reporter: ¶300-350)

Year	Restricted deduction[1]
2017–18	75%
2018–19	50%
2019–20	25%
2020–21	0%

Note

[1] In calculating for income tax purposes the profits of a property business, the deduction allowed for finance costs of a dwelling-related loan is restricted to the percentage shown of the amount that would be allowed apart from the restriction. A tax reduction for such costs is available instead and calculated by reference to the basic rate of income tax. The restriction and tax reduction will have effect for costs incurred on or after 6 April 2017.

[¶3-530] Mileage rates for unincorporated property businesses

(Autumn Budget 2017; Finance Bill 2017–18)

Autumn Budget 2017 announced that legislation will be introduced in Finance Bill 2017-18 to add the use of mileage rates as an allowable method of calculating the allowable deduction in respect of motoring expenses incurred for the purposes of a property business.

Expenditure on vehicles	From 6 April 2017[1]
Cars or goods vehicles	
– First 10,000 miles	£0.45/mile
– Above 10,000 miles	£0.25/mile
Motorcycle	£0.24/mile

Note

[1] Legislation in Finance Bill 2017–18 will add ITTOIA 2005, s. 94C to 94G to the list of trading provisions applied in calculating the profit of a property business by ITTOIA 2005, s. 272(2). Mileage rates will not be available in respect of vehicles for which capital allowances have already been claimed, or for which expenditure in acquiring the vehicle has been deducted in a business using the cash basis. Transitional arrangements will apply for property businesses who claimed capital allowances in relation to a vehicle in the tax years 2013–14 to 2016–17, and who wish to start using mileage rates for use of the same vehicle from the 2017–18 tax year, to prevent the deduction of any further capital allowances in this circumstance.

[¶3-550]   Settlements on children

(ITTOIA 2005, s. 629(3))

(Tax Reporter: ¶356-300)

Income paid to or for the benefit of a minor child arising from capital provided by a parent is not treated as parents' income if it does not exceed £100 per tax year.

[¶3-700]   Time limits for elections and claims

(TMA 1970, s. 43)

In the absence of any provision to the contrary, for the purposes of income tax, the normal rule is that claims are to be made within four years from the end of the tax year to which they relate.

In certain cases, HMRC *may* permit an extension of the strict time limit in relation to certain elections and claims.

Provision	Time limit	Statutory reference
Averaging election for furnished holiday accommodation	12 months from 31 January following year to which claim applies	ITTOIA 2005, s. 326 (Tax Reporter: ¶303-170)
Set-off of property business loss against income of current or next year	12 months from 31 January following year of set-off	ITA 2007, s. 124 (Tax Reporter: ¶303-220)
Property business post-cessation relief	12 months from 31 January following year in which deduction to be made	ITA 2007, s. 125 (Tax Reporter: ¶303-230)
Set-off of loss on disposal of shares in unquoted trading company against income	12 months from 31 January following year in which loss arose	ITA 2007, s. 132 (Tax Reporter: ¶330-000ff.)
EIS, SEIS and SI relief	Five years from 31 January following tax year in which shares are issued (or previous tax year in relation to carry back claims)	ITA 2007, s. 202, 257EA and 257P (Tax Reporter: ¶323-120; ¶319-120)

Taxation of Investment Income

TAXATION OF EARNINGS

Company cars

[¶4-000] Car benefits from 2020–21

(ITEPA 2003, s. 139, 140 and 142 as prospectively amended by F(No. 2)A 2017; Autumn Budget 2017)

The benefit is calculated as a percentage of the list price of the car multiplied by the relevant percentage:

Car with a CO_2 emissions figure: the appropriate percentage

CO_2 emissions figure	Electric range figure	2020–21[1]
0		2%
1–50	130 or more	2%
	70–129	5%
	40–69	8%
	30–39	12%
	Less than 30	14%
51–54		15%
55–59		16%
60–64		17%
65–69		18%
70–74		19%
75 or more:		20%
Plus		1% per 5g/km
Up to maximum		37%
75–79		20%
80–84		21%
85–89		22%
90–94		23%
95–99		24%
100–104		25%
105–109		26%
110–114		27%

CO$_2$ emissions figure	2020–21[1]
115–119	28%
120–124	29%
125–129	30%
130–134	31%
135–139	32%
140–144	33%
145–149	34%
150–154	35%
155–159	36%
160+	37%
Diesel supplement[3]	[4%]

Car without a CO$_2$ emissions figure: the appropriate percentage

Cylinder capacity of car in cubic centimetres	2020–21[2]
1,400 or less	24%
More than 1,400 but not more than 2,000	35%
More than 2,000	37%
Cannot in any circumstances emit CO$_2$ by being driven	2%
Any other case	37%
Diesel supplement[3]	[4%]

Car first registered before 1 January 1998: the appropriate percentage

Cylinder capacity of car in cubic centimetres	2020–21[4]
1,400 or less	24%
More than 1,400 but not more than 2,000	35%
More than 2,000	37%
Any other case	37%

Notes
[1] Rates per F(No. 2)A 2017, s. 2 amending ITEPA 2003, s. 139.
[2] Rates per F(No. 2)A 2017, s. 2 amending ITEPA 2003, s. 140.
[3] Diesel supplement due to be increased to 4% from 6 April 2018 by legislation in Finance Bill 2017–18 (Autumn Budget 2017). The diesel supplement is subject to the maximum cap at 37%.
[4] Rates per F(No. 2)A 2017, s. 2 amending ITEPA 2003, s. 142.

[¶4-001]   Car benefits to 2019–20

(ITEPA 2003, s. 139)

(Tax Reporter: ¶415-050ff.)

The benefit is calculated as a percentage of the list price of the car appropriate to the level of the car's CO_2 emissions. The 'appropriate percentage' depends upon whether the car was first registered on or after 1 January 1998 and whether it has a CO_2 emissions figure or is a diesel car. Relevant percentages are set out below.

For cars registered on or after 1 January 1998 (with CO_2 emissions figures)

CO_2 emissions[5]	2013–14 & 2012–13	2014–15	2015–16	2016–17	2017–18	2018–19[3]	2019–20[4]
50g/km or below	5%	5%	5%	7%	9%	13%	16%
51–75g/km			9%	11%	13%	16%	19%
Above 75g/km up to relevant threshold	10%	11%	13%	15%	17%	19%	22%
Equal to relevant threshold[1]	11%	12%	14%	16%	18%	20%	23%
Above relevant threshold: Increase per 5g/km[1]	1%	1%	1%	1%	1%	1%	1%
Up to maximum	35%	35%	37%	37%	37%	37%	37%
Diesel supplement[2]	3%	3%	3%	3%	3%	4%	4%

Notes

[1] Where CO_2 emissions are not a multiple of five, round down to the nearest multiple of five.

[2] All diesel cars are currently subject to a 3% addition (but subject to the absolute cap). The diesel supplement will be increased to 4% (subject to the absolute cap) from 6 April 2018 by legislation in Finance Bill 2017–18 (Autumn Budget 2017).

[3] In 2018–19, the appropriate percentage of list price subject to tax will increase by two percentage points for cars emitting more than 75g/km CO_2, to a maximum of 37%. In 2018–19, there will be a three percentage point differential between the 0–50g/km and 51–75g/km CO_2 bands and between the 51–75g/km and 76–94g/km CO_2 bands (FA 2015, s. 8).

[4] In 2019–20, the appropriate percentage of list price subject to tax will increase by three percentage points for cars emitting more than 75g/km CO_2, to a maximum of 37%. There will be a three-percentage point differential between the 0–50g/km and 51–75g/km CO_2 bands (FA 2016, s. 8).

The relevant threshold is as follows:

Year	Relevant threshold
2017–18	95g/km
2013–14 to 2016–17	95g/km
2012–13	100g/km

Cars registered on or after 1 January 1998 without CO₂ emissions, or cars first registered before 1 January 1998

	2014–15 Registered		2015–16 Registered		2016–17	2017–18	2018–19[2]	2019–20[3]
	on or after 01/01/1998	before 01/01/1998	on or after 01/01/1998	before 01/01/1998				
Cylinder capacity of car with internal combustion engine in cubic centimetres								
• 1,400 or less	15%	15%	15%	15%	16%	18%	20%	23%
• more than 1,400 but not more than 2,000	25%	22%	25%	22%	27%	29%	31%	34%
• more than 2,000	35%	32%	37%	32%	37%	37%	37%	37%
Cars without an internal combustion engine								
• zero-emission cars registered on or after 1 January 1998	0%[1]	—	5%	—	7%	9%	13%	16%
• any other case	35%	32%	37%	32%	37%	37%	37%	37%
Diesel supplement[1]	3%	N/A	3%	N/A	3%	3%	4%	4%

Notes
[1] All diesel cars registered on or after 1 January 1998 are currently subject to a 3% addition (but subject to the absolute cap). The diesel supplement will be increased to 4% (subject to the absolute cap) from 6 April 2018 by legislation in Finance Bill 2017–18 (Autumn Budget 2017).
[2] Rates per FA 2015, s. 8 (amending ITEPA 2003, s. 140 and 142).
[3] Rates per FA 2016, s. 8 (amending ITEPA 2003, s. 140 and 142).

[¶4-002] Car benefits: table of percentages to 2019–20

Table of taxable percentages

(ITEPA 2003, s. 139)

(Tax Reporter: ¶415-720)

CO₂ emissions	Appropriate percentage						
	2013–14[1]	2014–15[1]	2015–16[1]	2016–17[1]	2017–18[1]	2018–19[1][2]	2019–20[1][3]
0	0	0	5	7	9	13	16
1–50	5	5					
51–75			9	11	13	16	19
76–94	10	11	13	15	17	19	22
95–99	11	12	14	16	18	20	23

CO$_2$ emissions	Appropriate percentage						
	2013–14[1]	2014–15[1]	2015–16[1]	2016–17[1]	2017–18[1]	2018–19[1][2]	2019–20[1][3]
100–104	12	13	15	17	19	21	24
105–109	13	14	16	18	20	22	25
110–114	14	15	17	19	21	23	26
115–119	15	16	18	20	22	24	27
120–124	16	17	19	21	23	25	28
125–129	17	18	20	22	24	26	29
130–134	18	19	21	23	25	27	30
135–139	19	20	22	24	26	28	31
140–144	20	21	23	25	27	29	32
145–149	21	22	24	26	28	30	33
150–154	22	23	25	27	29	31	34
155–159	23	24	26	28	30	32	35
160–164	24	25	27	29	31	33	36
165–169	25	26	28	30	32	34	
170–174	26	27	29	31	33	35	
175–179	27	28	30	32	34	36	
180–184	28	29	31	33	35		
185–189	29	30	32	34	36		
190–194	30	31	33	35			37
195–199	31	32	34	36			
200–204	32	33	35			37	
205–209	33	34	36		37		
210–214	34			37			
215–219	35	35	37				
220+							

Notes

[1] All diesel cars are subject to a 3% loading, but not to take the maximum figure above 37% (from 2015–16, previously, 35%). The diesel supplement will be increased to 4% (subject to the absolute cap) from 6 April 2018 by legislation in Finance Bill 2017–18 (Autumn Budget 2017).

[2] In 2018–19, the appropriate percentage of list price subject to tax will increase by two percentage points for cars emitting more than 75g/km CO_2, to a maximum of 37%. In 2018–19, there will be a three percentage point differential between the 0–50g/km and 51–75g/km CO_2 bands and between the 51–75g/km and 76–94g/km CO_2 bands (FA 2015, s. 8).

[3] In 2019–20, the appropriate percentage of list price subject to tax will increase by three percentage points for cars emitting more than 75g/km CO_2 to a maximum of 37%. There will be a three percentage point differential between the 0–50g/km and 51–75g/km CO_2 bands (FA 2016, s. 8).

[¶4-015] Diesel cars: loading of appropriate percentage

(ITEPA 2003, s. 141)

(Tax Reporter: ¶415-740)

Most diesel cars have an appropriate percentage that is three points higher than an equivalent petrol car (but still subject to a 37% overall cap). See ¶4-000ff. for details of the petrol figures. The diesel supplement is due to be increased to 4% from 6 April 2018 by legislation in Finance Bill 2017–18 (Autumn Budget 2017).

Fuel for company cars

[¶4-140] Fuel benefit charges

(ITEPA 2003, s. 150)

(Tax Reporter: ¶416-000ff.)

The additional taxable benefit of free fuel provided for a company car is calculated using the same CO_2 percentages as are used for calculating the company car charge.

The fuel benefit is reduced to nil if the employee is required to make good the full cost of all fuel provided for private use, and does so.

A proportionate reduction is made where the company car is only available for part of the year, where car fuel ceases to be provided part-way through the year, or where the benefit of the company car is shared.

The CO_2 percentage figure is applied to a fixed amount in accordance with the following table:

Tax year	£
2018–19	23,400
2017–18	22,600
2016–17	22,200
2015–16	22,100
2014–15	21,700
2013–14	21,100

[¶4-160] Fuel types

Employers must notify HMRC of the type of fuel (or other power) used by an employer provided car by entering the appropriate 'key letter' on the forms P11D and P46(Car). The key letters in use are as follows:

Key letter	Fuel or power type description
A	All other cars
D	Diesel (all Euro standards)

[¶4-180] Advisory fuel rates for company cars: recent rates
(Tax Reporter: ¶416-040)

HMRC publish rates that can be used by employers wishing to pay their employees the cost of fuel for business journeys in company cars (or, where the employer initially pays for all fuel, for reimbursement of private mileage by company car drivers to their employers). Passenger payments may be made for company cars as for private cars (see ¶4-220). Hybrid cars are treated as either petrol or diesel cars for this purpose.

HMRC now review the rates four times a year – on 1 March, 1 June, 1 September and 1 December. For one month from the date of change, employers may use either the previous or new current rates, as they choose.

Engine size	Cost per mile		
	Petrol	Diesel	LPG
Rates applying from 1 December 2017			
1400cc or less	11p	—	7p
1600cc or less	—	9p	—
1401cc to 2000cc	14p	—	9p
1601cc to 2000cc	—	11p	—
Over 2000cc	21p	13p	14p
Rates applying from 1 September 2017			
1400cc or less	11p	—	7p
1600cc or less	—	9p	—
1401cc to 2000cc	13p	—	8p
1601cc to 2000cc	—	11p	—
Over 2000cc	21p	12p	13p
Rates applying from 1 June 2017			
1400cc or less	11p	—	7p
1600cc or less	—	9p	—
1401cc to 2000cc	14p	—	9p
1601cc to 2000cc	—	11p	—
Over 2000cc	21p	13p	14p
Rates applying from 1 March 2017			
1400cc or less	11p	—	7p
1600cc or less	—	9p	—
1401cc to 2000cc	14p	—	9p
1601cc to 2000cc	—	11p	—
Over 2000cc	22p	13p	14p
Rates applying from 1 December 2016			
1400cc or less	11p	—	7p
1600cc or less	—	9p	—
1401cc to 2000cc	14p	—	9p
1601cc to 2000cc	—	11p	—
Over 2000cc	21p	13p	13p

Taxation of Earnings

	Cost per mile		
Engine size	Petrol	Diesel	LPG
Rates applying from 1 September 2016			
1400cc or less	11p	—	7p
1600cc or less	—	9p	—
1401cc to 2000cc	13p	—	9p
1601cc to 2000cc	—	11p	—
Over 2000cc	20p	13p	13p
Rates applying from 1 June 2016			
1400cc or less	10p	—	7p
1600cc or less	—	9p	—
1401cc to 2000cc	13p	—	9p
1601cc to 2000cc	—	10p	—
Over 2000cc	20p	12p	13p
Rates applying from 1 March 2016			
1400cc or less	10p	—	7p
1600cc or less	—	8p	—
1401cc to 2000cc	12p	—	8p
1601cc to 2000cc	—	10p	—
Over 2000cc	19p	11p	13p

Private vehicles

[¶4-200] Mileage allowance payments

(ITEPA 2003, s. 230)

(Tax Reporter: ¶432-100ff.)

Statutory rates are set for mileage allowance payments. An employer may, of course, reimburse business mileage driven in a privately-owned car at more or less than the statutory rates but any excess is taxable. Any shortfall is tax deductible and the employee may claim relief accordingly.

Kind of vehicle	Rate per mile from 6 April 2011
Car or van	45p for the first 10,000 miles 25p after that
Motorcycle	24p
Cycle	20p

[¶4-220]   Passenger payments

(ITEPA 2003, s. 233)

(Tax Reporter: ¶432-150)

No liability to income tax arises in respect of an approved passenger payment made to an employee for a car or a van, whether the vehicle is privately owned or provided by the employer. The approved amount is 5p per passenger mile.

Company vans

[¶4-300]   Taxable benefit

(ITEPA 2003, s. 114, 154–164)

(Tax Reporter: ¶416-200ff.)

	£
2018–19	3,350
2017–18	3,230
2016–17	3,170
2015–16	3,150
2014–15	3,090
2013–14 (from April 2007)	3,000

But nil if:

(1)   the restricted private use conditions are met (available and used only for ordinary commuting and business travel);

(2)   private use in the tax year is insignificant.

Zero-emission vans

For tax year 2014–15, the cash equivalent of the benefit of a van was nil if the van could not produce any CO_2 emissions under any circumstances by being driven (e.g. an electric van). From 2015–16, the charge for zero-emission vans is calculated as the 'relevant percentage' per the table below of the main rate as per the table above.

	Appropriate percentage
2015–16	20%
2016–17	20%
2017–18	20%
2018–19	40%
2019–20	60%
2020–21	80%
2021–22	90%

[¶4-345]   Fuel for company vans

(ITEPA 2003, s. 160ff.)

(Tax Reporter: ¶416-200ff.)

Tax Year	£
2018–19	633
2017–18	610
2016–17	598
2015–16	594
2014–15	581
2013–14	564

But nil if:

(1)   the restricted private use conditions are met (available and used only for ordinary commuting and business travel);

(2)   private use in the tax year is insignificant.

Buses

[¶4-360]   Bus services

(ITEPA 2003, s. 242 and 243)

(Tax Reporter: ¶432-600ff.)

An exemption applies to:

(1)   works transport services, which must be a bus or minibus:
  (a)   available to employees generally;
  (b)   used mainly for qualifying journeys; and
  (c)   used substantially by employees or their children;

(2)   support for public bus services:
  (a)   available to employees generally;
  (b)   used for qualifying journeys by employees of one or more employers; and
  (c)   either:
    (i)   a local bus service; or
    (ii) the bus must be provided to other passengers on terms that are as favourable as the terms on which the bus is provided to employees.

Used cycles

[¶4-380] Used cycles: valuation table
(Tax Reporter: ¶419-090)

HMRC allow used cycles to be transferred to employees using disposal values as follows:

Age of cycle	Original price less than £500	Original price £500+
1 year	18%	25%
18 months	16%	21%
2 years	13%	17%
3 years	8%	12%
4 years	3%	7%
5 years	Negligible	2%
6 years & over	Negligible	Negligible

Beneficial loans

[¶4-390] Beneficial loans threshold
(ITEPA 2003, Pt. 3, Ch. 7; s. 180)

(Tax Reporter: ¶417-000ff.)

A taxable benefit may arise where an employee (or a relative of an employee) is provided with a loan either interest-free or at a favourable rate of interest. A tax charge does not arise where the amount outstanding on the loan does not exceed the threshold at all times during the year. Threshold is as follows:

Period	Threshold £
2014–15 and subsequent years	10,000
2013–14 and earlier years (post-6 April 1994)	5,000

Official rates of interest

[¶4-400]   Official rate of interest

(ITEPA 2003, s. 181)

(Tax Reporter: ¶417-100)

The official rate of interest is used to calculate the cash equivalent of the benefit of an employment-related loan which is a taxable cheap loan. HMRC review the level of the official rate of interest on a quarterly basis but normally set a single rate in advance for the whole tax year in line with a commitment given in January 2000, that (following announcement of the rate for any given tax year) the official rate may be reduced but will not be increased in the light of interest rate changes generally.

Date	Rate %	SI No.
From 6 April 2017	2.50	SI 2017/305
6 April 2016 to 5 April 2017	3.00	–
6 April 2015 to 5 April 2016	3.00	SI 2015/411
6 April 2014 to 5 April 2015	3.25	SI 2014/496
6 April 2010 to 5 April 2014	4.00	SI 2010/415

The average official rates of interest are given at ¶4-405.

[¶4-405]   Official rate of interest: average rates

(ITEPA 2003, s. 181)

(Tax Reporter: ¶417-100)

Official rates of interest are given at ¶4-400. Average official rates of interest, given below, should be used if the loan was outstanding throughout the tax year and the normal averaging method of calculation is being used. Average rates were last published by HMRC for 2013–14.

Year	Average official rate %
2013–14	4.00
2012–13	4.00
2011–12	4.00

[¶4-420]   Official rate of interest: foreign currency loans
(ITEPA 2003, s. 181; SI 1989/1297)

(Tax Reporter: ¶418-100)

Period	Switzerland[1] %	Japan[1] %
From 6 July 1994	5.5	3.9

Note
[1] These rates apply to loans made in the currency of a country or territory outside the UK, and to an employee who normally lives in that country or territory, and who has lived in that country or territory at some time in the tax year or in the previous five years. The intention of the rules is to give relief for employees working temporarily in the UK, where interest rates in the overseas country are lower than interest rates in the UK. The relief does not apply to employees who come to the UK and live here permanently.

Travel and subsistence

[¶4-500]   Subsistence scale rates
(Tax Reporter: ¶457-560)

(SI 2015/1948)

(Tax Reporter: 457-560)

Employers wishing to pay or reimburse expenses may use the benchmark rates set out below without needing the prior approval of HMRC (or for tax years up to 2015–16, without needing to apply for a dispensation).

Duration of qualifying travel	Amount from 2016–17
5 hours or more	£5
10 hours or more	£5
Supplementary rate for travel ongoing at 8 p.m.[1]	£10
15 hours or more and ongoing at 8 p.m.	£15
Description	**Amount to 2015–16**
Breakfast rate (before 6 a.m.)	£5
One meal (5 hour) rate	£5
Two meal (10 hour) rate	£10
Late evening meal rate (after 8 p.m.)	£10

Note
[1] The supplementary allowance is paid in additon to the allowance given at the 5 or 10 hour rates where travel is ongoing at 8 p.m.

Taxation of Earnings

[¶4-520] Accommodation and subsistence – overseas rates

(Tax Reporter: ¶457-570)

Employers can reimburse subsistence to employees by making a scale rate payment. HMRC usually publish the rates in October or November every year. Legislation in Finance Bill 2018–19 will place the existing concessionary travel and subsistence overseas scale rates on a statutory basis from 6 April 2019 (Autumn Budget 2017).

Recent rates are available as follows:

From October 2014[(1)]: www.gov.uk/government/uploads/system/uploads/ attachment_data/file/359797/2014_Worldwide_subsistence_ rates.pdf

Note
[(1)] The rates published in October 2014 will continue to apply for the year commencing October 2017.

[¶4-540] Incidental overnight expenses and benefits

(ITEPA 2003, s. 240)

(Tax Reporter: ¶432-900)

Benefits, reimbursements and expenses provided by an employer for employees' minor, personal expenditure whilst on business-related activities requiring overnight accommodation away from home are not taxable provided that the total amount reimbursed, etc. does not exceed the relevant maximum amount(s) per night, multiplied by the number of nights' absence. If the limit is exceeded, the whole amount provided remains taxable.

	Authorised maximum per night	
	In UK	Overseas
From	£	£
6 April 1995	5	10

[¶4-550] Lorry drivers subsistence allowances

(ITEPA 2003, s. 337 and 338)

(Tax Reporter: ¶455-020; ¶455-040)

A subsistence allowance paid to long distance lorry drivers will not be taxed provided they are paid or reimbursed in an approved way and both of the following conditions are met.

(1) The payer, or another person, operates system for checking that the employees are in fact incurring and paying amounts in respect of expenses of the same kind and that a fully matching deduction would be allowed under ITEPA 2003, Pt. 5, Ch. 2 or 5 in respect of those amounts.

(2) Neither the payer nor any other person operating the system for checking knows or suspects, or could reasonably be expected to know or suspect, that the employee had not incurred an amount in respect of the expense, or that a deduction under ITEPA 2003, Pt. 5, Ch. 2 or 5 would not be allowed in respect of those amounts.

HMRC accept the following amounts as reasonable for nights in the UK.

Year ended	Payment per night	
	Drivers with non-sleeper cabs £	**Drivers with sleeper cabs**[1] £
31 December 2017	34.90	26.20
31 December 2013 to 2016	34.90	26.20

Note

[1] The mere fact that a lorry has a sleeper cab does not prevent the employer paying an amount tax free up to the limit shown for drivers with non-sleeper cabs (or locally agreed limits) provided that the employer is satisfied that the driver did incur expenses on overnight accommodation (for example by staying in a hotel) and meals. HMRC accept that a payment of 75% of the figure shown for drivers with non-sleeper cabs does no more than reimburse the expense incurred when the driver uses the sleeper cab overnight.

Shares and share incentives

[¶4-600]   Share incentive plans

(TCGA 1992, s. 236A, 238A, Sch. 7C, 7D, Pt. 1; ITEPA 2003, s. 488ff., Sch. 2)

(Tax Reporter: ¶468-000ff.)

	Free shares	Partnership shares	Matching shares	Dividend shares
Employment before eligibility[1]	Up to 18 months employment	Up to 18 months employment[4] where no accumulation period, up to six months with accumulation period	Only awarded to employees who buy partnership shares	Must be acquired with dividends from plan shares
Limits	Up to £3,600 per tax year	Up to £1,800 per tax year or 10% of salary, if less	Up to two matching shares for each partnership share bought	Dividends from shares in the plan reinvested: – no limit
Minimum amount if stated[1]	—	no more than £10 per month	—	—
Performance measures[1]	Yes	No	No	No
Holding period	At least three years from award[2]	None	At least three years from award[2]	Three years from acquisition

Taxation of Earnings

	Free shares	Partnership shares	Matching shares	Dividend shares
Forfeiture on cessation of employment[1]	Yes[5]	No	Yes[5]	No
Tax on award	None	None – tax relief for salary used to buy shares	None	None
Tax on removal of shares from plan within three years of award[3]	On market value when taken out	On market value when taken out	On market value when taken out	Original dividend taxable but in year when shares taken out of plan
Tax on removal between three and five years of award[2]	On lower of: – value at award – value on removal	On lower of: – salary used to buy shares – value on removal	On lower of: – value at award – value on removal	None
Tax on removal after five years	None	None	None	None
CGT on removal – any time	None	None	None	None

Notes

[1] These conditions can be included at the option of the company.

[2] The holding period may be up to five years at the option of the company.

[3] PAYE and NICs will be operated in relation to any income tax charge where the shares are readily convertible assets.

[4] Maximum accumulation period for partnership shares is 12 months.

[5] Restrictions apply to provisions for forfeiture that may be applied including a maximum forfeiture period of up to three years from award, that forfeiture provisions cannot relate to cesation of employment through injury, disability, redundancy, TUPE transfers, changes of control, retirement (at normal age), death, or be linked to the performance of any person. From 15 September 2016, rules for share incentive plans previously repealed will be reinstated to enforce the principle that shares with preferential rights cannot be issued to selected employees only (amendments by FA 2016, Sch. 3).

[¶4-610] Company share option plan

(TCGA 1992, s. 238A and Sch. 7D, Pt. 3; ITEPA 2003, s. 521–526 and Sch. 4)

(Tax Reporter: ¶467-000ff.)

Maximum options[1][2]	£30,000

Notes

[1] This includes options granted under the scheme, or under any other approved CSOP scheme established by the scheme organiser or an associated company of the scheme organiser.

[2] The 'market value' of shares is calculated at the date of grant, or of each relevant option grant (if more than one grant); or if any agreement relating to any such shares has been made under ITEPA 2003, Sch. 4, para. 22, the earlier time or times stated in the agreement.

[¶4-620] Enterprise management incentives (EMI)

(TCGA 1992, s. 238A and Sch. 7D, Pt. 4; ITEPA 2003, s. 527–541 and Sch. 5)

(Tax Reporter: ¶466-000ff.)

Qualifying company	• Gross assets not exceeding £30m • Fewer than 250 employees (full-time or equivalent)
Maximum options	£250,000

Notes
[1] The above limits are qualified as follows:
(a) options held by the employee under a (HMRC-approved) Company Share Ownership Plan (CSOP), that are unexercised at the date of grant of an EMI option, are taken into account in applying the maximum figure above;
(b) by the 'three-year restriction period' rule; the grant of an option to an employee within three years from the most recent EMI option grant to him, cannot itself qualify as an EMI option if the value of the shares which were the subject of all previous EMI option grants, down to and including the most recent grant, amounted to £250,000 (or other applicable threshold figure in earlier periods). This applies whether or not any of such previously granted options have been exercised; and
(c) there is an overriding company limit; the total value (as defined) of shares in the company that are the subject of unexercised EMI options cannot exceed £3,000,000.
For purposes of (a) and (b) above, one takes into account all options granted by reason of the same employment, or employment by any member of the same group of companies.

[¶4-635] SAYE

(TCGA 1992, s. 238A and Sch. 7D, Pt. 2; ITEPA 2003, s. 516–520 and Sch. 3)

(Tax Reporter: ¶470-000ff.)

Limits	Savings periods	Monthly contributions
Minimum	36 months	£5–£10[1]
Maximum	60 months	£500

Note
[1] Company may impose a minimum monthly payment of up to £10 per month; otherwise the minimum is £5 per month.

[¶4-640] SAYE bonus rates: multiple of monthly payments

(ITEPA 2003, Sch. 3)

(Tax Reporter: ¶470-000ff.)

The bonus rate applicable to a scheme is set at the time the savings contract is entered into and is unaffected by any subsequent change to the rates. Current and historical rates are shown below. See ¶4-660 for details of the 'early leaver rate' applying for those who withdraw their funds after 12 monthly contributions, but before the three-year anniversary.

From	3-year	5-year	7-year[1]
27 December 2014	0.0	0.0	—
28 July 2014	0.0	0.6	—
1 August 2012	0.0	0.0	0.0
23 September 2011	0.0	0.0	1.6
12 August 2011	0.0	0.9	3.5
27 February 2011	0.1	1.7	4.8

Note
[1] The seven-year savings period of Save As You Earn (SAYE) Share Option Schemes was withdrawn with effect from 23 July 2013. Employees already saving under existing SAYE contracts before that date were not affected by the change.

[¶4-660]   SAYE 'early leaver rates'

(ITEPA 2003, Sch. 3)

(Tax Reporter: ¶470-000ff.)

The following 'early leaver rates' have applied for employees whose SAYE contracts are cancelled after 12 monthly contributions but before the maturity date:

Dates	Rates %
27 December 2014	0.00
28 July 2014	0.00
1 August 2012	0.00
23 September 2011	0.00
12 August 2011	0.00
27 February 2011	0.12

Note
The relevant date is that on which the employee starts saving under the contract, not the date on which the contract is cancelled.

[¶4-680]   SAYE effective interest rates

(ITEPA 2003, Sch. 3)

(Tax Reporter: ¶470-000ff.)

From	3-year	5-year	7-year[1]
27 December 2014	0.00	0.00	—
28 July 2014	0.00	0.39	—
1 August 2012	0.00	0.00	0.00
23 September 2011	0.00	0.00	0.58
12 August 2011	0.00	0.59	1.25
27 February 2011	0.18	1.10	1.70

Note
[1] The seven-year savings period of Save As You Earn (SAYE) Share Option Schemes was withdrawn with effect from 23 July 2013. Employees already saving under existing SAYE contracts before that date were not affected by the change.

Taxation of Earnings

[¶4-690] Employee shareholder status

(ITEPA 2003, s. 226A–226D)

(Tax Reporter: ¶471-500ff.)

Finance Act 2017 removed the income tax relief in respect of employee shareholder shares received in return for entering into an employee shareholder agreement on or after 1 December 2016.

Previously, employees accepting a position under an employee shareholder employment contract could be awarded fully paid up shares in their employer or parent company, at no cost to the employee without incurring a liability to income tax (or National Insurance contributions).

See ¶5-050 for capital gains tax exemption on employee shareholder shares (also withdrawn for shares received on or after 1 December 2016).

	1 September 2013 to 30 November 2016 £
Minimum value of share award (market value on acquisition)	2,000
Income tax and NIC exemption[1] (market value on acquisition)	2,000

Note

[1] Employee was treated as having made a payment of £2,000 for the acquisition of shares and accordingly; any excess (of market value) over £2,000 was treated as earnings from the employment subject to income tax (and NIC as applicable).

[¶4-695] Employee ownership trusts

(ITEPA 2003, s. 312A–312I)

An exemption from income tax is available for any relevant bonus payment made in a tax year to an employee by a qualifying indirectly employee-owned company that meets the relevant conditions (a trading company in which a controlling interest is held by an employee-ownership settlement). A relevant bonus will be a cash award other than regular salary or wages that is paid to all employees on equal terms, although bonuses can be set by an employer by reference to a percentage of salary or length of service or hours worked. The exemption is available from 1 October 2014 and subject to an annual cap per employee for each qualifying company as set out below.

Period	£
From 1 October 2014	3,600

National minimum wage

[¶4-700]   National minimum wage: from 1 October 2010

(SI 2016/953)

Period	Workers aged 25 plus £	Workers aged at least 21 but under 25 £	Workers aged at least 18 but under 21 £	Workers aged under 18 £	Apprentices aged under 19 or in the first year of apprenticeship £
From 6 April 2017	7.50	7.05	5.60	4.05	3.50
1/10/16–05/04/16	7.20	6.95	5.55	4.00	3.40
1/04/16–30/09/16	7.20	6.70	5.30	3.87	3.30
1/10/15–31/03/16	–	6.70	5.30	3.87	3.30
1/10/14–30/09/15	–	6.50	5.13	3.79	2.73
1/10/13–30/09/14	–	6.31	5.03	3.72	2.68

[¶4-720]   National minimum wage: accommodation offset

The maximum permitted daily and weekly rates of accommodation offset in relation to the national minimum wage are as follows:

Period	Daily offset £	Weekly offset £
From 6/4/2017	6.40	44.80
1/10/16–5/4/17	6.00	42.00
1/10/15–30/09/16	5.35	37.45
1/10/14–30/09/15	5.08	35.56
1/10/13–30/09/14	4.91	34.37

Flat-rate expenses

[¶4-750]   Fixed sum deductions for repairing and maintaining equipment

(ITEPA 2003, s. 367)

(Tax Reporter: ¶457-500)

A tax deduction is given for certain amounts 'representing the average annual expenses incurred by employees of the class to which the employee belongs in respect of the repair and maintenance of work equipment'. The term 'flat-rate expenses' is often used for these figures. The following table is from EIM32712.

Manual and certain other employees: flat-rate expenses deduction for tools and special clothing

Industry	Occupation		Deduction for 2008–09 onwards £	Deduction for 2004–05 to 2007–08 £
Agriculture	All workers		100	70
Aluminium	a.	Continual casting operators, process operators, de-dimplers, driers, drill punchers, dross unloaders, firemen, furnace operators and their helpers, leaders, mouldmen, pourers, remelt department labourers, roll flatteners	140	130
	b.	Cable hands, case makers, labourers, mates, truck drivers and measurers, storekeepers	80	60
	c.	Apprentices	60	45
	d.	All other workers	120	100
Banks and building societies	Uniformed doormen and messengers		60	45
Brass and copper	Braziers, coppersmiths, finishers, fitters, moulders, turners and all other workers.		120	100
Building	a.	Joiners and carpenters	140	105
	b.	Cement works, roofing felt and asphalt labourers	80	55
	c.	Labourers and navvies	60	45
	d.	All other workers	120	85
Building materials	a.	Stone-masons	120	85
	b.	Tilemakers and labourers	60	45
	c.	All other workers	80	55
Clothing	a.	Lacemakers, hosiery bleachers, dyers, scourers and knitters, knitwear bleachers and dyers	60	45
	b.	All other workers	60	45
Constructional engineering	a.	Blacksmiths and their strikers, burners, caulkers, chippers, drillers, erectors, fitters, holders up, markers off, platers, riggers, riveters, rivet heaters, scaffolders, sheeters, template workers, turners, welders	140	115

Industry		Occupation	Deduction for 2008–09 onwards £	Deduction for 2004–05 to 2007–08 £
	b.	Banksmen labourers, shop-helpers, slewers, straighteners	80	60
	c.	Apprentices and storekeepers	60	45
	d.	All other workers	100	75
Electrical and electricity supply	a.	Those workers incurring laundry costs only (generally CEGB employees)	60	45
	b.	All other workers	120	90
Engineering	a.	Pattern makers	140	120
	b.	Labourers, supervisory and unskilled workers	80	60
	c.	Apprentices and storekeepers	60	45
	d.	Motor mechanics in garage repair shops	120	100
	e.	All other workers	120	100
Fire service		Uniformed fire fighters and fire officers	80	60
Food		All workers	60	45
Forestry		All workers	100	70
Glass		All workers	80	60
Healthcare staff in the National Health Service, private hospitals and nursing homes	a.	Ambulance staff on active service (i.e. excluding staff who take telephone calls or provide clerical support)	185 (but £140 to 5 April 2014)	110
	b.	Nurses, midwives, chiropodists, dental nurses, occupational, speech, physiotherapists and other therapists, healthcare assistants, phlebotomists and radiographers	125 (but £100 to 5 April 2014)	70
	c.	Plaster room orderlies, hospital porters, ward clerks, sterile supply workers, hospital domestics, hospital catering staff	125 (but £100 to 5 April 2014)	60
	d.	Laboratory staff, pharmacists, pharmacy assistants	80 (but £60 to 5 April 2014)	45
	e.	Uniformed ancillary staff – maintenance workers, grounds staff, drivers, parking attendants and security guards, receptionists and other uniformed staff	80 (but £60 to 5 April 2014)	45

Industry	Occupation		Deduction for 2008–09 onwards £	Deduction for 2004–05 to 2007–08 £
Heating	a.	Pipe fitters and plumbers	120	100
	b.	Coverers, laggers, domestic glaziers, heating engineers and their mates	120	90
	c.	All gas workers, all other workers	100	70
Iron mining	a.	Fillers, miners and underground workers	120	100
	b.	All other workers	100	75
Iron and steel	a.	Day labourers, general labourers, stockmen, time-keepers, warehouse staff and weighmen	80	60
	b.	Apprentices	60	45
	c.	All other workers	140	120
Leather	a.	Curriers (wet workers), fellmongering workers, tanning operatives (wet)	80	55
	b.	All other workers	60	45
Particular engineering	a.	Pattern makers	140	120
	b.	All chainmakers; cleaners, galvanisers, tinners and wire drawers in the wire drawing industry; tool-makers in the lock making industry	120	100
	c.	Apprentices and storekeepers	60	45
	d.	All other workers	80	60
Police force	Police officers (ranks up to and including Chief Inspector)		140	55 (but £110 for 2007–08)
Precious metals	All workers		100	70
Printing	a.	*Letterpress Section*: Electrical engineers (rotary presses), electrotypers, ink and roller makers, machine minders (rotary), maintenance engineers (rotary presses) and stereotypers	140	105

Taxation of Earnings

Industry	Occupation		Deduction for 2008–09 onwards £	Deduction for 2004–05 to 2007–08 £
	b.	Bench hands (periodical and bookbinding section), compositors (letterpress section), readers (letterpress section) telecommunications and electronic section wire room operators, warehousemen (paper box making section)	60	45
	c.	All other workers	100	70
Prisons	Uniformed prison officers		80	55
Public service	a.	*Dock and inland waterways* – Dockers, dredger drivers, hopper steerers	80	55
		– All other workers	60	45
	b.	*Public transport* – Garage hands (including cleaners)	80	55
		– Conductors and drivers	60	45
Quarrying	All workers		100	70
Railways	(See the appropriate category for craftsmen, e.g. engineers, vehicle, etc.)			
	All other workers		100	70
Seamen	a.	Carpenters (Seamen) Passenger liners	165	165
	b.	Carpenters (Seamen) Cargo vessels, tankers, coasters and ferries	140	130
Shipyards	a.	Blacksmiths and their strikers, boilermakers, burners, carpenters, caulkers, drillers, furnacemen (platers), holders up, fitters, platers, plumbers, riveters, sheet iron workers, shipwrights, tubers, welders	140	115
	b.	Labourers	80	60
	c.	Apprentices and storekeepers	60	45
	d.	All other workers	100	75
Textiles and textile printing	a.	Carders, carding engineers, overlookers and technicians in spinning mills	120	85
	b.	All other workers	80	60

Industry		Occupation	Deduction for 2008–09 onwards £	Deduction for 2004–05 to 2007–08 £
Vehicles	a.	Builders, railway vehicle repairers and railway wagon lifters	140	105
	b.	Railway vehicle painters, letterers, and builders' and repairers' assistants	80	60
	c.	All other workers	60	45
Wood and furniture (formerly Wood)	a.	Carpenters, cabinet makers, joiners, wood carvers and woodcutting machinists	140	115
	b.	Artificial limb makers (other than in wood), organ builders and packaging case makers	120	90
	c.	Coopers not providing own tools, labourers, polishers and upholsterers	60	45
	d.	All other workers	100	75

Note

'Workers' and 'all other workers' are references to manual workers or to workers who have to pay for the upkeep of tools and special clothing.

'Firemen' means persons engaged to light and maintain furnaces.

'Constructional engineering' means engineering undertaken on a construction site, including buildings, shipyards, bridges, roads and other similar operations.

'Particular engineering' means engineering undertaken on a commercial basis in a factory or workshop for the purposes of producing components such as wire, springs, nails and locks.

Miscellaneous

[¶4-800]   Mobile phones

(ITEPA 2003, s. 319)

(Tax Reporter: ¶437-700)

No tax charge on employer-provided mobile phones but exemption restricted to one phone per employee, with no exemption for phones provided for family members. Limited exemption for vouchers supplied for mobile phone use. The right of the employee to surrender the phone for additional pay does not trigger a tax charge.

[¶4-805]   Recommended medical treatment

(ITEPA 2003, s. 320C)

(Tax Reporter: ¶437-900)

No liability to income tax arises in respect of the provision to an employee of recommended medical treatment, or the payment or reimbursement, to or in respect of an employee of the cost of such treatment, if the provision, payment or reimbursement is not pursuant to relevant salary sacrifice arrangements or relevant flexible remuneration arrangements. The exemption does not apply if, and to the extent that, the value in the tax year exceeds the limit shown in the table below.

Period	Annual limit
From 1 January 2015	£500

[¶4-810]   Employer-provided childcare (workplace nurseries)

(ITEPA 2003, s. 318)

(Tax Reporter: ¶434-600)

No liability to income tax arises in respect of employer-provided childcare (workplace nurseries) provided certain conditions are met; including that the premises are made available by the employer alone, or that the care is provided under partnership arrangements by persons including the employer, one or more of whom makes the premises available, and under which arrangements the employer is wholly or partly responsible for financing and managing the provision of the care.

[¶4-815]   Employer-supported childcare

(ITEPA 2003, s. 270A, 318A)

(Tax Reporter: ¶434-800ff.)

A limited exemption is available for childcare vouchers and directly contracted childcare. Where the cash equivalent of the benefit falls above the limits set out in the table below, liability to income tax arises only in respect of so much as exceeds the exempt amount.

The *Childcare Payments Act* 2014 amends s. 270A and 318A to restrict the availability of the existing tax exemptions for employer-supported childcare where the employee has given their employer a 'chilcare account notice' to say that they no longer want to receive employer-supported childcare so that they or their partner can open a childcare account under the new scheme launched in 2017 (by gradual roll out) (see ¶10-560). At Budget 2016, it was announced that Employer Supported Childcare will remain open to new entrants until April 2018 to support the transition between the schemes.

	Basic rate[1] £	Higher rate £	Additional rate £
From 6 April 2013			
Weekly	55	28	25
Monthly	243	124	111
Annual	2,915	1,484	1,325
From 6 April 2011			
Weekly	55	28	22
Monthly	243	124	97
Annual	2,915	1,484	1,166

Note

[1] The restriction on the amount of the exemption available for higher rate and additional rate taxpayers from 6 April 2011 does not apply where an employee joined the scheme before 6 April 2011, has not ceased to be employed by the employer since that date and there has not been a continuous period of 52 weeks since that date throughout which vouchers were not, or care was not, being provided under the scheme and such employees continue to be entitled to relief at the rates that are otherwise available for basic rate earners only (FA 2011, Sch. 8, para. 8).

[¶4-830]   Relocation allowance

(ITEPA 2003, s. 271–289)

(Tax Reporter: ¶433-850)

Tax exemption for the provision by employers of removal benefits, or payment or reimbursement of removal expenses in connection with an employee's change of residence where the employee's job or place of work is changed is generally subject to a statutory maximum of £8,000. No tax relief is available for the employee where expenses are not reimbursed by the employer.

[¶4-840]   Payments and benefits on termination of employment

(ITEPA 2003, s. 401–416)

(Tax Reporter: ¶437-000ff.)

Period	Relief[1][2]
From 1998–99	£30,000 exempt

Notes

[1] The exemption is not available for any payment or other benefit chargeable to income tax under other legislation (ITEPA 2003, s. 401(3)). There is therefore no exemption for any amounts already taxable as earnings (e.g. payments made under a contract of employment).

[2] *Finance (No. 2) Act* 2017 aligns the employer National Insurance contributions (NIC) treatment of termination payments with income tax and tightens the scope of the £30,000 exemption by making it clear that all payments in lieu of notice (PILONs), not just contractual PILONs, are taxable earnings. All employees will pay tax and Class 1 NICs on the amount of basic pay that they would have received if they had worked their notice in full, even if they are not paid a contractual PILON. The existing £30,000 income tax exemption is retained and employees will continue to benefit from an unlimited employee NICs exemption for payments associated with the termination of employment.

[¶4-850]   Scholarships and sandwich courses

(SP 4/86)

(Tax Reporter: ¶419-200)

Subject to conditions, employers may make tax-free payments up to a specified figure to employees who are attending certain educational courses. The specified amount for recent years has been as follows:

Period	Specified amount
From 1/9/07	£15,480

[¶4-860]   Trivial benefits

(ITEPA 2003, s. 323A)

No liability to income tax arises in respect of a benefit provided by, or on behalf of, an employer to an employee or a member of the employee's family or household provided the benefit is not cash or a cash voucher, is not a reward for work or performance, is not in the terms of the employment contract and falls within the limits set out below:

From	Maximum benefit cost £	Annual exempt amount £
6 April 2016	50	300

[¶4-870]   Sporting testimonials

(ITEPA 2003, s. 306B)

A one-off exemption from income tax applies in respect of income arising from a non-contractual or non-customary sporting testimonial or benefit for an employed sportsperson. Testimonials granted or awarded under contract or custom are already subject to income tax and are not eligible for the exemption.

From	Exemption[1] £
6 April 2016[2]	300

Notes

[1] Applies to income arising from relevant events held in a maximum period of 12 calendar months only, beginning with the date the first event is held in a 'testimonial year' (even if that year straddles more than one tax year). If the level of the income arising from the testimonial or testimonial year falls below the value of the exemption, the unused exemption cannot be carried forward to any future sporting testimonial/benefit matches, or against any other testimonial events held after that 12-month period.

[2] Events held on or after 6 April 2017 from a testimonial that is awarded or arranged for a sportsperson prior to 25 November 2015 will continue to fall within guidance previously published by HMRC on the tax treatment of sporting testimonials and benefits for employed sportspersons which afforded a concessionary exemption.

PAYE

[¶4-900] PAYE thresholds
(SI 2003/2682)

(Tax Reporter: ¶493-240ff.)

| | Amount | |
| | Weekly | Monthly |
Tax year	£	£
2017–18	221.00	958.00
2016–17	212.00	917.00
2015–16	204.00	883.00
2014–15	192.00	833.00
2013–14	182.00	787.00
2012–13	156.00	675.00
2011–12	144.00	623.00

Note
Under normal circumstances, employers need not deduct tax from employees who earn less than the above amounts. The PAYE monthly and weekly thresholds are calculated arithmetically as 1/52 and 1/12 respectively of the personal allowance, rounded to the nearest pound (SI 2003/2682, reg. 9(8)).

[¶4-920] PAYE codes
The PAYE code enables an employer or payer of pension to give the employee or pensioner the approved amount of tax-free pay.

L	Entitled to the basic tax-free personal allowance – 1150L for the 2017–18 tax year. Also used for 'emergency' codes
M	Marriage allowance: people who have received a transfer of 10% of their partner's personal allowance
N	Marriage allowance: people who have transferred 10% of their personal allowance to their partner
S	Income or pension taxed at Scottish rate of income tax
T	Tax code includes other calculations to work out the personal allowance (i.e. income-related reduction to the personal allowance)
0T	Allowances fully used up or reduced to nil and income is taxed at the relevant rates, may also be used for a new job where the employee does not have a P45 or has not completed a P46 before the first pay day
BR	All income is taxed at the basic rate, currently 20%, most commonly used for a second job or pension
SBR	Scottish taxpayer; all income taxed at the basic rate, currently 20%
D0	All income taxed at the higher rate, currently 40%, most commonly used for a second job or pension
SD0	Scottish taxpayer; all income taxed at the higher rate, currently 40%

D1	All income taxed at the additional rate, currently 45%, most commonly used for a second job or pension
SD1	Scottish taxpayer; all income taxed at the additional rate, currently 45%
NT	No tax to be deducted from income or pension
K	Untaxed income exceeds tax-free allowances (e.g. tax due for previous tax year, taxable state benefits or taxable employment benefits)

Emergency codes

W1, M1, X are emergency tax code indicators and denote the tax code is operating on a non-cumulative basis. Also issued where the tax code is adjusted during the tax year and the adjustment is to reduce net allowances/increase taxable benefits (so that the new collects on a non-cumulative basis for the remainder of the year). Emergency tax codes for the 2017–18 tax year are 1150L M1, 1150L W1, 1150L X.

[¶4-925] PAYE coding out limits

Debts

(ITEPA 2003, s. 684; SI 2003/2682, reg. 14A–14C)

(Tax Reporter: ¶493-340)

HMRC may collect specified relevant debts up to the permitted limit through the PAYE system. The table below sets out the maximum amount that may be collected in this way (but see also the 'overall limit' and the 'overriding limit' below):

Tax year in which deduction made	Maximum deduction £
From 2015–16	17,000
2012–13 to 2014–15(1)	3,000

Note
(1) SI 2003/2682, reg. 14A which provides for determination of a tax code to recover a 'relevant debt' within the meaning of ITEPA 2003, s. 684 was introduced with effect from 6 April 2012.

To the extent that the payee does not object, HMRC may also determine a code to collect or repay income tax payable or overpaid in respect of the high income child benefit charge and, from 2015–16, to collect child or working tax credit debt.

Self-assessment balancing payments

(SI 2003/2682, reg.186)

(Tax Reporter: ¶493-330)

Payments due on or after	Maximum deduction £
6 April 2012	3,000

Overall limit

(SI 2003/2682, reg. 14D)

With effect for tax codes issued for the tax year 2015–16 onwards, and to coincide with the increase in the coding out limit above from £3,000 to £17,000, an overall limit on the total amount of 'relevant debt' (under SI 2003/2682, reg. 14A) and 'tax credit debt' (under SI 2003/2682, reg. 14C) that may be recovered from an employee in a tax year via their tax code will be introduced, based on the expected amount of the individual's PAYE income for the tax year and as set out in the table below (subject to the 'overriding limit' below):

Expected amount of PAYE income in the tax year for which the code is determined	Total amount of debt recoverable in that tax year
Less than £30,000	No more than £3,000
£30,000 or more but less than £40,000	No more than £5,000
£40,000 or more but less than £50,000	No more than £7,000
£50,000 or more but less than £60,000	No more than £9,000
£60,000 or more but less than £70,000	No more than £11,000
£70,000 or more but less than £80,000	No more than £13,000
£80,000 or more but less than £90,000	No more than £15,000
£90,000 or more	No more than £17,000

Overriding limit

(SI 2003/2682, reg. 2)

The 'overriding limit' is the limit on the amount of tax that may be deducted from a relevant payment and is an amount equal to 50% of the amount of the relevant payment. A relevant payment is defined as a payment of net PAYE income, except PAYE social security income, UK social security pensions, excluded relocation expenses, excluded business expenses, excluded pecuniary liabilities, and excluded notional payments (SI 2003/2682, reg. 4).

Additionally, HMRC will further not code out debts which result in the individual's liability for the year doubling, even though the debt might otherwise fall within the limits set out above (i.e. only debts that equate to less than the individual's expected liability for the tax year will be coded out) (see HMRC manuals, PAYE12070).

[¶4-930]   PAYE real time information returns

(SI 2012/822; SI 2003/2682)

(Tax Reporter: ¶493-015)

Since 6 April 2013 (or 5 April 2014 for businesses with 50 or less employees), reporting PAYE information in real time has been mandatory, unless HMRC have notified otherwise. Key RTI requirements are as follows:

Taxation of Earnings

Submissions	Deadlines	Details
Full Payment Submission (FPS)	On or before the day employees are paid Final submission by 19 April (cannot file an FPS after this date)	• include all employees that are paid (including those earning below the NIC lower earnings limit (e.g. students)) • information to be submitted includes: amounts paid, deductions (tax and National Insurance), starter and leaver dates (if applicable)
Employer Payment Submission (EPS)	19 April following tax year (by 19 May following tax year to avoid a penalty)	• to report a reduction in the amount you pay to HMRC or if you have not paid any employees in a pay period
Earlier Year Update (EYU)	Up to six years after original FPS or EPS filed (by 19 May following tax year to avoid a penalty)	• to correct, after 19 April, any of the year to date totals submitted in your final FPS for the previous tax year. This only applies to years after you started to send information in real time
National Insurance verification request (NVR)	–	• to verify or obtain an National Insurance number for new employees

[¶4-932]   PAYE RTI: forms no longer needed

Reporting PAYE pre-RTI	Reporting in real time
Forms P14 and P35 end of year returns – do not use after you have submitted your 2012–13 return	FPS each time you pay employees EPS each month for any adjustments to what you owe Earlier Year Update (EYU) to amend details for earlier years
P45 – do not send any parts to HMRC – only use for the employees own records after 6 April 2013	Include starters and leavers information on your FPS
P46, P46(Pen) or P46(Expat) – do not use these forms after 6 April 2013	Include starters and leavers on your FPS.
Form CA6855 to trace or check a National Insurance number – do not use after 6 April 2013	Use payroll software to issue a National Insurance number verification request (NVR) to trace or check a National Insurance number
Form P38(S) – do not use after 6 April 2013	Include on your payroll and in your FPS

[¶4-935]   PAYE RTI: procedures unchanged

- **PAYE** – remains the same, only reporting that changes;
- **Coding notices** – employers still choose how they receive coding notices as previously;
- **Reporting a change to HMRC**, e.g. updating employee's new name or address for HMRC records – a real time submission will not update HMRC records. It remains the responsibility of the individual employee to notify HMRC of changes to name, address, etc.;
- **HMRC messages to employers** – HMRC continue to use the Data Provisioning Services (DPS) and EDI outbound message services;
- **Payment dates** – remain unchanged;
- **Forms P60** – P60s remain the same;
- **Expenses and benefits** – real time reporting has not changed how expenses and benefits are reported. Employers continue to complete and file any forms P9D, P11D and P11D(b) due under existing arrangements;
- **The Construction Industry Scheme (CIS) payment and reporting process** – real time reporting has not changed the CIS process. Employers continue to complete and file monthly returns (CIS300) due under the existing CIS arrangements. But where a limited company acting as a subcontractor has suffered CIS deductions, amounts should be reported to HMRC on an EPS and, as existing practice, subtract these from the amounts of PAYE due to be paid to HMRC.

[¶4-938]   PAYE RTI: correcting errors

Error in a Full Payment Submission (FPS) or EPS in the current tax year

Submit an additional FPS or EPS in the week or month of discovery or include correction in the next FPS or EPS for the next payroll run.

Error in FPS or EPS for previous tax year

Errors can be corrected before 20 April by submitting an additional FPS or EPS.

After 20 April, it is not possible to submit an additional FPS and instead the correction must be made on an EYU, however, errors on an EPS may be corrected by submitting an additional EPS for the tax year even after 20 April.

[¶4-939]   PAYE RTI: collection of tax on benefits in kind and expenses

(ITEPA 2003, s. 289Aff. and 684(1ZA); FA 2015, s. 13; SI 2003/2682, Pt. 3, Ch. 3A; SI 2015/1948)

Finance Act 2015 included amending legislation to enable the voluntary payrolling of benefits in kind from the 2016–17 tax year. Where an employer opts to payroll benefits in kind for cars, car fuel, medical insurance and gym membership, they will no longer be obliged to make a return (form P11D) and employers will instead report the value of these benefits in kind through real time information (SI 2003/2682, Pt. 3, Ch. 3A).

Taxation of Earnings

Payrolling benefits in kind is extended by *Finance Act* 2016 to allow for the payrolling of non-cash vouchers and credit tokens from 2017–18 (amendments to SI 2003/2682, Pt. 3, Ch. 3A by SI 2016/1137).

From April 2016, the £8,500 a year threshold for the taxation of benefits in kind was abolished (FA 2015, s. 13) (meaning all benefits in kind are liable to income tax and National Insurance contributions, whatever the level of the employee's earnings and benefits in kind); and, also with effect from 6 April 2016, the dispensation regime for expenses was also replaced with an exemption for paid and reimbursed expenses (ITEPA 2003, s. 289Aff. and SI 2015/1948).

[¶4-940]   PAYE deadlines

(Tax Reporter: ¶494-700)

Reporting deadlines

Forms	Date	Provision	Penalty provisions
P14, P35, P38 and P38A (non-real time employers only)	19 May following tax year	*Income Tax (Pay As You Earn) Regulations 2003 (SI 2003/2682)*, reg. 73 and 74	TMA 1970, s. 98A
P60 (to employee)	31 May following tax year	*Income Tax (Pay As You Earn) Regulations 2003 (SI 2003/2682)*, reg. 67	TMA 1970, s. 98A
P11D	6 July following tax year	*Income Tax (Pay As You Earn) Regulations 2003 (SI 2003/2682)*, reg. 85	TMA 1970, s. 98
P46(Car)	3 May, 2 August, 2 November, 2 February	*Income Tax (Pay As You Earn) Regulations 2003 (SI 2003/2682)*, reg. 90	TMA 1970, s. 98

Other deadlines	Date
Employee payments in return for benefits in kind (making good) for 2017–18 and subsequent tax years[(1)]	6 July following tax year

Note

[(1)]   *Finance (No. 2) Act* 2017 introduces a date for 'making good' on benefits in kind which are not accounted for in real time through Pay As You Earn (PAYE). The date has effect for benefits in kind which give rise to a tax liability for the tax year 2017–18 or any subsequent tax year.

[¶4-942]   PAYE late filing penalties

(FA 2009, Sch. 55)

RTI

Where payment information is not received as expected on an FPS, or HMRC have not been notified that no employees have been paid in a tax period by submission of an EPS, late filing penalties will apply. The rules apply to each PAYE scheme, rather than each employer.

Late filing penalties will apply on a monthly basis, however, no penalty will apply for the first month in each tax year that returns are filed late.

New employers will not be penalised if their first FPS is received within 30 days of making their first payment to an employee.

In August 2017, HMRC announced they will continue with a risk-based approach to late filing PAYE penalties for the 2017–18 tax year. This includes not charging penalties if FPSs are filed late but within three days of the payment date and there is no pattern of persistent late filing.

Initial penalties

Number of employees[1]	Monthly penalty[2] £
1–9	100
10–49	200
50–249	300
250 or more	400

Notes
[1] HMRC will use the latest information available to determine the number of employees, and the size of the filing penalty for each period where a return is late.
[2] Filing penalty notices will be issued quarterly in July, October, January and April, if appropriate, showing the amount of the filing penalty for each tax month identified in that quarter.

Additional penalties for returns over three months late

	Penalty
3 months late	5%[1]

Note
[1] Calculated as a percentage of the tax/NICs that should have been shown on the late return.

Key deadlines	Penalty
Final FPS submitted by 19 April (last date for submission of an FPS)	None
EYU submitted after 19 April but by 19 May	None
Final payments unreported at 19 May	£100 per 50 employees for each month return outstanding[1]

Note
[1] Penalty notices issued after 19 September (once return outstanding for four months) and again, the following January and May.

Taxation of Earnings

Penalties (fixed) imposed for delays (TMA 1970, s. 98A)

Forms	First 12 months	Thereafter
P14, P35, P38 and P38A	£100 per 50 employees per month	Additional penalty not exceeding 100% of the tax and NIC payable for the year but remaining unpaid by 19 April following end of tax year

Penalties (mitigable) that may be imposed for delays (TMA 1970, s. 98)

Forms	Initial	Continuing
P11D	£300 per return	£60 per day

[¶4-945] PAYE penalties for incorrect returns

(FA 2007, Sch. 24)

(Tax Reporter: ¶184-850)

HMRC use a risk-based approach to identify employers they think may be submitting incorrect returns. Where HMRC discover careless or deliberate errors, the penalties that could apply will be based on the behaviour that led to the error and the amount of potential lost revenue for that return. Errors that arise despite taking reasonable care attract no penalty at all and penalties for errors due to failure to take reasonable care can be reduced to zero with full and unprompted disclosure to HMRC.

The maximum penalty for an incorrect return is 100% of the potential lost revenue (deliberate and concealed action), 70% (deliberate but not concealed) or 30% (careless action).

[¶4-946] PAYE: late payment penalties

(FA 2009, s. 107 and Sch. 56)

(Tax Reporter: ¶184-975)

Late payment penalties will be charged in-year on a late payment of monthly, quarterly or annual PAYE, student loan deductions, CIS deductions or Class 1, 1A and 1B NICs. Late payment penalty notices are issued quarterly in July, October, January and April showing the amount of the penalty due for each tax month. The total penalty charged can be made up of:

- a default penalty, for failure to pay monthly/quarterly payments on time and in full; and
- penalties for amounts still unpaid after six and 12 months.

Penalties for late monthly or quarterly PAYE payments

No penalty if only one PAYE amount is late in a tax year, unless that payment is over six months late.

No. defaults in a tax year	Penalty percentage	Amount to which penalty percentages apply
1–3[(1)]	1%	The total amount that is late in the relevant tax month (ignoring the first late payment in the tax year)
4–6	2%	
7–9	3%	
10 or more	4%	

Note
[(1)] The first failure to pay on time does not count as a default.

Additional penalties	Amount
6 months late	5%
12 months late	Further 5%

Amounts due annually or occasionally (Class 1A and 1B NIC)

Penalty date	5%
5 months after initial penalty date	further 5%
11 months after initial penalty date	further 5%

Penalty dates

The penalty date varies according to the type of payment. For payments such as Class 1A and Class 1B NICs, HMRC determinations, assessments and amendments, or corrections to returns the 'penalty date' is 30 days after the due date. In most other cases, the penalty date is the day after the due date.

[¶4-948]   Interest on certain PAYE paid late

(FA 2009, s. 101 and 102)

(Tax Reporter: ¶494-900; ¶494-910)

HMRC charge in-year, rather than annual, interest on all unpaid:

- PAYE tax, Class 1 National Insurance contributions (NICs) and student loan deductions, including specified charges (estimates HMRC make in the absence of a PAYE submission);
- Construction Industry Scheme charges;
- In-year late filing penalties; and
- In-year late payment penalties.

Interest will also be charged on underpayments that arise because of adjustments reported on Earlier Year Updates submitted.

Taxation of Earnings

For annual payments such as Class 1A and Class 1B NICs, HMRC will continue to charge interest on any amount which remains unpaid after the due date.

Interest is charged daily, from the date a payment is due and payable to the date it is paid in full.

Repayment interest will apply where a payment is made and the charge is then reduced resulting in an overpayment which is either reallocated to a later charge or repaid.

[¶4-962]   PAYE electronic communications penalty: form P45 (Part 1 or Part 3), P46 or P46(Pen)

(SI 2003/2682, reg. 210BA)

(Tax Reporter: ¶498-745)

2013–14 and subsequent years Table 9AA		2011–12 and 2012–13 Table 9A	
Number of items	Penalty	Number of items	Penalty
		1–2	nil
1–49	£100	3–49	£100
50–149	£300	50–149	£300
150–299	£600	150–299	£600
300–399	£900	300–399	£900
400–499	£1,200	400–499	£1,200
500–599	£1,500	500–599	£1,500
600–699	£1,800	600–699	£1,800
700–799	£2,100	700–799	£2,100
800–899	£2,400	800–899	£2,400
900–999	£2,700	900–999	£2,700
1,000+	£3,000	1,000+	£3,000

Note
[1]   Number of items of specified information the employer has failed to deliver in the tax year. (Each item mentioned in reg. 207(1), para. (a)–(d) counts as a separate item of specified information.) An item of specified information counts even if it relates to the same employee as one or more other items.

[¶4-965] PAYE electronic communications penalty: forms P35 and P14

(SI 2003/2682, reg. 210AA)

(Tax Reporter: ¶498-745)

2010–11 and subsequent years Table 9ZA	
Number of employees[1]	Penalty
1–5	£100
6–49	£300
50–249	£600
250–399	£900
400–499	£1,200
500–599	£1,500
600–699	£1,800
700–799	£2,100
800–899	£2,400
900–999	£2,700
1,000+	£3,000

Note
[1] Number of employees for whom particulars should have been included with the specified information.

[¶4-975] PAYE monthly accounting periods

(SI 2003/2682, reg. 69)

(Tax Reporter: ¶494-510)

Period	Month no.	Payment due (electronic)	Payment due (other)
6 Apr to 5 May	1	22 May	19 May
6 May to 5 June	2	22 June	19 June
6 June to 5 July	3	22 July	19 July
6 July to 5 Aug	4	22 August	19 August

Period	Month no.	Payment due (electronic)	Payment due (other)
6 Aug to 5 Sept	5	22 September	19 September
6 Sept to 5 Oct	6	22 October	19 October
6 Oct to 5 Nov	7	22 November	19 November
6 Nov to 5 Dec	8	22 December	19 December
6 Dec to 5 Jan	9	22 January	19 January
6 Jan to 5 Feb	10	22 February	19 February
6 Feb to 5 Mar	11	22 March	19 March
6 Mar to 5 Apr	12	22 April	19 April

[¶4-976] PAYE quarterly accounting periods

(SI 2003/2682, reg. 70)

(Tax Reporter: ¶494-570)

Period	Month no.	Payment due (electronic)	Payment due (other)
6 Apr to 5 July	1–3	22 July	19 July
6 July to 5 Oct	4–6	22 October	19 October
6 Oct to 5 Jan	7–9	22 January	19 January
6 Jan to 5 Apr	10–12	22 April	19 April

[¶4-980] Payroll giving scheme

(ITEPA 2003, s. 713)

(Tax Reporter: ¶457-500)

Employees whose remuneration is subject to deduction of tax at source under PAYE can make unlimited tax-deductible donations to charity by requesting that their employers deduct the donations from their pay.

[¶4-985] Student loan deductions

(SI 2009/470, reg. 29; SI 2016/606)

There are now three categories of student loans: Plan 1 loans (pre-2012 loans); Plan 2 loans (post-2012 loans) and postgraduate master's degree loans. Each type of loan carries different repayment terms although all repayment provisions, in respect both student loans and postgraduate master's degree loans in England and Wales, are now consolidated in the 2009 Regulations (SI 2017/831).

Postgraduate master's degree loans[1]

Year	Percentage	Threshold[2]
From 6 April 2019	6%	£25,000

Note
[1] Postgraduate master's degree loans are available to eligible students for postgraduate master's degree courses which begin on or after 01 August 2016. No repayment of a postgraduate master's degree loan is required until on or after 6 April 2019.
[2] Postgraduate master's degree loans repayment threshold aligned with post-2012 repayment threshold by SI 2017/831, reg. 20(6), with effect from 5 September 2017.

Plan 2 (post-2012[1]) student loans

Year	Percentage	Threshold[2]
2018–19[2]	9%	£25,000
2017–18	9%	£21,000
2016–17	9%	£21,000

Notes
[1] Plan 2 loans are loans taken out by new students starting courses on or after 1 September 2012 (and as defined by SI 2009/470, reg. 3(2)). Repayment of post-2012 loans commenced from 6 April 2016.
[2] Rates announced by Department for Education in October 2017.

Plan 1 (pre-2012) student loans

Year	Percentage	Threshold[1]
2018–19[2]	9%	£18,330
2017–18	9%	£17,775
2016–17	9%	£17,495
2015–16	9%	£17,335
2014–15	9%	£16,910
2013–14	9%	£16,365
2012–13	9%	£15,795
2011–12	9%	£15,000

Notes
[1] Repayment threshold uprated by RPI for tax years ending after 6 April 2012 (SI 2009/470, reg. 29(7)).
[2] Rates announced by Department for Education in October 2017.

[¶4-990] Apprenticeship levy

(FA 2016, Pt. 6)

Apprenticeship levy is charged where:

- a person has a pay bill for a tax year (beginning with 6 April 2017 or any subsequent year); and
- the relevant percentage of the pay bill exceeds the person's levy allowance (if any) for that tax year.

Amount of charge

The amount of the charge is equal to:

N – A

where:

N is the relevant percentage of the pay bill for the tax year; and

A is the amount of the levy allowance (if any) to which the person is entitled for the tax year.

From	Levy allowance[1] £	Relevant percentage %	Pay bill threshold[2] £
6 April 2017	15,000	0.5	3,000,000

Notes
[1] Two or more companies which form a 'company unit' share a single levy allowance.
[2] Paybill threshold is calculated as the amount by which the employer's pay bill must exceed in order for a positive charge to arise after deducting the levy allowance (i.e. equals the levy allowance divided by the relevant percentage).

[¶4-992]   Apprenticeship levy: monthly cumulative levy allowance

(SI 2003/2682, reg. 147E)

(Tax Reporter: ¶495-943)

The table below may be used for the purposes of calculating the apprenticeship levy charge for the relevant month (based on the cumulative amount of the monthly pay bill, multiplied by 0.5%, minus the monthly cumulative levy allowance).

Relevant month in the tax year	Monthly cumulative levy allowance £
Month 1	1,250
Month 2	2,500
Month 3	3,750
Month 4	5,000
Month 5	6,250
Month 6	7,500
Month 7	8,750
Month 8	10,000
Month 9	11,250
Month 10	12,500
Month 11	13,750
Month 12	15,000

TAXATION OF CAPITAL GAINS

[¶5-000] Rates

(TCGA 1992, s. 4)

(Tax Reporter: ¶500-220)

Tax year	Gains eligible for:		Individuals		Trustees and PRs	
	Entrepreneurs' relief	Investors' relief[3]	Main rates[1]	Residential property/ carried interest[2]	Main rate	Residential property/ carried interest[2]
2018–19[4]	10	[10]	10/20	18/28	20	28
2017–18	10	[10]	10/20	18/28	20	28
2016–17	10	[10]	10/20	18/28	20	28
2015–16	10	—	18/28	18/28	28	28
2014–15	10	—	18/28	18/28	28	28
2013–14	10	—	18/28	18/28	28	28
2012–13	10	—	18/28	18/28	28	28

Notes

[1] For disposals on or after 6 April 2016, the chargeable gains arising from those disposals are aggregated with the individual's taxable income and to the extent that the aggregate falls above the threshold of the income tax basic rate, capital gains tax is charged at 20% (taking the chargeable gains as being the highest part of that aggregate). If the aggregate falls below the threshold, the capital gains tax rate is 10% (TCGA 1992, s. 4, as amended by FA 2016, s. 83).

[2] Gains accruing on the disposal of interests in residential properties that do not qualify for private residence relief and carried interest remain chargeable at the 18% and 28% rates as applicable for disposals before 6 April 2016 (TCGA 1992, s. 4, as amended by FA 2016, s. 83).

[3] *Finance Act* 2016 introduces a new relief for investors in unlisted trading companies. The relief applies a lower (10%) rate of capital gains tax on disposals of qualifying holdings (of newly issued shares purchased on or after 17 March 2016), providing they are held for a minimum of three years from 6 April 2016 (meaning that effectively, the relief will not be available until 2019–20) (TCGA 1992, Pt. 5, Ch. 5).

[4] Rates per Autumn Budget 2017.

[¶5-010] Exemptions

(TCGA 1992, s. 3 and 262)

(Tax Reporter: ¶509-050; ¶535-100)

Tax year	Annual exempt amount[1]		Chattel exemption (max sale proceeds)[4] £
	Individuals, PRs[2], trusts for mentally disabled £	Other trusts[3] £	
2018–19[5]	11,700	5,850	6,000
2017–18	11,300	5,650	6,000
2016–17	11,100	5,550	6,000
2015–16	11,100	5,550	6,000

Tax year	Annual exempt amount[1]		Chattel exemption (max sale proceeds)[4] £
	Individuals, PRs[2], trusts for mentally disabled £	Other trusts[3] £	
2014–15	11,000	5,500	6,000
2013–14	10,900	5,450	6,000

Notes

[1] The annual exempt amount is increased annually, unless Parliament determines otherwise, by reference to the increase in CPI (from 2013–14, previously by reference to RPI).

[2] For year of death and next two years in the case of personal representatives (PRs) of deceased persons.

[3] Multiple trusts created by the same settlor; each attracts relief equal to the annual amount divided by the number of such trusts (subject to a minimum of 10% of the full amount).

[4] Where disposal proceeds exceed the exemption limit, marginal relief restricts any chargeable gain to $5/3$ of the excess. Where there is a loss and the proceeds are less than £6,000, the proceeds are deemed to be £6,000.

[5] Rates per Autumn Budget 2017.

[¶5-020] ATED-related capital gains on high value residential property

(TCGA 1992, s. 2B, Sch. 4ZZA)

(Tax Reporter: ¶808-015)

From 6 April 2013, capital gains tax applies to companies and other corporate bodies on disposals of UK residential property valued at over the 'threshold amount'. If a residential property which has been subject to annual tax on enveloped dwellings (ATED) is disposed of some or all of the gains or losses will be 'ATED-related' and charged to capital gains tax.

Tax year	Threshold amount	Rate
2016–17 to 2018–19	£500,000	28%
2015–16	£1,000,000	28%
2014–15 and 2013–14	£2,000,000	28%

The charge applies to any of the following that own an interest in residential property that is subject to ATED:

- companies that are resident in the UK for tax purposes;
- companies that are not UK resident;
- companies (both UK resident and non-UK resident) which are a partner in a partnership; and
- some collective investment schemes, depending on the terms and nature of the scheme.

The charge arises in respect of ATED-related gains only, which, normally, will be gains attributable to periods after 5 April 2013. However, it is possible to elect out of the rules of apportionment between pre- and post-April 2013 periods, and calculate the ATED-related gain by reference to the entire period of ownership. In most cases, such an election will only be beneficial where the market value at 5 April 2013 is greater than the value at the time of disposal.

Gains and losses that are ATED-related are ring-fenced from non-ATED-related gains and losses, and a general computational feature of the rules is that indexation allowance is available only against non-ATED-related gains.

[¶5-030]   Disposals of UK residential property by non-residents, etc.

(TCGA 1992, s. 14B–14H)

(Tax Reporter: ¶510-750ff.)

The charge to capital gains tax is extended, with effect in relation to disposals made on or after 6 April 2015, to chargeable gains accruing to non-UK resident persons on the disposal of an interest in UK residential property.

Tax year	Rate		
	Individuals	Trustees and PRs	Companies
From 2015–16	18%/28%	28%	20%

Non-UK resident persons include:

*   non-UK resident individuals;
*   non-UK resident trusts;
*   personal representatives of a deceased person who was non-UK resident; and
*   non-UK resident companies controlled by five or fewer persons, except where the company itself, or at least one of the controlling persons, is a 'qualifying institutional investor'.

'UK residential property' is broadly, an interest in UK land that has consisted of or included a dwelling at any time during the relevant ownership period, being the period from acquisition or 6 April 2015 (whichever is later) to the day before the date of disposal.

The charge only applies to the portion of any gain that relates to the post-6 April 2015 ownership period calculated by rebasing the property at its 5 April 2015 market value to calculate a notional pre- and post-5 April 2015 gain or loss. An election for straight-line time apportionment will also be possible.

NRCGT losses accruing by a person on chargeable non-resident disposals of UK residential property interests when non-UK resident will be general allowable losses for use against chargeable gains when UK resident but are otherwise ring-fenced and can only be relieved against gains from other UK residential property in the same or a subsequent tax year and cannot be carried back.

[¶5-040]   Entrepreneurs' relief and investors' relief

(TCGA 1992, s. 169H–169S)

(Tax Reporter: ¶572-500ff.)

Chargeable gains arising on disposals of qualifying business assets on or after 23 June 2010 are charged to tax at a rate of 10%.

Period	Lifetime limit for entrepreneurs[1] £	Lifetime limit for investors[2] £
From 2019–20	–	10,000,000
From 06.04.11	10,000,000	–

Taxation of Capital Gains

Notes
(1) The limit is a lifetime limit applying to disposals on or after 6 April 2008. Transitional provisions allow relief to be claimed in certain circumstances where gains deferred from disposals made on or before 5 April 2008 subsequently become chargeable (FA 2008, Sch. 3, para. 7 and 8).
(2) *Finance Act* 2016 introduces a new relief for investors in unlisted trading companies. The relief applies a lower (10%) rate of capital gains tax on disposals of qualifying holdings (of newly issued shares purchased on or after 17 March 2016), providing they are held for a minimum of three years from 6 April 2016 (meaning that effectively, the relief will not be available until 2019-20). The relief is subject to a separate lifetime limit of £10m of gains (TCGA 1992, Pt. 5, Ch. 5).

Restrictions

- **Goodwill on incorporation:** with effect for transfers on or after 3 December 2014, individuals are prevented from claiming entrepreneurs' relief on disposals of the reputation and customer relationships associated with a business ('goodwill') when they transfer the business to a related close company. The restriction does not extend to partners in a firm who do not hold or acquire any stake in the successor company (TCGA 1992, s. 169LA). However, entrepreneurs' relief may still be claimed, subject to certain conditions, on gains on the goodwill of a business when that business is transferred to a company controlled by five or fewer persons or by its directors. The principal condition is that the claimant must hold less than 5% of the acquiring company's shares. There are special rules to allow relief where the acquiring company is then sold to a third party.

- **Associated disposals:** with effect for disposals on or after 18 March 2015, individuals are prevented from claiming entrepreneurs' relief in respect of gains on disposals of privately held assets used in a business, unless they are associated with a significant material disposal, that is to say a disposal of at least a 5% shareholding in the company or of at least a 5% share in the assets of the partnership carrying on the business (TCGA 1992, s. 169K). However, entrepreneurs' relief may be claimed on a disposal of a privately-held asset when the accompanying disposal of business assets is to a family member.

- **Joint ventures and partnerships:** with effect for disposals on or after 18 March 2015, individuals are prevented from claiming entrepreneurs' relief in respect of gains on shares in certain companies which invest in joint venture companies, or which are members of partnerships. Relief is denied where the investing company has no trade (or no relevant trade) of its own (TCGA 1992, s. 169S). However, entrepreneurs' relief may be claimed in some cases involving joint ventures and partnerships where the disposal of business assets does not meet the existing 5% minimum holding conditions. The definitions of a trading company and trading group which apply for entrepreneurs' relief purposes have been amended. To allow a percentage of the activities of a joint venture company to be treated as carried on by a company which holds shares in that company. Accordingly, trading activities of a company in its capacity as a partner in a firm may be taken into account as such rather than treated as being non-trading (TCGA 1992, s. 169SA and Sch. 7ZA).

[¶5-050]   Other exemptions and reliefs

EMI shares

(TCGA 1992, s. 169I(7A)–(7R))

(Tax Reporter: ¶572-950)

With effect in relation to disposals on or after 6 April 2013 of shares acquired pursuant to the exercise of a qualifying EMI option, entrepreneurs' relief will be available in respect of the disposal notwithstanding that the 'personal company' requirement (5% holding) may not be satisfied. To qualify, the shares must be:

- acquired since 6 April 2012;
- disposed of at least one year after the grant of the option; and
- the individual must have been an employee of the company, or a company in the same trading group, throughout the one year period ending with the disposal.

Employee shareholder status

(TCGA 1992, s. 236B–236G)

(Tax Reporter: ¶565-050)

Finance Act 2017 removes the capital gains tax exemption and relief associated with shares received in return for entering into an employee shareholder agreement on or after 1 December 2016.

Period	Gains exemption[1] £	Lifetime limit[2] £
From 17 March 2016	50,000	100,000
From 1 September 2013	50,000	—

Notes

[1] Gains on the disposal of up to £50,000 worth of shares (based on acquisition value) acquired in respect of agreements entered into before 1 December 2016 (extended to 2 December in certain cases) are exempt from capital gains tax. Where a particular acquisition of shares caused the £50,000 limit to be breached, the remainder of the £50,000 limit was applied against the total value of the particular share acquisition and only that portion of the total number of shares acquired by the particular acquisition will be exempt from capital gains tax. The capital gains tax exemption was not available if the shareholder or connected person had a material interest (25% or more) in the company or parent undertaking. Normal share pooling and share identification rules do not apply to exempt employee shareholder shares.

[2] *Finance Act* 2016 introduced a lifetime limit of £100,000 in respect of capital gains tax exempt gains arising on employee shareholder shares. The limit applies to employee shareholder shares issued as consideration for entering into employee shareholder agreements from midnight at the end of 16 March 2016. Any past or future gains, realised or unrealised, on employee shareholder shares that were issued in respect of employee shareholder agreements before midnight at the end of 16 March 2016 do not count towards the limit (TCGA 1992, s. 236B).

See ¶4-690 for further details on employee shareholder status and income tax reliefs. (also withdrawn from 1 December 2016).

Employee-ownership trusts

(TCGA 1992, s. 236H–236U)

(Tax Reporter: ¶361-400ff.)

Disposals of shares to a trust with specific characteristics which benefits all employees of a company (or a group) may be wholly relieved from capital gains tax if certain criteria are met. The relief requirements are:

- the trading requirement: the company whose shares are disposed of must be a trading company, or the parent company of a trading group;

- the all-employee benefit requirement: the trust which acquires the shares must operate for the benefit of all employees;

- the controlling interest requirement: the trust must have a controlling interest in the company at the end of the tax year, which it did not have at the start of that year;

- the limited participation requirement: certain participators must be excluded from being beneficiaries of the trust; and

- neither the claimant (nor anyone connected with him) has previously received relief on the same company's (or any group company's) shares.

The relief operates by disapplying TCGA 1992, s. 17(1) (market value disposals) and treats the disposal (and acquisition by the trustees) as a no gain, no loss disposal. The relief is available on disposals which take place in a single tax year; disposals may be made by more than one person and can be of any number of shares. Where a disqualifying event (broadly, the relief requirements cease to be met) occurs in the following tax year, any relief given is withdrawn and where a disqualifying event occurs in any later tax year, this triggers a deemed disposal and reacquisition at market value by the trustees.

Rollover relief

(TCGA 1992, s. 152)

(Tax Reporter: ¶570-100)

To qualify for rollover relief, an asset must fall within one of the 'relevant classes of assets' and the reinvestment must generally take place within the period from 12 months before to three years after the disposal of the old asset. Classes of assets qualifying for relief are as follows, but see TCGA 1992, s. 156ZB for the interaction of this section with the corporation tax rules for gains and losses on intangible fixed assets:

- land and buildings occupied and used exclusively for the purposes of a trade;

- fixed plant or machinery (not forming part of a building);

- ships, aircraft, hovercraft;

- satellites, space stations and spacecraft (including launch vehicles);

- goodwill;

- milk quotas and potato quotas, ewe and suckler cow premium quotas, fish quotas;

- entitlements under the single farm payments scheme;

- entitlements under the basic payment scheme (with effect in relation to disposals of old assets or acquisitions of new assets on or after 20 December 2013); and

- Lloyd's members' syndicate rights and assets treated as acquired by members.

Private residence relief

(TCGA 1992, s. 222)

(Tax Reporter: ¶540-000)

Relief is given on gains arising on the disposal of a dwelling house and on land enjoyed with the residence as its garden or grounds (up to the permitted area of half a hectare, or more if required for the reasonable enjoyment of the property).

Gains are apportioned across the period of ownership between periods of occupation (including deemed occupation) and other periods, with relief available for the portion of the gain attributable to periods of occupation. The final period of ownership is always eligible for relief provided the property was at some time the only or main residence. For disposals on or after 6 April 2014, the final period exemption applies to the last 18 months of ownership (previously, 36 months) except for individuals who are disabled or in a care home and with no other property who continue to get a 36-month final period exemption.

Where a residence is let during a period of non-occupation, relief is available on the portion of the gain attributable to the let period up to £40,000.

Enterprise investment scheme

(TCGA 1992, s. 150A; Pt. 5, Ch. 4 and Sch. 5B)

(Tax Reporter: ¶564-400ff.; ¶568-000)

A disposal of shares on which income tax relief has not been withdrawn is exempt from capital gains tax. The exemption applies where EIS shares are held for more than three years from their issue. Losses arising are eligible for relief in the normal way, but the base cost is treated as reduced by any EIS income tax relief which has been given and not withdrawn.

A CGT deferral relief permits the postponement of a capital gain to be claimed where an investor subscribes for EIS shares within the period of one year prior to and three years after the gain accrues.

See ¶3-400 for EIS income tax relief.

Gains that are eligible for entrepreneurs' relief and deferred into investment under the enterprise investment scheme on or after 3 December 2014 will benefit from entrepreneurs' relief when the gain is realised.

Seed enterprise investment scheme

(TCGA 1992, Sch. 5BB)

(Tax Reporter: ¶568-500)

Disposal relief

The exemption from capital gains applies where SEIS shares are held for more than three years from their issue. Losses are eligible for relief in the normal way but the base cost is treated as reduced by any SEIS income tax relief which has been given and not withdrawn.

Reinvestment relief

The reinvestment exemption is available in respect of a gain arising on the disposal of any asset to the extent that the individual makes a qualifying investment under SEIS in the same tax year, with so much of the gain that is matched with the relevant percentage of

Taxation of Capital Gains

qualifying SEIS investment expenditure being exempt from CGT (subject to the £100,000 investment limit). *Finance Act* 2013 extended the relief and *Finance Act* 2014 made it permanent.

Relevant year[1]	Relevant percentage[2]
2017–18	50%
2013–14 to 2016–17	50%
2012–13	100%

Notes
[1] The relevant year is year in which the investor is eligible for and makes a claim for SEIS income tax relief in respect of an amount subscribed for an issue of shares which must be the same tax year as the disposal of the asset and year in which the chargeable gain accrues.
[2] The relevant percentage of the 'available SEIS expenditure' is to be set against a corresponding amount of the original gain. The 'available SEIS expenditure' is the amount specified in the claim (provided that the amount has not been previously set against a gain) but cannot exceed the amount of the gain which remains unmatched after any previous claims or claims under the EIS deferral relief. To the extent that the gain is matched with the relevant percentage of the amount subscribed, it is not a chargeable gain.

Investment in social enterprises

(TCGA 1992, s. 255A–255E; Pt. 5, Ch. 4 and Sch. 8B)

(Tax Reporter: ¶569-300ff.)

Disposal relief

The disposal relief provides an exemption from capital gains tax in respect of the disposal of an investment where the investor has received income tax relief (which has not subsequently been withdrawn) on the cost of the investment, and the investment is disposed of after it has been held for at least three years. However, if no claim to income tax relief is made, then any subsequent disposal of the investment will not qualify for exemption from capital gains tax.

Deferral relief

The deferral relief enables the payment of tax on a capital gain to be deferred where the gain is reinvested in shares or debt investments which also qualify for SITR income tax relief. It is not, however, necessary for the investor to have made a claim for SITR income tax relief. The gain can arise from the disposal of any kind of asset, but must arise in the period from 6 April 2014 to 5 April 2019. The SITR qualifying investment must be made in the period one year before or three years after the gain arose. There is no minimum period for which the investment must be held; the deferred capital gain is brought back into charge whenever the investment is disposed of or the social enterprise ceases to meet the requirements of the scheme, but if an amount equal to the gain is once more invested in shares or debt investments which also qualify for SITR income tax relief then the gain may be held over again.

Gains that are eligible for entrepreneurs' relief and deferred into investment under the enterprise investment scheme on or after 3 December 2014 will benefit from entrepreneurs' relief when the gain is realised.

Charities

(TCGA 1992, s. 256, 257; ITA 2007, s. 518ff.; CTA 2010, s. 466ff.)

(Tax Reporter: ¶815-440)

The gains of charities are not taxable provided they are applicable, and applied, for charitable purposes only. The legislation is designed to charge charities to tax on the amount of their income and gains that has not been invested, lent or spent in an approved way.

A charge to capital gains tax arises if a charity ceases to be a charity, when there is a deemed sale and reacquisition of the trust property by the trustees at market value.

Gifts to the nation

(TCGA 1992, s. 258; FA 2012, Sch. 14)

(Tax Reporter: ¶535-620)

Gains arising on gifts of pre-eminent property to be held for the benefit of the public or the nation are not chargeable to capital gains tax.

For the tax year 2012–13 and subsequent tax years, a reduction in income tax and/or capital gains tax is available where an individual makes a gift of pre-eminent property to be held for the benefit of the public or the nation. The tax reduction is 30% of the value of the gift. A gift offer must be made and registered in accordance with the scheme and relief is available against the individual's liability for the year in which the gift offer is registered and/or any of the succeeding four tax years.

Pre-eminent property includes any picture, print, book, manuscript, work of art, scientific object or other thing that is pre-eminent for its national, scientific, historic or artistic interest, collections of such items and any object kept in a significant building where it is desirable that it remain associated with the building.

Disincorporation relief

(TCGA 1992, s. 162B and 162C; CTA 2009, s. 849A; FA 2013, s. 58–60)

Disincorporation relief is due to expire on 31 March 2018 and will not be extended (Autumn Budget 2017).

Disincorporation relief is a form of rollover or deferral relief which allows a company to transfer certain assets to its shareholders who continue the business in an unincorporated form. The assets are deemed to be transferred at below market value so that no corporation tax charge arises to the company, although shareholders may still be liable to income tax or capital gains tax on the transfer of assets to them by the company. Shareholders will be liable to capital gains tax, as usual, on a future sale of the assets, for which purpose the assets are treated as having been acquired at the reduced transfer value.

The relief applies in relation to a 'qualifying transfer' of a business with a disposal date falling within the period of five years beginning 1 April 2013. A qualifying transfer is one which meets the following conditions:

- the business must be transferred as a going concern;
- the business must be transferred together with all the assets of the business or together with all the assets of the business apart from cash;
- the total market value of the 'qualifying assets' at the time of the transfer must not be more than £100,000;
- the shareholders that the business is transferred to must be individuals; and
- those shareholders must have held shares in the company throughout the 12 months before the transfer.

Taxation of Capital Gains

108

Qualifying assets are interests in land (other than land held as trading stock) and goodwill. Special rules apply to determine the transfer value of any post-FA 2002 goodwill.

A claim for disincorporation relief must be made jointly by the company and all the shareholders to whom the business is transferred. The claim must be made within two years of the business transfer date.

[¶5-100] Leases which are wasting assets

Restrictions of allowable expenditure

(TCGA 1992, s. 240 and Sch. 8, para. 1)

(Tax Reporter: ¶509-600ff.)

Fraction equal to $\dfrac{P(1) - P(3)}{P(1)}$ excluded from expenditure under TCGA 1992, s. 38(1)(a),

and fraction equal to $\dfrac{P(2) - P(3)}{P(2)}$ excluded from expenditure under TCGA 1992, s. 38(1)(b),

where:

P(1) = table percentage for duration of lease at time of acquisition (or 31 March 1982 where applicable);

P(2) = table percentage for duration of lease at time expenditure incurred; and

P(3) = table percentage for duration of lease at time of disposal.

Years	%	Monthly[1] increment
50 or more	100	—
49	99.657	0.029
48	99.289	0.031
47	98.902	0.032
46	98.490	0.034
45	98.059	0.036
44	97.595	0.039
43	97.107	0.041
42	96.593	0.043
41	96.041	0.046
40	95.457	0.049
39	94.842	0.051
38	94.189	0.054
37	93.497	0.058
36	92.761	0.061
35	91.981	0.065
34	91.156	0.069
33	90.280	0.073

Years	%	Monthly[1] increment
32	89.354	0.077
31	88.371	0.082
30	87.330	0.087
29	86.226	0.092
28	85.053	0.098
27	83.816	0.103
26	82.496	0.110
25	81.100	0.116
24	79.622	0.123
23	78.055	0.131
22	76.399	0.138
21	74.635	0.147
20	72.770	0.155
19	70.791	0.165
18	68.697	0.175
17	66.470	0.186
16	64.116	0.196
15	61.617	0.208
14	58.971	0.221
13	56.167	0.234
12	53.191	0.248
11	50.038	0.263
10	46.695	0.279
9	43.154	0.295
8	39.399	0.313
7	35.414	0.332
6	31.195	0.352
5	26.722	0.373
4	21.983	0.395
3	16.959	0.419
2	11.629	0.444
1	5.983	0.470
0	0	0.499

Note

[1] Where duration is *not* an *exact* number of years, the table percentage for the whole number of years is increased by $1/12$ of the difference between that and the next highest percentage for each odd month. Fourteen odd days or more are rounded up and treated as a month; less than 14 odd days are ignored.

Taxation of Capital Gains

[¶5-150]   Premiums for short leases: CGT/IT charge

(ITTOIA 2005, s. 277)

(Tax Reporter: ¶509-950)

The chart at ¶3-500 shows the proportion of any premium received in respect of a lease of less than 50 years which is chargeable to capital gains tax and that which is chargeable to income tax as property business profits.

[¶5-200]   CGT exempt gilt-edged securities

(TCGA 1992, s. 16(2), 115(1) and Sch. 9)

(Tax Reporter: ¶559-000)

Gains on the following securities are not chargeable gains and any losses are not allowable losses.

Stocks and bonds charged on the National Loans Funds	
2½%	Annuities 1905 or after
2¾%	Annuities 1905 or after
2½%	Consolidated Stock 1923 or after
3½%	War Loan 1952 or after
4%	Consolidated Loan 1957 or after
3½%	Conversion Loan 1961 or after
3%	Treasury Stock 1966 or after
2½%	Treasury Stock 1975 or after
12¾%	Treasury Loan 1992
8%	Treasury Loan 1992
10%	Treasury Stock 1992
3%	Treasury Stock 1992
12¼%	Exchequer Stock 1992
13½%	Exchequer Stock 1992
10½%	Treasury Convertible Stock 1992
2%	Index-Linked Treasury Stock 1992
12½%	Treasury Loan 1993
6%	Funding Loan 1993
13¾%	Treasury Loan 1993
10%	Treasury Loan 1993
8¼%	Treasury Stock 1993
14½%	Treasury Loan 1994
12½%	Exchequer Stock 1994
9%	Treasury Loan 1994
10%	Treasury Loan 1994
13½%	Exchequer Stock 1994
8½%	Treasury Stock 1994

	Stocks and bonds charged on the National Loans Funds – cont'd
8½%	Treasury Stock 1994 'A'
2%	Index-Linked Treasury Stock 1994
3%	Exchequer Gas Stock 1990–95
12%	Treasury Stock 1995
10¼%	Exchequer Stock 1995
12¾%	Treasury Loan 1995
9%	Treasury Loan 1992–96
15¼%	Treasury Loan 1996
13¼%	Exchequer Loan 1996
14%	Treasury Stock 1996
2%	Index-Linked Treasury Stock 1996
10%	Conversion Stock 1996
10%	Conversion Stock 1996 'A'
10%	Conversion Stock 1996 'B'
13¼%	Treasury Loan 1997
10½%	Exchequer Stock 1997
8¾%	Treasury Loan 1997
8¾%	Treasury Loan 1997 'B'
8¾%	Treasury Loan 1997 'C'
8¾%	Treasury Loan 1997 'D'
8¾%	Treasury Loan 1997 'E'
15%	Exchequer Stock 1997
7%	Treasury Convertible Stock 1997
6¾%	Treasury Loan 1995–98
15½%	Treasury Loan 1998
12%	Exchequer Stock 1998
12%	Exchequer Stock 1998 'A'
9¾%	Exchequer Stock 1998
9¾%	Exchequer Stock 1998 'A'
7¼%	Treasury Stock 1998 'A'
7¼%	Treasury Stock 1998 'B'
12%	Exchequer Stock 1998 'B'
4⅝%	Index-Linked Treasury Stock 1998
7¼%	Treasury Stock 1998
9½%	Treasury Loan 1999
10½%	Treasury Stock 1999
12¼%	Exchequer Stock 1999
12¼%	Exchequer Stock 1999 'A'

Taxation of Capital Gains

Stocks and bonds charged on the National Loans Funds – cont'd	
12¼%	Exchequer Stock 1999 'B'
2½%	Index-Linked Treasury Convertible Stock 1999
10¼%	Conversion Stock 1999
6%	Treasury Stock 1999
	Floating Rate Treasury Stock 1999
9%	Conversion Stock 2000
9%	Conversion Stock 2000 'A'
9%	Conversion Stock 2000 'B'
9%	Conversion Stock 2000 'C'
8½%	Treasury Loan 2000
8%	Treasury Stock 2000
8%	Treasury Stock 2000 'A'
13%	Treasury Stock 2000
13%	Treasury Stock 2000 'A'
7%	Treasury Stock 2001
7%	Treasury Stock 2001 'A'
14%	Treasury Stock 1998–2001
2½%	Index-Linked Treasury Stock 2001
9¾%	Conversion Stock 2001
10%	Treasury Stock 2001
9½%	Conversion Loan 2001
10%	Treasury Stock 2001 'A'
10%	Treasury Stock 2001 'B'
	Floating Rate Treasury Stock 2001
12%	Exchequer Stock 1999–2002
12%	Exchequer Stock 1999–2002 'A'
9½%	Conversion Stock 2002
10%	Conversion Stock 2002
9%	Exchequer Stock 2002
7%	Treasury Stock 2002
9¾%	Treasury Stock 2002
9¾%	Treasury Stock 2002 'A'
9¾%	Treasury Stock 2002 'B'
9¾%	Treasury Stock 2002 'C'
13¾%	Treasury Stock 2000–2003
13¾%	Treasury Stock 2000–2003 'A'
2½%	Index-Linked Treasury Stock 2003
9¾%	Conversion Loan 2003

	Stocks and bonds charged on the National Loans Funds – cont'd
6½%	Treasury Stock 2003
8%	Treasury Stock 2003
8%	Treasury Stock 2003 'A'
10%	Treasury Stock 2003
10%	Treasury Stock 2003 'A'
10%	Treasury Stock 2003 'B'
3½%	Funding Stock 1999–2004
11½%	Treasury Stock 2001–2004
9½%	Conversion Stock 2004
10%	Treasury Stock 2004
6¾%	Treasury Stock 2004
5%	Treasury Stock 2004
6¾%	Treasury Stock 2004 'A'
4⅜%	Index-Linked Treasury Stock 2004
9½%	Conversion Stock 2004 'A'
12½%	Treasury Stock 2003–2005
12½%	Treasury Stock 2003–2005 'A'
10½%	Exchequer Stock 2005
9½%	Conversion Stock 2005
9½%	Conversion Stock 2005 'A'
8½%	Treasury Stock 2005
8%	Treasury Loan 2002–2006
8%	Treasury Loan 2002–2006 'A'
2%	Index-Linked Treasury Stock 2006
9¾%	Conversion Stock 2006
7½%	Treasury Stock 2006
7¾%	Treasury Stock 2006
11¾%	Treasury Stock 2003–2007
11¾%	Treasury Stock 2003–2007 'A'
7¼%	Treasury Stock 2007
4½%	Treasury Stock 2007
8½%	Treasury Loan 2007
8½%	Treasury Loan 2007 'A'
8½%	Treasury Loan 2007 'B'
8½%	Treasury Loan 2007 'C'
13½%	Treasury Stock 2004–2008
9%	Treasury Loan 2008
9%	Treasury Loan 2008 'A'

Taxation of Capital Gains

	Stocks and bonds charged on the National Loans Funds – cont'd
9%	Treasury Loan 2008 'B'
9%	Treasury Loan 2008 'C'
9%	Treasury Loan 2008 'D'
5%	Treasury Stock 2008
2½%	Index-Linked Treasury Stock 2009
5¾%	Treasury Stock 2009
8%	Treasury Stock 2009
4%	Treasury Stock 2009
8%	Treasury Stock 2009 'A'
6¼%	Treasury Stock 2010
4¾%	Treasury Stock 2010
4¼%	Treasury Gilt 2011
3¼%	Treasury Gilt 2011
2½%	Index-Linked Treasury Stock 2011
9%	Conversion Loan 2011
9%	Conversion Loan 2011 'A'
9%	Conversion Loan 2011 'B'
9%	Conversion Loan 2011 'C'
9%	Conversion Loan 2011 'D'
5½%	Treasury Stock 2008–2012
9%	Treasury Stock 2012
9%	Treasury Stock 2012 'A'
5%	Treasury Stock 2012
5¼%	Treasury Gilt 2012
2½%	Index-Linked Treasury Stock 2013
8%	Treasury Stock 2013
4½%	Treasury Gilt 2013
5%	Treasury Stock 2014
2¼%	Treasury Gilt 2014
7¾%	Treasury Loan 2012–2015
4¾%	Treasury Stock 2015
2¾%	Treasury Gilt 2015
8%	Treasury Stock 2015
8%	Treasury Stock 2015 'A'
2½%	Treasury Stock 1986–2016
2½%	Index-Linked Treasury Stock 2016
2½%	Index-Linked Treasury Stock 2016 'A'
4%	Treasury Gilt 2016

	Stocks and bonds charged on the National Loans Funds – cont'd
2%	Treasury Gilt 2016
12%	Exchequer Stock 2013–2017
1%	Treasury Gilt 2017
1¼%	Index-Linked Treasury Gilt 2017
1¾%	Treasury Gilt 2017
8¾%	Treasury Stock 2017
8¾%	Treasury Stock 2017 'A'
1¼%	Treasury Gilt 2018
5%	Treasury Gilt 2018
0⅛%	Index-Linked Treasury Gilt 2019
1¾%	Treasury Gilt 2019
4½%	Treasury Gilt 2019
3¾%	Treasury Gilt 2019
2½%	Index-Linked Treasury Stock 2020
2%	Treasury Gilt 2020
3¾%	Treasury Gilt 2020
4¾%	Treasury Stock 2020
1½%	Treasury Gilt 2021
3¾%	Treasury Gilt 2021
8%	Treasury Stock 2021
0½%	Treasury Gilt 2022
1¾%	Treasury Gilt 2022
4%	Treasury Gilt 2022
1⅞%	Index-Linked Treasury Gilt 2022
2¼%	Treasury Gilt 2023
0⅛%	Index-Linked Treasury Gilt 2024
2½%	Index-Linked Treasury Stock 2024
2¾%	Treasury Gilt 2024
2%	Treasury Gilt 2025
5%	Treasury Stock 2025
0⅛%	Index-Linked Treasury Gilt 2026
1½%	Treasury Gilt 2026
1¼%	Index-Linked Treasury Gilt 2027
4¼%	Treasury Gilt 2027
6%	Treasury Stock 2028
0⅛%	Index-Linked Treasury Gilt 2029
4⅛%	Index-Linked Treasury Stock 2030
4¾%	Treasury Gilt 2030

Taxation of Capital Gains

Stocks and bonds charged on the National Loans Funds – cont'd	
4¼%	Treasury Stock 2032
1¼%	Index-Linked Treasury Gilt 2032
0¾%	Index-Linked Treasury Gilt 2034
4½%	Treasury Gilt 2034
2%	Index-Linked Treasury Stock 2035
0⅛%	Index-Linked Treasury Gilt 2036
4¼%	Treasury Stock 2036
1⅛%	Index-Linked Treasury Gilt 2037
1¾%	Treasury Gilt 2037
4¾%	Treasury Stock 2038
4¼%	Treasury Gilt 2039
0⅝%	Index-Linked Treasury Gilt 2040
4¼%	Treasury Gilt 2040
4½%	Treasury Gilt 2042
0⅝%	Index-Linked Treasury Gilt 2042
0⅛%	Index-Linked Treasury Gilt 2044
3¼%	Treasury Gilt 2044
3½%	Treasury Gilt 2045
0⅛%	Index-Linked Treasury Gilt 2046
4¼%	Treasury Gilt 2046
0¾%	Index-Linked Treasury Gilt 2047
1½%	Treasury Gilt 2047
4¼%	Treasury Gilt 2049
0½%	Index-Linked Treasury Gilt 2050
0¼%	Index-Linked Treasury Gilt 2052
3¾%	Treasury Gilt 2052
1¼%	Indexed-Linked Treasury Gilt 2055
4¼%	Treasury Gilt 2055
0⅛%	Index-Linked Treasury Gilt 2058
4%	Treasury Gilt 2060
0½%	Index-Linked Treasury Gilt 2060
0⅜%	Index-Linked Treasury Gilt 2062
0⅛%	Index-Linked Treasury Gilt 2065
2½%	Treasury Gilt 2065
0⅛%	Index-Linked Treasury Gilt 2068
3½%	Treasury Gilt 2068

Securities issued by certain public corporations and guaranteed by the Treasury	
3%	North of Scotland Electricity Stock 1989–92

[¶5-250] Securities of negligible value

(TCGA 1992, s. 24(2))

(Tax Reporter: ¶515-150)

The HMRC website contains a list, constantly updated, of shares or securities formerly quoted (largely) on the London Stock Exchange which have been officially declared of negligible value for the purposes of a claim under s. 24(2). The list was last updated as at 30 September 2017 and can be found at www.gov.uk/guidance/negligible-value-agreements-to-30-june-2014.

The time limit for a claim is two years from the end of the tax year (or accounting period of a company) in which the deemed disposal and reacquisition take place.

[¶5-300] Identification of securities

(TCGA 1992, s. 104–109)

(Tax Reporter: ¶556-525ff.)

Disposals by individuals and trustees: 2008–09 onwards

Disposals on or after 6 April 2008 are to be identified with acquisitions in the following order:

(1) same-day acquisitions, but subject to an election under s. 105A (see below);

(2) acquisitions within the following 30 days on the basis of earlier acquisitions in that period, rather than later ones (a FIFO basis); and

(3) securities within the expanded s. 104 holding, which specifically does not include acquisitions under (1) and (2) above.

Where the number of securities which comprise the disposal exceed those identified under the above rules, that excess is identified with subsequent acquisitions beyond the 30-day period referred to above.

Where an individual acquires shares of the same class on the same day and some of those shares are acquired pursuant to the exercise of approved scheme share options, a s. 105A election may be made. The election treats the option scheme shares as a separate holding from the other shares acquired and as being disposed of after the remainder of the other shares.

Disposals by companies

The order of identification is:

(1) any acquisition on the same day;

(2) acquisitions within the previous nine days;

(3) acquisitions since 1 April 1982, 'the s. 104 holding', previously termed 'the new holding';

(4) acquisitions in the period 6 April 1965 to 31 March 1982, 'the 1982 holding'; and

(5) those held on 6 April 1965, in respect of which no election has been made to include them in the pre-1982 pool; these will be identified on a last-in, first-out (LIFO) basis.

In respect of disposals before 5 December 2005, where a company or group of companies held at least 2% of the shares or securities of that class, acquisitions and disposals within one month (for most quoted shares or securities) or six months (for most other shares or securities) could be matched.

[¶5-350] Expenses incurred by personal representatives

(SP 2/04)

(Tax Reporter: ¶367-575)

In respect of deaths after 5 April 2004, the scale of expenses allowable in computing the gains or losses of personal representatives on the sale of assets in a deceased person's estate is as follows:

Gross value of estate	Allowable expenditure
Up to £50,000	1.8% of probate value of assets sold by personal representatives
£50,001–£90,000	£900, divided among all assets in the estate in proportion to their probate values and allowed in those proportions on assets sold by personal representatives
£90,001–£400,000	1% of probate value of assets sold
£400,001–£500,000	£4,000, divided as above
£500,001–£1,000,000	0.8% of probate value of assets sold
£1,000,001–£5,000,000	£8,000, divided as above
Over £5,000,000	0.16% of the probate value of the assets sold, subject to a maximum of £10,000

Note
Computations based either on the above scale or on actual expenditure incurred are accepted.

[¶5-500] Compliance and administration

(TMA 1970, s. 8ff.)

(Tax Reporter: ¶180-000ff.)

For summary of the main provisions which relate both to capital gains tax and income tax, see ¶1-250ff.

Capital gains can be reported straightaway using HMRC's capital gains tax online service (www.gov.uk/capital-gains-tax/report-and-pay-capital-gains-tax) or are otherwise reported annually in a self-assessment tax return.

Submission dates for 2017–18 capital gains tax returns

Gain	Filing date	References
Gains within self-assessment (UK resident individuals, trustees, personal representatives)	31 January following tax year of disposal	See ¶1-250ff.
ATED-related gains	31 January following tax year or 5 October where tax return not issued	See www.gov.uk/ guidance/pay-annual-tax-on-enveloped-dwellings
Non-resident capital gains tax returns (NRCGT returns)	Within 30 days of the completion date of the disposal	TCGA 1992, s. 222A; TMA 1970, s. 12ZB (Tax Reporter: ¶545-975)

[¶5-950]   Time limits for elections and claims

In the absence of any specific provision to the contrary, under self-assessment the normal rule is that claims by individuals, trustees and companies are to be made within four years from the end of the tax year or chargeable period to which they relate (TMA 1970, s. 43(1) and FA 1998, Sch. 18, para. 55).

In certain cases, HMRC *may* permit an extension of the strict time limit in relation to certain elections and claims.

Provision	Time limit	References
Post-cessation expenses relieved against gains	12 months from 31 January next following the tax year in which expenses paid	TCGA 1992, s. 261D(6) (Tax Reporter: ¶524-125)
Trading losses relieved against gains	12 months from 31 January next following the tax year loss arose	TCGA 1992, s. 261B(8) (Tax Reporter: ¶524-100)
Value of asset negligible	Two years from end of tax year (or accounting period if a company) in which deemed disposal/reacquisition takes place	TCGA 1992, s. 24(2) (Tax Reporter: ¶515-150)
Re-basing of all assets to 31 March 1982 values (companies only from 06/04/08)	Two years from end of accounting period of disposal for company	TCGA 1992, s. 35(6) (Tax Reporter: ¶520-350)
50% relief if deferred charge on gains before 31 March 1982 (companies only from 06/04/08)	Two years from end of accounting period of disposal for company	TCGA 1992, s. 36 and Sch. 4, para. 9(1) (Tax Reporter: ¶520-600)
Variation within two years of death not to have CGT effect	Six months from date of variation	TCGA 1992, s. 62 (Tax Reporter: ¶367-825)
Specifying which 'same day' share acquisitions (through employee share schemes) should be treated as disposed of first	Within 12 months from 31 January next following the tax year of disposal	TCGA 1992, s. 105A (Tax Reporter: ¶556-650)
Replacement of business assets (rollover relief)	Four years from the end of the tax year/accounting period Replacement asset to be purchased between 12 months before and three years after disposal of old asset	TCGA 1992, s. 152(1) (Tax Reporter: ¶570-250)

Taxation of Capital Gains

Provision	Time limit	References
Disapplication of incorporation relief under TCGA 1992, s. 162	Two years from 31 January following the end of the year of assessment in which the business is transferred	TCGA 1992, s. 162A (Tax Reporter: ¶574-125)
Holdover of gain on gift of business asset	Four years from the end of the tax year	TCGA 1992, s. 165(1) (Tax Reporter: ¶574-550)
Determination of main residence	Two years from acquisition of second property (see ESC D21)	TCGA 1992, s. 222(5) (Tax Reporter: ¶545-950)
Determination of main residence: non-resident CGT disposals	Notice must be given in NRCGT return in respect of the disposal which must be filed within 30 days following the completion date for the disposal	TCGA 1992, s. 222A; TMA 1970, s. 12ZB (Tax Reporter: ¶545-975)
Irrecoverable loan to a trader	Four years from the end of the tax year/accounting period	TCGA 1992, s. 253(4A) (Tax Reporter: ¶511-150)
Deemed disposal/reacquisition on expiry of mineral lease	Four years from the date of the relevant event	TCGA 1992, s. 203(2) (Tax Reporter: ¶799-475)
Delayed remittances of foreign gains	Four years from the end of the tax year/accounting period	TCGA 1992, s. 279(5) (Tax Reporter: ¶591-150)
Deferred unascertainable consideration: election for treatment of loss	12 months from 31 January next following the tax year loss arose	TCGA 1992, s. 279A and 279D (Tax Reporter: ¶524-250)
Earn out right treated as a security	Within 12 months from 31 January next following the tax year in which the right is received for individuals or two years from the end of the accounting period for companies	TCGA 1992, s. 138A (Tax Reporter: ¶561-600)
Appropriations of assets to trading stock; no deemed disposal at market value on transfer to stock but subsequent trading profits adjusted by gain or loss that would have arisen	Within 12 months from 31 January next following tax year of assessment for the period of account in which the appropriation is made for capital gains tax purposes, or within two years from the end of the accounting period in which the appropriation is made for corporation tax	TCGA 1992, s. 161 (Tax Reporter: ¶573-800)
Entrepreneurs' relief	Within 12 months from 31 January next following tax year in which qualifying disposal is made	TCGA 1992, s. 169M (Tax Reporter: ¶572-550)
Small part disposals of land; no disposal but base cost on subsequent disposal reduce by consideration received	Within 12 months from 31 January next following tax year in which part disposal is made for individuals, or two years from end of accounting period in which part disposal is made for companies	TCGA 1992, s. 242 (Tax Reporter: ¶510-350)
Holdover relief on gifts chargeable to inheritance tax	Four years from end of the tax year of gift	TCGA 1992, s. 260 (Tax Reporter: ¶548-700)
Disincorporation relief	Within two years beginning with the business transfer date	FA 2013, s. 60
EIS/SEIS/SI deferral relief	Five years from 31 January following tax year in which shares are issued/ investment is made	TCGA 1992, Sch. 5B, para. 6; Sch. 5BB, para. 3; Sch. 8B, para. 8 (Tax Reporter: ¶565-600; ¶569-200; ¶569-800)

INHERITANCE TAX

[¶6-000] Rates of tax

(IHTA 1984, s. 7 and Sch. 1)

(Tax Reporter: ¶607-000; ¶624-000)

From 15 March 1988

	Gross rate of tax
Lifetime transfers	
Gross transfers up to cumulative limit	Nil
Gross transfers over cumulative limit	20%
Grossing-up fraction	$1/4$
Death transfers	
Gross transfers up to cumulative limit	Nil
Gross transfers over cumulative limit	40%
Grossing-up fraction	$2/3$
Reduced rate[1]	36%

Note

[1] For deaths occurring on or after 6 April 2012, a reduced rate of inheritance tax of 36% applies where 10% or more of a deceased person's net estate (after deducting IHT exemptions, reliefs and the nil-rate band) is left to charity. To determine whether the lower rate will apply, the estate is broken down into three components (with the nil-rate band apportioned): the survivorship component (property passing automatically to the survivor), the settled property component (settled property in which the deceased held an interest in possession) and the general component (all other property excluding gifts with reservation of benefit to which the lower rate cannot apply). The 10% test is applied to each component separately and the lower rate applied to those components which satisfy the 10% test. An election to merge components of the estate and apply the 10% test in aggregate is possible, as is an election to opt out of the lower rate for one or more components of the estate. Both elections must be made within two years of the date of death and may be withdrawn within two years and one month of the date of death.

[¶6-050] Cumulative chargeable transfers limit

(IHTA 1984, s. 7 and Sch. 1)

Period	Cumulative chargeable transfers limit[1] £
2017–18[2]	325,000
2009–10 to 2016–17	325,000
2008–09	312,000

Notes

[1] A claim can be made to transfer any unused nil-rate band of the first deceased spouse or civil partner to the estate of their surviving spouse or civil partner.

[2] The inheritance tax nil-rate band has been frozen since 2012–13 and is set to remain at £325,000 until April 2021 (F(No. 2)A 2015, s. 10).

[¶6-075]   Residence nil-rate band
(IHTA 1984, s. 8D–8M)

Year	Residential enhancement £
2017–18	100,000
2018–19	125,000
2019–20	150,000
2020–21	175,000

Note
(1) For deaths on or after 6 April 2017, an additional nil-rate band is available when a residence is passed on death to direct descendants. Amounts are set for years 2017–18 to 2020–21 as per the table above and the amount will then increase in line with CPI from 2021–22 onwards. Any unused nil-rate band will be transferred to a surviving spouse or civil partner. It will also be available when a person downsizes or ceases to own a home on or after 8 July 2015 and assets of an equivalent value, up to the value of the additional nil-rate band, are passed on death to direct descendants. There will also be a tapered withdrawal of the additional nil-rate band for estates with a net value of more than £2m. This will be at a withdrawal rate of £1 for every £2 over this threshold (IHTA 1984, s. 8D–8M, as amended by FA 2016, s. 93 and Sch. 15).

[¶6-200]   Annual and small gift exemption
(IHTA 1984, s. 19 and 20)

(Tax Reporter: ¶643-200; ¶643-700)

	On or after 6 April 1981 £
Annual	3,000
Small gift (to the same person)	250

[¶6-250]   Gifts in consideration of marriage/civil partnership
(IHTA 1984, s. 22)

(Tax Reporter: ¶644-450)

Donor	Exemption limit £
Parent of party to the marriage/civil partnership	5,000
Remote ancestor of party to the marriage/civil partnership	2,500
Party to the marriage/civil partnership	2,500
Any other person	1,000

[¶6-300] Transfers by UK-domiciled spouse/civil partner to non-UK domiciled spouse/civil partner

(IHTA 1984, s. 18)

(Tax Reporter: ¶644-900)

Transfer on or after	Exemption limit £
6 April 2013	325,000[1]
9 March 1982	55,000

Note
[1] The rate is aligned with the exemption limit at the time of the transfer per IHTA 1984, Sch. 1 (the nil-rate band).

[¶6-325] Election to be treated as domiciled in UK

(IHTA 1984, s. 267ZA–267ZB)

(Tax Reporter: ¶684-575)

A person who is not domiciled in the UK but who is, or has been married to, or in a civil partnership with, someone who is domiciled in the UK can elect to be treated as domiciled in the UK for the purposes of inheritance tax. There are two types of elections:

(1) A lifetime election by the non-domiciled individual who is at any time on or after 6 April 2013 and during the period of seven years ending with the date of the election married to or in a civil partnership with a UK-domiciled individual.

(2) A death election by the personal representatives of a deceased person who was at any time on or after 6 April 2013, and during the period of seven years ending with the date of death themselves domiciled in the UK and married to or in a civil partnership with a non-domiciled person who is, by virtue of the election, to be treated as domiciled in the UK.

The election is irrevocable but ceases to have effect if the individual is not resident in the UK for income tax purposes for four successive tax years. The election must be in writing and in the case of a death election made within two years of the date of death. The election cannot relate back to before 6 April 2013, or more than seven years before either the election is made or the date of death and any date the election relates back to must be a date when the individual was married, or in a civil partnership, and either the individual or their spouse (as the case may be) was UK domiciled on that date.

[¶6-335]   Non-domiciles

(Tax Reporter: ¶684-300)

Deemed domicile

Non-domiciled individuals pay inheritance tax only in respect of their UK assets. However, an individual who is not domiciled in the UK can become deemed UK-domiciled for inheritance tax purposes in certain circumstances. Then, they pay UK inheritance tax on their worldwide assets.

Finance (No. 2) Act 2017 amends the inheritance tax legislation relating to individuals who will be treated as domiciled in the UK. The amendments provide that an individual will be treated as domiciled for IHT purposes if they have been resident in the UK for at least 15 out of the previous 20 tax years (rather than 17 out of the 20 tax years ending with the tax year in question). The changes take effect from the start of the 2017–18 tax year.

Those who become deemed domicile in April 2017, excepting those who were born in the UK with a UK domicile of origin, can treat the cost base of their non-UK based assets as the market value of that asset on 5 April 2017.

The returning UK dom

Finance (No. 2) Act 2017 also introduces a separate rule to provide that an individual born in the UK with a UK domicile of origin who has acquired a domicile of choice elsewhere will be treated as domiciled for inheritance tax purposes if at any time they are resident in the UK and have been resident in the UK in at least one out of the two previous tax years. The provisons take effect from the start of the 2017–18 tax year.

Residential property of non-domiciles

Under IHTA 1984, an individual who is domiciled outside the UK is not liable to tax on any property they own which is situated overseas (because it falls within the definition of excluded property in IHTA 1984, s. 6), unlike UK domiciled individuals who are liable to inheritance tax on their worldwide property. This difference in treatment has been used by some non-doms as a means of avoiding inheritance tax by holding UK residential properties indirectly through overseas structures such as companies, trusts and partnerships. *Finance (No. 2) Act* 2017 extends the scope of inheritance tax to include the value of overseas structures or financing that is attributable to residential properties situated in the UK where they are held through overseas structures by amending the definition of excluded property in IHTA 1984 so that any value attributable to UK residential properties does not fall to be treated as 'excluded property'. Minor interests in UK residential property (less than 5%) are disregarded. The extended charge will be effective from 6 April 2017.

[¶6-350]   Gifts to the nation

(IHTA 1984, s. 25; FA 2012, Sch. 14)

(Tax Reporter: ¶646-050)

Gifts of pre-eminent property to be held for the benefit of the public or the nation are exempt from inheritance tax. Pre-eminent property includes any picture, print, book, manuscript, work of art, scientific object or other thing that is pre-eminent for its national, scientific, historic or artistic interest, collections of such items and any object kept in a significant building where it is desirable that it remain associated with the building.

[¶6-360]   Employee ownership trusts

(IHTA 1984, s. 13A, 28A, 72(3A), 75A, 86)

(Tax Reporter: ¶646-750; ¶363-770; ¶364-750)

An exemption from inheritance tax applies to transfers on or after 6 April 2014 by individuals of shares in a company to an employee ownership trust and for transfers of cash and other assets by a close company to the employee ownership trust (such transfers are not transfers of value for IHT purposes). Employee ownership trusts are also excluded from the definition of 'relevant property' and, therefore, not subject to the ten-year charge or the exit charge under the relevant property regime (from 6 April 2014).

[¶6-400]   Agricultural and business property relief

(IHTA 1984, s. 103ff. and 115ff.)

(Tax Reporter: ¶664-000; ¶658-000)

Type of relief	Rate of relief for disposals on or after 6/4/96 %
Agricultural property[1]	
Vacant possession or right to obtain it within 12 months	100
Tenanted land with vacant a possession value	100
Entitled to 50% relief at 9 March 1981 and not since able to obtain vacant possession	100
Agricultural land let on or after 1 September 1995	100
Other circumstances	50
Business property	
Nature of property	
Business or interest in business	100
Controlling shareholding in quoted company	50
Controlling shareholding in unquoted[2] company	100
Settled property used in life tenant's business	100/50[3]
Shareholding in unquoted[2] company: more than 25% interest	100
Minority shareholding in unquoted[2] company: 25% or less	100
Land, buildings, machinery or plant used by transferor's company or partnership	50

Notes

[1] Applies to property in the European Economic Area.

[2] 'Unquoted' means shares not quoted on a recognised stock exchange and therefore includes shares dealt in on the Unlisted Securities Market (USM) or Alternative Investment Market (AIM).

[3] The higher rate applies if the settled property is transferred along with business itself.

Inheritance Tax

[¶6-450]   Quick succession relief

(IHTA 1984, s. 141)

(Tax Reporter: ¶627-400)

Years between transfers		Percentage applied to
More than	Not more than	formula below
0	1	100
1	2	80
2	3	60
3	4	40
4	5	20

Formula

$$\text{Tax charge on earlier transfer} \times \frac{\text{Increase in transferee's estate}}{\text{Diminution in transferor's estate}}$$

[¶6-475]   Intestate rules

(*Administration of Estates Act* 1925, s. 46(1) and Sch. 1A)

Note: See ¶26-500 for succession and intestacy rules applicable in Scotland.

Surviving family	Beneficiaries	
	Deaths before 1 October 2014[1]	Deaths on or after 1 October 2014[2]
Spouse or civil partner but no issue Spouse or civil partner only (no issue, parents, brothers or sisters of the whole blood (or their issue)).	Spouse or civil partner takes everything, absolutely.	Spouse or civil partner takes everything, absolutely.
Spouse or civil partner (no issue) and parent or whole blood brother or sister, or issue of whole blood brother or sister.	Spouse or civil partner takes: • personal chattels; • £450,000 absolutely (or the entire estate where this is less); • one-half share of residue (if any) absolutely.	Spouse or civil partner takes everything, absolutely.
	Remainder distributable to: • parent(s); • failing a parent then on trust for the deceased's whole blood brothers and sisters, (nephews and nieces step into their parent's shoes if the latter is dead).	Parents/siblings receive nothing.

Surviving family	Beneficiaries	
	Deaths before 1 October 2014[1]	**Deaths on or after 1 October 2014**[2]
Spouse or civil partner and issue	Spouse or civil partner takes: • personal chattels (e.g. furniture, pictures, clothing, jewellery, etc.), absolutely; • £250,000 absolutely (or the entire estate where this is less); • **life interest** in one-half of the residue (if any). Issue receive: • one half of residue (if any) on statutory trusts; • the other half of residue on statutory trusts upon the death of the spouse or civil partner.	Spouse or civil partner takes: • personal chattels (e.g. furniture, pictures, clothing, jewellery, etc.), absolutely; • £250,000[3] absolutely (or the entire estate where this is less); • one half of the residue (if any) **absolutely**. Issue receive: • one half of residue (if any) on statutory trusts.
No spouse or civil partner	Everything is taken by: • Issue, but if none; • Parent(s), but if none; • Brothers and sisters of the whole blood (nephews and nieces step into their parent's shoes), but if none; • Brothers and sisters of the half blood (nephews and nieces step into their parent's shoes), but if none; • Grandparents, but if none; • Uncles and aunts of the whole blood and the issue of any deceased uncle or aunt, but if none; • Uncles and aunts of the half blood and the issue of any deceased uncle or aunt, but if none; • the Crown.	

Notes
[1] For deaths on or after 1 February 2009 under the *Administration of Estates Act* 1925, s. 46(1); not applicable in Scotland.
[2] For deaths after 1 October 2014 (2014/2039) under the *Administration of Estates Act* 1925, s. 46(1) (as amended by the *Inheritance and Trustees' Powers Act* 2014); not applicable in Scotland.
[3] The fixed sum statutory legacy is to be index-linked using the consumer prices index and amended by statutory instrument (*Administration of Estates Act* 1925, Sch. 1A (as inserted by the *Inheritance and Trustees' Powers Act* 2014)).

[¶6-500] Instalment option

(IHTA 1984, s. 227)

(Tax Reporter: ¶183-215)

Interest-free:

• controlling shareholdings;
• holdings of 10% or more of unquoted shares with value over £20,000;
• certain other death transfers of unquoted shares;

- business or interest in business;
- agricultural value of agricultural property; and
- woodlands.

Not interest-free:

- land, wherever situated, other than within categories above; and
- shareholdings in certain land investment and security dealing companies, or market makers or discount houses.

[¶6-550]   Fall in value relief

(IHTA 1984, s. 179, 191 and 197A)

(Tax Reporter: ¶627-900)

Type of property	Period after death
Quoted securities sold	One year
Qualifying investments[1]	One year
Interests in land – deaths after 15 March 1990	Four years

Note

[1] Qualifying investments mean shares or securities which are quoted at the date of death in question, holdings in a unit trust which at that date is an authorised unit trust, shares in an open-ended investment company and shares in any common investment fund established under the *Administration of Justice Act* 1982, s. 42.

[¶6-600]   Taper relief

(IHTA 1984, s. 7(4))

(Tax Reporter: ¶611-400)

Years between gift and death		Percentage of full tax charge at death – rates actually due
More than	Not more than	%
3	4	80
4	5	60
5	6	40
6	7	20

[¶6-650]   Pre-owned assets

(FA 2004, s. 84 and Sch. 15)

(Tax Reporter: ¶614-800)

A freestanding income tax charge where individuals continue to enjoy property previously owned by them with effect from 6 April 2005. The charge to tax arises under three main heads, relating to:

- land;
- chattels; and
- intangible property in settlor interested trusts.

In determining whether charges arise in respect of land or chattels, certain transactions are excluded and there are a number of exemptions.

Limited reliefs prevent double charges to tax. Special rules apply to individuals not resident or not domiciled in the UK. Provisions allow for opting out of the pre-owned assets charge arising in respect of any property, with inheritance tax consequences.

Land

The chargeable amount in the case of land or any interest in land is the 'appropriate rental value' less an amount paid under any legal obligation in respect of the occupation of the land. The appropriate rental value is:

$$R \times \frac{DV}{V}$$

Where:

R is the 'rental value' of the relevant land for the 'taxable period';

DV is the value at the 'valuation date' of the interest in the relevant land that was disposed of by the chargeable person or, where the disposal was a non-exempt sale, the appropriate proportion of that value; and

V is the value of the relevant land at the valuation date.

The 'taxable period' is the year of assessment, or part of the year of assessment, during which the relevant conditions are met.

The 'rental value' is based on the assumption of a letting from year-to-year where the tenant pays the taxes, rates and charges and the landlord is responsible for repair and insurance. Land may be valued on a five-yearly rather than an annual valuation (SI 2005/724).

Chattels

In respect of chattels, the chargeable amount is the 'appropriate amount' less an amount paid under a legal obligation to the owner of the chattel. The 'appropriate amount' is:

$$N \times \frac{DV}{V}$$

Where:

N is the notional interest for the taxable period, at the prescribed rate, on the value of the chattel at the valuation date;

DV is the value at the valuation date of the interest in the relevant chattel that was disposed of by the chargeable person or, where the disposal was a non-exempt sale, the appropriate proportion of that asset; and

V is the value of the chattel at the valuation date.

Inheritance Tax

Intangible property in settlor interested trusts

The chargeable amount in relation to the relevant property is:

N – T

Where:

N is the notional amount of interest for the taxable period, at the prescribed rate, on the value of the property at the valuation date; and

T is the amount of income tax or capital gains tax payable by the chargeable person in the taxable period on gains from contracts of life assurance, income where settlor retains an interest, transfer of assets abroad, charge on settlor with interest in settlement and attribution of gains to settlors with interest in non-resident or dual resident settlements.

Where the aggregate amount attributable to a chargeable person in respect of land, chattels and intangibles does not exceed £5,000, there is no income tax payable. If benefits exceed £5,000, the charge is on the full amount including the first £5,000.

[¶6-700]   Delivery of accounts

(IHTA 1984, s. 216)

(Tax Reporter: ¶180-725)

Nature of transfer	Due Date
Chargeable lifetime transfer	Later of: – 12 months after end of month in which transfer occurred – three months after person became liable
Potentially exempt transfers which have become chargeable	12 months after end of month in which death of transferor occurred
Transfers on death	Later of: – 12 months after end of month in which death occurred – three months after personal representatives first act or have reason to believe an account is required
Gifts subject to reservation included in donor's estate at death	12 months after end of month in which death occurred
National heritage property	Six months after end of month in which chargeable event occurred
Relevant property settlements: ten-year anniversary and exit charges	Six months from end of month in which the occasion occurs

Values below which no account required

(SI 2008/605)

(Tax Reporter: ¶180-775)

Excepted lifetime chargeable transfers on or after 6 April 2007	£
Where the property given away, or in which the interest subsists, is wholly attributable to cash or quoted stocks and securities, the cumulative total of all chargeable transfers made by the transfer in the seven years before the transfer must not exceed the nil-rate band.	
Where the property given away, or in which the interest subsists, is wholly or partly attributable to property other than cash or quoted stocks and securities: (1) the value transferred by the chargeable transfer together with the cumulative total of all chargeable transfers made by the transferor in the seven years before the transfer must not exceed 80% of the relevant IHT nil-rate band; (2) the value transferred must not exceed the nil-rate band that is available to the transferor at the time the disposal takes place.	
Excepted lifetime chargeable transfers from 1 April 1981 to 5 April 2007	
Transfer in question, together with all other chargeable transfers in same 12-month period ending on 5 April	10,000
Transfer in question, together with all previous chargeable transfers during preceding ten years	40,000

Excepted settlements

(SI 2008/606)

(Tax Reporter: ¶180-905)

Excepted settlements: chargeable events on or after 6 April 2007
No qualifying interest in possession subsists and: **Either:**   • Cash is and has always been the only property comprised in the settlement;   • No further property has been added to the settlement (since it was made);   • The trustees are and have always been UK resident;   • Gross value of settled property less than **£1,000** throughout; and   • No related settlements.   **Or:**   • UK domiciled settlor (when settlement made until earlier of the chargeable event or death of settlor);   • Trustees are and have always been UK resident;   • No related settlements; and   • One of following conditions satisfied.

Inheritance Tax

> **Chargeable event:**
> 1) **Ten-year anniversary** (IHTA 1984, s. 64)
>   Value transferred does not exceed 80% of IHT threshold.
> 2) **Exit charge before first ten-year anniversary** (IHTA 1984, s. 65)
>   Value transferred does not exceed 80% of IHT threshold.
> 3) **Exit charge after one or more ten-year anniversaries** (IHTA 1984, s. 65)
>   Value transferred (under IHTA 1984, s. 66(3), taking into account s. 69) does not exceed 80% of IHT threshold.
> 4) **Exit charge age 18–25 trusts** (IHTA 1984, s. 71E)
>   Value transferred (under IHTA 1984, s. 71F) does not exceed 80% of IHT threshold.

Excepted estates

(SI 2004/2543)

(Tax Reporter: ¶180-855)

Domiciled in the United Kingdom

Deaths on and after	But on or before	Total gross value[1][2][3][4][5] £	Total gross value of property outside UK £	Total value of settled property £	Aggregate value of 'specified transfers' £
6 April 2017	5 April 2018	325,000	100,000	150,000	150,000
6 April 2009	5 April 2017	325,000	100,000	150,000	150,000

Notes

[1] The aggregate of the gross value of that person's estate, the value transferred by any specified transfers made by that person, and the value transferred by any specified exempt transfers made by that person, must not exceed the IHT threshold. (Where the deceased dies after 5 April and before 6 August and application for probate or confirmation is made before 6 August in the same year as death, the inheritance tax threshold used is that for the preceding tax year.)

[2] An estate will qualify as an excepted estate where the gross value of the estate, plus the chargeable value of any transfers in the seven years to death, does not exceed £1m and the net chargeable estate after deduction of spouse or civil partner and/or charity exemption only is less than the IHT threshold, and the total value transferred on that person's death by a spouse, civil partner or charity transfer must be greater than nil (SI 2004/2543).

[3] The limit applies to the aggregate of the gross value of the estate *plus* the value of 'specified transfers' including chargeable transfers, within seven years prior to death, of cash, quoted shares or securities, or an interest in land and furnishings and chattels disposed of at the same time to the same person (excluding property transferred subject to a reservation or property which becomes settled property).

[4] The IHT threshold for these purposes is increased by 100% where (SI 2004/2543):
(a) the deceased is a surviving spouse or civil partner;
(b) a claim has been made for the transfer of the unused nil-rate band of their deceased spouse or civil partner;
(c) all of the first deceased spouse's or civil partner's nil-rate band was unused; and
(d) the first deceased met similar criteria to those listed above for excepted estates.

[5] Where, in any tax year in the seven years prior to death, a person has transferred over £3,000 that is considered to be exempt as part of normal expenditure out of income, the amount will be included in the value of a person's estate for the purposes of determining whether the estate is an excepted estate, even though the transfer itself may qualify for the exemption (SI 2004/2543).

[¶6-750]   Due dates for payment
(IHTA 1984, s. 226)

(Tax Reporter: ¶183-205)

Transfer	Due date
Chargeable lifetime transfers between 6 April and 30 September	30 April in following year
Chargeable lifetime transfers between 1 October and 5 April	Six months after end of month in which transfer made
Potentially exempt transfers which become chargeable	Six months after end of month in which death occurred
Transfers on death; extra tax payable on chargeable lifetime transfers within seven years before death	Six months after end of month in which death occurred or on delivery of accounts by personal representatives, if earlier
Relevant property settlements: ten-year anniversary and exit charges	Six months after end of month in which the occasion occurs

[¶6-800]   Penalties for failure in relation to obligations falling due after 22 July 2004
(IHTA 1984, s. 245–253; FA 2007, Sch. 24; FA 2008, Sch. 36)

(Tax Reporter: ¶181-550)

Failure to deliver an IHT account (IHTA 1984, s. 245)	Account outstanding at end of statutory period	Fixed penalty of £100 (but not exceeding tax due)
	Daily penalty after failure declared by a court or the tribunal	Up to £60 a day
	Penalty after six months from end of statutory period, if proceedings for declaring the failure not started before then	Fixed penalty of further £100 (but not exceeding tax due)
	Penalty after 12 months from end of statutory period where tax is payable	Up to £3,000

Inheritance Tax

Failure by professional person to deliver a return of a settlement by a UK-domiciled person but with non-resident trustees (IHTA 1984, s. 245A)	Account outstanding at end of statutory period (three months from making of settlement)	Up to £300
	Daily penalty after failure declared by a court or the tribunal	Up to £60 a day
Failure to report a deed of variation which increases the IHT liability (IHTA 1984, s. 245A)	Penalty for failure to report within 18 months of deed of variation being executed	Up to £3,000
	Penalty	Up to £100
	Daily penalty after failure declared by a court or the tribunal	Up to £60 a day
Failure to comply with a notice requiring information (FA 2008, Sch. 36)	Penalty	Up to £300
	Daily penalty	Up to £60 a day
	Penalty where continued failure and significant tax at stake, determined by tribunal	Tax related
Incorrect information or document provided in compliance with information notice (FA 2008, Sch. 36)	Penalty	Up to £3,000 per inaccuracy
Incorrect information provided by any person (IHTA 1984, s. 247(3))	Fraud or negligence	Up to £3,000
Error in taxpayer's document (careless or deliberate) (FA 2007, Sch. 24, para. 1) For reductions for disclosure, see ¶1-350 (but note FA 2016, Sch. 22 increases in offshore penalties apply for inheritance tax purposes in relation to transfers of value occurring on or after 1 April 2017).	Standard amount (careless behaviour) Where the inaccuracy is deliberate but not concealed Where the inaccuracy is deliberate and concealed	30% of potential revenue lost 70% of potential lost revenue 100% of the potential lost revenue
Error in taxpayer's document attributable to another person (FA 2007, Sch. 24, para. 1A)[1]	Penalty	Tax geared

Offshore asset moves (FA 2015, Sch. 21)	Additional penalty for offshore asset moves from specified territory[2] to non-specified territory on or after 26 March 2015 following an original deliberate failure penalty under: FA 2007, Sch. 24, para. 1; or FA 2009, Sch. 55, para. 6.	50% of original penalty
Enabling offshore tax evasion or non-compliance (FA 2016, Sch. 20) from 1 January 2017 Penalty for engaging in offshore tax evasion of non-compliance where the tax at stake is inheritance tax.	Standard penalty:	The higher of: 100% of the potential lost revenue; or £3,000
	Where a penalty under FA 2015, Sch. 21, para. 1 arises:	The higher of: 50% of the potential lost revenue; or £3,000
Asset based penalty for offshore inaccuracies and failures: (FA 2016, Sch. 22) in relation to transfers of value made on or after 1 April 2017 Additional penalty where one or more standard offshore penalties and the offshore potential lost revenue in relation to a tax year exceeds £25,000. Standard offshore penalties means penalties under: FA 2007, Sch. 24, para. 1; or FA 2009, Sch. 55, para. 6 imposed involving offshore matters or offshore transfers and deliberate behaviour.	Lower of 10% of value of asset and offshore PLR x 10.	

Reductions for:	Reduction factors	
	Unprompted disclosure 50%	**Prompted disclosure** 20%
• disclosing to HMRC • providing a reasonable value • providing information or access to records to assist HMRC value the asset • special circumstances		

Notes

(1) Where it can be shown that the other person deliberately withheld information or supplied false information to the liable person, with the intention that the account or return would contain an inaccuracy, a penalty may be charged on that other person. But that will not necessarily mean that the personal representative themselves may not also be chargeable to a penalty. If the withheld or false information gave rise to inconsistencies in the information they had received about the estate and they did not question those inconsistencies; the liable person may still be charged a penalty for failing to take reasonable care as well.

(2) See ¶1-370 for table of specified territories.

[¶6-850]   Prescribed rates of interest

(IHTA 1984, s. 233 and 235)

Interest is charged at the following rates on late payments or repayments of inheritance tax or capital transfer tax.

Interest period	Interest rate %	Repayment interest rate %	Days
From 23 August 2016	2.75	0.5	—
29 September 2009 to 22 August 2016	3	0.5	2,520

Note

(1) Fixed by Treasury Order under SI 1989/1297. Interest is charged on late payments of tax at the Bank of England base rate plus 2.5% and the interest rate on overpayments is the Bank of England rate minus 1, subject to a minimum rate of 0.5% on repayment.

TAXATION OF COMPANIES

[¶7-000]   Rates of corporation tax

(Tax Reporter: ¶704-000ff.)

Financial year[1]	Main rate[2][4]	Main ring fence profits rate[3]	Small ring fence profits rate[3]	Special IP rate[5]	Diverted profits rate[6]
	%	%	%	%	%
2018 & 2019[8]	19	30	19	10	[25]
2017	19	30	19	10	25
2016	20	30	19	10	25
2015	20	30	19	10	25

Notes

[1] A financial year begins on 1 April and ends on 31 March. The financial year 2017 began on 1 April 2017 and will end on 31 March 2018.

[2] F(No. 2)A 2015, s. 7 sets the main rate of corporation tax for the financial years 2018 and 2019 at 19%. FA 2016, s. 46 reduces the rate (as set by F(No. 2)A 2015) for financial year 2020 to 17%.

[3] The small ring fence profits rate applies to profits falling below the lower limit of £300,000 and the main ring fence rate applies otherwise. However, where ring fence profits exceed the lower limit of £300,000 but do not exceed the upper limit of £1,500,000, the amount of corporation tax (calculated at the main rates) is reduced by an amount equal to:

$$R \times (U - A) \times \frac{N}{A}$$

Where:

R is the marginal relief fraction of 11/400ths;

U is the upper limit of £1,500,000;

A is the amount of the augmented profits (CTA 2010, s. 279G); and

N is the amount of the taxable total profits.

The lower and upper limits are reduced proportionally for accounting periods of less than 12 months; and where a company has one or more related 51% group companies by dividing the limits by one plus the number of those related 51% group companies (CTA 2010, Ch. 3A).

[4] Special rules apply to companies in liquidation and administration (CTA 2010, s. 628 and 630) and to open-ended investment companies and authorised unit trusts (CTA 2010, s. 614 and 618).

[5] Qualifying companies may elect that relevant intellectual property profits of a trade are chargeable at a lower rate of corporation tax (CTA 2010, s. 357A) (see ¶7-050).

[6] Diverted profits tax is charged at a rate of 25% where multinational companies use artificial arrangements to divert profits overseas in order to avoid UK tax (FA 2015, Pt. 3).

[7] Recent and future changes:

- *Finance Act* 2016 reduced the restriction on the amount of banking companies' profits that can be offset by carried-forward losses to 25%, with effect for the purposes of determining the taxable profits of companies for accounting periods beginning on or after 1 April 2016 (with periods straddling 1 April 2016 treated as separate accounting periods before and after that date). The restriction was first introduced at 50% from 1 April 2015 (to ensure banks continued to contribute through corporation tax payments notwithstanding having large accumulated losses), subject to an exemption for losses incurred in the first five years of a bank's authorisation (CTA 2010, Pt. 7A).

- A special 45% rate of corporation tax on income is applied to restitution interest, with effect in relation to interest (whether arising before or on or after 21 October 2015) which falls within F(No. 2)A 2015, s. 38(11) (a determination by a court becoming final on or after 21 October 2015 or an agreement between HMRC and a company in final settlement of a claim for restitution made on or after 21 October 2015) (CTA 2009, Pt. 8C).
- A restriction on the amount of interest and other financing amounts that a company may deduct in computing its profits for corporation tax purposes, with effect from 1 April 2017. These rules limit deductions where a group has net interest expenses of more than £2m to 30% of the earnings before interest, tax, depreciation and amortisation (EBITDA) that is taxable in the UK. An optional group ratio rule, based on the net-interest to EBITDA ratio for the worldwide group, may permit a greater amount to be deducted in some cases. The legislation also provides for repeal of the existing debt cap legislation and its replacement by a modified debt cap which will ensure that the net UK interest deduction does not exceed the total net interest expense of the worldwide group. All groups will be able to deduct up to £2m of net interest expense per annum, so groups below this threshold will not need to apply the rules (F(No. 2)A 2017, Sch. 5).
- The ability for all companies to utilise carried forward losses arising on or after 1 April 2017 against profits from different types of income and other group companies, subject to a restriction on the use of carried forward losses so that they cannot reduce their profits arising on or after 1 April 2017 by more than 50%. This restriction applies to a company or group's profits above £5m (banking companies remain subject to separate bank loss restriction). Profits and losses subject to the oil and gas ring-fence regime are excluded from the loss reform (F(No. 2)A 2017, Sch. 4).

[8] Rates per Autumn Budget 2017. Rates shown in square brackets not announced at Autumn Budget 2017, therefore, shown as per current legislation.

[¶7-020] Charge on loan to participators

(CTA 2010, s. 455)

(Tax Reporter: ¶776-900ff.)

Loans and benefits conferred	Rate
On or after 6 April 2016	32.5%[1]
Pre-5 April 2016	25.00%

Note
[1] The rate is set at such percentage as corresponds to the dividend upper rate specified in ITA 2007, s. 8(2) for the tax year in which the loan or advance is made.

The charge itself is separate from other liabilities, being treated as if it were an amount of corporation tax chargeable on the company.

The charge is not applied to qualifying loans or advances made on or after 25 November 2015, by close companies to charity trustees for charitable purposes (CTA 2010, s. 456(2A)).

[¶7-050] Patent profits election

(CTA 2010, Pt. 8A)

(Tax Reporter: ¶705-000ff.)

The patent box enables companies to apply a lower rate of corporation tax to profits earned after 1 April 2013 from its patented inventions and certain other innovations. The lower rate of corporation tax to be applied is 10%. The relief is subject to a number of conditions.

A company must elect into the regime, the election must be in writing, and specify the first accounting period for which the election will apply. The election will apply for all subsequent accounting periods until the election is revoked by notice in writing.

Any revocation must be in writing, specifying the accounting period for which it is to take effect. Any new election will have no effect for any accounting period which begins less than five years after the last day of the accounting period following the period identified in the revocation notice.

In order to avoid complications where losses and other reliefs are claimed, the reduced 10% rate is applied by subtracting an additional trading deduction from corporation tax profits as calculated below.

Additional deduction

The amount of the deduction is:

$$RP \times FY\% \times (\frac{MR - IPR}{MR})$$

Where:

RP is the relevant IP (patent box) profits of the trade of the company;

FY% is the appropriate percentage for each financial year;

MR is the main rate of corporation tax; and

IPR is the special IP rate of corporation tax.

Financial year	Appropriate percentage
2013	60%
2014	70%
2015	80%
2016	90%
2017 and subsequent years	100%

[¶7-100]   Additional relief for research and development

(CTA 2009, Pt. 13)

(Tax Reporter: ¶715-000ff.)

Additional relief is available for companies incurring expenditure on qualifying research and development (R&D). The relief is subject to a number of conditions. SMEs with losses can claim a payable tax credit.

	Expenditure incurred on or after					
	1 April 2016	1 April 2015	1 April 2014	1 April 2013	1 April 2012	1 April 2011
Additional deduction where SME qualifies for main or pre-trading relief	130%	130%	125%	125%	125%	100%
Rate of payable tax credit (SME only)	14.5%	14.5%	14.5%	11%	11%	12.5%
Additional deduction where R&D subcontracted to SME	—(1)	30%	30%	30%	30%	30%

	Expenditure incurred on or after					
	1 April 2016	1 April 2015	1 April 2014	1 April 2013	1 April 2012	1 April 2011
Additional deduction where expenditure of SME is subsidised or capped	—[1]	30%	30%	30%	30%	30%
Additional deduction for non-SME	—[1]	30%	30%	30%	30%	30%
R&D expenditure credit[1]	11%	11%	10%	10%	—	—

Note
[1] The 'above the line credit' (ATL) scheme is mandatory from 1 April 2016. The credit is taxable but paid net of tax to companies with no corporation tax liability. Prior to 31 March 2016, the ATL scheme was optional, as an alternative to (but not in addition to) the former large company enhanced deduction scheme of R&D relief. Rate of the R&D expenditure credit will be increased from 11% to 12% from 1 January 2018 (Autumn Budget 2017).

Limits applying for SMEs:

A company must pass the headcount test and either the turnover test or the Balance Sheet total test.

Staff headcount less than	500
Turnover not exceeding	€100m
Balance sheet total not exceeding	€86m

[¶7-125]   Creative industry tax reliefs

(CTA 2009, Pt. 15, 15A, 15B, 15C and 15D)

(Tax Reporter: ¶714-000ff.)

Creative industry tax reliefs allow qualifying companies to claim a larger deduction, or in some circumstances, claim a payable tax credit when calculating their taxable profits. The reliefs work by increasing the amount of allowable expenditure, which may be surrendered in exchange for a payable tax credit if the company makes a loss.

Additional relief is available for companies incurring expenditure on (i) qualifying film production, (ii) animation and high-end television production (including children's television programmes), (iii) video games development, (iv) theatrical productions and (v) production of orchestral concerts.

The creative industry tax reliefs are all subject to a number of conditions (in particular, that the film, animation, high-end television programme or game must be certified as culturally British to qualify).

	Financial year			
	From 2016–17	2015–16	2014–15	2013–14 (and earlier)
Minimum expenditure (% of core expenditure)				
Film (UK expenditure)	10%	10%	10%	25%
Animation/television (UK expenditure)	10%	10%	25%	25%
Video games development/theatrical productions/orchestral concert production (EEA expenditure)	25%	25%	25%	25%

	Financial year			
	From 2016–17	2015–16	2014–15	2013–14 (and earlier)
Additional deduction (% of qualifying core expenditure)				
Film: limited budget[1]	100%	100%	100%	100%
Film: any other[1]	100%	100%	80%	80%
Animation/television/video games development/theatrical productions/ orchestral concert production[2]	100%	100%	100%	100%
Maximum qualifying core expenditure (% of total core expenditure)	80%	80%	80%	80%
Tax credits (% of surrendered loss)				
Film: first £20m	25%	25%	25%	—
Film: remainder	25%	25%	20%	—
Film: limited budget[1]	—	—	—	25%
Film: any other	—	—	—	20%
Animation/television/video games development/theatrical productions/ orchestral concert production[2]	25%	25%	25%	25%

Notes
[1] Limited-budget films are those with a total core expenditure of £20m or less.
[2] Film production relief has been available since 1 January 2007. Animation and television reliefs were introduced from 1 April 2013, video games development relief from 1 April 2014, theatrical productions relief from 1 September 2014 and orchestra tax relief from 1 April 2016.

[¶7-130]   Museum and galleries tax relief
(CTA 2009, Pt. 15E)

Museum and gallery exhibitions tax relief allows qualifying companies engaged in the production of exhibitions to claim an additional deduction in computing their taxable profits and where that additional deduction results in a loss, to surrender those losses for a payable tax credit.

Expenditure incurred on or after 1 April 2017 until 31 March 2022	
Additional deduction (the lesser of):	
Qualifying expenditure which is EEA expenditure	100%
Total amount of qualifying expenditure	80%
Payable tax credit	
Non-touring exhibitions	20% up to £80,000
Touring exhibitions	25% up to £100,000
Maximum equivalent expenditure cap	£500,000
Maximum qualifying core expenditure (% of total core expenditure)	80%

[¶7-150]   Gifts to the nation

(FA 2012, Sch. 14)

(Tax Reporter: ¶716-685ff.)

For accounting periods beginning on or after 1 April 2012, a reduction in corporation tax is available where a company makes a gift of pre-eminent property to be held for the benefit of the public or the nation. The tax reduction is 20% of the value of the gift. A gift offer must be made and registered in accordance with the scheme and relief is available against the company's liability for the accounting period in which the gift offer is registered.

Pre-eminent property includes any picture, print, book, manuscript, work of art, scientific object or other thing that is pre-eminent for its national, scientific, historic or artistic interest, collections of such items and any object kept in a significant building where it is desirable that it remain associated with the building.

[¶7-200]   Car hire

(CTA 2009, s. 56ff.)

(Tax Reporter: ¶707-860ff.)

Leased cars, where the lease begins from 1 April 2009, suffer a 15% disallowance of relevant payments if CO_2 emissions exceed the limits set out below, otherwise no disallowance. This applies to all cars (not just those costing more than £12,000).

	CO_2 emissions
On or after 1 April 2018	Over 110g/km
1 April 2013 to 31 March 2018	Over 130g/km
1 April 2009 to 31 March 2013	Over 160g/km

For leased cars where the lease began before 1 April 2009, the restricted deduction for hire charges of motor cars with a retail price greater than £12,000 is calculated as follows:

$$\text{Allowable amount} = \frac{£12{,}000 + \tfrac{1}{2}\,(\text{retail price} - £12{,}000)}{\text{retail price}} \times \text{hire charge}$$

[¶7-300]   Bank levy

(FA 2011, Sch. 19)

(Tax Reporter: ¶807-000)

The rates of charge are as follows:

Period	Chargeable equity and long-term chargeable liabilities[1][2][3] %	Short-term chargeable liabilities[1][2][3] %
1 Jan. 2017–31 Dec. 2017	0.085	0.17
1 Jan. 2016–31 Dec. 2016	0.09	0.18
1 Jan. 2015–31 Dec. 2015	0.105	0.21
1 Jan. 2014–31 Dec. 2014	0.078	0.156
1 Jan. 2013–31 Dec. 2013	0.065	0.130

Notes
[1] F(No. 2)A 2015, s. 16 and Sch. 2 set future long-term and short-term rates as follows:

Period	Long-term rate	Short-term rate
1 Jan. 2018–31 Dec. 2018	0.08%	0.16%
1 Jan. 2019–31 Dec. 2019	0.075%	0.15%
1 Jan. 2020–31 Dec. 2020	0.07%	0.14%
Any time on or after 1 Jan. 2021	0.05%	0.10%

[2] Double tax relief is available against the UK bank levy for payments made to the Eurozone Single Resolution Fund. Affected banks may claim relief in relation to accounting periods ending on or after 1 January 2016 (SI 2016/1212).
[3] The bank levy charge will be restricted to UK balance sheet liabilities from 1 January 2021, subject to an exemption for certain UK liabilities relating to the funding of non-UK companies and an exemption for UK liabilities relating to the funding of non-UK branches (Autumn Budget 2017, as previously announced).

[¶7-325] Banking companies: surcharge

(CTA 2010, Pt. 7A, Ch. 4)

(Tax Reporter: ¶807-000)

Accounting periods beginning on or after	Surcharge[1]
1 January 2016	8%

Note
[1] A surcharge of 8% is levied on the taxable profits of banking companies arising on or after 1 January 2016. Taxable profits are calculated before the offset of losses that arose before the commencement date or from non-banking companies, and before the surrender of group relief from non-banking companies. An annual surcharge allowance of £25m is available to groups and individual banking companies which reduces the profits liable to the surcharge.

[¶7-350] Annual tax on enveloped dwellings (ATED)

(FA 2013, Pt. 3; SI 2014/854; SI 2016/1244)

(Tax Reporter: ¶807-800ff.)

Annual tax on enveloped dwellings (ATED) is a tax payable by companies and other corporate bodies (partnerships with corporate partners or other collective investment vehicle) that own UK residential property valued above the threshold amount.

The tax is charged for the chargeable period (a period of 12 months beginning 1 April and ending 31 March) concerned.

Property value		Annual charge[1]					
More than £	Less than £	2018–19[2] £	2017–18 £	2016–17 £	2015–16 £	2014–15 £	2013–14 £
500,000	1,000,000	3,600	3,500	3,500	0	0	0
1,000,000	2,000,000	7,250	7,050	7,000	7,000	0	0
2,000,000	5,000,000	24,250	23,550	23,350	23,350	15,400	15,000
5,000,000	10,000,000	56,550	54,950	54,450	54,450	35,900	35,000
10,000,000	20,000,000	113,400	110,100	109,050	109,050	71,850	70,000
20,000,000		226,950	220,350	218,200	218,200	143,750	140,000

Note
[1] The annual charge will be increased by consumer prices index inflation each year.
[2] Rates per Autumn Budget 2017.

Reliefs[1]	References
Property rental businesses	FA 2013, s. 133 (Tax Reporter: ¶807-922)
Rental property: preparation for sale, etc.	FA 2013, s. 134
Dwellings opened to the public	FA 2013, s. 137 (Tax Reporter: ¶807-923)
Property developers	FA 2013, s. 138
Property developers: exchange of dwellings	FA 2013, s. 139
Property traders	FA 2013, s. 141
Financial institutions acquiring dwellings in the course of lending	FA 2013, s. 143
Occupation by certain employees or partners	FA 2013, s. 145 (Tax Reporter: ¶807-924)
Farmhouses	FA 2013, s. 148 (Tax Reporter: ¶807-925)
Providers of social housing	FA 2013, s. 150

Exemptions	References
Charitable companies	FA 2013, s. 151 (Tax Reporter: ¶807-927)
Public bodies	FA 2013, s. 153 (Tax Reporter: ¶807-928)
Bodies established for national purpose	FA 2013, s. 154 (Tax Reporter: ¶807-929)
Dwelling conditionally exempt from inheritance tax	FA 2013, s. 155 (Tax Reporter: ¶807-930)

Note
[1] *Finance Act* 2016 extends the reliefs available from ATED (and the 15% higher rate of SDLT) to equity release schemes (home reversion plans) and properties occupied by employees from 1 April 2016 (FA 2013, s. 144A and 145).

Administration

[¶7-400]   Filing deadlines

(FA 1998, Sch. 18, para. 14)

(Tax Reporter: ¶181-075ff.)

The filing date for a return of profits (CT600) is generally the **later** of the dates outlined below:

- 12 months from the end of the return period;
- where the period of account is 18 months or less, 12 months from the end of the period of account;
- where the period of account is greater than 18 months, 30 months from the start of the period of account; and
- three months after the issue of a notice to deliver a corporation tax return.

Notes

Obligation to file a return is not automatic but is imposed by notice.

Every company which is chargeable to corporation tax in respect of any accounting period, and which has not made a return of its profits for that period, nor received a notice to make such a return, is under a duty to give notice to the inspector that it is so chargeable. The notice must be given not later than 12 months after the end of that accounting period.

A company must notify HMRC that its first accounting period has begun within three months of the accounting period beginning. This also applies to dormant companies which cease to be dormant.

An amended return under self-assessment may not be made later than 12 months after the filing date stipulated above.

[¶7-450]   Due and payable dates

(TMA 1970, s. 59D–59FA; ITA 2007, Pt. 15; SI 1998/3175)

(Tax Reporter: ¶183-410ff.; ¶117-000ff.)

Liability	Due date
Corporation tax	Nine months and one day after end of an accounting period[1]
Corporation tax in instalments[2][3]	The 14th day of the 7th, 10th, 13th and 16th months after start of a 12-month accounting period
Income tax on interest, annual payments, etc.	14 days after end of return period

Notes

[1] The *Taxes Management Act* 1970, s. 59G provides for companies to enter into voluntary payment plans with HMRC under which corporation tax liabilities can be paid in instalments spread equally before and after the due date. It should be noted that only corporation tax payable in accordance with TMA 1970, s. 59D (i.e. tax payable nine months and one day after the end of the accounting period) can be the subject of a managed payment plan. This excludes corporation tax payable by large companies in accordance with the quarterly instalment payment scheme. In addition, companies which have entered into a group payment arrangement can not enter into a managed payment plan.

[2] The *Taxes Management Act* 1970, s. 59E and SI 1998/3175 provide for the payment of corporation tax by 'large' companies (defined in accordance with the small profits marginal relief upper limit) in instalments.

Companies which are 'large' because of the number of associated companies or because of substantial dividend income will not have to pay by instalments if their corporation tax liabilities are less than £10,000. Companies which become 'large' in an accounting period, having previously had profits below the upper limit, may be exempt from instalment arrangements in certain circumstances. Groups containing 'large' companies are able to pay corporation tax on a group-wide basis.

Taxation of Companies

Corporation tax and the supplementary charge payable by oil companies on ring fence profits are payable in three equal instalments. Corporation tax due on other profits (i.e. non-ring fence) continues to be payable in quarterly instalments as above.

The payment dates for the three instalments once the transitional period (see below) has passed are as follows:

(1) one-third payable six months and 13 days from the start of the accounting period (unless the date for instalment (3) is earlier);

(2) one-third payable three months from the first instalment due date (unless (3) is earlier); and

(3) the balance payable 14 days from the end of the accounting period (regardless of the length of the period).

Transitional arrangements apply for the first accounting period affected. These arrangements leave the first two quarterly instalments unchanged (at one-quarter each of the estimated liability for the period) but then require payment of the remainder of the estimated liability on ring fence profits for that accounting period to be paid on the new third instalment date.

[3] Return periods end on 31 March, 30 June, 30 September, 31 December and at the end of an accounting period. Summer Budget 2015 announced that the Government will introduce new payment dates for companies with annual taxable profits of £20m or more. Where a company is a member of a group, the £20m threshold will be divided by the number of companies in the group. Affected companies will be required to pay corporation tax in quarterly instalments in the third, sixth, ninth and twelfth months of their accounting period. The measure was due to apply to accounting periods starting on or after 1 April 2017, however, the commencement of rules has been deferred for two years, so will now have effect for accounting periods commencing on or after 1 April 2019 (Budget 2016).

[¶7-500] Penalties

(Tax Reporter: ¶181-350ff.)

Infringement penalised[5][6][7]	Maximum penalty	Provision
Failure to notify chargeability • deliberate and concealed act or failure • deliberate but not concealed act or failure • any other case	*Standard amount* 100% of potential lost revenue 70% of potential lost revenue 30% of potential lost revenue	FA 2008, Sch. 41, para. 1, 6
Failure to make return[1] • up to three months after filing date • more than three months after filing date • at least 18 months but less than 24 months after end of return period • 24 months or more after end of return period	*Fixed rate penalty*[2] £100 (persistent failure, £500) £200 (persistent failure, £1,000) *Tax-geared penalty*[3] 10% of tax unpaid at 18 months after end of return period 20% of tax unpaid at 18 months after end of return period	FA 1998, Sch. 18, para. 17(2), (3) FA 1998, Sch. 18, para. 18
Error in a return (careless or deliberate) • standard amount • where the inaccuracy is deliberate but not concealed • where the inaccuracy is deliberate and concealed	 30% of potential lost revenue 70% of potential lost revenue 100% of potential lost revenue	FA 2007, Sch. 24, para. 4

Infringement penalised[5][6][7]	Maximum penalty	Provision
Failure to keep and preserve records (subject to specific exceptions)	Up to £3,000	FA 1998, Sch. 18, para. 23
Failure to produce document required in connection with an enquiry[4]		FA 2008, Sch. 36, para. 39 and 40
• standard amount	£300	
• continued failure	daily penalty of £60	

Notes

[1] From a date yet to be announced, FA 2009 introduced a new flat-rate and tax-geared penalty regime for the late filing of corporation tax returns (FA 2009, Sch. 55).

[2] Fixed rate penalty does not apply if return filed by date allowed by registrar of companies.

[3] Tax geared penalty is charged in addition to fixed penalty. Where more than one tax-geared penalty is incurred the total penalty shall not exceed the largest individual penalty on that part.

[4] An additional tax-related penalty can be imposed under FA 2008, Sch. 36, para. 50.

[5] From a date yet to be announced, FA 2009 introduced a new penalty regime for late payment of corporation tax (FA 2009, Sch. 56).

[6] For financial years beginning on or after 21 July 2009, the senior accounting officer of a qualifying company is obliged to ensure that the company establishes and maintains appropriate tax accounting arrangements, and to provide a certificate to HMRC indicating whether or not this was the case for each financial year (FA 2009, Sch. 46; see Tax Reporter: ¶191-660ff.). Qualifying companies are obliged to provide details of their senior accounting officer to HMRC. Failure to comply with these requirements will make the senior accounting officer and/or the company liable to a penalty.

[7] A criminal offence for corporates which fail to prevent their agents from criminally facilitating tax evasion by an individual or entity was introduced by the *Criminal Finances Act* 2017, with effect from 30 September 2017 (SI 2017/739).

[¶7-550] Interest on overdue tax

(Tax Reporter: ¶183-430ff.)

Interest on	Interest runs from	Provision in TMA 1970[2]
Overdue corporation tax	Date tax due and payable (nine months and one day after end of accounting period)[1]	s. 87A
Corporation tax payable in instalments	Date instalment is due to be paid	s. 87A
Overdue income tax deducted from certain payments	14 days after end of return period	s. 87
Overdue tax due on loans to participators	Date tax due and payable	s. 109

Notes

[1] Where one group company is liable to interest and another group company with the same accounting period is due a repayment of corporation tax an election may be made for the overpayment to be surrendered so as to reduce the interest liability of the first company which will be treated as having paid tax at the same time as the surrendering company (CTA 2010, s. 963).

[2] *Finance (No. 3) Act* 2010 contains provisions to apply the harmonised interest regime introduced by FA 2009 to corporation tax and PRT. The provisions will be brought into force by Treasury Order.

[¶7-650] Interest on tax repayments

(ICTA 1988, s. 826; SI 1998/3175, reg. 8)

(Tax Reporter: ¶183-430ff.)

Repayment interest on corporation tax runs from later of:

(1) due and payable date (nine months after end of accounting period); and

(2) date of actual payment except for:

    (a) overpayments of instalments of corporation tax, when interest runs from the first instalment date on which the excess amount would have been due and payable or, if later, the date on which that excess arises; and

    (b) for companies outside the instalments regime, if tax was paid earlier than the normal due date, then interest on repayments in advance of agreement of liability runs from the first instalment date on which the excess amount would have been due and payable had the instalments regime applied or, the date on which the amount repayable was originally paid, whichever is later.

Interest on repayments of income tax deducted at source from income will run from the day after the end of the accounting period in which the income was received for accounting periods under self-assessment.

Finance (No. 3) Act 2010 contains provisions to apply the harmonised interest regime introduced by *Finance Act* 2009 to corporation tax and PRT. The provisions will be brought into force by Treasury Order.

[¶7-700] Rates of interest

With effect for interest periods commencing on 6 February 1997, the rates of interest for the purposes of corporation tax are different from those for other taxes. The rate of interest on corporation tax will depend on the accounting period for which the tax is due and, under self-assessment, the nature of the tax due or repayable.

Self-assessment

For accounting periods within the self-assessment regime (CTSA), i.e. APs on or after 1 July 1999, the rates of interest are distinct from those for pre-CTSA periods, because the interest is taxable and tax deductible (see below).

In addition, there are separate provisions for:

• overpaid instalments of corporation tax; and

• payments of corporation tax made after the normal due date.

CTSA

1. CT (other than instalments and CT not due by instalments)

From	Late payment %	Repayment %
23 August 2016	2.75	0.5
29 September 2009 to 22 August 2016	3.00	0.50

2. Instalments and CT not due by instalments

From	Late payment %	Repayment %
15 August 2016	1.25	0.5
21 September 2009 to 14 August 2016	1.50	0.50

[¶7-900] Time limits for elections and claims

(Tax Reporter: ¶191-835)

In the absence of any provision to the contrary (some of which are considered below), the normal rule is that a claim must be made within four years of the end of the accounting period to which it relates (six years prior to 1 April 2010) (FA 1998, Sch. 18, para. 55).

In certain cases, HMRC *may* permit an extension of the strict time limit in relation to certain elections and claims.

Provision	Time limit	References
Stock transferred to a connected party on cessation of trade to be valued at higher cost or sale price	Two years from end of accounting period in which trade ceased	CTA 2009, s. 167(4)
Carry-forward of trading losses	Relief is given automatically	CTA 2010, s. 45
Set-off of trading losses against profits of the same, or an earlier, accounting period	Two years from end of accounting period in which loss incurred	CTA 2010, s. 37(7)
Group relief	Claims to group relief must be made (or withdrawn) by the later of: (1) 12 months after the claimant company's filing date for the return for the accounting period covered by the claim; (2) 30 days after a closure notice is issued on the completion of an enquiry[(1)]; (3) 30 days after HMRC issue a notice of amendment to a return following the completion of an enquiry (issued where the company fails to amend the return itself); or (4) 30 days after the determination of any appeal against an HMRC amendment (as in (3) above).	FA 1998, Sch. 18, para. 74
Set-off of loss on disposal of shares in unquoted trading company against income of investment company	Two years from end of accounting period	CTA 2010, s. 70(4)
Surrender of company tax refund within group	Before refund made to surrendering company	CTA 2010, s. 963(3)

Provision	Time limit	References
Relief for a non-trading deficit on loan relationships (including any non-trading exchange losses) – set off against profits of deficit or earlier periods – carry forward to later periods	– two years from end of period in which deficit arises – two years from end of the accounting period following the deficit period, or such further period as an officer of HMRC allows	CTA 2009, s. 458(2) and 460(1)
Appropriation of asset to trading stock: election to adjust trading profit by the amount of the gain or loss on the deemed disposal at market value	Two years from the end of the accounting period in which the asset is appropriated as trading stock	TCGA 1992, s. 161(3)
Terminal loss relief on cessation of trade	Two years from end of the loss making accounting period	CTA 2010, s. 39
Intangible fixed assets: election to write down cost for tax purposes at fixed rate	Two years from end of accounting period in which company creates or acquires the asset	CTA 2009, s. 730
Election by recipient that company distribution should not be exempt	Second anniversary of end of accounting period in which distribution received	CTA 2009, s. 931R
Claims included in a company tax return, including research and development tax relief claim, land remediation tax credits and life assurance company tax credits, and film tax credits	One year from filing date for return or a later date if an officer of HMRC allows it	FA 1998, Sch. 18, para. 83E, 83K, 83W
Election for special treatment of profits from patents, etc. (patent box)	Two years from end of first accounting period to which it relates	CTA 2010, s. 357G

Note
[1] 'Enquiry' in the above does not include a restricted enquiry into an amendment to a return (restricted because the time limit for making an enquiry into the return itself has expired), where the amendment consists of a group relief claim or withdrawal of claim.

These time limits have priority over any other general time limits for amending returns and are subject to HMRC permitting an extension to the time limits.

CAPITAL ALLOWANCES

[¶8-000]   Plant and machinery: overview of allowances
(CAA 2001)

(Tax Reporter: ¶235-000ff.)

Plant and machinery allowances are normally given by way of:

*   annual investment allowances: see ¶8-100;

*   first-year allowances: see ¶8-200; or

*   writing-down allowances: see ¶8-300.

In specified circumstances, balancing allowances may be due or balancing charges may be made.

[¶8-100]   Plant and machinery: annual investment allowances
(CAA 2001, s. 51A)

(Tax Reporter: ¶236-400ff.)

	Maximum (£)
1 January 2016	200,000
1/6 April 2014 to 31 December 2015	500,000[1]
1 January 2013 to 31 March/5 April 2014	250,000[1]
1/6 April 2012 to 31 December 2012	25,000
1/6 April 2010 to 31 March/5 April 2012	100,000

Note

[1] Temporary increase in the annual invesment allowance initially for the period of two years beginning with 1 January 2013 (FA 2013, s. 7 and Sch. 1) was extended to 31 December 2015 (and increased to £500,000) by FA 2014, s. 10 and Sch. 2.

This figure is adjusted pro rata for chargeable periods shorter or longer than one year.

Where a chargeable period spans the above dates of change (i.e. 1/6 April 2014, or 1 January 2016), the maximum AIA is calculated by splitting the chargeable period into separate periods falling before and after each of the dates of change. Transitional rules are then applied to determine the maximum AIA available in respect of the total chargeable period and the maximum AIA that may be allocated against qualifying expenditure incurred in each of the separate periods (FA 2014, Sch. 2; FA 2013, Sch. 1; FA 2011, s. 11).

Groups of companies, companies and qualifying activities carried on by individuals or partnerships, under common control which share premises and carry on similar activities are entitled to a single annual investment allowance only.

Capital Allowances

[¶8-200] Plant and machinery: 100% first-year allowances

(CAA 2001, s. 52)

(Tax Reporter: ¶237-000ff.)

Subject to the general exclusions listed at ¶8-210, full 100% allowances are available for the following types of expenditure incurred by a business of any size. If full FYAs are not claimed, WDA is normally available on a reducing balance basis (see ¶8-300).

Nature of expenditure	Authority (CAA 2001)	Notes
Energy-saving plant or machinery	s. 45A–45C; Sch. A1	Loss-making companies may claim tax rebate until 31 March 2018[(1)].
Cars with low CO_2 emissions	s. 45D	On expenditure incurred until 31 March 2021[(2)]. See also ¶8-500.
Zero-emission goods vehicles	s. 45DA	On expenditure incurred before 1 April 2021[(3)] (corporation tax) or 6 April 2021[(3)] (income tax).
Plant or machinery for certain refuelling stations	s. 45E	Expenditure incurred until 31 March 2021[(3)] (for both corporation tax and income tax).
Plant or machinery for electric vehicle charging point	s. 45EA	On expenditure incurred from 23 November 2016 until 31 March 2019 (corporation tax) or 5 April 2019 (income tax).
Plant or machinery (other than a long life asset) for use by a company wholly in a ring fence trade	s. 45F	
Environmentally beneficial plant or machinery	s. 45H–45J	Loss-making companies may claim tax rebate until 31 March 2018[(1)].
Expenditure on plant and machinery for use in designated assisted areas	s. 45K	Available for eight years from date expenditure incurred.

Notes

[(1)] First-year tax credits, for companies surrendering losses attributable to their expenditure on designated energy-saving or environmentally beneficial plant or machinery has been extended for a further five years until 31 March 2018 (SI 2013/464).
[(2)] First-year allowance for cars with low carbon dioxide emissions extended for a further three-year period ending on 31 March 2021 by SI 2016/984, art. 4(a) (and qualifying emissions threshold for the first-year allowance reduced from 75 grams to 50 grams per kilometre driven, in relation to expenditure incurred on or after 1 April 2018).
[(3)] First-year allowances for zero-emission goods vehicles and gas refuelling equipment to be extended to March/April 2021 by statutory instrument in December 2017 (Autumn Budget 2017).

[¶8-210] Plant and machinery: first-year allowances – general exclusions

(CAA 2001, s. 46(2))

(Tax Reporter: ¶237-150)

No first-year allowances are available for:

- expenditure incurred in the final chargeable period;
- cars (other than those with very low CO_2 emissions);
- items excluded from the long-life asset treatment only by virtue of the transitional provisions in CAA 2001, Sch. 3, para. 20;
- plant or machinery for leasing;
- in certain anti-avoidance cases where the obtaining of a FYA is linked to a change in the nature or conduct of a trade;
- where an asset was initially acquired for purposes other than those of the qualifying activity;
- where an asset was acquired by way of a gift; and
- where plant or machinery that was provided for long funding leasing starts to be used for other purposes.

[¶8-300] Plant and machinery: writing-down allowances

(CAA 2001, s. 56)

(Tax Reporter: ¶238-050ff.)

	Standard rate (%)	Special rate (%)
From April 2012	18	8
April 2008 to April 2012	20	10

Note
Different rules apply for certain cars (see ¶8-500).

WDA for small pools

Main pool or special rate pool only where tax written down value brought forward plus expenditure added to the pool during the period minus disposal receipts deducted from the pool during the period totals less than or equal to £1,000 (apportioned for periods of more or less than one year), an allowance may be claimed for the former amount in place of the standard rates above (CAA 2001, s. 56A).

Pooling

Expenditure is allocated to the main pool unless it is allocated to either a single asset pool or single class pool. Single asset and single class pools are as follows:

Single asset pools

- short life asset (CAA 2001, s. 86);
- ship (CAA 2001, s. 127);
- assets with partial non-qualifying use (CAA 2001, s. 206);

Capital Allowances

- expenditure in relation to which a partial depreciation subsidy is received (CAA 2001, s. 211); and
- contribution allowances: plant and machinery (CAA 2001, s. 538).

Single class pools
- special rate expenditure (see below) (CAA 2001, s. 104A); and
- overseas leasing (CAA 2001, s. 107).

Special rate expenditure

Expenditure	Incurred on or after	Provision
Thermal insulation of buildings	1 April 2008 (corporation tax) or 6 April 2008 (income tax)	CAA 2001, s. 28
Integral features	1 April 2008 (corporation tax) or 6 April 2008 (income tax)	CAA 2001, s. 33A
Long life asset expenditure	26 November 1996, or 1 January 2001 in pursuance of a contract entered into before 26 November 1996 or incurred before 26 November 1996 but allocated to a pool in a chargeable period beginning on or after that date	CAA 2001, Ch. 10
Cars (excluding main rate cars (first registered before 1 March 2001, cars with low CO_2 emissions, electrically-propelled cars))	1 April 2009 (corporation tax) or 6 April 2009 (income tax)	CAA 2001, s. 104AA
Provision of cushion gas	1 April 2010	CAA 2001, s. 70J(7)
Solar panels	1 April 2012 (corporation tax) or 6 April 2012 (income tax)	CAA 2001, s. 104A(1)(g)

[¶8-400]   Plant and machinery: integral features

(CAA 2001, s. 33A)

(Tax Reporter: ¶243-400ff.)

The following assets are designated as integral features:
- electrical systems (including lighting systems);
- cold water systems;
- space or water heating systems, powered systems of ventilation, air cooling or air purification, and any floor or ceiling comprised in such systems;
- lifts, escalators and moving walkways; and
- external solar shading.

[¶8-410]   Plant and machinery: expenditure unaffected by statutory restrictions re buildings

(CAA 2001, s. 23)

(Tax Reporter: ¶245-550)

The restrictions in CAA 2001, s. 21 and 22 (buildings, structures and other assets) do not apply to the following categories of expenditure:

- thermal insulation of buildings (CAA 2001, s. 28);
- personal security (CAA 2001, s. 33);
- integral features (CAA 2001, s. 33A); and
- software and rights to software (CAA 2001, s. 71).

Note
Before 1 April 2013, expenditure on safety at designated sports grounds, safety at regulated stands at sports grounds and safety at other sports grounds was also included in the list of exclusions.

The restrictions in CAA 2001, s. 21 and 22 (buildings, structures and other assets) also do not apply to expenditure in List C at CAA 2001, s. 23. List C, as amended, is as follows:

(1)   machinery (including devices for providing motive power) not within any other item in this list;

(2)   gas and sewerage systems provided mainly:

    (a)   to meet the particular requirements of the qualifying activity;

    (b)   to serve particular plant or machinery used for the purposes of the qualifying activity;

(3)   [omitted by *Finance Act* 2008];

(4)   manufacturing or processing equipment; storage equipment (including cold rooms); display equipment; and counters, checkouts and similar equipment;

(5)   cookers, washing machines, dishwashers, refrigerators and similar equipment; washbasins, sinks, baths, showers, sanitary ware and similar equipment; and furniture and furnishings;

(6)   hoists;

(7)   sound insulation provided mainly to meet the particular requirements of the qualifying activity;

(8)   computer, telecommunication and surveillance systems (including their wiring or other links);

(9)   refrigeration or cooling equipment;

(10)   fire alarm systems, sprinkler and other equipment for extinguishing or containing fires;

(11)   burglar alarm systems;

(12)   strong rooms in bank or building society premises, safes;

(13)   partition walls, where moveable and intended to be moved in the course of the qualifying activity;

(14)   decorative assets provided for the enjoyment of the public in hotel, restaurant or similar trades;

(15)   advertising hoardings, signs, displays and similar assets;

Capital Allowances

(16) swimming-pools (including diving boards, slides and structures on which such boards or slides are mounted);

(17) any glasshouse constructed so that the required environment (namely, air, heat, light, irrigation and temperature) for the growing of plants is provided automatically by means of devices forming an integral part of its structure;

(18) cold stores;

(19) caravans provided mainly for holiday lettings;

(20) buildings provided for testing aircraft engines run within the buildings;

(21) moveable buildings intended to be moved in the course of the qualifying activity;

(22) the alteration of land for the purpose only of installing plant or machinery;

(23) the provision of dry docks;

(24) the provision of any jetty or similar structure provided mainly to carry plant or machinery;

(25) the provision of pipelines or underground ducts or tunnels with a primary purpose of carrying utility conduits;

(26) the provision of towers to support floodlights;

(27) the provision of:

    (a) any reservoir incorporated into a water treatment works; or

    (b) any service reservoir of treated water for supply within any housing estate or other particular locality;

(28) the provision of:

    (a) silos provided for temporary storage; or

    (b) storage tanks;

(29) the provision of slurry pits or silage clamps;

(30) the provision of fish tanks or fish ponds;

(31) the provision of rails, sleepers and ballast for a railway or tramway;

(32) the provision of structures and other assets for providing the setting for any ride at an amusement park or exhibition;

(33) the provision of fixed zoo cages.

Items (1)–(16) of the above list do not, however, include any asset with the principal purpose of insulating or enclosing the interior of a building or of providing an interior wall, floor or ceiling that is intended to remain permanently in place (CAA 2001, s. 33A).

[¶8-420] Assets treated as buildings

(CAA 2001, s. 21)

(Tax Reporter: ¶245-550)

Plant and machinery allowances are not available on expenditure on the provision of a building, including its construction or acquisition. Building includes:

• an asset incorporated in the building;

- although not incorporated in the building (whether because the asset is moveable or for any other reason), is in the building and is of a kind normally incorporated in a building; or
- is in, or connected with the building and is in list A as follows:
    - walls, floors, ceilings, doors, gates, shutters, windows and stairs;
    - mains services, and systems, for water, electricity and gas;
    - waste disposal systems;
    - sewerage and drainage systems;
    - shafts or other structures in which lifts, hoists, escalators and moving walkways are installed;
    - fire safety systems.

[¶8-430] Excluded structures and other assets

(CAA 2001, s. 22)

Plant and machinery does not include expenditure on the provision of a structure or other asset within list B, or any works involving the alteration of land. List B is as follows:

(1)   a tunnel, bridge, viaduct, aqueduct, embankment or cutting;

(2)   a way, hard standing (such as a pavement), road, railway, tramway, a park for vehicles or containers, or an airstrip or runway;

(3)   an inland navigation, including a canal or basin or a navigable river;

(4)   a dam, reservoir or barrage, including any sluices, gates, generators and other equipment associated with the dam, reservoir or barrage;

(5)   a dock, harbour, wharf, pier, marina or jetty or any other structure in or at which vessels may be kept, or merchandise or passengers may be shipped or unshipped;

(6)   a dike, sea wall, weir or drainage ditch;

(7)   any structure not within items (1)–(6) other than:

    (a)   a structure (but not a building) within the meaning of 'industrial building';

    (b)   a structure in use for the purposes of an undertaking for the extraction, production, processing or distribution of gas; and

    (c)   a structure in use for the purposes of a trade which consists in the provision of telecommunication, television or radio services.

Note
Structure means a fixed structure of any kind, other than a building (as defined by s. 21(3) (see ¶8-420 above)). Land does not include buildings or other structures.

[¶8-450] Fixtures

(CAA 2001, s. 187A)

From April 2012, purchasers of buildings which include fixtures on which capital allowances have previously been claimed will only be able to claim capital allowances on the fixtures if either:

Capital Allowances

(1) the fixed value requirement is met whereby the value of the fixtures transferred is agreed within two years of the transfer either:

  • between the seller and purchaser by joint election under CAA 2001, s. 198–199; or

  • by determination of the First-tier Tribunal; or

(2) the purchaser obtains a written statement from the seller that the fixed value requirement has not been met and is no longer capable of being met and the purchaser obtains from a past owner a written statement of the disposal value brought into account by that owner (this will apply in cases where the seller is an intermediate owner or lessee not entitled to claim allowances but who acquired the fixtures from a past owner who was entitled to claim allowances).

From April 2014, it will also be necessary to show that historic expenditure has been pooled, or that the past owner claimed a first year allowance on the expenditure (or any part of it) before a subsequent transfer to another person.

[¶8-500] Plant and machinery: allowances for cars

(CAA 2001, s. 104A and 104AA)

(Tax Reporter: ¶238-500ff.)

	CO$_2$ emissions			
	2018–19 to 2020–21	2015–16 to 2017–18	2013–14 & 2014–15	2012–13 (from 2009–10)
100% FYAs (CAA 2001, s. 45D) (see also ¶8-200)	50g/km or less	75g/km or less	95g/km or less	110g/km or less
Main rate pool (18%)	Over 50g/km up to 110g/km	Over 75g/km up to 130g/km	Over 95g/km up to 130g/km	Over 110g/km up to 160g/km
Special rate pool (8%)	Over 110g/km	Over 130g/km	Over 130g/km	Over 160g/km

Cars with private use go to a single asset pool but still with WDA as above, but then adjusted for private use percentage.

[¶8-550] Enterprise zones: 100% capital allowances

(CAA 2001, s. 45K–45N)

(Tax Reporter: ¶237-610)

First year allowances (at 100%) are available in respect of expenditure incurred by companies (not unincorporated businesses) on new and unsued plant and machinery for use primarily in designated assisted areas in enterprise zones. The allowances are available for expenditure incurred during the period of eight years beginning with the date on which the area is (or is treated as) designated by Treasury Order[1]. Expenditure must be incurred for the purposes of a new or expanding business carried on by the company, must not be replacement expenditure and is limited to €125m per single investment project (as defined) (CAA 2001, s. 45K–45N). A full list of current zones and designated assisted areas is available at:

- http://enterprisezones.communities.gov.uk (see also maps at www.gov.uk/government/ publications/enterprise-zones);
- http://business.wales.gov.uk/enterprisezones/enhanced-capital-allowances;
- www.scotland.gov.uk/Topics/Economy/EconomicStrategy/Enterprise-Areas/ Incentives/Capital-Allowances.

Note
(1) The period of availability was originally introduced as five years beginnning with 1 April 2012 (FA 2012, s. 44 and Sch. 11, para. 3), extended to eight years from the same date by FA 2014, s. 64(5)(a) and has been further extended to eight years from the date of designation by FA 2016, s. 69.

[¶8-650]   Enterprise zones: industrial buildings, hotels, commercial buildings or structures

(Former CAA 2001, s. 271ff.; FA 2008, Sch. 27, para. 31)

(Tax Reporter: ¶250-950ff.)

No IBAs are given for any chargeable period beginning after 1 or 6 April 2011. For enterprise zone expenditure only, a balancing charge can still be incurred up to 5 April 2018.

[¶8-800]   Other allowances

Allowance	Date expenditure incurred (from)	Initial allowance (%)	WDA (%)	CAA 2001	Tax Reporter
[Business premises renovation(3)]	[11 April 2007 (to 31 March or 5 April 2017)]	[100]	[25]	[s. 360A]	¶252-500
[Flat conversion(1)]	[11 May 2001 (to 31 March or 5 April 2013)]	[100]	[25]	[former s. 393A]	¶254-000
Mineral extraction(4)	1 April 1986	—	25	s. 394	¶255-500
Research and development	6 November 1962	100	—	s. 437	¶256-000
Know-how(2)	1 April 1986	—	25	s. 452	¶257-000
Patents(2)	1 April 1986	—	25	s. 464	¶257-500
Dredging	6 November 1962	—	4	s. 484	¶258-000
Assured tenancy	10 March 1982 (to 31 March 1992)	—	4	s. 490	¶258-500

Notes
(1) Flat conversion allowances were abolished in respect of expenditure incurred on or after 1 April 2013 for corporation tax purposes and 6 April 2013 for income tax purposes (FA 2012, s. 227 and Sch. 39, para. 36 and 37). The entitlement to claim writing-down allowances on any residual expenditure is also withdrawn from that date.
(2) Capital allowances for know-how and patents still apply for income tax but were replaced for most corporation tax purposes by the intangible assets regime with effect from 1 April 2002.
(3) BPRA expired on 1 April 2017 (corporation tax) and 6 April 2017 (income tax), with effect in relation to expenditure incurred on or after those dates.

Capital Allowances

[¶8-950]   Time limits for elections and claims

(CAA 2001, s. 3; TMA 1970, s. 43; FA 1998, Sch. 18, para. 54–60)

(Tax Reporter: ¶235-050)

Capital allowances must be claimed in a tax return. However, the rules for claims outside a return for income tax (TMA 1970, s. 42) and corporation tax (FA 1998, Sch. 18, para. 54–60) apply in certain instances:

- special leasing plant and machinery allowance claims; and
- claims for patent allowances on non-trading expenditure (in income tax cases).

Provision	Time limit	Statutory reference
General claim to capital allowances under corporation tax self-assessment	Claims to capital allowances must be made (or amended or withdrawn) by the later of: (1) 12 months after the claimant company's filing date for the return for the accounting period covered by the claim; (2) 30 days after a closure notice is issued on the completion of an enquiry; (3) 30 days after HMRC issue a notice of amendment to a return following the completion of an enquiry (issued where the company fails to amend the return itself); or (4) 30 days after the determination of any appeal against an HMRC amendment (as in (3) above). 'Enquiry' in the above does not include a restricted enquiry into an amendment to a return (restricted because the time limit for making an enquiry into the return itself has expired), where the amendment consists of making, amending or withdrawing a claim for capital allowances. These time limits have priority over any other general time limits for amending returns to the extent that an amendment makes, amends or withdraws a claim for capital allowances. A claim for capital allowances may be made, amended or withdrawn at a later time if an officer of HMRC allows it.	FA 1998, Sch. 18, para. 82

Provision	Time limit	Statutory reference
Certain plant and machinery treated as 'short life' assets (income tax elections)	12 months from 31 January next following the tax year in which ends the chargeable period in which the qualifying expenditure was incurred	CAA 2001, s. 85
Certain plant and machinery treated as 'short life' assets (corporation tax elections)	Two years from end of the chargeable period in which the qualifying expenditure was incurred	CAA 2001, s. 85
Set-off of capital allowances on special leasing (corporation tax)	Two years from end of accounting period	CAA 2001, s. 260(3), (6)
Business successions: election between connected parties to transfer plant and machinery at tax written down value	Two years from date on which succession takes effect	CAA 2001, s. 266(4)
Transfer between connected parties of certain assets treated as being at market value; election for sale to be treated as being for an alternative amount value	Two years from date of sale	CAA 2001, s. 570(5)
Purchase of interest in land that includes a fixture – election to fix apportionment of disposal proceeds	Two years from the date of purchase	CAA 2001, s. 198, 201
Lease of interest in land that includes a fixture – election to fix apportionment of disposal proceeds	Two years from the date the lease is granted	CAA 2001, s. 199, 201

Capital Allowances

NATIONAL INSURANCE CONTRIBUTIONS

[¶9-000]   NIC rates: general

(NIC Reporter: ¶305-000ff.)

There are six classes of National Insurance contributions (NICs) payable according to the individual circumstances of the payer.

Class 1 contributions

Class 1 contributions are earnings-related and payable by employer and employee on earnings above the earnings thresholds. The primary threshold (PT) applies for employees and the secondary threshold (ST) for employers. Employees pay at the main rate up to the upper earnings limit (UEL) and the additional rate above the limit.

The *Pensions Act* 2014 abolished the contracting-out for salary-related occupational pensions schemes (from 6 April 2016) and introduced a new single-component state pension to replace the existing state pension comprising basic state pension and additional state pension (from 6 April 2016).

Contracting out for money purchase schemes (COMPS), mixed benefit schemes (COMB) contracted-out on a defined contribution basis, appropriate personal pension schemes (APP) and APP stakeholder schemes was abolished on 5 April 2012.

The reduced rate applies to married women or widows with a valid certificate of election and affects only primary contributions.

Individuals over state pension age pay no primary contributions, though employers still pay the secondary contribution regardless of the previous category of contribution liability. Children under 16 and their employers pay no contributions.

Employer NIC for the under 21s and apprentices under 25

(SSCBA 1992, s. 9A and 9B)

From 6 April 2015, employers with employees under the age of 21 are no longer required to pay Class 1 secondary NICs on earnings up to the upper earning limit (UEL), for those employees.

From 6 April 2016, employers of apprentices under the age of 25 are no longer required to pay secondary Class 1 (employer) NICs on earnings up to the UEL, for those employees.

[¶9-005]   National Insurance rate ceilings

(NIC(RC)A 2015)

(NIC Reporter: ¶305-600)

The *National Insurance Contributions (Rate Ceilings) Act* 2015 sets a ceiling on the main and additional primary percentages, the secondary percentage and the upper earnings limit in relation to Class 1 NICs. The Act came into force on 17 December 2015, with effect for tax years beginning after that date but before the date of the first Parliamentary

National Insurance Contributions

general election after that day (i.e. from 2016–17 until the tax year starting before the next general election thereafter). The Act prescribes the following limits:

Contribution/limit	Ceiling
Class 1 main primary percentage	12%
Class 1 additional primary percentage	2%
Class 1 secondary percentage	13.8%
Upper earnings limit	HRT[1]
	52

Note

[1] HRT is the proposed higher rate threshold for the tax year calculated as the sum of the basic rate limit for income tax for the tax year as proposed in the pre-budget proposals for that year, and the personal allowance for income tax for the tax year as so proposed.

[9-008] Class 1 NIC: 2018–19

(Autumn Budget 2017)

Class 1 contributions

Class 1 primary (employee) contributions 2018–19	
Lower earnings limit (LEL)[4]	£116 weekly £503[2] monthly £6,032[2] yearly
Primary threshold (PT)[4]	£162 weekly £702[3] monthly £8,424[3] yearly
Upper earnings limit (UEL)	£892 weekly £3,863[3] monthly £46,350[3] yearly
Rate on earnings up to PT[1]	0%
Rate	12% on £162.01 to £892 weekly 2% on excess over £892 weekly
Reduced rate	5.85% on £162.01 to £892 weekly 2% on excess over £892

Notes

[1] No national insurance contributions (NICs) are actually payable but a notional Class 1 NIC is deemed to have been paid in respect of earnings between the LEL and PT to protect contributory benefit entitlement.
[2] Monthly and annual LEL and UAP figures are calculated as per SI 2001/1004, reg. 11.
[3] Monthly and annual PT and UEL figures are prescribed by SI 2001/1004, reg. 11 and amended by Statutory Instrument. Figures for 2018-19 have yet to be specified and the amounts shown are calculated amounts (by reference to prior year equivalents) and may be subject to change.
[4] These thresholds are uprated by CPI.

Class 1 secondary (employer) contributions 2018–19	
Secondary earnings threshold (ST)[2]	£162 weekly £702[1] monthly £8,424[1] yearly
Upper secondary threshold (UST) for under 21s	£892 weekly £3,863[1] monthly £46,350[1] yearly
Apprentice upper secondary threshold (AUST) for under 25s	£892 weekly £3,863[1] monthly £46,350[1] yearly
Rate	13.8% on earnings above ST/UST/AUST
Employment allowance	£3,000 per year, per employer

Notes
[1] Monthly and annual ST, UST and AUST figures are prescribed by SI 2001/1004, reg. 11 and amended by Statutory Instrument. Figures for 2018-19 have yet to be specified and the amounts shown are calculated amounts (by reference to prior year equivalents) and may be subject to change.
[2] The weekly secondary threshold is uprated by CPI.

[¶9-010] Class 1 NIC: 2017–18

(SSCBA 1992; NICA 2014, s. 1, 8–9; SI 2001/1004, reg. 10–11 and 131)

(NIC Reporter: ¶305-575ff.)

Class 1 contributions

Class 1 primary (employee) contributions 2017–18	
Lower earnings limit (LEL)[4]	£113 weekly £490[2] monthly £5,876[2] yearly
Primary threshold (PT)[4]	£157 weekly £680[3] monthly £8,164[3] yearly
Upper earnings limit (UEL)	£866 weekly £3,750[3] monthly £45,000[3] yearly
Rate on earnings up to PT[1]	0%
Rate	12% on £157.01 to £866 weekly 2% on excess over £866 weekly
Reduced rate	5.85% on £157.01 to £866 weekly 2% on excess over £866

Notes
[1] No National Insurance contributions (NICs) are actually payable but a notional Class 1 NIC is deemed to have been paid in respect of earnings between the LEL and PT to protect contributory benefit entitlement.
[2] Monthly and annual LEL and UAP figures are calculated as per SI 2001/1004, reg. 11.
[3] Monthly and annual PT and UEL figures are prescribed by SI 2001/1004, reg. 11 and amended by Statutory Instrument.
[4] These thresholds are uprated by CPI.

National Insurance Contributions

Class 1 secondary (employer) contributions 2017–18	
Secondary earnings threshold (ST)[2]	£157 weekly £680[1] monthly £8,164[1] yearly
Upper secondary threshold (UST) for under 21s	£866 weekly £3,750[1] monthly £45,000[1] yearly
Apprentice upper secondary threshold (AUST) for under 25s	£866 weekly £3,750[1] monthly £45,000[1] yearly
Rate	13.8% on earnings above ST/UST/AUST
Employment allowance	£3,000 per year, per employer

Notes
[1] Monthly and annual ST, UST and AUST figures are prescribed by SI 2001/1004, reg. 11 and amended by Statutory Instrument.
[2] The weekly secondary threshold is uprated by CPI.

[¶9-015]   Class 1 NIC: 2016–17

(SSCBA 1992, NICA 2014, s. 1, 8–9; SI 2001/1004, reg. 10–11 and 131)

(NIC Reporter: ¶305-575ff.)

Class 1 contributions

Class 1 primary (employee) contributions 2016–17	
Lower earnings limit (LEL)[4]	£112 weekly £486[2] monthly £5,824[2] yearly
Primary threshold (PT)[4]	£155 weekly £672[3] monthly £8,060[3] yearly
Upper earnings limit (UEL)	£827 weekly £3,583[3] monthly £43,000[3] yearly
Rate on earnings up to PT[1]	0%
Rate	12% on £155.01 to £827 weekly 2% on excess over £827 weekly
Reduced rate	5.85% on £155.01 to £827 weekly 2% on excess over £827 weekly

Notes
[1] No National Insurance contributions (NICs) are actually payable but a notional Class 1 NIC is deemed to have been paid in respect of earnings between the LEL and PT to protect contributory benefit entitlement.
[2] Monthly and annual LEL and UAP figures are calculated as per SI 2001/1004, reg. 11.
[3] Monthly and annual PT and UEL figures are prescribed by SI 2001/1004, reg. 11 and amended by Statutory Instrument.
[4] These thresholds are uprated by CPI.

Class 1 secondary (employer) contributions 2016–17

Secondary earnings threshold (ST)[4]	£156 weekly £676[1] monthly £8,112[1] yearly
Upper secondary threshold (UST) for under 21s[2]	£827 weekly £3,583[1] monthly £43,000[1] yearly
Apprentice upper secondary threshold (AUST) for under 25s[3]	£827 weekly £3,583[1] monthly £43,000[1] yearly
Rate	13.8% on earnings above ST/UST[2]/AUST[3]
Employment allowance[5]	£3,000 per year, per employer

Notes
[1] Monthly and annual ST, UST and AUST figures are prescribed by SI 2001/1004, reg. 11 and amended by Statutory Instrument.
[2] Upper secondary threshold (UST) introduced from April 2015 for employees under the age of 21. The rate of secondary NICs for employees under the age of 21 on earnings between the ST and UST is 0%.
[3] Apprentice upper secondary threshold (AUST) introduced from April 2016. The rate of secondary NICs for apprentices under the age of 25 on earnings between the ST and AUST is 0%.
[4] The weekly secondary threshold is uprated by CPI.
[5] From 6 April 2016, companies where the director is the sole employee are no longer able to claim the allowance (NICA 2014, s. 2(4A)).

[¶9-020] Class 1 NIC: 2015–16

(NIC Reporter: ¶305-575ff.)

Class 1 contributions

Class 1 primary (employee) contributions 2015–16

Lower earnings limit (LEL)[4]	£112 weekly £486[2] monthly £5,824[2] yearly
Primary threshold (PT)[4]	£155 weekly £672[3] monthly £8,060[3] yearly
Upper earnings limit (UEL)	£815 weekly £3,532[3] monthly £42,385[3] yearly
Upper accruals point (UAP)	£770 weekly £3,337[2] monthly £40,040[2] yearly
Rate on earnings up to PT[1]	0%
Not contracted-out rate	12% on £155.01 to £815 weekly 2% on excess over £815 weekly

168   ¶9-020

Class 1 primary (employee) contributions 2015–16	
Contracted-out rate	10.6% on £155.01 to £770 weekly 12% on £770.01 to £815 weekly 2% on excess over £815 weekly
Reduced rate	5.85% on £155.01 to £815 weekly 2% on excess over £815 (no rebate even if contracted out)

Notes

[1] Earnings from the LEL, up to and including the PT, count towards the employee's basic state pension, even though no contributions are paid on those earnings. Similarly, earnings between the LEL and the PT count towards the employee's entitlement to certain benefits including the second state pension (S2P). Employees in contracted-out employment earn no S2P rights and receive a rebate of contributions of 1.4%. This applies from the LEL to the UAP, so earnings from LEL to PT attract a 'negative' contribution of 1.4% and the rate for earnings from PT to UAP becomes 10.6%. Earnings from UAP to UEL are subject to the main not contracted-out rate.

[2] Monthly and annual LEL and UAP figures are calculated as per SI 2001/1004, reg. 11.

[3] Monthly and annual PT and UEL figures are prescribed by SI 2001/1004, reg. 11 and amended by Statutory Instrument.

[4] These thresholds are uprated by CPI.

Class 1 secondary (employer) contributions 2015–16	
Secondary earnings threshold (ST)[4]	£156 weekly £676[2] monthly £8,112[2] yearly
Upper secondary threshold (UST) for under 21s[3]	£815 weekly £3,532 monthly £42,385 yearly
Not contracted-out rate	13.8% on earnings above ST
Contracted-out rate[1]	10.4% for salary related (COSR) on earnings from ST to UAP (plus 3.4% rebate for earnings from LEL to ST), then 13.8% above UAP
Employment allowance[5]	£2,000 per year, per employer

Notes

[1] Although employer contributions do not per se give any benefit entitlements, earnings between the LEL and ST are those classed as relevant for S2P. Employers with contracted-out occupational pension schemes receive a rebate of contributions for scheme members of 3.4% (COSR). This applies from the LEL to the UAP, so earnings from LEL to ST attract a 'negative' contribution and the rate for earnings from ST to UAP is reduced as shown.

[2] Monthly and annual ST figures are prescribed by SI 2001/1004, reg. 11 and amended by Statutory Instrument.

[3] Upper secondary threshold (UST) introduced from April 2015 for employees under the age of 21. The rate of secondary NICs for employees under the age of 21 on earnings between the ST and UST will be 0%.

[4] The weekly secondary threshold is uprated by RPI.

[5] From 6 April 2015, the allowance is extended to care and support workers (NICA 2014, s. 2(3A)).

[¶9-025]   Class 1 NIC: 2014–15

(NIC Reporter: ¶305-575ff.)

Class 1 contributions

Class 1 primary (employee) contributions 2014–15	
Lower earnings limit (LEL)	£111 weekly £481[2] monthly £5,772[2] yearly
Primary threshold (PT)	£153 weekly £663[3] monthly £7,956[3] yearly
Upper earnings limit (UEL)	£805 weekly £3,489[3] monthly £41,865[3] yearly
Upper accruals point (UAP)	£770 weekly £3,337[2] monthly £40,040[2] yearly
Rate on earnings up to PT[1]	0%
Not contracted-out rate	12% on £153.01 to £805 weekly 2% on excess over £805 weekly
Contracted-out rate	10.6% on £153.01 to £770 weekly 12% on £770.01 to £805 weekly 2% on excess over £805 weekly
Reduced rate	5.85% on £153.01 to £805 weekly 2% on excess over £805 (no rebate even if contracted-out)

Notes

[1] Earnings from the LEL, up to and including the PT, count towards the employee's basic state pension, even though no contributions are paid on those earnings. Similarly, earnings between the LEL and the PT count towards the employee's entitlement to certain benefits including the second state pension (S2P). Employees in contracted-out employment earn no S2P rights and receive a rebate of contributions of 1.4%. This applies from the LEL to the UAP, so earnings from LEL to PT attract a 'negative' contribution of 1.4% and the rate for earnings from PT to UAP becomes 10.6%. Earnings from UAP to UEL are subject to the main not contracted-out rate.

[2] Monthly and annual LEL and UAP figures are calculated as per SI 2001/1004, reg. 11.

[3] Monthly and annual PT and UEL figures are prescribed by SI 2001/1004, reg. 11 and amended by Statutory Instrument.

Class 1 secondary (employer) contributions 2014–15	
Secondary earnings threshold (ST)	£153 weekly £663[2] monthly £7,956[2] yearly
Not contracted-out rate	13.8% on earnings above ST
Contracted-out rate[1]	10.4% for salary related (COSR) on earnings from ST to UAP (plus 3.4% rebate for earnings from LEL to ST), then 13.8% above UAP
Employment allowance	£2,000 (per year, per employer)

National Insurance Contributions

Notes
(1) Although employer contributions do not per se give any benefit entitlements, earnings between the LEL and ST are those classed as relevant for S2P. Employers with contracted-out occupational pension schemes receive a rebate of contributions for scheme members of 3.4% (COSR). This applies from the LEL to the UAP, so earnings from LEL to ST attract a 'negative' contribution and the rate for earnings from ST to UAP is reduced as shown.
(2) Monthly and annual ST figures are prescribed by SI 2001/1004, reg. 11 and amended by Statutory Instrument.

[¶9-030]   Class 1 NIC: 2013–14

(NIC Reporter: ¶305-575ff.)

Class 1 contributions

Class 1 primary (employee) contributions 2013–14	
Lower earnings limit (LEL)	£109 weekly £473(2) monthly £5,668(2) yearly
Primary threshold (PT)	£149 weekly £646 monthly £7,755 yearly
Upper earnings limit (UEL)	£797 weekly £3,454 monthly £41,450 yearly
Upper accruals point (UAP)	£770 weekly £3,337(2) monthly £40,040(2) yearly
Rate on earnings up to PT(1)	0%
Not contracted-out rate	12% on £149.01 to £797 weekly 2% on excess over £797 weekly
Contracted-out rate	10.6% on £149.01 to £770 weekly 12% on £770.01 to £797 weekly 2% on excess over £797 weekly
Reduced rate	5.85% on £149.01 to £797 weekly 2% on excess over £797 (no rebate even if contracted-out)

Notes
(1) Earnings from the LEL, up to and including the PT, count towards the employee's basic state pension, even though no contributions are paid on those earnings. Similarly, earnings between the LEL and the PT count towards the employee's entitlement to certain benefits including the second state pension (S2P). Employees in contracted-out employment earn no S2P rights and receive a rebate of contributions of 1.4%. This applies from the LEL to the UAP, so earnings from LEL to PT attract a 'negative' contribution of 1.4% and the rate for earnings from PT to UAP becomes 10.6%. Earnings from UAP to UEL are subject to the main not contracted-out rate.
(2) Monthly and annual LEL and UAP figures are calculated as per SI 2001/1004, reg. 11.

Class 1 secondary (employer) contributions 2013–14(2)	
Secondary earnings threshold (ST)	£148 weekly £641 monthly £7,696 yearly
Not contracted-out rate	13.8% on earnings above ST

Class 1 secondary (employer) contributions 2013–14[2]	
Contracted-out rate[1]	10.4% for salary related (COSR) on earnings from ST to UAP (plus 3.4% rebate for earnings from LEL to ST), then 13.8% above UAP

Notes

[1] Although employer contributions do not per se give any benefit entitlements, earnings between the LEL and ST are those classed as relevant for S2P. Employers with contracted-out occupational pension schemes receive a rebate of contributions for scheme members of 3.4% (COSR). This applies from the LEL to the UAP, so earnings from LEL to ST attract a 'negative' contribution and the rate for earnings from ST to UAP is reduced as shown.

[2] From 22 June 2010 until 5 September 2013, qualifying businesses will be exempt (when a claim is made and accepted) from the first £5,000 of Class 1 NICs due in respect of the first ten qualifying employees hired in the first year of business (*National Insurance Contributions Act* 2011, s. 4).

[¶9-350]   Class 1A contributions

(SSCBA 1992, s. 10)

(NIC Reporter: ¶310-000ff.)

Employers (but not employees) pay NIC on an annual basis on benefits in kind provided to all employees (other than lower paid ministers of religion), from 2016–17. Prior to 5 April 2016 (since 6 April 2000), NICs were payable only on benefits provided to employees earning at a rate of £8,500 p.a. or more or to directors (SSCBA 1992, s. 10). Contributions for the year are due by 19 July following the end of the tax year to which they relate (22 July for electronic payment). Rates applying are always the full Class 1 secondary (employer) rate for each year, as follows:

Period	%
2011–12 to 2017–18	13.8

For rates of interest on late paid Class 1A contributions, see ¶9-650.

[¶9-400]   Return deadlines for Class 1 and 1A contributions

(NIC Reporter: ¶310-425; ¶340-000ff.)

Forms	Date	Penalty provision
Real time employers (RTI) (see ¶4-930)	Each time a payment is made to an employee	FA 2009, Sch. 55 (see also ¶4-942) (previously TMA 1970, s. 98A)
Non-real time employers End of year returns P14, P35, P38 and P38A	19 May following year of assessment	TMA 1970, s. 98A
All employers P11D(b)	6 July following year of assessment	SI 2001/1004, reg. 81(2)

Note

In cases of PAYE and NIC default, there are provisions to prevent double charging. Class 1A contributions are recorded annually in arrears.

[¶9-450]   Class 1B contributions

(SSCBA 1992, s. 10A)

(NIC Reporter: ¶311-400ff.)

Class 1B contributions are payable by employers on the amount of earnings in a PAYE settlement agreement (PSA) that are chargeable to Class 1 or Class 1A NICs, together with the total amount of income tax payable under the agreement (SSCBA 1992, s. 10A). Class 1B contributions are charged at the same rate as Class 1A contributions (see above) and are payable by 19 October after the end of the tax year to which the PSA applies (22 October for electronic payment).

[¶9-500]   Class 2 contributions

(SSCBA 1992, s. 11)

(NIC Reporter: ¶315-000ff.)

Class 2 contributions are paid at a flat rate by a self-employed and are collected through self-assessment alongside income tax and Class 4 contributions (from 2015–16). Only those with profits at or above the small profits threshold (SPT) are liable to Class 2 NICs. Prior to 2015–16, a person had to pay Class 2 NICs unless he had applied for and been granted exception because his earnings were below the small earnings exception (SEE) limit. Persons with profits below the small profits threshold (or who were previously granted exception for earnings below the SEE limit) can (could) still pay voluntary contributions in order to protect entitlement to contributory benefits.

The Government has announced that Class 2 NICs will be abolished and self-employed contributory benefit entitlement will be accessed through Class 3 and Class 4 NICs. The changes are due to be legislated for in a NIC Bill. In November 2017, HM Treasury issued a written statement to the House of Commons announcing that the NIC Bill will be introduced in 2018 but the measures it will implement, including the abolition of Class 2 NICs, will now take effect from April 2019 (one year later than was originally announced).

Rates and small profits threshold

Tax year	Weekly contribution rate[1]			Small profits threshold[2] £
	Rate £	Share fishermen £	Volunteer development workers £	
2018–19[3]	2.95	3.60	5.80	6,205
2017–18	2.85	3.50	5.65	6,025
2016–17	2.80	3.45	5.60	5,965
2015–16	2.80	3.45	5.60	5,965
2014–15	2.75	3.40	5.55	5,885
2013–14	2.70	3.35	5.45	5,725

Notes
[1] These rates are uprated by CPI.
[2] The 'small profits threshold' replaced the 'small earnings exception' from 6 April 2015. This threshold is uprated by CPI.
[3] Rates per Autumn Budget 2017.

[¶9-550]   Class 3 contributions

(SSCBA 1992, s. 13)

(NIC Reporter: ¶320-000ff.)

Class 3 contributions are paid voluntarily by persons not liable for contributions, or who have been excepted from Class 2 contributions, or whose contribution record is insufficient to qualify for benefits (i.e. Class 3 contributions allow people to fill gaps in their contributions record for basic state pension purposes). They are paid at a flat-rate. Class 3 contributions may not be paid where an individuals earnings factor (earnings on which primary Class 1 or Class 2 contributions have been paid) equals or exceeds the qualifying limit for the year.

Rate and earnings factor

Tax year	Weekly contribution rate[1] £	Earnings factor for each contribution in col. 2 £
2018–19[2]	14.65	116.00
2017–18	14.25	113.00
2016–17	14.10	112.00
2015–16	14.10	112.00
2014–15	13.90	111.00
2013–14	13.55	109.00

Notes
[1] Rate is uprated by CPI.
[2] Rates per Autumn Budget 2017.

[¶9-570]   Class 3A contributions

(SSCBA 1992, s. 14A–14C; PA 2014, Sch. 15, para. 4; SI 2014/3240)

(NIC Reporter: ¶321-500)

From 12 October 2015 until 5 April 2017, existing pensioners and those reaching state pension age before 6 April 2016 had the opportunity to gain additional state pension by paying Class 3A voluntary NICs. There were two conditions:

*   contributors must have had entitlement to a UK state pension; and
*   contributors must have reached state pension age before 6 April 2016.

The measure was in addition to Class 3 voluntary contributions (see above).

The maximum number of units of additional pension that a person could obtain was 25 and each unit equated to £1 per week of additional pension (i.e. a maximum of £25 per week of additional pension could be acquired).

Age at payment date (12 October 2015 to 5 April 2017)	Rate for each additional pension unit of £1 per week £	Age at payment date (12 October 2015 to 5 April 2017)	Rate for each additional pension unit of £1 per week £
62 (women only)	956	82	484
63 (women only)	934	83	454
64 (women only)	913	84	424
65	890	85	394

National Insurance Contributions

Age at payment date (12 October 2015 to 5 April 2017)	Rate for each additional pension unit of £1 per week £	Age at payment date (12 October 2015 to 5 April 2017)	Rate for each additional pension unit of £1 per week £
66	871	86	366
67	847	87	339
68	827	88	314
69	801	89	291
70	779	90	270
71	761	91	251
72	738	92	232
73	719	93	216
74	694	94	200
75	674	95	185
76	646	96	172
77	625	97	159
78	596	98	148
79	574	99	137
80	544	100	127
81	514		

[¶9-600] Class 4 contributions

(SSCBA 1992, s. 15)

(NIC Reporter: ¶317-650ff.)

Self-employed people whose profits or gains are over a certain amount have to pay Class 4 contributions as well as Class 2 contributions. These contributions are earnings-related and paid at a main rate on trading profits (earnings) between the lower and upper annual limits (which are the same as the Class 1 earnings threshold and upper earnings limit), with an additional 2% on profits above the upper limit since 6 April 2011.

Tax year	Rate on profits between upper and lower limits %	Annual lower profits limit[1] £	Annual upper profits limit £	Rate on profits in excess of upper limit %	Maximum contribution £
2018–19[2]	9	8,424	46,350	2	unlimited
2017–18	9	8,164	45,000	2	unlimited
2016–17	9	8,060	43,000	2	unlimited
2015–16	9	8,060	42,385	2	unlimited
2014–15	9	7,956	41,865	2	unlimited
2013–14	9	7,755	41,450	2	unlimited

Notes
[1] This threshold is uprated by CPI.
[2] Rates per Autumn Budget 2017.

[¶9-650] Rates of interest on National Insurance contributions

(SSCBA 1992, Sch. 1, para. 6(2))

(NIC Reporter: ¶341-875ff.)

The same rates of interest apply in relation to overdue and overpaid National Insurance as apply in relation to overdue and overpaid income tax (see ¶1-500).

From 15 September 2016, late payment interest rates and the special repayment rate for debts owed to or by HMRC under a court judgment or order are extended to National Insurance related debts (F(No. 2)A 2015, s. 52) (see ¶1-500).

Interest on **overdue** National Insurance contributions is payable from the due date of payment:

- **Class 1:** from 2014–15, see ¶4-948: interest on certain PAYE paid late (previously 19 April, or 22 April (electronic payments) following end of the tax year in respect of which the NIC was due (SI 2001/1004, Sch. 4, para. 17(3))).

- **Class 1A:** 19 July, or 22 July (where payment is made electronically) following the end of the tax year in respect of which the NIC was due to the date of payment (SI 2004/1004, reg. 76(3)).

- **Class 1B:** 19 October, or 22 October (where payment is made electronically) following the end of the tax year in respect of which the NIC was due to the date of payment (SI 2004/1004, Sch. 4, para. 17(3)).

The qualifying period for repayment interest on **overpaid** National Insurance contributions is as set out below:

- **Class 1:** from 2014–15, see ¶4-948: interest on certain PAYE paid late (previously from 19 April following the end of the tax year in respect of which the NIC was paid to the date on which the order for the repayment is issued. Contributions paid late, i.e. after 19 April, and later repaid carry interest from the actual date of payment (SI 2001/1004, Sch. 4, para. 18(3))).

- **Class 1A:** from 19 April following the end of the tax year in respect of which the NIC was paid, or if the contribution was paid later, from the date of actual payment – usually 19 July in practice – to the date on which the order for the repayment is issued (SI 2001/1004, reg. 77(2)).

- **Class 1B:** from 19 October following the end of the tax year in respect of which the NIC was paid to the date on which the order for the repayment is issued. Contributions paid late, i.e. after 19 October, and later repaid carry interest from the actual date of payment (SI 2001/1004, Sch. 4, para. 18(3)).

National Insurance Contributions

TAX CREDITS

[¶10-000] Working tax credits
(SI 2002/2005)

Maximum rates 2012–13 to 2018–19

Element	2018–19[1][2] £	2017–18[1] £	2016–17[1] £	2015–16 £	2014–15 £	2013–14 £
Basic element	1,960	1,960	1,960	1,960	1,940	1,920
Disabled worker element	3,090	3,000	2,970	2,970	2,935	2,855
Severe disability element	1,330	1,290	1,275	1,275	1,255	1,220
30-hour element	810	810	810	810	800	790
Couple and lone parent element	2,010	2,010	2,010	2,010	1,990	1,970
Childcare element: percentage of eligible costs covered	70%	70%	70%	70%	70%	70%
• maximum eligible cost for one child (per week)	175	175	175	175	175	175
• maximum eligible cost of two or more children (per week)	300	300	300	300	300	300

Notes
[1] Working age benefits, including tax credits and the local housing allowances (but excluding disability benefits which will continue to be indexed by CPI) frozen for four years from 2016–17 to 2019–20 (Summer Budget 2015).
[2] Rates per Autumn Budget 2017.

[¶10-100] Child tax credits
(SI 2002/2007)

Maximum rates 2012–13 to 2018–19

Element	Circumstance	2018–19[1][4] £	2017–18[1] £	2016–17[1] £	2015–16 £	2014–15 £	2013–14 £
Family[3]	Normal case	545	545	545	545	545	545
Individual	Each child or young person[2]	2,780	2,780	2,780	2,780	2,750	2,720
	Each disabled child or young person	6,055	5,955	5,920	5,920	5,850	5,735
	Each severely disabled child or young person	7,380	7,245	7,195	7,195	7,105	6,955

Income thresholds and withdrawal rates 2012–13 to 2018–19

	2018–19[1][4]	2017–18[1]	2016–17[1]	2015–16	2014–15	2013–14
First income threshold	£6,420	£6,420	£6,420	£6,420	£6,420	£6,420
First withdrawal rate	41%	41%	41%	41%	41%	41%
First threshold for those entitled to child tax credit only	£16,105	£16,105	£16,105	£16,105	£16,010	£15,910
Income rise disregard	£2,500	£2,500	£2,500	£5,000	£5,000	£5,000
Income fall disregard	£2,500	£2,500	£2,500	£2,500	£2,500	£2,500

Notes
[1] Working age benefits, including tax credits and the local housing allowances (but excluding disability benefits which will continue to be indexed by CPI) frozen for four years from 2016–17 to 2019–20 (Summer Budget 2015).
[2] Tax credits support to be limited to two children from 6 April 2017 (SI 2002/2007, reg. 7(2)).
[3] Not available to those starting a family after 6 April 2017 (SI 2002/2007, reg. 7(2A)).
[4] Rates per Autumn Budget 2017.

STATE BENEFITS AND STATUTORY PAYMENTS

[¶10-500] Taxable state benefits

(ITEPA 2003, s. 577, 660)

(Tax Reporter: ¶490-000ff.)

The following benefits are liable to income tax.

Rates were most recently updated by SI 2017/349.

Benefit	Weekly rate from				
	April 2017[5] £	April 2016 £	April 2015 £	April 2014 £	April 2013 £
Bereavement					
Bereavement allowance[3]	113.70	112.55	112.55	111.20	108.30
Widowed parent's allowance[4]	113.70	112.55	112.55	111.20	108.30
Carer's allowance	62.70	62.10	62.10	61.35	59.75
Dependent adults					
with retirement pension[1]	66.35	65.70	65.70	64.90	63.20
with carer's allowance[1]	36.90	36.55	36.55	36.10	35.15
with long-term incapacity	61.80	61.20	61.20	60.45	58.85
with short-term incapacity (under pensionable age)	48.15	47.65	47.65	47.10	45.85
with short-term incapacity (over pensionable age)	59.50	58.90	58.90	58.20	56.65
Employment & support allowance					
Age 25+ contributions-based ESA	73.10	73.10	73.10	72.40	71.70
Industrial death benefit: Widow's pension					
Permanent rate:					
higher	122.30	119.30	115.95	113.10	110.15
lower	36.69	35.79	34.79	33.93	33.05
Widower's pension	122.30	119.30	115.95	113.10	110.15
Incapacity benefit (long-term)					
Rate	106.40	105.35	105.35	104.10	101.35
Increase for age:					
higher rate	11.25	11.15	11.15	11.00	10.70
lower rate	6.25	6.20	6.20	6.15	6.00
Jobseeker's allowance See ¶10-600.					

	Weekly rate from				
Benefit	**April 2017**[5] **£**	**April 2016 £**	**April 2015 £**	**April 2014 £**	**April 2013 £**
Incapacity benefit (short-term)					
Higher rate:					
under pensionable age[2]	95.00	94.05	94.05	92.95	90.50
over pensionable age[2]	106.40	105.35	105.35	104.10	101.35
Non-contributory retirement pension					
Standard rate[6]	73.30	71.50	69.50	67.80	66.00
Age addition (at age 80)	0.25	0.25	0.25	0.25	0.25
Retirement pension					
Standard rate	122.30	119.30	115.95	113.10	110.15
Age addition (at age 80)	0.25	0.25	0.25	0.25	0.25
SSP, SMP, SPP and SAP See ¶10-650ff.					
New state pension	159.55	155.65	—	—	—
Widow's pension[3]	113.70	112.55	112.55	111.20	108.30
Widowed mother's allowance[4]	113.70	112.55	112.55	111.20	108.30

Notes

[1] No new claims for adult dependency increases payable with the state retirement pension or the carer's allowance may be made on or after 6 April 2010. Adult dependency increases already in payment immediately before 6 April 2010 will be phased out between 2010 and 2020.

[2] A man born before 6 December 1953 still attains pensionable age at age 65, whilst a woman born before 6 April 1950 attained pensionable age at age 60. The date the pensionable age is attained by individuals born after those dates is set out in the tables at ¶3-175.

[3] Bereavement allowance replaced widow's pension from 9 April 2001 for all new claims by widows and widowers.

[4] Widowed parent's allowance replaced widowed mother's allowance from 9 April 2001 for all new claims.

[5] Working age benefits, including tax credits and the local housing allowances (but excluding SMA, SMP, SPP, SSP and disability benefits which will continue to be indexed by CPI) frozen for four years from 2016–17 to 2019–20 (Summer Budget 2015).

From April 2011, the consumer price index is used for the indexation of benefits.

[¶10-550] Non-taxable state benefits

(ITEPA 2003, s. 677(1): see also EIM76100)

(Tax Reporter: ¶490-000ff.)

The following UK social security benefits are wholly exempt from tax, except where indicated otherwise.

- Attendance allowance
- Back to work bonus (see EIM76223)
- Bereavement payment (see EIM76171)
- Child benefit
- Child's special allowance
- Child tax credit
- Constant attendance allowance: see industrial disablement benefit
- Council tax benefit

- Disability living allowance
- Income related employment and support allowance (see EIM76186)
- Exceptionally severe disablement allowance: see industrial disablement benefit
- Guardian's allowance
- Housing benefit
- Incapacity benefit for first 28 weeks of entitlement, taxable thereafter (see EIM76180)
- Income support, certain payments (see EIM76190)
- Industrial injuries benefit, a general term covering industrial injuries pension, reduced earnings allowance, retirement allowance, constant attendance allowance and exceptionally severe disablement allowance
- Invalidity benefit, replaced by incapacity benefit from April 1995 but still payable where invalidity commenced before April 1995
- In-work credit, In-work emergency discretion fund payment, In-work emergency fund payment
- Maternity allowance (see EIM76361)
- Pensioner's Christmas bonus
- Personal independence payment
- State pension credit
- Reduced earnings allowance: see industrial disablement benefit
- Retirement allowance: see industrial injuries benefit
- Return to work credit and self-employment credit
- Severe disablement allowance
- Social fund payments – help with maternity expenses, funeral costs, financial crisis, community care grants and interest free loans.
- Universal credit
- War widow's pension (see EIM76103)
- Winter fuel payment (or 'cold weather payment')
- Working tax credit

With regard to wounds and disability pensions for service with the forces see EIM74302 and for allowances payable to civilians in respect of war injuries see EIM74700.

Certain foreign social security payments are exempt from UK tax (see EIM76009).

The new bereavement support payment, which replaces three current benefits paid in respect of bereavement from April 2017 (*Pensions Act* 2014) will be exempt from income tax.

Benefit rates

	Weekly rate from				
Benefit	**April 2017**[5] **£**	**April 2016 £**	**April 2015 £**	**April 2014 £**	**April 2013 £**
Attendance allowance					
Higher rate	83.10	82.30	82.30	81.30	79.15
Lower rate	55.65	55.10	55.10	54.45	53.00
Child benefit[1][6]					
For the eldest qualifying child	20.70	20.70	20.70	20.50	20.30
For each other child	13.70	13.70	13.70	13.55	13.40

Benefit	Weekly rate from				
	April 2017[5] £	April 2016 £	April 2015 £	April 2014 £	April 2013 £
Guardian's allowance[6]	16.70	16.55	16.55	16.35	15.90
Child dependency addition					
Payable with: state pension; widowed mothers/parents allowance; short-term incapacity benefit – higher rate or over state pension age; long-term incapacity benefit; carer's allowance; severe disablement unemployability supplement.	11.35	11.35	11.35	11.35	11.35
Reduced rate[2]	8.00	8.00	8.00	8.05	8.10
Constant attendance allowance					
Exceptional rate	135.80	134.40	134.40	132.80	129.40
Intermediate rate	101.85	100.80	100.80	99.60	97.05
Normal maximum rate	67.90	67.20	67.20	66.40	64.70
Part-time rate	33.95	33.60	33.60	33.20	32.35
Exceptionally severe disablement allowance	67.90	67.20	67.20	66.40	64.70
Employment & support allowance – income-related based (ESA(IR))					
Involves over 30 potential components					
Maternity allowances (where SMP not available)					
Standard rate	140.98	139.58	139.58	138.18	136.78
MA threshold	30.00	30.00	30.00	30.00	30.00
Disability living allowance (care component)[5]					
Higher rate	83.10	82.30	82.30	81.30	79.15
Middle rate	55.65	55.10	55.10	54.45	53.00
Lower rate	22.00	21.80	21.80	21.55	21.00

Benefit	Weekly rate from				
	April 2017[5] £	April 2016 £	April 2015 £	April 2014 £	April 2013 £
Disability living allowance (mobility component)[5]					
Higher rate	58.00	57.45	57.45	56.75	55.25
Lower rate	22.00	21.80	21.80	21.55	21.00
Incapacity benefit (short-term)[3]					
Lower rate:					
under pensionable age[4]	80.25	79.45	79.45	78.50	76.45
over pensionable age[4]	102.10	101.10	101.10	99.90	97.25
Severe disablement allowance					
Basic rate	75.40	74.65	74.65	73.75	71.80
Age addition (from Dec 1990)					
• Higher rate	11.25	11.15	11.15	11.00	10.70
• Middle rate	6.25	6.20	6.20	6.15	6.00
• Lower rate	6.25	6.20	6.20	6.15	6.00
Adult dependency increase	37.10	36.75	36.75	36.30	35.35
Pensions credit					
Standard					
Single	159.35	155.60	151.20	148.35	145.40
Couple	243.25	237.55	230.85	226.50	222.05
Additional amount for severe disability					
Single	62.45	61.85	61.85	61.10	59.50
Couple (one qualifies)	62.45	61.85	61.85	61.10	59.50
Couple (both qualify)	124.90	123.70	123.70	122.20	119.00
Additional amount for carers	34.95	34.60	34.60	34.20	33.30
Savings credit					
Threshold – single	137.35	133.82	126.50	120.35	115.30
Threshold – couple	218.42	212.97	201.80	192.00	183.90
Maximum award – single	13.20	13.07	14.82	16.80	18.06
Maximum award – couple	14.90	14.75	17.43	20.70	22.89

State Benefits and Statutory Payments

Benefit	Weekly rate from				
	April 2017[5] £	April 2016 £	April 2015 £	April 2014 £	April 2013 £
Polygamous marriage amounts					
Claimant and first spouse	243.25	237.55	230.85	226.50	222.05
Additional amount for additional spouse	83.90	81.95	79.65	78.15	76.65
Personal independence payment					
Daily living component					
Standard rate	55.65	55.10	55.10	54.45	53.00
Enhanced rate	83.10	82.30	82.30	81.30	79.15
Mobility component					
Standard rate	22.00	21.80	21.80	21.55	21.00
Enhanced rate	58.00	57.45	57.45	56.75	55.25

Notes
(1) High income child benefit charge applies from 7 January 2013 (see ¶1-110).
(2) The rate of child dependency increase is adjusted where it is payable for the eldest child for whom child benefit is also paid. The weekly rate in such cases is reduced by the difference between ChB rates for the eldest and subsequent children.
(3) Incapacity benefit and contributory employment & support allowance (ESA(C)) are taxable, under the *Income Tax (Earnings and Pensions) Act* 2003, Pt. 10, Ch. 3, except for short-term benefit payable at the lower rate. It is not taxable, however, if the recipient started receiving invalidity benefit or sickness benefit before 6 April 1995 and has continued receiving long-term incapacity benefit since then.
(4) See ¶3-175 for pensionable age tables.
(5) Working age benefits, including tax credits and the local housing allowances (but excluding SMA, SMP, SPP, SSP and disability benefits which will continue to be indexed by CPI) frozen for four years from 2016–17 to 2019–20 (Summer Budget 2015).
(6) Rates announced for 2018–19 at Autumn Budget 2017: Child benefit as per 2017–18 rates; Guardian's allowance £17.20.

From April 2011, the consumer price index is used for the indexation of benefits.

[¶10-560] Childcare accounts
(CPA 2014; SI 2015/448; SI 2015/522)

(Tax Reporter: ¶434-500)

The *Childcare Payments Act* 2014 introduces a new scheme which provides financial support to help working families with the cost of childcare. Once the scheme is implemented, the Government will make a top-up payment of £2 for every £8 which a person pays towards childcare. Government support will be capped at a maximum of £4,000 in the case of a disabled child and £2,000 in the case of any other child, per year, although there will be no restriction on the number of children for whom support is available. The scheme will be managed by HMRC and rolled out in 2017 following a trial which will run for six months from 14 November 2016 to 15 May 2017 (SI 2016/1083).

A person will be eligible to receive government support (referred to as a 'top-up payment') if they meet the eligibility conditions; provide information to demonstrate their eligibility in a declaration to HMRC, and HMRC agree, based on that information, that they are eligible; have a child who qualifies for support (broadly, a child under the age of 12 years old, or if disabled, 17 years old); have opened a childcare account in accordance with the scheme; and they, or another person, pay money into the childcare account.

Existing tax and NIC reliefs (see ¶4-815) will be withdrawn from employees and employers where the employee enters a childcare voucher or directly contracted childcare scheme after the new scheme has come into force, however, as part of the transition to tax-free childcare, employer-supported childcare will remain open to new entrants until April 2018 (Budget 2016).

A top-up payment made into a childcare account is not to be regarded as income of the account holder for the purposes of the Income Tax Acts (CPA 2014, s. 66).

[¶10-600]   Income support and jobseeker's allowance
(Tax Reporter: ¶490-250)

	Weekly rate from				
Benefit: Income support	April 2017(1) £	April 2016 £	April 2015 £	April 2014 £	April 2013 £
Single					
Under 25	57.90	57.90	57.90	57.35	56.80
25 or over	73.10	73.10	73.10	72.40	71.70
Lone parent					
Under 18	57.90	57.90	57.90	57.35	56.80
18 or over	73.10	73.10	73.10	72.40	71.70
Couple					
Both under 18	57.90	57.90	57.90	57.35	56.80
Both under 18 – higher rate	87.50	87.50	87.50	86.65	85.80
One under 18, one under 25	57.90	57.90	57.90	57.35	56.80
One under 18, one 25 and over	73.10	73.10	73.10	72.40	71.70
Both 18 or over	114.85	114.85	114.85	113.70	112.55
Dependent children	66.90	66.90	66.90	66.33	65.62

State Benefits and Statutory Payments

Benefit: Jobseeker's allowance	Weekly rate from				
	April 2017[(1)] £	April 2016 £	April 2015 £	April 2014 £	April 2013 £
Contributions based JSA – personal rates					
under 25	57.90	57.90	57.90	57.35	56.80
25 or over	73.10	73.10	73.10	72.40	71.70
Income based JSA – personal allowances					
under 25	57.90	57.90	57.90	57.35	56.80
25 or over	73.10	73.10	73.10	72.40	71.70
Lone parent					
Under 18	57.90	57.90	57.90	57.35	56.80
18 or over	73.10	73.10	73.10	72.40	71.70
Couple					
Both under 18	57.90	57.90	57.90	57.35	56.80
Both under 18 – higher rate	87.50	87.50	87.50	86.65	85.80
One under 18, one under 25	57.90	57.90	57.90	57.35	56.80
One under 18, one 25 and over	73.10	73.10	73.10	72.40	71.70
Both 18 or over	114.85	114.85	114.85	113.70	112.55
Dependent children	66.90	66.90	66.90	66.33	65.62

Premium: Income support and Jobseeker's allowance	Weekly rate from				
	April 2017[(1)] £	April 2016 £	April 2015 £	April 2014 £	April 2013 £
Family/lone parent	17.45	17.45	17.45	17.45	17.40
Pensioner					
Single (JSA only)	86.25	82.50	78.10	75.95	73.70
Couple	128.40	122.70	116.00	112.80	109.50
Disability					
Single	32.55	32.25	32.25	31.85	31.00
Couple	46.40	45.95	45.95	45.40	44.20
Enhanced disability					
Single	15.90	15.75	15.75	15.55	15.15
Disabled child	24.78	24.43	24.43	24.08	23.45
Couple	22.85	22.60	22.60	22.35	21.75
Severe disability					
Single	62.45	61.85	61.85	61.10	59.50
couple (lower rate)	62.45	61.85	61.85	61.10	59.50
couple (higher rate)	124.90	123.70	123.70	122.20	119.00
Disabled child	60.90	60.06	60.06	59.50	57.89
Carer	34.95	34.60	34.60	34.20	33.30

Note
(1) Working age benefits, including tax credits and the local housing allowances (but excluding SMA, SMP, SPP, SSP and disability benefits which will continue to be indexed by CPI) frozen for four years from 2016–17 to 2019–20 (Summer Budget 2015).

From April 2011, the consumer price index is used for the indexation of benefits.

[¶10-625]   Benefits cap
(SI 2006/213, reg. 75CA; SI 2013/376, reg. 80A)

The benefits cap limits the total amount of benefit that working age people can receive.

Benefit capped	Limits from		
	7 Nov. 2016		15 Apr. 2013
Housing benefit	Annual £	Weekly(1) £	Weekly £
Single claimants			
Greater London	15,410	296.35	350.00
Outside Greater London	13,400	257.69	350.00
Couples and lone parents			
Greater London	23,000	442.31	500.00
Outside Greater London	20,000	384.62	500.00
Universal credit	Annual £	Monthly(2) £	Monthly £
Single claimants with no dependent children			
Greater London	15,410	1,284.17	1,517
Outside Greater London	13,400	1,116.67	1,517
Joint claimants and single claimants with children			
Greater London	23,000	1,916.67	2,167
Outside Greater London	20,000	1,666.67	2,167

Notes
(1) Rates expressed as annual limits with weekly amount calculated as annual limit divide by 52, rounding up or down to the nearest whole penny (SI 2006/213, reg. 75CA).
(2) Rates expressed as annual rates with monthly equivalent calculated as annual rates divide by 12 (SI 2013/376, reg. 80A(1)).

Benefits to which cap is applicable
The cap will apply to household income from the following:
- Bereavement Allowance
- Child Benefit
- Child Tax Credit
- Employment and Support Allowance (except where paid with support component)
- Housing Benefit
- Incapacity Benefit
- Income Support
- Jobseeker's Allowance
- Maternity Allowance
- Severe Disablement Allowance

- Widowed Parent's Allowance (or widowed mother's allowance or widow's pension)
- Universal credit

Note
Carer's allowance and Guardian's allowance added to list of excluded benefits from 7 November 2016 (SI 2013/376, reg. 83).

Households not affected by the cap

A partner or any dependant child qualifies for Working Tax Credit, or in receipt of any of the following:

- Armed Forces Compensation Scheme
- Armed Forces Independence Payment
- Attendence Allowance
- Carer's Allowance
- Disability Living Allowance
- Employment and Support Allowance
- Guardian's Allowance
- Industrial Injuries Benefit
- Personal Independence Payment
- Universal Credit (payments towards carer's costs or for 'limited capability for work and work-related activity')
- War pensions
- War Widow's or Widower's pension

[¶10-650]   Statutory sick pay (SSP)

Employers are liable to pay SSP in any period of incapacity for work to a maximum of 28 weeks at the SSP rate in force. Statutory sick pay is treated as wages and is subject to PAYE income tax and to National Insurance contributions. Statutory sick pay is not payable for certain periods in which statutory maternity pay is being paid.

The amount of SSP payable to an employee depends on the earnings band into which he or she falls. The earnings bands and the associated SSP payments are as follows:

Period (from)	Average gross weekly earnings £	Weekly SSP rate[1] £
6 April 2017	113.00 or more	89.35
6 April 2016	112.00 or more	88.45
6 April 2015	112.00 or more	88.45
6 April 2014	111.00 or more	87.55
6 April 2013	109.00 or more	86.70

Notes
[1] The daily rate of SSP is ascertained by dividing the weekly rate by the number of qualifying days in the week (beginning on Sunday), then multiplying by the number of qualifying days of incapacity in the week, rounded up to the nearest penny.

From April 2011, the consumer price index is used for the indexation of benefits.

Maximum entitlement

An employee reaches his maximum entitlement to SSP in one spell of incapacity when he has been paid 28 times the appropriate rate, i.e. £89.35 × 28 = £2,501.80.

[¶10-700]   Statutory maternity pay (SMP)

Women expecting a baby who satisfy the qualifying conditions are entitled to a maximum of 39 weeks' SMP. These include having 'average weekly earnings' of:

- £113 if their baby is due between 16 July 2017 and 14 July 2018;
- £112 if their baby is due between 19 July 2015 and 15 July 2017.

In other words, 'average weekly earnings' must reach or exceed the then current NIC LEL in the eight weeks leading up to the 15th week before the expected week of childbirth (or placement of an adopted child).

Period (from)	First six weeks	Remaining weeks
6 April 2017	90% average weekly earnings	Lower of 90% average weekly earnings and £140.98
6 April 2016	90% average weekly earnings	Lower of 90% average weekly earnings and £139.58
6 April 2015	90% average weekly earnings	Lower of 90% average weekly earnings and £139.58
6 April 2014	90% average weekly earnings	Lower of 90% average weekly earnings and £138.18
6 April 2013	90% average weekly earnings	Lower of 90% of weekly earnings and £136.78

Note
From April 2011, the consumer price index is used for the indexation of benefits.

[¶10-725]   Statutory shared parental pay (ShPP)

Shared parental leave (SPL) and statutory shared parental pay (ShPP) is available in respect of:

- children with an expected week of birth ending on or after 5 April 2015;
- children placed for adoption on or after 5 April 2015.

SPL is available where both parents are eligible and one partner ends maternity or adoption leave or pay (or maternity allowance) early. The remaining leave will be available as SPL. The remaining weeks of pay will be available as ShPP.

State Benefits and Statutory Payments

The mother must take a minimum of two weeks' maternity leave following the birth (four if she works in a factory). Thereafter:

• the rest of the 52 weeks of leave (up to a maximum of 50 weeks) can be taken as SPL;

• the rest of the 39 weeks of pay or maternity allowance (up to a maximum of 37 weeks) can be taken as ShPP.

ShPP is paid at the rate of £140.98 (2017–18) a week or 90% of average weekly earnings, whichever is lower. This is the same as statutory maternity pay (see ¶10-700) except that during the first six weeks, SMP is paid at 90% of earnings (with no maximum).

[¶10-800]   Statutory adoption pay (SAP)

SAP was introduced in April 2003.

Employees who are adopting a child and are notified that they have been matched with a child or received official notification that they are eligible to adopt a child from abroad who satisfy the qualifying conditions are entitled to a maximum of 39 weeks' SAP. These include having average weekly earnings of:

Eligible to adopt on or after	Average weekly earnings
2 April 2017	£113.00
5 April 2015	£112.00
6 April 2014	£111.00
31 March 2013	£109.00

The weekly rate of statutory adoption pay is the same as the standard rate of statutory maternity pay (see ¶10-700). The adoptive parents are treated in effect as if they have had a baby and qualified for SMP.

[¶10-900]   Universal credit

(SI 2013/376)
(Tax Reporter: ¶490-670)

Universal credit is a new benefit that has started to replace six existing benefits with a single monthly payment. Universal credit will eventually replace all of the following tax credits and benefits:

• tax credits – both child tax credit and working tax credit;

• income-based Jobseeker's Allowance;

• income-related employment and support allowance;

• income support; and

• housing benefit.

Universal credit will not replace child benefit.

Universal credit started to be introduced in stages from April 2013. Existing claimants of the above benefits will be moved to universal credit during 2016 and 2017. Universal credit is exempt from income tax.

Universal credit	Per month				
	2017[1] £	2016 £	2015 £	2014 £	2013 £
Universal credit amounts					
Standard allowance					
– single under 25	251.77	251.77	251.77	249.28	246.81
– single over 25	317.82	317.82	317.82	314.67	311.55
– joint claimants, both under 25	395.20	395.20	395.20	391.29	387.42
– joint claimants, one or both 25 or over	498.89	498.89	498.89	493.95	489.06
Child element					
– first child[2]	277.08	277.08	277.08	274.58	272.08
– second/subsequent child[2]	231.67	231.67	231.67	229.17	226.67
Disabled child additions					
– lower rate	126.11	126.11	126.11	124.86	123.62
– higher rate	372.30	367.92	367.92	362.92	352.92
LCW and WRA elements					
– limited capability for work	126.11	126.11	126.11	124.86	123.62
– limited capability for work and work related activity	318.76	315.60	315.60	311.86	303.66
Carer element	151.89	150.39	150.39	148.61	144.70
Childcare costs element					
– max for one child	646.35	646.35	532.29	532.29	532.29
– max for two or more children	1,108.04	1,108.04	912.50	912.50	912.50
Non-dependants' housing cost contributions	70.06	69.37	69.37	68.68	68.00
Work allowances					
Higher work allowance (no housing element)					
– single claimant, no dependent children	Nil	Nil	111.00	111.00	111.00
– single claimant, one or more children	397.00	397.00	734.00	734.00	734.00
– single claimant, limited capability for work	397.00	397.00	647.00	647.00	647.00
– joint claimant, no dependent children	Nil	Nil	111.00	111.00	111.00
– joint claimant, one or more children	397.00	397.00	536.00	536.00	536.00
– joint claimant, limited capability for work	397.00	397.00	647.00	647.00	647.00

State Benefits and Statutory Payments

Universal credit	Per month				
	2017[1] £	2016 £	2015 £	2014 £	2013 £
Lower work allowance					
– single claimant, no dependent children	Nil	Nil	111.00	111.00	111.00
– single claimant, one or more children	192.00	192.00	263.00	263.00	263.00
– single claimant, limited capability for work	192.00	192.00	192.00	192.00	192.00
– joint claimant, no dependent children	Nil	Nil	111.00	111.00	111.00
– joint claimant, one or more children	192.00	192.00	222.00	222.00	222.00
– joint claimant, limited capability for work	192.00	192.00	192.00	192.00	192.00
Assumed income from capital (for every £250 or part thereof)	4.35	4.35	4.35	4.35	4.35

Notes

[1] Working age benefits (but excluding disability benefits which will continue to be indexed by CPI) frozen for four years from 2016–17 to 2019–20 (Summer Budget 2015).

[2] New claims from April 2017 limited to two children and first child premium also withdrawn for new claims from April 2017 (*Welfare Reform and Work Act* 2016, s. 13).

GENERAL

Retail prices index

[¶11-000]   Retail prices index: general

The retail prices index (RPI), issued by the Office for National Statistics, is used to calculate the indexation allowance for the purposes of calculating capital gains on corporation tax.

Indexation allowance will be frozen for corporate disposals on or after 1 January 2018 at the amount due based on the RPI for December 2017, by legislation in Finance Bill 2017–18 (Autumn Budget 2017). Indexation allowance ceased to be available to individuals from April 1998.

With effect from February 1987, the reference date to which the price level in each subsequent month is related was changed from 'January 1974 = 100' to 'January 1987 = 100'.

Movements in the RPI in the months after January 1987 are calculated with reference to January 1987 = 100. (With a base of January 1974 = 100, January 1987's RPI was 394.5). A new formula was provided by the then Department of Employment for calculating movements in the index over periods which span January 1987:

> 'The index for the later month (January 1987 = 100) is multiplied by the index for January 1987 (January 1974 = 100) and divided by the index for the earlier month (January 1974 = 100). 100 is subtracted to give the percentage change between the two months.'

The following table has been prepared in accordance with this formula:

	1982	1983	1984	1985	1986	1987	1988	1989	1990	1991
Jan.		82.61	86.84	91.20	96.25	100.0	103.3	111.0	119.5	130.2
Feb.		82.97	87.20	91.94	96.60	100.4	103.7	111.8	120.2	130.9
March	79.44	83.12	87.48	92.80	96.73	100.6	104.1	112.3	121.4	131.4
April	81.04	84.28	88.64	94.78	97.67	101.8	105.8	114.3	125.1	133.1
May	81.62	84.64	88.97	95.21	97.85	101.9	106.2	115.0	126.2	133.5
June	81.85	84.84	89.20	95.41	97.79	101.9	106.6	115.4	126.7	134.1
July	81.88	85.30	89.10	95.23	97.52	101.8	106.7	115.5	126.8	133.8
Aug.	81.90	85.68	89.94	95.49	97.82	102.1	107.9	115.8	128.1	134.1
Sept.	81.85	86.06	90.11	95.44	98.30	102.4	108.4	116.6	129.3	134.6
Oct.	82.26	86.36	90.67	95.59	98.45	102.9	109.5	117.5	130.3	135.1
Nov.	82.66	86.67	90.95	95.92	99.29	103.4	110.0	118.5	130.0	135.6
Dec.	82.51	86.89	90.87	96.05	99.62	103.3	110.3	118.8	129.9	135.7

	1992	1993	1994	1995	1996	1997	1998	1999	2000	2001
Jan.	135.6	137.9	141.3	146.0	150.2	154.4	159.5	163.4	166.6	171.1
Feb.	136.3	138.8	142.1	146.9	150.9	155.0	160.3	163.7	167.5	172.0
March	136.7	139.3	142.5	147.5	151.5	155.4	160.8	164.1	168.4	172.2
April	138.8	140.6	144.2	149.0	152.6	156.3	162.6	165.2	170.1	173.1
May	139.3	141.1	144.7	149.6	152.9	156.9	163.5	165.6	170.7	174.2
June	139.3	141.0	144.7	149.8	153.0	157.5	163.4	165.6	171.1	174.4
July	138.8	140.7	144.0	149.1	152.4	157.5	163.0	165.1	170.5	173.3

	1992	1993	1994	1995	1996	1997	1998	1999	2000	2001
Aug.	138.9	141.3	144.7	149.9	153.1	158.5	163.7	165.5	170.5	174.0
Sept.	139.4	141.9	145.0	150.6	153.8	159.3	164.4	166.2	171.7	174.6
Oct.	139.9	141.8	145.2	149.8	153.8	159.5	164.5	166.5	171.6	174.3
Nov.	139.7	141.6	145.3	149.8	153.9	159.6	164.4	166.7	172.1	173.6
Dec.	139.2	141.9	146.0	150.7	154.4	160.0	164.4	167.3	172.2	173.4

	2002	2003	2004	2005	2006	2007	2008	2009	2010	2011
Jan.	173.3	178.4	183.1	188.9	193.4	201.6	209.8	210.1	217.9	229.0
Feb.	173.8	179.3	183.8	189.6	194.2	203.1	211.4	211.4	219.2	231.3
March	174.5	179.9	184.6	190.5	195.0	204.4	212.1	211.3	220.7	232.5
April	175.7	181.2	185.7	191.6	196.5	205.4	214.0	211.5	222.8	234.4
May	176.2	181.5	186.5	192.0	197.7	206.2	215.1	212.8	223.6	235.2
June	176.2	181.3	186.8	192.2	198.5	207.3	216.8	213.4	224.1	235.2
July	175.9	181.3	186.8	192.2	198.5	206.1	216.5	213.4	223.6	234.7
Aug.	176.4	181.6	187.4	192.6	199.2	207.3	217.2	214.4	224.5	236.1
Sept.	177.6	182.5	188.1	193.1	200.1	208.0	218.4	215.3	225.3	237.9
Oct.	177.9	182.6	188.6	193.3	200.4	208.9	217.7	216.0	225.8	238.0
Nov.	178.2	182.7	189.0	193.6	201.1	209.7	216.0	216.6	226.8	238.5
Dec.	178.5	183.5	189.9	194.1	202.7	210.9	212.9	218.0	228.4	239.4

	2012	2013	2014	2015	2016	2017	2018	2019	2020	2021
Jan.	238.0	245.8	252.6	255.4	258.8	265.5				
Feb.	239.9	247.6	254.2	256.7	260.0	268.4				
March	240.8	248.7	254.8	257.1	261.1	269.3				
April	242.5	249.5	255.7	258.0	261.4	270.6				
May	242.4	250.0	255.9	258.5	262.1	271.7				
June	241.8	249.7	255.9	258.9	263.1	272.3				
July	242.1	249.7	256.0	258.6	263.4	272.9				
Aug.	243.0	251.0	257.0	259.8	264.4	274.7				
Sept.	244.2	251.9	257.6	259.6	264.9	275.1				
Oct.	245.6	251.9	257.7	259.5	264.8					
Nov.	245.6	252.1	257.1	259.8	265.5					
Dec.	246.8	253.4	257.5	260.6	267.1					

[¶11-350]   RPI: January 2017 to September 2017

Tables follow showing the indexed rise to be used for disposals between January 2017 and September 2017. The amount of indexation allowances is restricted where the indexation allowance gives rise to a loss.

RD Month (January 2017 to September 2017) January 1987 = 100

RI Month		Jan	Feb	Mar	Apr	May	Jun	Jul	Aug	Sept
						2017				
1982	Mar.	2.342	2.379	2.390	2.406	2.420	2.428	2.435	2.433	2.463
	April	2.276	2.312	2.323	2.339	2.353	2.360	2.368	2.365	2.395
	May	2.253	2.288	2.299	2.315	2.329	2.336	2.343	2.341	2.370
	June	2.244	2.279	2.290	2.306	2.319	2.327	2.334	2.332	2.361
	July	2.243	2.278	2.289	2.305	2.318	2.326	2.333	2.331	2.360
	Aug.	2.242	2.277	2.288	2.304	2.317	2.325	2.332	2.330	2.359
	Sept.	2.244	2.279	2.290	2.306	2.319	2.327	2.334	2.332	2.361
	Oct.	2.228	2.263	2.274	2.290	2.303	2.310	2.318	2.315	2.344
	Nov.	2.212	2.247	2.258	2.274	2.287	2.294	2.301	2.299	2.328
	Dec.	2.218	2.253	2.264	2.280	2.293	2.300	2.307	2.305	2.334
1983	Jan.	2.214	2.249	2.260	2.276	2.289	2.296	2.303	2.301	2.330
	Feb.	2.200	2.235	2.246	2.262	2.275	2.282	2.289	2.287	2.316
	Mar.	2.194	2.229	2.240	2.256	2.269	2.276	2.283	2.281	2.310
	April	2.150	2.184	2.195	2.211	2.224	2.231	2.238	2.235	2.264
	May	2.137	2.171	2.182	2.197	2.210	2.217	2.224	2.222	2.250
	June	2.129	2.164	2.174	2.189	2.202	2.210	2.217	2.214	2.243
	July	2.113	2.147	2.157	2.172	2.185	2.192	2.199	2.197	2.225
	Aug.	2.099	2.133	2.143	2.158	2.171	2.178	2.185	2.183	2.211
	Sept.	2.085	2.119	2.129	2.144	2.157	2.164	2.171	2.169	2.197
	Oct.	2.074	2.108	2.118	2.133	2.146	2.153	2.160	2.158	2.185
	Nov.	2.063	2.097	2.107	2.122	2.135	2.142	2.149	2.147	2.174
	Dec.	2.055	2.089	2.099	2.114	2.127	2.134	2.141	2.138	2.166
1984	Jan.	2.057	2.091	2.101	2.116	2.129	2.136	2.142	2.140	2.168
	Feb.	2.045	2.078	2.088	2.103	2.116	2.123	2.130	2.127	2.155
	Mar.	2.035	2.068	2.078	2.093	2.106	2.113	2.120	2.117	2.145
	April	1.995	2.028	2.038	2.053	2.065	2.072	2.079	2.076	2.103
	May	1.984	2.017	2.027	2.041	2.054	2.060	2.067	2.065	2.092
	June	1.976	2.009	2.019	2.034	2.046	2.053	2.059	2.057	2.084

General

RI Month		2017								
		Jan	Feb	Mar	Apr	May	Jun	Jul	Aug	Sept
	July	1.980	2.012	2.022	2.037	2.049	2.056	2.063	2.061	2.088
	Aug.	1.952	1.984	1.994	2.009	2.021	2.028	2.034	2.032	2.059
	Sept.	1.946	1.978	1.988	2.003	2.015	2.022	2.028	2.026	2.053
	Oct.	1.928	1.960	1.970	1.984	1.997	2.003	2.010	2.008	2.034
	Nov.	1.919	1.951	1.961	1.975	1.987	1.994	2.001	1.998	2.025
	Dec.	1.922	1.954	1.963	1.978	1.990	1.996	2.003	2.001	2.027
1985	Jan.	1.911	1.943	1.953	1.967	1.979	1.986	1.992	1.990	2.016
	Feb.	1.888	1.919	1.929	1.943	1.955	1.962	1.968	1.966	1.992
	Mar.	1.861	1.892	1.902	1.916	1.928	1.934	1.941	1.939	1.964
	April	1.801	1.832	1.841	1.855	1.867	1.873	1.879	1.877	1.903
	May	1.789	1.819	1.829	1.842	1.854	1.860	1.866	1.864	1.889
	June	1.783	1.813	1.822	1.836	1.848	1.854	1.860	1.858	1.883
	July	1.788	1.818	1.828	1.841	1.853	1.859	1.866	1.863	1.889
	Aug.	1.780	1.811	1.820	1.834	1.845	1.852	1.858	1.856	1.881
	Sept.	1.782	1.812	1.822	1.835	1.847	1.853	1.859	1.857	1.883
	Oct.	1.778	1.808	1.817	1.831	1.842	1.849	1.855	1.853	1.878
	Nov.	1.768	1.798	1.808	1.821	1.833	1.839	1.845	1.843	1.868
	Dec.	1.764	1.795	1.804	1.817	1.829	1.835	1.841	1.839	1.864
1986	Jan.	1.758	1.789	1.798	1.811	1.823	1.829	1.835	1.833	1.858
	Feb.	1.748	1.778	1.788	1.801	1.813	1.819	1.825	1.823	1.848
	Mar.	1.745	1.775	1.784	1.797	1.809	1.815	1.821	1.819	1.844
	April	1.718	1.748	1.757	1.771	1.782	1.788	1.794	1.792	1.817
	May	1.713	1.743	1.752	1.766	1.777	1.783	1.789	1.787	1.812
	June	1.715	1.745	1.754	1.767	1.778	1.784	1.791	1.788	1.813
	July	1.723	1.752	1.762	1.775	1.786	1.792	1.799	1.796	1.821
	Aug.	1.714	1.744	1.753	1.766	1.778	1.784	1.790	1.788	1.812
	Sept.	1.701	1.730	1.740	1.753	1.764	1.770	1.776	1.774	1.799
	Oct.	1.697	1.726	1.735	1.748	1.760	1.766	1.772	1.770	1.794
	Nov.	1.674	1.703	1.712	1.725	1.736	1.742	1.749	1.746	1.771
	Dec.	1.665	1.694	1.703	1.716	1.727	1.733	1.739	1.737	1.762
1987	Jan.	1.655	1.684	1.693	1.706	1.717	1.723	1.729	1.727	1.751
	Feb.	1.644	1.673	1.682	1.695	1.706	1.712	1.718	1.716	1.740
	Mar.	1.639	1.668	1.677	1.690	1.701	1.707	1.713	1.711	1.735

RI Month		2017								
		Jan	Feb	Mar	Apr	May	Jun	Jul	Aug	Sept
	April	1.608	1.637	1.645	1.658	1.669	1.675	1.681	1.679	1.702
	May	1.605	1.634	1.643	1.656	1.666	1.672	1.678	1.676	1.700
	June	1.605	1.634	1.643	1.656	1.666	1.672	1.678	1.676	1.700
	July	1.608	1.637	1.645	1.658	1.669	1.675	1.681	1.679	1.702
	Aug.	1.600	1.629	1.638	1.650	1.661	1.667	1.673	1.671	1.694
	Sept.	1.593	1.621	1.630	1.643	1.653	1.659	1.665	1.663	1.687
	Oct.	1.580	1.608	1.617	1.630	1.640	1.646	1.652	1.650	1.673
	Nov.	1.568	1.596	1.604	1.617	1.628	1.633	1.639	1.637	1.661
	Dec.	1.570	1.598	1.607	1.620	1.630	1.636	1.642	1.640	1.663
1988	Jan.	1.570	1.598	1.607	1.620	1.630	1.636	1.642	1.640	1.663
	Feb.	1.560	1.588	1.597	1.609	1.620	1.626	1.632	1.630	1.653
	Mar.	1.550	1.578	1.587	1.599	1.610	1.616	1.622	1.620	1.643
	April	1.509	1.537	1.545	1.558	1.568	1.574	1.579	1.578	1.600
	May	1.500	1.527	1.536	1.548	1.558	1.564	1.570	1.568	1.590
	June	1.491	1.518	1.526	1.538	1.549	1.554	1.560	1.558	1.581
	July	1.488	1.515	1.524	1.536	1.546	1.552	1.558	1.556	1.578
	Aug.	1.461	1.487	1.496	1.508	1.518	1.524	1.529	1.527	1.550
	Sept.	1.449	1.476	1.484	1.496	1.506	1.512	1.518	1.516	1.538
	Oct.	1.425	1.451	1.459	1.471	1.481	1.487	1.492	1.490	1.512
	Nov.	1.414	1.440	1.448	1.460	1.470	1.475	1.481	1.479	1.501
	Dec.	1.407	1.433	1.442	1.453	1.463	1.469	1.474	1.472	1.494
1989	Jan.	1.392	1.418	1.426	1.438	1.448	1.453	1.459	1.457	1.478
	Feb.	1.375	1.401	1.409	1.420	1.430	1.436	1.441	1.439	1.461
	Mar.	1.364	1.390	1.398	1.410	1.419	1.425	1.430	1.428	1.450
	April	1.323	1.348	1.356	1.367	1.377	1.382	1.388	1.386	1.407
	May	1.309	1.334	1.342	1.353	1.363	1.368	1.373	1.371	1.392
	June	1.301	1.326	1.334	1.345	1.354	1.360	1.365	1.363	1.384
	July	1.299	1.324	1.332	1.343	1.352	1.358	1.363	1.361	1.382
	Aug.	1.293	1.318	1.326	1.337	1.346	1.351	1.357	1.355	1.376
	Sept.	1.277	1.302	1.310	1.321	1.330	1.335	1.340	1.339	1.359
	Oct.	1.260	1.284	1.292	1.303	1.312	1.317	1.323	1.321	1.341
	Nov.	1.241	1.265	1.273	1.284	1.293	1.298	1.303	1.301	1.322
	Dec.	1.235	1.259	1.267	1.278	1.287	1.292	1.297	1.295	1.316

General

RI Month		2017								
		Jan	Feb	Mar	Apr	May	Jun	Jul	Aug	Sept
1990	Jan.	1.222	1.246	1.254	1.264	1.274	1.279	1.284	1.282	1.302
	Feb.	1.209	1.233	1.240	1.251	1.260	1.265	1.270	1.269	1.289
	Mar.	1.187	1.211	1.218	1.229	1.238	1.243	1.248	1.246	1.266
	April	1.122	1.145	1.153	1.163	1.172	1.177	1.181	1.180	1.199
	May	1.104	1.127	1.134	1.144	1.153	1.158	1.162	1.161	1.180
	June	1.096	1.118	1.125	1.136	1.144	1.149	1.154	1.152	1.171
	July	1.094	1.117	1.124	1.134	1.143	1.147	1.152	1.151	1.170
	Aug.	1.073	1.095	1.102	1.112	1.121	1.126	1.130	1.129	1.148
	Sept.	1.053	1.076	1.083	1.093	1.101	1.106	1.111	1.109	1.128
	Oct.	1.038	1.060	1.067	1.077	1.085	1.090	1.094	1.093	1.111
	Nov.	1.042	1.065	1.072	1.082	1.090	1.095	1.099	1.098	1.116
	Dec.	1.044	1.066	1.073	1.083	1.092	1.096	1.101	1.099	1.118
1991	Jan.	1.039	1.061	1.068	1.078	1.087	1.091	1.096	1.094	1.113
	Feb.	1.028	1.050	1.057	1.067	1.076	1.080	1.085	1.083	1.102
	Mar.	1.021	1.043	1.049	1.059	1.068	1.072	1.077	1.075	1.094
	April	0.995	1.017	1.023	1.033	1.041	1.046	1.050	1.049	1.067
	May	0.989	1.010	1.017	1.027	1.035	1.040	1.044	1.043	1.061
	June	0.980	1.001	1.008	1.018	1.026	1.031	1.035	1.034	1.051
	July	0.984	1.006	1.013	1.022	1.031	1.035	1.040	1.038	1.056
	Aug.	0.980	1.001	1.008	1.018	1.026	1.031	1.035	1.034	1.051
	Sept.	0.973	0.994	1.001	1.010	1.019	1.023	1.027	1.026	1.044
	Oct.	0.965	0.987	0.993	1.003	1.011	1.016	1.020	1.019	1.036
	Nov.	0.958	0.979	0.986	0.996	1.004	1.008	1.013	1.011	1.029
	Dec.	0.957	0.978	0.985	0.994	1.002	1.007	1.011	1.010	1.027
1992	Jan.	0.958	0.979	0.986	0.996	1.004	1.008	1.013	1.011	1.029
	Feb.	0.948	0.969	0.976	0.985	0.993	0.998	1.002	1.001	1.018
	Mar.	0.942	0.963	0.970	0.980	0.988	0.992	0.996	0.995	1.012
	April	0.913	0.934	0.940	0.950	0.957	0.962	0.966	0.965	0.982
	May	0.906	0.927	0.933	0.943	0.950	0.955	0.959	0.958	0.975
	June	0.906	0.927	0.933	0.943	0.950	0.955	0.959	0.958	0.975
	July	0.913	0.934	0.940	0.950	0.957	0.962	0.966	0.965	0.982
	Aug.	0.911	0.932	0.939	0.948	0.956	0.960	0.965	0.963	0.981
	Sept.	0.905	0.925	0.932	0.941	0.949	0.953	0.958	0.956	0.973

		2017							
RI Month		Jan	Feb	Mar	Apr	May	Jun	Jul	Aug	Sept
	Oct.	0.898	0.919	0.925	0.934	0.942	0.946	0.951	0.949	0.966
	Nov.	0.901	0.921	0.928	0.937	0.945	0.949	0.953	0.952	0.969
	Dec.	0.907	0.928	0.935	0.944	0.952	0.956	0.960	0.959	0.976
1993	Jan.	0.925	0.946	0.953	0.962	0.970	0.975	0.979	0.978	0.995
	Feb.	0.913	0.934	0.940	0.950	0.957	0.962	0.966	0.965	0.982
	Mar.	0.906	0.927	0.933	0.943	0.950	0.955	0.959	0.958	0.975
	April	0.888	0.909	0.915	0.925	0.932	0.937	0.941	0.940	0.957
	May	0.882	0.902	0.909	0.918	0.926	0.930	0.934	0.933	0.950
	June	0.883	0.904	0.910	0.919	0.927	0.931	0.935	0.934	0.951
	July	0.887	0.908	0.914	0.923	0.931	0.935	0.940	0.938	0.955
	Aug.	0.879	0.900	0.906	0.915	0.923	0.927	0.931	0.930	0.947
	Sept.	0.871	0.891	0.898	0.907	0.915	0.919	0.923	0.922	0.939
	Oct.	0.872	0.893	0.899	0.908	0.916	0.920	0.925	0.923	0.940
	Nov.	0.875	0.895	0.902	0.911	0.919	0.923	0.927	0.926	0.943
	Dec.	0.871	0.891	0.898	0.907	0.915	0.919	0.923	0.922	0.939
1994	Jan.	0.879	0.900	0.906	0.915	0.923	0.927	0.931	0.930	0.947
	Feb.	0.868	0.889	0.895	0.904	0.912	0.916	0.920	0.919	0.936
	Mar.	0.863	0.884	0.890	0.899	0.907	0.911	0.915	0.914	0.931
	April	0.841	0.861	0.868	0.877	0.884	0.888	0.893	0.891	0.908
	May	0.835	0.855	0.861	0.870	0.878	0.882	0.886	0.885	0.901
	June	0.835	0.855	0.861	0.870	0.878	0.882	0.886	0.885	0.901
	July	0.844	0.864	0.870	0.879	0.887	0.891	0.895	0.894	0.910
	Aug.	0.835	0.855	0.861	0.870	0.878	0.882	0.886	0.885	0.901
	Sept.	0.831	0.851	0.857	0.866	0.874	0.878	0.882	0.881	0.897
	Oct.	0.829	0.848	0.855	0.864	0.871	0.875	0.879	0.878	0.895
	Nov.	0.827	0.847	0.853	0.862	0.870	0.874	0.878	0.877	0.893
	Dec.	0.818	0.838	0.845	0.853	0.861	0.865	0.869	0.868	0.884
1995	Jan.	0.818	0.838	0.845	0.853	0.861	0.865	0.869	0.868	0.884
	Feb.	0.807	0.827	0.833	0.842	0.850	0.854	0.858	0.856	0.873
	Mar.	0.800	0.820	0.826	0.835	0.842	0.846	0.850	0.849	0.865
	April	0.782	0.801	0.807	0.816	0.823	0.828	0.832	0.830	0.846
	May	0.775	0.794	0.800	0.809	0.816	0.820	0.824	0.823	0.839
	June	0.772	0.792	0.798	0.806	0.814	0.818	0.822	0.820	0.836

General

RI Month		2017								
		Jan	Feb	Mar	Apr	May	Jun	Jul	Aug	Sept
	July	0.781	0.800	0.806	0.815	0.822	0.826	0.830	0.829	0.845
	Aug.	0.771	0.791	0.797	0.805	0.813	0.817	0.821	0.819	0.835
	Sept.	0.763	0.782	0.788	0.797	0.804	0.808	0.812	0.811	0.827
	Oct.	0.772	0.792	0.798	0.806	0.814	0.818	0.822	0.820	0.836
	Nov.	0.772	0.792	0.798	0.806	0.814	0.818	0.822	0.820	0.836
	Dec.	0.762	0.781	0.787	0.796	0.803	0.807	0.811	0.810	0.825
1996	Jan.	0.768	0.787	0.793	0.802	0.809	0.813	0.817	0.816	0.832
	Feb.	0.759	0.779	0.785	0.793	0.801	0.805	0.808	0.807	0.823
	Mar.	0.752	0.772	0.778	0.786	0.793	0.797	0.801	0.800	0.816
	April	0.740	0.759	0.765	0.773	0.780	0.784	0.788	0.787	0.803
	May	0.736	0.755	0.761	0.770	0.777	0.781	0.785	0.784	0.799
	June	0.735	0.754	0.760	0.769	0.776	0.780	0.784	0.782	0.798
	July	0.742	0.761	0.767	0.776	0.783	0.787	0.791	0.789	0.805
	Aug.	0.734	0.753	0.759	0.767	0.775	0.779	0.782	0.781	0.797
	Sept.	0.726	0.745	0.751	0.759	0.767	0.770	0.774	0.773	0.789
	Oct.	0.726	0.745	0.751	0.759	0.767	0.770	0.774	0.773	0.789
	Nov.	0.725	0.744	0.750	0.758	0.765	0.769	0.773	0.772	0.788
	Dec.	0.720	0.738	0.744	0.753	0.760	0.764	0.767	0.766	0.782
1997	Jan.	0.720	0.738	0.744	0.753	0.760	0.764	0.767	0.766	0.782
	Feb.	0.713	0.732	0.737	0.746	0.753	0.757	0.761	0.759	0.775
	Mar.	0.708	0.727	0.733	0.741	0.748	0.752	0.756	0.755	0.770
	April	0.699	0.717	0.723	0.731	0.738	0.742	0.746	0.745	0.760
	May	0.692	0.711	0.716	0.725	0.732	0.736	0.739	0.738	0.753
	June	0.686	0.704	0.710	0.718	0.725	0.729	0.733	0.731	0.747
	July	0.686	0.704	0.710	0.718	0.725	0.729	0.733	0.731	0.747
	Aug.	0.675	0.693	0.699	0.707	0.714	0.718	0.722	0.721	0.736
	Sept.	0.667	0.685	0.691	0.699	0.706	0.709	0.713	0.712	0.727
	Oct.	0.665	0.683	0.688	0.697	0.703	0.707	0.711	0.710	0.725
	Nov.	0.664	0.682	0.687	0.695	0.702	0.706	0.710	0.709	0.724
	Dec.	0.659	0.678	0.683	0.691	0.698	0.702	0.706	0.704	0.719
1998	Jan.	0.665	0.683	0.688	0.697	0.703	0.707	0.711	0.710	0.725
	Feb.	0.656	0.674	0.680	0.688	0.695	0.699	0.702	0.701	0.716
	Mar.	0.651	0.669	0.675	0.683	0.690	0.693	0.697	0.696	0.711

RI Month		2017								
		Jan	Feb	Mar	Apr	May	Jun	Jul	Aug	Sept
	April	0.633	0.651	0.656	0.664	0.671	0.675	0.678	0.677	0.692
	May	0.624	0.642	0.647	0.655	0.662	0.665	0.669	0.668	0.683
	June	0.625	0.643	0.648	0.656	0.663	0.666	0.670	0.669	0.684
	July	0.629	0.647	0.652	0.660	0.667	0.671	0.674	0.673	0.688
	Aug.	0.622	0.640	0.645	0.653	0.660	0.663	0.667	0.666	0.681
	Sept.	0.615	0.633	0.638	0.646	0.653	0.656	0.660	0.659	0.673
	Oct.	0.614	0.632	0.637	0.645	0.652	0.655	0.659	0.658	0.672
	Nov.	0.615	0.633	0.638	0.646	0.653	0.656	0.660	0.659	0.673
	Dec.	0.615	0.633	0.638	0.646	0.653	0.656	0.660	0.659	0.673
1999	*Jan.*	0.625	0.643	0.648	0.656	0.663	0.666	0.670	0.669	0.684
	Feb.	0.622	0.640	0.645	0.653	0.660	0.663	0.667	0.666	0.681
	Mar.	0.618	0.636	0.641	0.649	0.656	0.659	0.663	0.662	0.676
	April	0.607	0.625	0.630	0.638	0.645	0.648	0.652	0.651	0.665
	May	0.603	0.621	0.626	0.634	0.641	0.644	0.648	0.647	0.661
	June	0.603	0.621	0.626	0.634	0.641	0.644	0.648	0.647	0.661
	July	0.608	0.626	0.631	0.639	0.646	0.649	0.653	0.652	0.666
	Aug.	0.604	0.622	0.627	0.635	0.642	0.645	0.649	0.648	0.662
	Sept.	0.597	0.615	0.620	0.628	0.635	0.638	0.642	0.641	0.655
	Oct.	0.595	0.612	0.617	0.625	0.632	0.635	0.639	0.638	0.652
	Nov.	0.593	0.610	0.615	0.623	0.630	0.633	0.637	0.636	0.650
	Dec.	0.587	0.604	0.610	0.617	0.624	0.628	0.631	0.630	0.644
2000	*Jan.*	0.594	0.611	0.616	0.624	0.631	0.634	0.638	0.637	0.651
	Feb.	0.585	0.602	0.608	0.616	0.622	0.626	0.629	0.628	0.642
	Mar.	0.577	0.594	0.599	0.607	0.613	0.617	0.621	0.619	0.634
	April	0.561	0.578	0.583	0.591	0.597	0.601	0.604	0.603	0.617
	May	0.555	0.572	0.578	0.585	0.592	0.595	0.599	0.598	0.612
	June	0.552	0.569	0.574	0.582	0.588	0.591	0.595	0.594	0.608
	July	0.557	0.574	0.579	0.587	0.594	0.597	0.601	0.599	0.613
	Aug.	0.557	0.574	0.579	0.587	0.594	0.597	0.601	0.599	0.613
	Sept.	0.546	0.563	0.568	0.576	0.582	0.586	0.589	0.588	0.602
	Oct.	0.547	0.564	0.569	0.577	0.583	0.587	0.590	0.589	0.603
	Nov.	0.543	0.560	0.565	0.572	0.579	0.582	0.586	0.585	0.598
	Dec.	0.542	0.559	0.564	0.571	0.578	0.581	0.585	0.584	0.598

General

RI Month		2017								
		Jan	Feb	Mar	Apr	May	Jun	Jul	Aug	Sept
2001	Jan.	0.552	0.569	0.574	0.582	0.588	0.591	0.595	0.594	0.608
	Feb.	0.544	0.560	0.566	0.573	0.580	0.583	0.587	0.585	0.599
	Mar.	0.542	0.559	0.564	0.571	0.578	0.581	0.585	0.584	0.598
	April	0.534	0.551	0.556	0.563	0.570	0.573	0.577	0.575	0.589
	May	0.524	0.541	0.546	0.553	0.560	0.563	0.567	0.565	0.579
	June	0.522	0.539	0.544	0.552	0.558	0.561	0.565	0.564	0.577
	July	0.532	0.549	0.554	0.561	0.568	0.571	0.575	0.574	0.587
	Aug.	0.526	0.543	0.548	0.555	0.561	0.565	0.568	0.567	0.581
	Sept.	0.521	0.537	0.542	0.550	0.556	0.560	0.563	0.562	0.576
	Oct.	0.523	0.540	0.545	0.552	0.559	0.562	0.566	0.565	0.578
	Nov.	0.529	0.546	0.551	0.559	0.565	0.569	0.572	0.571	0.585
	Dec.	0.531	0.548	0.553	0.561	0.567	0.570	0.574	0.573	0.587
2002	Jan.	0.532	0.549	0.554	0.561	0.568	0.571	0.575	0.574	0.587
	Feb.	0.528	0.544	0.549	0.557	0.563	0.567	0.570	0.569	0.583
	Mar.	0.521	0.538	0.543	0.551	0.557	0.560	0.564	0.563	0.577
	April	0.511	0.528	0.533	0.540	0.546	0.550	0.553	0.552	0.566
	May	0.507	0.523	0.528	0.536	0.542	0.545	0.549	0.548	0.561
	June	0.507	0.523	0.528	0.536	0.542	0.545	0.549	0.548	0.561
	July	0.509	0.526	0.531	0.538	0.545	0.548	0.551	0.550	0.564
	Aug.	0.505	0.522	0.527	0.534	0.540	0.544	0.547	0.546	0.560
	Sept.	0.495	0.511	0.516	0.524	0.530	0.533	0.537	0.535	0.549
	Oct.	0.492	0.509	0.514	0.521	0.527	0.531	0.534	0.533	0.546
	Nov.	0.490	0.506	0.511	0.519	0.525	0.528	0.531	0.530	0.544
	Dec.	0.487	0.504	0.509	0.516	0.522	0.525	0.529	0.528	0.541
2003	Jan.	0.488	0.504	0.510	0.517	0.523	0.526	0.530	0.529	0.542
	Feb.	0.481	0.497	0.502	0.509	0.515	0.519	0.522	0.521	0.534
	Mar.	0.476	0.492	0.497	0.504	0.510	0.514	0.517	0.516	0.529
	April	0.465	0.481	0.486	0.493	0.499	0.503	0.506	0.505	0.518
	May	0.463	0.479	0.484	0.491	0.497	0.500	0.504	0.502	0.516
	June	0.464	0.480	0.485	0.493	0.499	0.502	0.505	0.504	0.517
	July	0.464	0.480	0.485	0.493	0.499	0.502	0.505	0.504	0.517
	Aug.	0.462	0.478	0.483	0.490	0.496	0.499	0.503	0.502	0.515
	Sept.	0.455	0.471	0.476	0.483	0.489	0.492	0.495	0.494	0.507

RI Month		2017							
		Jan	Feb	Mar	Apr	May	Jun	Jul	Aug	Sept
	Oct.	0.454	0.470	0.475	0.482	0.488	0.491	0.495	0.493	0.507
	Nov.	0.453	0.469	0.474	0.481	0.487	0.490	0.494	0.493	0.506
	Dec.	0.447	0.463	0.468	0.475	0.481	0.484	0.487	0.486	0.499
2004	Jan.	0.450	0.466	0.471	0.478	0.484	0.487	0.490	0.489	0.502
	Feb.	0.445	0.460	0.465	0.472	0.478	0.482	0.485	0.484	0.497
	Mar.	0.438	0.454	0.459	0.466	0.472	0.475	0.478	0.477	0.490
	April	0.430	0.445	0.450	0.457	0.463	0.466	0.470	0.468	0.481
	May	0.424	0.439	0.444	0.451	0.457	0.460	0.463	0.462	0.475
	June	0.421	0.437	0.442	0.449	0.454	0.458	0.461	0.460	0.473
	July	0.421	0.437	0.442	0.449	0.454	0.458	0.461	0.460	0.473
	Aug.	0.417	0.432	0.437	0.444	0.450	0.453	0.456	0.455	0.468
	Sept.	0.411	0.427	0.432	0.439	0.444	0.448	0.451	0.450	0.463
	Oct.	0.408	0.423	0.428	0.435	0.441	0.444	0.447	0.446	0.459
	Nov.	0.405	0.420	0.425	0.432	0.438	0.441	0.444	0.443	0.456
	Dec.	0.398	0.413	0.418	0.425	0.431	0.434	0.437	0.436	0.449
2005	Jan.	0.406	0.421	0.426	0.433	0.438	0.442	0.445	0.444	0.456
	Feb.	0.400	0.416	0.420	0.427	0.433	0.436	0.439	0.438	0.451
	Mar.	0.394	0.409	0.414	0.420	0.426	0.429	0.433	0.431	0.444
	April	0.386	0.401	0.406	0.412	0.418	0.421	0.424	0.423	0.436
	May	0.383	0.398	0.403	0.409	0.415	0.418	0.421	0.420	0.433
	June	0.381	0.396	0.401	0.408	0.414	0.417	0.420	0.419	0.431
	July	0.381	0.396	0.401	0.408	0.414	0.417	0.420	0.419	0.431
	Aug.	0.379	0.394	0.398	0.405	0.411	0.414	0.417	0.416	0.428
	Sept.	0.375	0.390	0.395	0.401	0.407	0.410	0.413	0.412	0.425
	Oct.	0.374	0.389	0.393	0.400	0.406	0.409	0.412	0.411	0.423
	Nov.	0.371	0.386	0.391	0.398	0.403	0.407	0.410	0.409	0.421
	Dec.	0.368	0.383	0.387	0.394	0.400	0.403	0.406	0.405	0.417
2006	Jan.	0.373	0.388	0.392	0.399	0.405	0.408	0.411	0.410	0.422
	Feb.	0.367	0.382	0.387	0.393	0.399	0.402	0.405	0.404	0.417
	Mar.	0.362	0.376	0.381	0.388	0.393	0.396	0.399	0.398	0.411
	April	0.351	0.366	0.370	0.377	0.383	0.386	0.389	0.388	0.400
	May	0.343	0.358	0.362	0.369	0.374	0.377	0.380	0.379	0.392
	June	0.338	0.352	0.357	0.363	0.369	0.372	0.375	0.374	0.386

General

		2017								
RI Month		**Jan**	**Feb**	**Mar**	**Apr**	**May**	**Jun**	**Jul**	**Aug**	**Sept**
	July	0.338	0.352	0.357	0.363	0.369	0.372	0.375	0.374	0.386
	Aug.	0.333	0.347	0.352	0.358	0.364	0.367	0.370	0.369	0.381
	Sept.	0.327	0.341	0.346	0.352	0.358	0.361	0.364	0.363	0.375
	Oct.	0.325	0.339	0.344	0.350	0.356	0.359	0.362	0.361	0.373
	Nov.	0.320	0.335	0.339	0.346	0.351	0.354	0.357	0.356	0.368
	Dec.	0.310	0.324	0.329	0.335	0.340	0.343	0.346	0.345	0.357
2007	*Jan.*	0.317	0.331	0.336	0.342	0.348	0.351	0.354	0.353	0.365
	Feb.	0.307	0.322	0.326	0.332	0.338	0.341	0.344	0.343	0.355
	Mar.	0.299	0.313	0.318	0.324	0.329	0.332	0.335	0.334	0.346
	April	0.293	0.307	0.311	0.317	0.323	0.326	0.329	0.328	0.339
	May	0.288	0.302	0.306	0.312	0.318	0.321	0.323	0.323	0.334
	June	0.281	0.295	0.299	0.305	0.311	0.314	0.316	0.315	0.327
	July	0.288	0.302	0.307	0.313	0.318	0.321	0.324	0.323	0.335
	Aug.	0.281	0.295	0.299	0.305	0.311	0.314	0.316	0.315	0.327
	Sept.	0.276	0.290	0.295	0.301	0.306	0.309	0.312	0.311	0.323
	Oct.	0.271	0.285	0.289	0.295	0.301	0.303	0.306	0.305	0.317
	Nov.	0.266	0.280	0.284	0.290	0.296	0.299	0.301	0.300	0.312
	Dec.	0.259	0.273	0.277	0.283	0.288	0.291	0.294	0.293	0.304
2008	*Jan.*	0.265	0.279	0.284	0.290	0.295	0.298	0.301	0.300	0.311
	Feb.	0.256	0.270	0.274	0.280	0.285	0.288	0.291	0.290	0.301
	Mar.	0.252	0.265	0.270	0.276	0.281	0.284	0.287	0.286	0.297
	April	0.241	0.254	0.258	0.264	0.270	0.272	0.275	0.274	0.286
	May	0.234	0.248	0.252	0.258	0.263	0.266	0.269	0.268	0.279
	June	0.225	0.238	0.242	0.248	0.253	0.256	0.259	0.258	0.269
	July	0.226	0.240	0.244	0.250	0.255	0.258	0.261	0.260	0.271
	Aug.	0.222	0.236	0.240	0.246	0.251	0.254	0.256	0.256	0.267
	Sept.	0.216	0.229	0.233	0.239	0.244	0.247	0.250	0.249	0.260
	Oct.	0.220	0.233	0.237	0.243	0.248	0.251	0.254	0.253	0.264
	Nov.	0.229	0.243	0.247	0.253	0.258	0.261	0.263	0.263	0.274
	Dec.	0.247	0.261	0.265	0.271	0.276	0.279	0.282	0.281	0.292
2009	*Jan.*	0.264	0.277	0.282	0.288	0.293	0.296	0.299	0.298	0.309
	Feb.	0.256	0.270	0.274	0.280	0.285	0.288	0.291	0.290	0.301
	Mar.	0.257	0.270	0.274	0.281	0.286	0.289	0.292	0.291	0.302
	April	0.255	0.269	0.273	0.279	0.285	0.287	0.290	0.289	0.301

RI Month		2017								
		Jan	Feb	Mar	Apr	May	Jun	Jul	Aug	Sept
	May	0.248	0.261	0.266	0.272	0.277	0.280	0.282	0.281	0.293
	June	0.244	0.258	0.262	0.268	0.273	0.276	0.279	0.278	0.289
	July	0.244	0.258	0.262	0.268	0.273	0.276	0.279	0.278	0.289
	Aug.	0.238	0.252	0.256	0.262	0.267	0.270	0.273	0.272	0.283
	Sept.	0.233	0.247	0.251	0.257	0.262	0.265	0.268	0.267	0.278
	Oct.	0.229	0.243	0.247	0.253	0.258	0.261	0.263	0.263	0.274
	Nov.	0.226	0.239	0.243	0.249	0.254	0.257	0.260	0.259	0.270
	Dec.	0.218	0.231	0.235	0.241	0.246	0.249	0.252	0.251	0.262
2010	Jan.	0.218	0.232	0.236	0.242	0.247	0.250	0.252	0.251	0.263
	Feb.	0.211	0.224	0.229	0.234	0.240	0.242	0.245	0.244	0.255
	Mar.	0.203	0.216	0.220	0.226	0.231	0.234	0.237	0.236	0.246
	April	0.192	0.205	0.209	0.215	0.219	0.222	0.225	0.224	0.235
	May	0.187	0.200	0.204	0.210	0.215	0.218	0.220	0.220	0.230
	June	0.185	0.198	0.202	0.207	0.212	0.215	0.218	0.217	0.228
	July	0.187	0.200	0.204	0.210	0.215	0.218	0.220	0.220	0.230
	Aug.	0.183	0.196	0.200	0.205	0.210	0.213	0.216	0.215	0.225
	Sept.	0.178	0.191	0.195	0.201	0.206	0.209	0.211	0.210	0.221
	Oct.	0.176	0.189	0.193	0.198	0.203	0.206	0.209	0.208	0.218
	Nov.	0.171	0.183	0.187	0.193	0.198	0.201	0.203	0.202	0.213
	Dec.	0.162	0.175	0.179	0.185	0.190	0.192	0.195	0.194	0.204
2011	Jan.	0.159	0.172	0.176	0.182	0.186	0.189	0.192	0.191	0.201
	Feb.	0.148	0.160	0.164	0.170	0.175	0.177	0.180	0.179	0.189
	Mar.	0.142	0.154	0.158	0.164	0.169	0.171	0.174	0.173	0.183
	April	0.133	0.145	0.149	0.154	0.159	0.162	0.164	0.163	0.174
	May	0.129	0.141	0.145	0.151	0.155	0.158	0.160	0.159	0.170
	June	0.129	0.141	0.145	0.151	0.155	0.158	0.160	0.159	0.170
	July	0.131	0.144	0.147	0.153	0.158	0.160	0.163	0.162	0.172
	Aug.	0.125	0.137	0.141	0.146	0.151	0.153	0.156	0.155	0.165
	Sept.	0.116	0.128	0.132	0.137	0.142	0.145	0.147	0.146	0.156
	Oct.	0.116	0.128	0.132	0.137	0.142	0.144	0.147	0.146	0.156
	Nov.	0.113	0.125	0.129	0.135	0.139	0.142	0.144	0.143	0.153
	Dec.	0.109	0.121	0.125	0.130	0.135	0.137	0.140	0.139	0.149
2012	Jan.	0.116	0.128	0.132	0.137	0.142	0.144	0.147	0.146	0.156
	Feb.	0.107	0.119	0.123	0.128	0.133	0.135	0.138	0.137	0.147

RI Month		2017								
		Jan	Feb	Mar	Apr	May	Jun	Jul	Aug	Sept
	Mar.	0.103	0.115	0.118	0.124	0.128	0.131	0.133	0.132	0.142
	April	0.095	0.107	0.111	0.116	0.120	0.123	0.125	0.125	0.134
	May	0.095	0.107	0.111	0.116	0.121	0.123	0.126	0.125	0.135
	June	0.098	0.110	0.114	0.119	0.124	0.126	0.129	0.128	0.138
	July	0.097	0.109	0.112	0.118	0.122	0.125	0.127	0.126	0.136
	Aug.	0.093	0.105	0.108	0.114	0.118	0.121	0.123	0.122	0.132
	Sept.	0.087	0.099	0.103	0.108	0.113	0.115	0.118	0.117	0.127
	Oct.	0.081	0.093	0.096	0.102	0.106	0.109	0.111	0.110	0.120
	Nov.	0.081	0.093	0.096	0.102	0.106	0.109	0.111	0.110	0.120
	Dec.	0.076	0.088	0.091	0.096	0.101	0.103	0.106	0.105	0.115
2013	*Jan.*	0.080	0.092	0.096	0.101	0.105	0.108	0.110	0.109	0.119
	Feb.	0.072	0.084	0.088	0.093	0.097	0.100	0.102	0.101	0.111
	Mar.	0.068	0.079	0.083	0.088	0.092	0.095	0.097	0.097	0.106
	Apr.	0.064	0.076	0.079	0.085	0.089	0.091	0.094	0.093	0.103
	May	0.062	0.074	0.077	0.082	0.087	0.089	0.092	0.091	0.100
	June	0.063	0.075	0.078	0.084	0.088	0.091	0.093	0.092	0.102
	July	0.063	0.075	0.078	0.084	0.088	0.091	0.093	0.092	0.102
	Aug.	0.058	0.069	0.073	0.078	0.082	0.085	0.087	0.086	0.096
	Sept.	0.054	0.066	0.069	0.074	0.079	0.081	0.083	0.083	0.092
	Oct.	0.054	0.066	0.069	0.074	0.079	0.081	0.083	0.083	0.092
	Nov.	0.053	0.065	0.068	0.073	0.078	0.080	0.083	0.082	0.091
	Dec.	0.051	0.063	0.066	0.071	0.076	0.078	0.080	0.080	0.089
2014	*Jan.*	0.051	0.063	0.066	0.071	0.076	0.078	0.080	0.080	0.089
	Feb.	0.044	0.056	0.059	0.065	0.069	0.071	0.074	0.073	0.082
	Mar.	0.042	0.053	0.057	0.062	0.066	0.069	0.071	0.070	0.080
	Apr.	0.038	0.050	0.053	0.058	0.063	0.065	0.067	0.066	0.076
	May	0.038	0.049	0.052	0.057	0.062	0.064	0.066	0.066	0.075
	June	0.036	0.047	0.051	0.056	0.060	0.062	0.065	0.064	0.073
	July	0.037	0.048	0.052	0.057	0.061	0.064	0.066	0.065	0.075
	Aug.	0.033	0.044	0.048	0.053	0.057	0.060	0.062	0.061	0.070
	Sept.	0.031	0.042	0.045	0.050	0.055	0.057	0.059	0.059	0.068
	Oct.	0.030	0.042	0.045	0.050	0.054	0.057	0.059	0.058	0.068
	Nov.	0.033	0.044	0.047	0.053	0.057	0.059	0.061	0.061	0.070
	Dec.	0.031	0.042	0.046	0.051	0.055	0.057	0.060	0.059	0.068

RI Month		2017								
		Jan	Feb	Mar	Apr	May	Jun	Jul	Aug	Sept
2015	Jan.	0.040	0.051	0.054	0.060	0.064	0.066	0.069	0.068	0.077
	Feb.	0.034	0.046	0.049	0.054	0.058	0.061	0.063	0.062	0.072
	Mar.	0.033	0.044	0.047	0.053	0.057	0.059	0.061	0.061	0.070
	Apr.	0.029	0.040	0.044	0.049	0.053	0.055	0.058	0.057	0.066
	May	0.027	0.038	0.042	0.047	0.051	0.053	0.056	0.055	0.064
	June	0.025	0.037	0.040	0.045	0.049	0.052	0.054	0.053	0.063
	July	0.027	0.038	0.041	0.046	0.051	0.053	0.055	0.055	0.064
	Aug.	0.022	0.033	0.037	0.042	0.046	0.048	0.050	0.050	0.059
	Sept.	0.023	0.034	0.037	0.042	0.047	0.049	0.051	0.050	0.060
	Oct.	0.023	0.034	0.038	0.043	0.047	0.049	0.052	0.051	0.060
	Nov.	0.022	0.033	0.037	0.042	0.046	0.048	0.050	0.050	0.059
	Dec.	0.019	0.030	0.033	0.038	0.043	0.045	0.047	0.046	0.056
2016	Jan.	0.026	0.037	0.041	0.046	0.050	0.052	0.054	0.054	0.063
	Feb.	0.021	0.032	0.036	0.041	0.045	0.047	0.050	0.049	0.058
	Mar.	0.017	0.028	0.031	0.036	0.041	0.043	0.045	0.044	0.054
	Apr.	0.016	0.027	0.030	0.035	0.039	0.042	0.044	0.043	0.052
	May	0.013	0.024	0.027	0.032	0.037	0.039	0.041	0.040	0.050
	June	0.009	0.020	0.024	0.029	0.033	0.035	0.037	0.036	0.046
	July	0.008	0.019	0.022	0.027	0.032	0.034	0.036	0.035	0.044
	Aug.	0.004	0.015	0.019	0.023	0.028	0.030	0.032	0.031	0.040
	Sept.	0.002	0.013	0.017	0.022	0.026	0.028	0.030	0.029	0.039
	Oct.	0.003	0.014	0.017	0.022	0.026	0.028	0.031	0.030	0.039
	Nov.	Nil	0.011	0.014	0.019	0.023	0.026	0.028	0.027	0.036
	Dec.	Nil	0.005	0.008	0.013	0.017	0.019	0.022	0.021	0.030
2017	Jan.		0.011	0.014	0.019	0.023	0.026	0.028	0.027	0.036
	Feb.			0.003	0.008	0.012	0.015	0.017	0.016	0.025
	Mar.			Nil	0.005	0.009	0.011	0.013	0.013	0.022
	Apr.				Nil	0.004	0.006	0.008	0.008	0.017
	May					Nil	0.002	0.004	0.004	0.013
	June						Nil	0.002	0.001	0.010
	July							Nil	Nil	0.008
	Aug.								Nil	0.001
	Sept.									Nil

General

Foreign exchange rates

[¶12-000]   Foreign exchange rates: general

HMRC publish annually currency exchange rates for the purposes of converting foreign currencies into sterling.

The currency exchange rates for the US dollar, German deutschmark, Japanese yen and euro are reproduced below.

Average exchange rates for year to 31 December

Average for year to 31 December	US $	Yen	Euro
2013	1.562598	151.646301	1.178398
2014	1.65073	173.790568	1.224907
2015	1.530538	185.286343	1.37576
2016	1.376045	150.168417	1.240784

Average exchange rates for year to 31 March

Average for year to 31 March	US $	Yen	Euro
2013	1.580925	130.738615	1.228351
2014	1.584390	158.325192	1.185417
2015	1.598652	176.516505	1.270009
2016	1.508298	181.381545	1.368138
2017	1.327506	144.307083	1.207700

[¶12-640]   Foreign exchange rates 2016–17

Average for the year to 31 December 2016 and 31 March 2017

Country	Unit of currency	Average for the year to 31 December 2016		Average for the year to 31 March 2017	
		Sterling value of currency unit £	Currency units per £1	Sterling value of currency unit £	Currency units per £1
Abu Dhabi	Dirham	0.1978	5.056488	0.2053	4.870015
Albania	Lek	0.0059	170.723375	0.0061	165.255417
Algeria	Dinar	0.0067	150.356917	0.0069	145.760208
Angola	Readj Kwanza	0.0045	223.259667	0.0046	219.334167
Antigua	E Caribbean Dollar	0.269	3.716987	0.2793	3.579938
Argentina	Peso	0.0499	20.039292	0.0505	19.813125
Armenia	Dram	0.0015	661.087208	0.0016	635.039167

General

Country	Unit of currency	Average for the year to 31 December 2016		Average for the year to 31 March 2017	
		Sterling value of currency unit £	Currency units per £1	Sterling value of currency unit £	Currency units per £1
Aruba	Florin	0.4058	2.464473	0.4213	2.37361
Australia	Dollar	0.5398	1.852649	0.566	1.766681
Azerbaijan	New Manat	0.4582	2.182317	0.4615	2.166667
Bahamas	Dollar	0.7267	1.376045	0.7533	1.327506
Bahrain	Dinar	1.9263	0.519127	2.0001	0.499965
Bangladesh	Taka	0.0093	108.051708	0.0096	104.331667
Barbados	Dollar	0.3632	2.753181	0.3771	2.651663
Belarus	Rouble	0.3887	2.57286	0.3936	2.54075
Belize	Dollar	0.3632	2.753017	0.3767	2.654854
Benin	CFA Franc	0.0012	814.319917	0.0013	791.886667
Bermuda	Dollar (US)	0.7267	1.376045	0.7533	1.327506
Bhutan	Ngultrum	0.0108	92.449	0.0112	89.215625
Bolivia	Boliviano	0.1052	9.505183	0.109	9.170683
Bosnia-Herzegovinia	Marka	0.4119	2.428067	0.4235	2.361131
Botswana	Pula	0.0665	15.039908	0.0702	14.237492
Brazil	Real	0.206	4.854893	0.2256	4.433554
Brunei	Dollar	0.2934	3.408618	0.2991	3.34355
Bulgaria	Lev	0.4118	2.428196	0.4235	2.361273
Burkina Faso	CFA Franc	0.0012	814.319917	0.0013	791.886667
Burundi	Franc	0.0004	2222.357583	0.0005	2181.28875
Cambodia	Riel	0.0002	5330.036625	0.0002	5123.295
Cameroon Republic	CFA Franc	0.0012	814.319917	0.0013	791.886667
Canada	Dollar	0.5501	1.817877	0.5778	1.730748
Cape Verde Islands	Escudo	0.0073	136.919417	0.0075	133.193333
Cayman Islands	Dollar	0.8858	1.128863	0.9199	1.087065
Central African Republic	CFA Franc	0.0012	814.319917	0.0013	791.886667
Chad	CFA Franc	0.0012	814.319917	0.0013	791.886667
Chile	Peso	0.0011	937.166708	0.0011	886.574792
China	Yuan	0.1099	9.098112	0.1127	8.870269
Colombia	Peso	0.0002	4207.046542	0.0003	3943.479375
Comoros	Franc	0.0016	610.738583	0.0017	593.913958
Congo (Brazaville)	CFA Franc	0.0012	814.319917	0.0013	791.886667
Congo (DemRep)	Congo Franc	0.0008	1217.051375	0.0008	1272.947917
Costa Rica	Colon	0.0013	745.827167	0.0014	724.224375

Country	Unit of currency	Average for the year to 31 December 2016		Average for the year to 31 March 2017	
		Sterling value of currency unit £	Currency units per £1	Sterling value of currency unit £	Currency units per £1
Cote d'Ivoire	CFA Franc	0.0012	814.319917	0.0013	791.886667
Croatia	Kuna	0.1069	9.354187	0.1104	9.058758
Cuba	Peso	0.7264	1.376575	0.7542	1.325902
Czech Republic	Koruna	0.0298	33.553167	0.0307	32.624567
Denmark	Krone	0.1082	9.239276	0.1113	8.985713
Djibouti	Franc	0.0041	244.655458	0.0042	235.63375
Dominica	E Caribbean Dollar	0.269	3.716987	0.2793	3.579938
Dominican Republic	Peso	0.0158	63.174	0.0163	61.189167
Dubai	Dirham	0.1978	5.056488	0.2053	4.870015
Ecuador	Dollar	0.7267	1.376045	0.7533	1.327506
Egypt	Pound	0.0784	12.756667	0.0644	15.525625
El Salvador	Colon	0.083	12.041875	0.0862	11.59625
Equatorial Guinea	CFA Franc	0.0012	814.319917	0.0013	791.886667
Eritrea	Nakfa	0.0484	20.6435	0.0503	19.882083
Ethiopia	Birr	0.0334	29.935083	0.0342	29.262083
Eurozone	Euro	0.8059	1.240784	0.828	1.2077
Fiji Islands	Dollar	0.3469	2.88288	0.3625	2.758275
Fr. Polynesia	CFP Franc	0.0068	148.136792	0.0069	144.055417
Gabon	CFA Franc	0.0012	814.319917	0.0013	791.886667
Gambia	Dalasi	0.0173	57.703958	0.0175	57.026875
Georgia	Lari	0.3119	3.206053	0.3159	3.165079
Ghana	Cedi	0.1853	5.395412	0.1877	5.328192
Grenada	E Caribbean Dollar	0.269	3.716987	0.2793	3.579938
Guatemala	Quetzal	0.0954	10.486725	0.0996	10.041267
Guinea Bissau	CFA Franc	0.0012	814.319917	0.0013	791.886667
Guinea Republic	Franc	0.0001	9424.586583	0.0001	9557.783333
Guyana	Dollar	0.0035	285.108708	0.0036	274.8625
Haiti	Gourde	0.0116	86.077125	0.0117	85.69875
Honduras	Lempira	0.0319	31.304417	0.0328	30.48125
Hong Kong	Dollar	0.0937	10.676933	0.0971	10.296783
Hungary	Forint	0.0026	386.828917	0.0027	375.333958
Iceland	Krona	0.0059	168.441917	0.0064	156.928542
India	Rupee	0.0108	92.449	0.0112	89.215625
Indonesia	Rupiah	0.0001	18335.22346	0.0001	17584.31896

Country	Unit of currency	Average for the year to 31 December 2016		Average for the year to 31 March 2017	
		Sterling value of currency unit £	Currency units per £1	Sterling value of currency unit £	Currency units per £1
Iraq	Dinar	0.0006	1616.382625	0.0006	1567.59125
Israel	Shekel	0.1892	5.285135	0.1977	5.057563
Jamaica	Dollar	0.0058	171.248417	0.006	167.475417
Japan	Yen	0.0067	150.168417	0.0069	144.307083
Jordan	Dinar	1.0244	0.976191	1.0637	0.940108
Kazakhstan	Tenge	0.0021	469.985917	0.0023	443.701458
Kenya	Schilling	0.0072	139.787417	0.0074	135.004375
Kuwait	Dinar	2.4045	0.415885	2.4895	0.401694
Kyrgyz Republic	Som	0.0104	96.609792	0.011	91.083333
Lao People's Dem Rep	Kip	0.0001	11193.88567	0.0001	10799.85042
Lebanon	Pound	0.0005	2076.391292	0.0005	1999.26
Lesotho	Loti	0.049	20.421333	0.0529	18.895
Liberia	Dollar (US)	0.7216	1.385863	0.7533	1.327506
Libya	Dinar	0.5337	1.873744	0.5469	1.82859
Macao	Pataca	0.0909	11.001733	0.0944	10.592617
Macedonia	Denar	0.0131	76.4425	0.0135	74.335625
Madagascar	Malagasy Ariary	0.0002	4370.964	0.0002	4223.932083
Malawi	Kwacha	0.001	975.086042	0.0011	944.816875
Malaysia	Ringgit	0.1767	5.660823	0.181	5.525885
Maldive Islands	Rufiyaa	0.0475	21.074542	0.0492	20.336667
Mali Republic	CFA Franc	0.0012	814.319917	0.0013	791.886667
Mauritania	Ouguiya	0.0021	481.10375	0.0021	471.101667
Mauritius	Rupee	0.0205	48.857917	0.0213	47.026042
Mexico	Mexican Peso	0.0393	25.431792	0.0393	25.433958
Moldova	Leu	0.0366	27.330792	0.038	26.318958
Mongolia	Tugrik	0.0003	2891.671958	0.0003	2935.9775
Montserrat	E Caribbean Dollar	0.269	3.716987	0.2793	3.579938
Morocco	Dirham	0.0742	13.476167	0.0766	13.060625
Mozambique	Metical	0.012	83.258833	0.0114	87.956667
Myanmar	Kyat	0.0006	1693.940542	0.0006	1659.734167
Nepal	Rupee	0.0068	147.969542	0.007	142.607917
New Caledonia	CFP Franc	0.0068	148.136792	0.0069	144.055417
New Zealand	Dollar	0.5039	1.984533	0.5316	1.881252
Nicaragua	Gold Cordoba	0.0255	39.258144	0.0261	38.249977

Country	Unit of currency	Average for the year to 31 December 2016		Average for the year to 31 March 2017	
		Sterling value of currency unit £	Currency units per £1	Sterling value of currency unit £	Currency units per £1
Niger Republic	CFA Franc	0.0012	814.319917	0.0013	791.886667
Nigeria	Naira	0.0029	347.059917	0.0027	372.817917
Norway	Norwegian Krone	0.0865	11.563583	0.0903	11.078125
Oman	Rial	1.8866	0.53006	1.9587	0.510533
Pakistan	Rupee	0.0069	144.189208	0.0072	138.893542
Panama	Balboa	0.7264	1.376654	0.7542	1.325902
Papua New Guinea	Kina	0.2325	4.301563	0.2385	4.192831
Paraguay	Guarani	0.0001	7789.234917	0.0001	7464.89875
Peru	New Sol	0.2157	4.635137	0.2261	4.4238
Philippines	Peso	0.0154	65.009792	0.0157	63.514375
Poland	Zloty	0.1851	5.402822	0.1902	5.256254
Qatar	Riyal	0.1995	5.01264	0.2071	4.82779
Romania	New Leu	0.1794	5.575248	0.1844	5.422944
Russia	Rouble	0.0108	92.835625	0.0119	84.216875
Rwanda	Franc	0.0009	1075.026417	0.0009	1056.958125
Sao Tome and Principe	Dobra	0	27787.62243	0	26963.36918
Saudi Arabia	Riyal	0.1938	5.160259	0.2008	4.978908
Senegal	CFA Franc	0.0012	814.319917	0.0013	791.886667
Serbia	Dinar	0.0065	152.777667	0.0067	148.926458
Seychelles	Rupee	0.0546	18.33075	0.0565	17.704583
Sierra Leone	Leone	0.0002	6389.390333	0.0001	7017.53375
Singapore	Dollar	0.5272	1.896978	0.5452	1.834148
Soloman Islands	Dollar	0.092	10.874433	0.0965	10.367517
Somali Republic	Schilling	0.0012	819.771	0.0013	776.039167
South Africa	Rand	0.049	20.428208	0.0529	18.90375
South Korea	Won	0.0006	1598.662625	0.0007	1529.039792
Sri Lanka	Rupee	0.005	200.72675	0.0051	195.195625
St Christopher and Anguilla	E Caribbean Dollar	0.269	3.716987	0.2793	3.579938
St Lucia	E Caribbean Dollar	0.269	3.716987	0.2793	3.579938
St Vincent	E Caribbean Dollar	0.269	3.716987	0.2793	3.579938
Sudan Republic	Pound	0.1187	8.427427	0.1216	8.224729
Surinam	Dollar	0.121	8.26306	0.1095	9.132498

General

Country	Unit of currency	Average for the year to 31 December 2016		Average for the year to 31 March 2017	
		Sterling value of currency unit £	Currency units per £1	Sterling value of currency unit £	Currency units per £1
Swaziland	Lilangeni	0.049	20.421575	0.0529	18.895
Sweden	Krona	0.0857	11.667417	0.0876	11.421667
Switzerland	Franc	0.7393	1.35263	0.7638	1.3093
Taiwan	Dollar	0.0225	44.499375	0.0236	42.342708
Tanzania	Schilling	0.0003	3009.647958	0.0003	2909.941875
Thailand	Baht	0.0206	48.517458	0.0214	46.692083
Togo Republic	CFA Franc	0.0012	814.319917	0.0013	791.886667
Tonga Islands	Pa'anga (AUS)	0.5398	1.852649	0.566	1.766681
Trinidad/Tobago	Dollar	0.1097	9.113027	0.1128	8.867246
Tunisia	Dinar	0.3423	2.921115	0.3447	2.901442
Turkey	Turkish Lira	0.2453	4.076891	0.2395	4.175619
Turkmenistan	New Manat	0.2074	4.821745	0.2153	4.644727
UAE	Dirham	0.1978	5.056488	0.2053	4.870015
Uganda	Schilling	0.0002	4676.453958	0.0002	4556.602917
Ukraine	Hryvnia	0.0286	34.921333	0.0293	34.161667
Uruguay	Peso	0.0239	41.794083	0.0254	39.41375
USA	Dollar	0.7267	1.376045	0.7533	1.327506
Uzbekistan	Sum	0.0002	4039.4335	0.0002	4029.228958
Vanuatu	Vatu	0.0066	152.664458	0.0068	146.318125
Venezuela	Bolivar Fuerte	0.0812	12.311973	0.0761	13.1331
Vietnam	Dong	0	30756.86363	0	29726.64333
Wallis and Futuna Islands	CFP Franc	0.0068	148.136792	0.0069	144.055417
Western Samoa	Tala	0.285	3.509119	0.2984	3.351075
Yemen (Rep of)	Rial	0.003	329.298792	0.003	329.275
Zambia	Kwacha	0.0703	14.221917	0.0756	13.219792
Zimbabwe	Dollar	0.002	498.20875	0.0021	479.838958

Table of spot rates on 31 December 2016 and 31 March 2017

Country	Unit of currency	Spot rate on 31 December 2016		Spot rate on 31 March 2017	
		Sterling value of currency unit £	Currency units per £1	Sterling value of currency unit £	Currency units per £1
Australia	AUD Dollar	0.586	1.7065	0.6143	1.6279
Canada	CAD Dollar	0.6035	1.6571	0.6022	1.6605
Denmark	DKK Krone	0.1148	8.7108	0.1155	8.6547
Eurozone	EUR Euro	0.8536	1.1715	0.8593	1.1637
Hong Kong	HKD Dollar	0.1044	9.5802	0.103	9.7076
Japan	JPY Yen	0.0069	144.12	0.0072	139.03
Norway	NOK Norwegian Krone	0.0941	10.63	0.0938	10.66
South Africa	ZAR Rand	0.0592	16.89	0.0624	16.03
Sweden	SEK Krona	0.0891	11.22	0.0899	11.12
Switzerland	CHF Franc	0.7962	1.2559	0.8036	1.2444
USA	USD Dollar	0.8093	1.2357	0.8004	1.2493

Residence of individuals

[¶13-000]   Statutory residence: from 2013–14

(FA 2013, Sch. 45)

(Tax Reporter: ¶199-000ff.)

From 6 April 2013, with effect for the tax year 2013–14 and subsequent tax years, a new statutory residence test (SRT) applies to determine the residence of an individual for tax purposes. The test applies for the purposes of income tax, capital gains tax and so far as relevant inheritance tax and corporation tax.

Tests	Status
Automatic overseas test is satisfied	Not resident
Automatic UK residence test is satisfied (at least one of the automatic tests is satisfied **and** none of the automatic overseas tests are satisfied)	Resident
None of automatic overseas or automatic UK tests are satisfied: • sufficient ties test is satisfied; • sufficient ties test is not satisfied.	• UK resident • Not resident

Automatic tests

An individual is automatically resident or not resident if they meet any of the four tests:

Automatic overseas test (any one)	Automatic UK test (any one plus none of the overseas tests)
Resident in the UK for one or more of the three previous tax years and spend fewer than 16 days in the UK in the current tax year	Spend at least 183 days in the UK during the tax year
Not resident in the UK for any of the previous three tax years and spend fewer than 46 days in the UK in the current tax year	A period of more than 90 days, part of which falls into the tax year, when the individual has a home in the UK, and no overseas home (disregarding any home at which they are present for fewer than 30 days in the tax year)

General

Automatic overseas test (any one)	Automatic UK test (any one plus none of the overseas tests)
Work full-time overseas in the tax year and spends fewer than 91 days in the UK in the tax year, incl. fewer than 31 working days	Work full time in the UK in the current tax year
Die in the current tax year subject to conditions which include spending fewer than 46 days in the current tax year	Die in current tax year subject to conditions which include having been UK resident in the previous three tax years

Sufficient ties tests

Where none of the automatic overseas and none of the automatic UK tests are satisfied, an individual will need to look at the number of ties in conjunction with the number of days spent in the UK during the tax year and whether they have been resident in the previous three tax years to determine whether the sufficient ties test is satisfied. Ties to be considered are as follows:

- UK resident family;
- Substantive UK employment (including self-employment);
- Available accommodation in the UK;
- More than 90 days spent in the UK in either or both of the previous two tax years; and
- A country tie (but only if individual resident in one or more three previous tax years).

Days spent in the UK during the tax year	Number of ties that are sufficient	
	Not resident in previous three tax years	Resident in any of the previous three tax years
More than 15 but not more than 45	[Automatic overseas test is satisfied]	At least four
More than 45 but not more than 90	All four	At least three
More than 90 but not more than 120	At least three	At least two
More than 120	At least two	At least one

Definition of ties
Family tie (either):
• Individual has a UK resident spouse (unless separated), or partner (if living together as husband and wife or civil partners); or
• Individual has a UK resident child under 18-years old (unless spends fewer than 61 days with the child in the tax year),
(an individual will not be considered to have a family tie with a child who is UK resident and under 18 years who is in full-time education and would not be a UK resident if the time spent in full-time education were disregarded and the child spends fewer than 21 days in the UK outside term time (half-term counts as term time)).
Work tie
Individual does more than three hours of work a day in the UK on at least 40 days in that year (whether continuously or intermittently). [NB. special rules apply as to what constitutes three hours work for workers on board a vehicle, aircraft or ship.]
Accommodation tie
Individual has a place to live in the UK (including a home, holiday home, temporary retreat of other accommodation) that is:
• available for a continuous period of 91 days or more during the year;
• the individual spends one or more nights there during the year; or
• if it is at the home of a close relative (parent, grandparent, sibling, child or grandchild over 18 years old), the individual spends 16 or more nights there during the year.
90-day tie
Individual spends more than 90 days (counting midnights) in the UK in either or both of the previous two tax years
Country tie
(applicable only where resident in any of previous three tax years)
UK is the country in which the individual was present at midnight for the greatest number of days in the tax year.
If the number of days an individual is present in a country at midnight is the same for two or more countries in a tax year, and one of those countries is the UK, then the individual will have a country tie for that tax year if that is the greatest number of days spent in any country in that tax year.

[¶13-400]   Split year treatment

(FA 2013, Sch. 45, Pt. 3)

(Tax Reporter: ¶199-375)

Under the SRT, an individual is either UK resident or non-UK resident for a full tax year and at all times in that tax year. However, if during a year that individual either starts to live or work abroad or comes from abroad to live or work in the UK, the tax year will be split into two parts if their circumstances meet specific criteria:

• a UK part for which they are charged to UK tax as a UK resident;

• an overseas part for which, for most purposes, they are charged to UK tax as a non-UK resident.

General

The taxpayer must be UK resident for a tax year under the SRT to meet the criteria for split year treatment for that year. They will not meet the split year criteria for a tax year for which they are non-UK resident under the SRT. Split year treatment only applies to an individual in their individual capacity and not to individuals acting as personal representatives. It applies in a limited way to individuals acting as trustee of a settlement.

[¶13-500]   Abolition of ordinary residence
(FA 2013, Sch. 46)

(Tax Reporter: ¶199-975)

The concept of ordinary resident for tax purposes has been abolished for tax years 2013–14 onwards. Transitional provisions apply to ensure those who currently benefit from being ordinarily resident will continue to be able to benefit for a maximum of two complete tax years.

[¶13-600]   Overseas workday relief
(ITEPA 2013, Pt. 2, Ch. 5)

(Tax Reporter: ¶199-960ff.)

Overseas workday relief (OWR) is available to certain resident, but non-UK domiciled individuals with an employment the duties of which are carried out partly in the UK and partly overseas. If relevant conditions are met, the earnings which relation to the duties performed overseas are only taxable on the remittance basis and if not remitted, are not taxable – this is OWR. OWR is available to all non-UK domiciled individuals who arrive in the UK after 5 April 2013 having been non-UK resident for the previous three tax years. It will be available for the whole of the tax year that the individual becomes resident in the UK (or for the UK part of the year if that year is a split year) and for the following two tax years.

[¶13-800]   Remittance basis
(ITA 2007, Pt. 14, Ch. A1)

(Tax Reporter: ¶199-675)

Non-domiciled individuals can elect to pay tax on the remittance basis so that UK tax is paid on foreign income or gains only to the extent that (and when) they are brought into the UK. A charge for claiming the remittance basis applies where the individual satisfies one of the three residence tests (is a 'long-term UK resident'), as shown in the table below.

No. of years UK resident	Remittance basis charge[1][2][3]			
	2017–18 to 2018–19 £	2015–16 to 2016–17 £	2012–13 to 2014–15 £	2008–09 to 2011–12 £
7-year test (7 out of past 9 tax years)	30,000	30,000	30,000	30,000
12-year test (12 out of past 14 tax years)	60,000	60,000	50,000	–
17-year test (17 out of past 20 tax years)	–	90,000	–	–

Notes

[1] Since 2008, where the remittance basis is claimed, the individual is not entitled to any personal allowance, blind person's allowance, tax reductions for married couples or civil partners, life assurance payments relief or capital gains tax annual exempt amount (ITA 2007, s. 809G).

[2] The remittance basis applies automatically (without a claim) to:

- individuals whose unremitted foreign income or gains for the year are less than £2,000 (unless they satisfy the conditions for the exemption from income tax for non-domiciliaries on foreign income described under ITA 2007, s. 828B, or give notice that the remittance basis is not to apply) (ITA 2007, s. 809D);

- individuals who:

  - do not have UK source income or gains (other than taxed investment income) exceeding £100 for the tax year concerned;

  - do not remit in that year any foreign income or gains which arose in a year in which the remittance basis has applied; and

  - have been UK resident for not more than six of the immediately preceding nine tax years, or are under the age of 18 throughout the tax year concerned (ITA 2007, s. 809E).

[3] Where a claim for the remittance basis is made, the claimant is required to 'nominate' all or part of his unremitted foreign income or gains for the year of claim, to be taxed on the arising basis. That amount must be such as would produce a 'relevant tax increase' of not more than the amount of the charge that applies (depending on which of the residence tests is satisfied) (ITA 2007, s. 809C(2)–(4)). These amounts are termed the 'applicable amounts' (ITA 2007, s. 809H(5A)).

Reform of domicile rules

(ITA 2007, s. 835BA; *Finance (No. 2) Act* 2017, s. 29)

Finance (No. 2) Act 2017 legislates for a series of reforms to the tax rules for individuals who are not domiciled in the UK under the general law.

The reforms provide that certain non-domiciled individuals will be treated as if they were domiciled in the UK for the purposes of income tax and capital gains tax from the start of the 2017–18 tax year.

Individuals who are not domiciled in the UK will be deemed to be UK domiciled for tax purposes if they are either resident in the UK for 15 of the past 20 tax years, or if they are born in the UK with a UK domicile of origin and return to the UK having obtained a domicile of choice elsewhere. They will be taxed on any arising worldwide income and gains in the same way as UK domiciles. At the same time, the existing inheritance tax deeming provisions will be aligned with the new 15 out of 20 rule.

Transitional protections will be given where an individual becomes deemed-UK domicile under the 15 out of 20 rule in April 2017, including the facility to rebase offshore assets for capital gains tax purposes. Those who become deemed domicile in April 2017, excepting those who were born in the UK with a UK domicile of origin, will be able to treat the cost base of their non-UK based assets as the market value of that asset on 6 April 2017.

General

The new rules will also ensure that any non-dom who sets up a qualifying trust before becoming deemed domiciled would not pay income tax/capital gains tax on income/ gains in the trust, as long as they did not receive a benefit from the trust. However, once a benefit is taken, capital gains tax would be payable on trust gains and income tax on family benefits received.

There will also be a facility for remittance basis taxpayers to rearrange their overseas mixed funds to allow them to remit clean capital from overseas ahead of income and gains. Non-doms will be able to segregate amounts of income, gains and capital within their overseas mixed funds to provide certainty on how amounts remitted to the UK will be taxed. This treatment will be extended by government amendment to income, gains and capital held in mixed funds from years before 2007–08, as well as those from subsequent years.

[¶14-000]   Double tax treaties

The following table lists all the territories with which the UK has concluded agreements to avoid international double taxation and also facilitate the exchange of information to prevent tax evasion.

Albania (C)
Algeria (C)
Andorra (EC)
Anguilla (SIE/TIE)
Antigua and Barbuda (C/TIE)
Argentina (C)
Aruba (SIE/TIE)
Armenia (C)
Australia (C)
Austria (C)
Azerbaijan (C)
Bahamas (TIE)
Bahrain (C)
Bangladesh (C)
Barbados (C)
Belarus (C)[(1)]
Belgium (C)
Belize (C/TIE)
Bermuda (TIE/IGA)
Bolivia (C)
Bosnia-Herzegovina (C)[(2)]
Botswana (C)
Brazil (SA/AC/TIE)
British Virgin Islands (SIE/TIE/IGA)
Brunei Darussalam (C)
Bulgaria (C)
Burma (C)
Cameroon (A)
Canada (C)
Cayman Islands (C/SIE/IGA)
Chile (C)[(3)]
China (C/A)
Croatia (C)
Cyprus (C)
Czech Republic (C)
Denmark (C)
Dominica (TIE)
Egypt (C)
Estonia (C)[(1)]
Ethiopia (C/A)
Falkland Islands (C)
Faroe Islands (C)
Fiji (C)
Finland (C)
France (includes Guadeloupe, Guyane, Martinique and Réunion (C/EIG)
Gambia (C)
Georgia (C)
Germany (C)
Ghana (C)
Gibraltar (SIE/IGA)
Greece (C)

Grenada (C/TIE)
Guernsey (includes Alderney, Herm and Lithou) (C/TIE/IGA)
Guyana (C)
Hong Kong SAR (C/SA)
Hungary (C)
Iceland (C)
India (C/EIG)[(3)]
Indonesia (C)
Iran (A)
Ireland (C/EIG)
Isle of Man (SIE) (C/TIE/IGA)
Israel (C)
Italy (C/EIG)
Ivory Coast (Cote d'Ivoire) (C)
Jamaica (C)
Japan (C)
Jersey (SIE/C/TIE/IGA)
Jordan (C)
Kazakstan (C)
Kenya (C)
Kiribati and Tuvalu (C)
Korea (C)
Kosovo (C)
Kuwait (C)
Latvia (C)
Lebanon (SA)
Lesotho (C)
Liberia (TIE)
Libya (C)
Liechtenstein (EC/TIE/C)
Lithuania (C)
Luxembourg (C)
Macao (TIE)
Macedonia (C)
Malawi (C)
Malaysia (C)
Malta (C)
Marshall Islands (TIE)
Mauritius (C)
Mexico (C)
Moldova (C)
Monaco (EC/TIE)
Mongolia (C)
Montenegro (C)[(2)]
Montserrat (SIE/C/TIE/IGA)
Morocco (C)
Namibia (C)
Netherlands (C/EIG/BT)
Netherlands Antilles (SIE/TIE)
New Zealand (C)
Nigeria (C)
Norway (C)

Oman (C)
Pakistan (EIG unchecked[(3)]/C)
Panama (C)
Papua New Guinea (C)
Philippines (C)
Poland (C)
Portugal (C)
Qatar (C)
Romania (C)
Russia (C)
St Christopher (St. Kitts) & Nevis (C/TIE)
St Lucia (TIE)
St Vincent and the Grenadines (TIE)
San Marino (EC/TIE)
Saudi Arabia (C/A)
Senegal (C)
Serbia (C)[(2)]
Sierra Leone (C)
Singapore (C)
Slovak Republic (C)
Slovenia (C)
Solomon Islands (C)
South Africa (C/EIG)
Spain (C)
Sri Lanka (C)
Sudan (C)
Swaziland (C)
Sweden (C/EIG)
Switzerland (TC/C/EC/EIG/EC/TIE)
Taiwan (C)
Tajikistan (C)
Thailand (C)
Trinidad and Tobago (C)
Tunisia (C)
Turkey (C)
Turkmenistan (C)[(1)]
Turks & Caicos Islands (SIE/TIE/IGA)
Tuvula (UK/Gilbert and Ellice Islands) (C)
Uganda (C)
Ukraine (C)
United Arab Emirates (C)
Uruguay (C/TIE)
USA (C/EIG)
Uzbekistan (C)
Venezuela (C)
Vietnam (C)
Zaire (SA)
Zambia (C)
Zimbabwe (C)

General

These agreements may be of various types which are indicated below by the following letters:

- (C) – comprehensive agreements covering a wide range of areas of possible double taxation of income and capital gains;
- (SA) – agreements limited to shipping and air transport profits;
- (A) – agreements limited to air transport profits only;
- (AC) – agreements limited to salaries of aircrew only;
- (EIG) – agreements relating to tax on estates, inheritances and gifts;
- (SIE) – tax information exchange agreements: agreements relating to the EU Directive on taxation of savings income in the form of interest payments;
- (TIE) – tax information exchange agreements: bilateral agreements for co-operation in tax matters through exchange of information;
- (EC) – tax information exchange agreements concluded by the EC on behalf of its member states with third countries;
- (TC) – tax co-operation agreements;
- (BT) – convention in respect of bank taxes; and
- (IGA) – inter-governmental agreement to improve international tax compliance.

Notes
[1] The Convention of 31 July 1985 with the former USSR is regarded as continuing in force (see SP 04/01). The Convention between UK and Turkmenistan was signed on 10 June 2016 but has not yet entered into force.
[2] The Convention of 5 November 1981 with the former Yugoslavia is regarded as continuing in force (see SP 03/07).
[3] The estate, inheritance and gifts agreements with India and Pakistan have not been formally terminated despite the fact that estate duties in those countries were abolished on 15 March 1985 and 29 July 1979 respectively.

Recognised exchanges

[¶15-000] Recognised stock exchanges

(ITA 2007, s. 1005)

With effect from 19 July 2007, a 'recognised stock exchange' is defined for the purposes of the Income Tax Acts as being one which is designated as such by an Order of the Commissioners for HMRC and which falls within one of two categories:

- 'recognised investment exchanges' designated by the Financial Conduct Authority (formerly the Financial Services Authority); and
- markets outside the UK (see below).

Designated 'recognised stock exchanges' by Order

Below is a list of stock exchanges designated as 'recognised stock exchanges' by Order of the Commissioners for HMRC, together with the date of recognition.

The Athens[1] Stock Exchange	14 Jun 1993
The Australian[1] Stock Exchange and any of its subsidiaries	22 Sep 1988
The Bahamas International Securities Exchange	19 Apr 2010
The Bermuda Stock Exchange	4 Dec 2007
The Bond Exchange of South Africa[1]	16 Apr 2008
The Cayman Islands Stock Exchange	4 Mar 2004
The Colombo[1] Stock Exchange	21 Feb 1972
The Copenhagen[1] Stock Exchange	22 Oct 1970
The Cyprus[1] Stock Exchange	22 Jun 2009
The Dutch Caribbean Securities Exchange	8 Dec 2014
Euronext London Ltd	4 Feb 2015
European Wholesale Securities Market	18 Jan 2013
Gibraltar Stock Exchange Limited	16 Aug 2016
Global Board of Trade	30 Jul 2013
GXG Official List	16 May 2013
GXG Main Quote[1]	23 Sep 2013
The Helsinki[1] Stock Exchange	22 Oct 1970
The Iceland[1] Stock Exchange	31 Mar 2006
ICAP Securities[1] & Derivatives Exchange Ltd	25 Apr 2013
The Johannesburg[1] Stock Exchange	22 Oct 1970
The Korea[1] Stock Exchange	10 Oct 1994
The Kuala Lumpa[1] Stock Exchange	10 Oct 1994
LIFFE[1] Administration and Management	26 Sep 2011
The London[1] Stock Exchange	19 Jul 2007
The Malta Stock Exchange	29 Dec 2005
The Mexico[1] Stock Exchange	10 Oct 1994

General

The MICEX[1] Stock Exchange	5 Jan 2011
The NASDAQ OMX Tallinn[1]	5 May 2010
The NASDAQ OMX Vilnius[1]	12 Mar 2012
The National Stock Exchange of Australia	19 Jun 2014
The New Zealand[1] Stock Exchange	22 Sep 1988
The Rio De Janeiro Stock Exchange	17 Aug 1995
The Sao Paulo[1] Stock Exchange	11 Dec 1995
The Singapore Exchange Limited (SGX)	7 Oct 2014 (30 Jun 1977)
The Stockholm[1] Stock Exchange	16 Jul 1985
The Stock Exchange of Mauritius[1]	31 Jan 2011
The Stock Exchange of Thailand[1]	10 Oct 1994
The Swiss Stock Exchange	12 May 1997
The Warsaw[1] Stock Exchange	25 Feb 2010

Note

[1] Markets of the above recognised exchanges on which securities would not meet HMRC definition of 'listed' are as follows:

- Athens Stock Exchange: The Alternative Market (EN.A)
- Australian Stock Exchange: The Sydney Futures Exchange (SFX)
- Bond Exchange of South Africa: Over-the Counter (OTC) market
- Colombo Stock Exchange: Diri Savi Board
- Copenhagen Stock Exchange (part of the OMX Nordic Exchange which is part of the NASDAQ OMX Group): First North
- Cyprus Stock Exchange: Emerging Companies Market (a Multi-lateral trading facility)
- GXG Main Quote: GXG Main Quote
- Helsinki Stock Exchange (part of the OMX Nordic Exchange which is part of the NASDAQ OMX Group): First North
- Iceland Stock Exchange (part of the OMX Nordic Exchange which is part of the NASDAQ OMX Group): First North
- ICAP Securities & Derivatives Exchange Ltd: ISDX Growth Market and ISDX Secondary Market
- Johannesburg Stock Exchange: Alt-X, Venture Capital Market (VCM) and Development Capital Market (DCM)
- Korean Stock Exchange: KOSDAQ and Korean Derivatives Market
- Kuala Lumpa Stock Exchange: ACE Market
- LIFFE Administration and Management (LIFFE A&M): London International Financial Futures and Options Market (LIFFE) the Derivatives Market
- London Stock Exchange: the Alternative Investment Market (AIM), Specialist Fund Market (SFM) and High Growth Segment (HGS)
- Mexico Stock Exchange: OTC Market
- MICEX Stock Exchange: Quotation list B, Quotation list V, Quotation list I, Over the Counter and unlisted security segments
- NASDAQ OMX Tallinn: First North
- NASDAQ OMX Vilnius: First North
- New Zealand Stock Exchange: NZAX Market (Alternative Market)
- Sao Paulo Stock Exchange: Over-the Counter (OTC) market
- Stockholm Stock Exchange (part of the OMX Nordic Exchange which is part of the NASDAQ OMX Group): First North
- Stock Exchange of Mauritius: Development and Enterprise Market (DEM)
- Stock Exchange of Thailand: Market for Alternative Investment (MAI) and the Thailand Futures Exchange (TFEX), and securities traded over the counter (OTC)
- Warsaw Stock Exchange: New Connect Market and Catalyst Market for Bonds (Retail Market) Multi-lateral Trading Facility (MTF)

In addition, a recognised stock exchange is any stock exchange in the following countries which is a stock exchange within the meaning of the law of the particular country relating to stock exchanges (or as specified below).

Austria[1]	22 Oct 1970
Belgium[1]	22 Oct 1970
Canada[1] (any stock exchange prescribed for the purpose of the Canadian Income Tax Act)	22 Oct 1970
France[1]	22 Oct 1970
Germany[1]	5 Aug 1971
Guernsey[2]	10 Dec 2002
Hong Kong[1]	26 Feb 1971
Ireland[1], Republic of	22 Oct 1970
Italy	3 May 1972
Japan	22 Oct 1970
Luxembourg	21 Feb 1972
Netherlands[1]	22 Oct 1970
Norway	22 Oct 1970
Portugal	21 Feb 1972
Spain	5 Aug 1971
USA[1] (any exchange registered with the Securities and Exchange Commission of the United States as a national securities exchange)	22 Oct 1970

Notes
[1] Markets of the above recognised exchanges on which securities would not meet HMRC definition of 'listed' are as follows:
• Austria: Third Market or Dritter Market
• Belgium: NYSE Alternext
• Canada: NEX
• France: NYSE Alternext
• Germany: Freiverkehr markets, Entry Markets (also known as open or unofficial markets)
• Hong Kong: The Growth and Enterprise Market (GEM)
• Ireland (Republic of): Enterprise Securities Market (ESM)
• Netherlands: NYSE Alternext
• USA: Over the counter transactions, Over the Counter Bulletin Board (OTCBB) and Pink Sheets
[2] The Channel Islands Stock Exchange restructured on 20 December 2013 with the business of the exchange being transferred to The Channel Islands Securities Exchange Authority Limited.

Alternative finance investment bonds

(TCGA 1992, s. 151N; ITA 2007, s. 564G; CTA 2009, s. 507)

'Alternative finance investment bonds' (Sharia compliant financial instruments commonly known as 'sukuk') must be listed on a recognised stock exchange. An alternative finance investment bond listed on an exchange recognised under ITA 2007, s. 1005 will meet this requirement. In addition, certain other exchanges are designated as recognised stock

General

exchanges **solely** for the purposes of ITA 2007, s. 564G. These are listed below, together with the dates of recognition.

Abu Dhabi Securities Market	1 April 2007
Bahrain Stock Exchange	1 April 2007
Dubai Financial Market	1 April 2007
NASDAQ Dubai (formerly the 'Dubai International Financial Exchange')	1 April 2007
Labuan International Financial Exchange	1 April 2007
Saudi Stock Exchange (Tadawul)	1 April 2007
Surabaya Stock Exchange	1 April 2007

[¶15-050]   Recognised futures exchanges

(TCGA 1992, s. 288(6))

The following futures exchanges have been designated by the Board of Her Majesty's Revenue and Customs as 'recognised futures exchanges' (when the Board recognises a futures exchange this is announced in the *London Gazette*):

Exchange	Date
International Petroleum Exchange of London London Metal Exchange	From 6 August 1985
London Gold Market London Silver Market	From 12 December 1985
CME Group (formerly Chicago Mercantile Exchange and Chicago Board of Trade[3]) Philadelphia Board of Trade New York Mercantile Exchange	From 19 December 1986
Montreal Exchange Mid-America Commodity Exchange	From 29 July 1987
Hong Kong Futures Exchange	From 15 December 1987
Commodity Exchange, Inc (COMEX)	From 25 August 1988
Sydney Futures Exchange Ltd	From 31 October 1988
OM Stockholm OMLX (formerly OM London)	From 18 March 1992
Euronext (London International Financial Futures and Options Exchange)[1]	From 22 March 1992
New York Board of Trade[2]	From 10 June 2004
Eurex Deutschland	From 13 March 2015

Notes

[1] Euronext (merged with NYSE group in 2007 to form NYSE Euronext) acquired London International Financial Futures and Options Exchange in January 2002. On 22 March 1992, London International Financial Futures Exchange and the London Traded Options Market merged forming London International Financial Futures and Options Exchange. In 1996, the LIFFE merged with the London Commodity Exchange (formerly FOX). Markets incorporated within former London Commodity Exchange, recognised from 6 August 1985 include: Baltic International Freight Futures Exchange; London Cocoa Terminal Market; London Coffee Terminal Market; London Futures and Options Exchange;

London Grain Futures Market; London Meat Futures Market; London Potato Futures Market; London Rubber Market; London Soya Bean Meal Futures Market and London Sugar Terminal Market.
(2) In June 2004, the New York Coffee Sugar and Cocoa Exchange (CS&CE) merged with the New York Cotton Exchange (NYCE) to form the New York Board of Trade. As a result of this merger, all previous exchanges and subsidiaries ceased to exist, including the Coffee, Sugar, & Cocoa Exchange, the New York Cotton Exchange, the Citrus Associates of the New York Cotton Exchange, the New York Futures Exchange (NYFE), and the FINEX Exchange. All markets are now referred to as the New York Board of Trade or NYBOT. [NY CS&CE was designated from 15 December 1987, and NYCE and Citrus Associates of the NYCE from 25 August 1988.]
(3) Chicago Board of Trade recognised from 24 April 1987.

[¶15-150]   Recognised investment exchanges

(ITEPA 2003, s. 702)

(Tax Reporter: ¶494-300)

A 'recognised investment exchange' (RIE) is an investment exchange in relation to which a recognition order made by the Financial Conduct Authority (FCA) (formerly Financial Services Authority) is in force (*Financial Services and Markets Act* 2000, s. 285ff.).

Where the FCA does issue a recognition order for a 'recognised investment exchange' this has consequences for the rules relating to the operation of PAYE on the provision of 'readily convertible asset' for employees. If an employer provides an employee with an asset that can be sold, or otherwise realised, on a recognised investment exchange (RIE); the London Bullion Market; the New York Stock Exchange; or any market specified in PAYE Regulations, that asset is a 'readily convertible asset' and the employer is obliged to operate PAYE (ITEPA 2003, s. 696, 702). Similarly, any asset, such as a gold bar, capable of sale or realisation on the London Bullion Market is a 'readily convertible asset'. As at November 2013, the FCA has currently issued recognition orders for the following RIEs:

Investment exchange	Effective date
UK	
ICE Futures Europe	22 November 2001
BATS Trading Limited	11 July 2013
ICAP Securities & Derivatives Exchange Limited	19 July 2007
LIFFE Administration and Management	22 November 2001
London Stock Exchange plc	22 November 2001
The London Metal Exchange Limited	22 November 2001
Overseas	
Australian Securities Exchange Limited	30 January 2002
Chicago Board of Trade [CBOT]	23 November 2001
EUREX [Zurich]	23 November 2001
ICE Futures U.S., Inc	17 May 2007
National Association of Securities Dealers Automated Quotations [NASDAQ]	23 November 2001
New York Mercantile Exchange Inc. [NYMEX Inc.]	23 November 2001
NYSE Liffe US	29 September 2009
SIX Swiss Exchange AG	23 November 2001
The Chicago Mercantile Exchange [CME]	23 November 2001

General

[¶15-200]   Recognised growth markets

(FA 1986, s. 99A)

Finance Act 2014 introduces an exemption from stamp duty and stamp duty reserve tax for transfers of securities admitted to trading on recognised growth markets, with effect from 28 April 2014.

To qualify as a recognised growth market, a market must be a recognised stock exchange (see ¶15-000) and meet one of two conditions:

- a majority of companies trading on that market are companies with market capitalisations of less than £170m in the qualifying period; or
- the market's rules require that companies seeking admission demonstrate at least 20% compounded annual growth in revenue or employment over the three years preceding admission.

List of recognised growth markets

Name	Effective date
Alternative Investment Market	28 April 2014
Enterprise Securities Market (ESM)	28 April 2014
GXG Markets A/S	28 April 2014
High Growth Segment	28 April 2014
ICAP Securities and Derivatives Exchange Limited (ISDX)	28 April 2014

HMRC information

Note: See ¶26-000 for opinions from Revenue Scotland in respect of Scottish taxes.

[¶15-500]   Clearances and approvals

(Source: www.gov.uk/seeking-clearance-or-approval-for-a-transaction)

HMRC may be able to provide advance clearance or approval to some transactions. HMRC will not provide clearances on the following matters:

- application of the 'settlements legislation' in ITTOIA 2005, Pt. 5, Ch. 5; or
- the tax consequences of executing non-charitable trust deeds or settlements.

Clearances and the General Anti-Abuse Rule (GAAR)

HMRC will not give either formal or informal clearances that the GAAR does not apply. However, as part of its model of direct engagement with large businesses and wealthy individuals HMRC will discuss commercial arrangements and confirm where appropriate that it does not regard particular arrangements as tax avoidance.

Code of Practice on Taxation for Banks

A bank which adopts the Code of Practice on Taxation for Banks commits not to undertake any tax planning that achieves a tax result contrary to the intentions of Parliament. When approached by a bank under the code, Customer Relationship Managers will continue to give HMRC's view of whether a transaction is 'code compliant'.

[¶15-550]   Non-statutory clearances

(Source: www.gov.uk/seeking-clearance-or-approval-for-a-transaction)

Transaction	Applications to:
Company migrations Notification of company migration and approval of arrangements for payment of tax liabilities in accordance with TMA 1970, s. 109B–109F (previously FA 1988, s. 130) (see SP 2/90).	Nicola Harris HM Revenue & Customs CTIS Business International, Foreign Profits Team 100 Parliament Street London SW1A 2BQ Telephone: 03000 543 476

General

Transaction	Applications to:
Controlled Foreign Companies Clearances in relation to Controlled Foreign Companies (CFC) in accordance with TIOPA 2010, Pt. 9A (new CFC rules) or ICTA 1988, s. 747–756 and Sch. 24–26 (old CFC Rules).	Electronically to Mary Sharp and copied to the UK group's Customer Relationship Manager or Customer Co-ordinator. (No paper copies of an application are needed.) If it is not possible to send applications for clearance electronically, applications should be sent to the following address: CTIS, Foreign Profits Team Registry (CFC clearances) 3rd floor 100 Parliament Street London SW1A 2BQ Telephone: 03000 585 623
Inward Investment Support service For information on inward investment and to discuss the tax implications of an investment.	Inward Investment Support HM Revenue & Customs CTIAA Business International 100 Parliament Street London SW1A 2BQ E-mail: inwardinvestmentsupport@hmrc. gsi.gov.uk.
Business Investment Relief Provisions For HMRC's view on whether a proposed investment can be treated as a qualifying investment as defined in ITA 2007, s. 809VC use the checklist at www.gov.uk/government/uploads/system/ uploads/attachment_data/file/377647/ annex-b.pdf.	Business Investment Relief HM Revenue & Customs BX9 1BN Telephone: 03000 527 416
Creative Industries Advice on the workings of the scheme as it applies to film tax, animation tax, high-end television tax and video games development reliefs.	Creative Industries Unit (film, television/ animation and video games tax reliefs) Local Compliance S0717 PO Box 3900 Glasgow G70 6AA Telephone: 03000 510 191
Enterprise investment scheme (EIS), seed enterprise investment scheme (SEIS) and venture capital trust (VCT) scheme Advice on the workings of these schemes, as well as providing non-statutory advance assurance to companies seeking investment under these schemes.	Local Compliance Small Company Enterprise Centre Admin Team SO777 PO Box 3900 Glasgow G70 6AA Telephone: 0300 123 1083

Transaction	Applications to:
Research and development tax relief: advance assurance Confirmation that a company will get R&D tax relief.	Apply online at www.gov.uk/government/publications/research-and-development-tax-relief-application-for-advance-assurance-for-research-and-development-tax-relief-ct-rd-aa By post to: Local Compliance I & R Unit Manchester (AA) SO717 Newcastle upon Tyne NE98 1ZZ

Other non-statutory clearances

(Source: www.gov.uk/non-statutory-clearance-service-guidance)

HMRC offer a further clearance service for customers and their advisers who need clarification on guidance or legislation in relation to a specific transaction that is not covered by a more appropriate clearance or approval route. HMRC will usually reply within 28 days.

HMRC will not provide advice under this service where:

- all the necessary information (per the checklists below) has not been provided;
- HMRC do not think that there are genuine points of uncertainty – they will explain why they think this and where the relevant online guidance can be found;
- the request is for HMRC to give tax planning advice, or to 'approve' tax planning products or arrangements;
- the application is about treatment of transactions which, in HMRC's view, are for the purposes of avoiding tax;
- HMRC are already checking the tax position for the period in question, in which case contact should be directed to the officer dealing with the check;
- any related return for the period in question is final; or
- there is a statutory clearance applicable for the transaction.

Other non-statutory clearances	Applications to:
All transactions other than Business Investment Relief and Business Property Relief See Annex A checklist at www.gov.uk/government/uploads/system/uploads/attachment_data/file/377646/annex-a.pdf – head the application letter 'Clearance service'.	HMRC Non-Statutory Clearance Team, 5th Floor Alexander House, 21 Victoria Avenue, Southend on Sea, Essex SS99 1AA E-mail: hmrc.southendteam@hmrc.gsi.gov.uk (HMRC Non-Statutory Clearance Team)

General

Other non-statutory clearances	Applications to:
Advance assurance on Business Investment Relief for non-domiciled persons taxed on the remittance basis See Annex B checklist at www.gov.uk/government/uploads/system/ uploads/attachment_data/file/377647/ annex-b.pdf – head the application letter 'Advance Assurance for Business Investment Relief'.	HM Revenue & Customs Business Investment Relief Team S1278 PO Box 202 Bootle L69 9AL
Inheritance Tax Business Property Relief clearances See Annex C checklist at www.gov.uk/government/uploads/system/ uploads/attachment_data/file/377648/ annex-c.pdf.	By e-mail to: mailpoint.e@hmrc.gsi.gov.uk (Trusts & Estates Technical Team (Clearances)). Please quote reference BP102/P1/08E By post to: HMRC Trusts & Estates Technical Team (Clearances) Ferrers House Castle Meadow Road Nottingham NG2 1BB
VAT clearances See Annex D checklist at www.gov.uk/government/uploads/system/ uploads/attachment_data/file/423806/ Annex_D_final_150416-5.pdf.	HM Revenue and Customs Non-Statutory Clearance Team 5th Floor Alexander House 21 Victoria Avenue Southend on Sea Essex SS99 1AA E-mail: hmrc.southendteam@hmrc.gsi. gov.uk

[¶15-600]   Statutory clearance or approval

Transaction	Applications to:
Qualifying life assurance policies ICTA 1988, Sch. 15 Applications to approve certification of qualifying life assurance policies.	HM Revenue & Customs CTISA Corporation Tax and Business Income Tax Financial Services Team 3rd Floor 100 Parliament Street London SW1A 2BQ Telephone: 03000 585 911

Transaction	Applications to:
Transfers of long-term business between life assurance companies under FA 2012, s. 133 Applications for clearance, including cases where the parties include non-UK resident companies or friendly societies	The transferor company's Customer Relationship Manager and to: HM Revenue & Customs CTISA Corporation Tax and Business Income Tax Financial Services Team 3rd Floor 100 Parliament Street London SW1A 2BQ Telephone: 03000 585911 Alternatively, by e-mail to Anthony Fawcett via link at www.hmrc.gov.uk/cap/
Transactions in shares or debentures under ICTA 1988, s. 765 and 765A The Treasury Consents regime was repealed by *Finance Act* 2009. Events or transactions taking place on or after 1 July 2009 are subject to a new reporting regime, detail of which can be found in HMRC's *International Manual*.	
Transfer pricing (advance pricing agreements) HMRC have run an Advanced Pricing Agreements programme since 1999 to assist businesses in identifying solutions for complex transfer pricing issues. HMRC issued Statement of Practice (SP) 2/10 in December 2010 to update an earlier Statement of Practice (SP 3/99) on Advance Pricing Agreements (APAs). The SP is intended as general guidance as to how HMRC interpret the APA legislation and how HMRC operate the UK APA Programme.	Nicholas Stevart (APA Team Leader) HM Revenue & Customs CTIS Business International East Spur, Euston Tower, 286 Euston Road, London NW1 3UH Telephone: 03000 585 659 Fax: 03000 543 795
Stamp taxes Queries on stamp taxes should be directed first to the Stamp Taxes Helpline and if the helpline is unable to answer the question, in writing to the Stamp Office. The Clearance and Counteraction Team (see below) does not handle applications for stamp duty land tax (SDLT) adjudications.	**Stamp Taxes Helpline** Tel: 0300 200 3510 Birmingham Stamp Office 9th Floor City Centre House 30 Union Street Birmingham B2 4AR

General

Transaction	Applications to:
Statutory applications for advance clearance HMRC's Clearance and Counteraction Team, Counter-Avoidance handles requests where advance clearance is required under statutory provisions relating to any one or more of the following:	Please ensure a 'Market sensitive' application is marked for the attention of 'The Team leader', and send it to: HM Revenue & Customs CA Clearance SO528 PO Box 194 Merseyside L69 9AA
Capital gains	Telephone: 03000 589 004
• share exchanges (TCGA 1992, s. 138(1))	Fax: 03000 589 802
• reconstruction involving the transfer of a business (TCGA 1992, s. 139(5))	E-mail: reconstructions@hmrc.gsi.gov.uk (Clearance and Counteraction Team) Where clearance is required under any
• collective investment schemes: exchanges, mergers and schemes of reconstruction (TCGA 1992, s. 103K)	one or more of the statutory provisions, a single letter should be sent to the Clearance and Counteraction Team,
• transfer of a UK trade between EU member states (TCGA 1992, s. 140B and 140D)	Counter-Avoidance at the address above. No extra copy is required as the same person will deal with each of the
Other shares, securities, demergers and reorganisations	clearances asked for. A single response will be given covering all of these. Please make clear at the top of the letter what
• purchase of own shares by unquoted trading companies (CTA 2010, s. 1044)	clearances are being requested.
• demergers (CTA 2010, s. 1091)	Please note the following points:
• EIS shares (acquisition by new company) (ITA 2007, s. 247(1)(f))	• HMRC acknowledge only those applications that request an acknowledgement;
• Company reorganisation involving intangible fixed assets (CTA 2009, s. 831)	• if a reply by e-mail is required, please write 'I confirm that I understand and accept the risks involved in using
• Transactions in securities (CTA 2010, s. 748 and ITA 2007, s. 701)	e-mail'. HMRC do not e-mail market sensitive applications;
Transactions in land	• enquiries about the progress of an application or making general enquiries
• under CTA 2009, s. 237 (for corporation tax purposes) and ITTOIA 2005, s. 300 (for income tax purposes) – confirmation of the customer's view of the tax consequences of assigning a lease granted at under value	should be made by telephone: 03000 589 004. Please allow ten days after receiving an acknowledgement before you contact to check progress;
• under CTA 2010, s. 831 (for corporation tax purposes) and ITA 2007, s. 770 (for income tax purposes).	

Transaction	Applications to:
Company finance • CTA 2009, s. 426/7 (loan relationships transfers) and 437 (loan relationships: mergers) • CTA 2009, s. 677 (derivative contracts: transfers) and 686 (derivative contracts: mergers) ***Targeted Anti-Avoidance Rule 3 (Capital Gains)*** Informal clearances: companies and their representatives may make requests for advice about the legislation in TCGA 1992, s. 184G–184H, including whether the provisions will apply to a planned series of transactions that may constitute an arrangement. ***Cross border transfers*** of a loan relationship, derivative contract or intangible fixed assets under TIOPA 2010, s. 117(4). ***Seed enterprise investment scheme (SEIS)*** continuity of relief under ITA 2007, s. 257HB.	• HMRC regard information that could affect the price of a stock market quoted company and information concerning the financial affairs of well known individuals as sensitive; • in March, September and December HMRC receive high volumes of applications which increases turn around time. Please bear this in mind when applying during these times.

[¶15-650]   HMRC websites

HMRC's homepage and website content has moved to the GOV.UK website and all content is now accessible through the GOV.UK site only.

HMRC home page

www.gov.uk/government/organisations/hm-revenue-customs

The HMRC section of the GOV.UK website contains full details of contact addresses and numbers, including in particular the following:

• Helplines and postal addresses for all taxes, National Insurance and VAT queries: www.gov.uk/government/organisations/hm-revenue-customs/contact;

• Dedicated helplines and contacts for authorised agents: www.gov.uk/topic/dealing-with-hmrc/tax-agent-guidance.

General

Other useful parts of the HMRC content are:

HMRC forms

http://search.hmrc.gov.uk/kb5/hmrc/forms/home.page

HMRC leaflets, factsheets and booklets

www.gov.uk/government/collections/hm-revenue-and-customs-leaflets-factsheets-and-booklets

HMRC manuals

www.gov.uk/government/collections/hmrc-manuals

HMRC self-assessment pages

www.gov.uk/personal-tax/self-assessment

HMRC employers information

www.gov.uk/business-tax/paye

HMRC tax credits

www.gov.uk/topic/benefits-credits/tax-credits

VAT

www.gov.uk/topic/business-tax/vat

Construction industry scheme

www.gov.uk/topic/business-tax/construction-industry-scheme

[¶15-800]   Other useful websites

Adjudicator

www.adjudicatorsoffice.gov.uk/

CIOT

www.tax.org.uk

Government Information Service

UK: www.direct.gov.uk

Scotland: www.scotland.gov.uk

Wales: http://wales.gov.uk/splash?orig=/

ICAEW Tax Faculty

www.icaew.com/en/technical/tax/tax-faculty

Legislation

www.legislation.gov.uk/

Parliament

UK: www.parliament.uk/

Scotland: www.scottish.parliament.uk/

Wales: www.assembly.wales/en/Pages/Home.aspx

Parliamentary Ombudsman

www.ombudsman.org.uk/

Revenue Scotland

www.revenue.scot/

Treasury Home Page

www.gov.uk/government/organisations/hm-treasury

Tribunals service

www.justice.gov.uk/tribunals/tax

Valuation Office Agency

www.voa.gov.uk/

Finance Acts

[¶15-950]   Finance Acts

Year	Budget		Royal Assent	
2013	20 March	2013	17 July	2013
2014	19 March	2014	17 July	2014
2015	18 March	2015	26 March	2015
2015 (No. 2)	8 July	2015	18 November	2015
2016	16 March	2016	15 September	2016
2017	8 March	2017	27 April	2017
2017 (No. 2)	-		16 November	2017

General

STAMP TAXES

Stamp duty land tax

Note: See ¶26-200 for rates applicable in Scotland from 1 April 2015.

[¶16-000]   Stamp duty land tax: general
(FA 2003, Pt. 4; SDLTA 2015)

(SLDT Reporter: ¶50-100ff.)

Applies to contracts entered into (or varied) after 10 July 2003 and completed after 30 November 2003 and to leases granted after that date.

SDLT also applies to transfers of an interest in land into or out of a partnership, and to an acquisition of an interest in a partnership where the partnership property includes an interest in land (from 22 July 2004). From 19 July 2006, SDLT additionally applies to transfers of partnership interests but only where the sole or main activity of the partnership is investing or dealing in interests in land.

[¶16-010]   SDLT: residential property rates
(FA 2003, s. 55; SDLTA 2015)

(SDLT Reporter: ¶50-105; ¶50-106)

Rate on portion of value above threshold

Period	Portion of value £	Rate %	Additional property rate[4] %
On or after 1 April 2016	0–125,000	0[5]	3
	125,001–250,000	2[5]	5
	250,001–925,000	5[5]	8
	925,001–1,500,000	10	13
	1,500,001 and over	12	15
	Over 500,000	15[1][2][3]	
On or after 4 December 2014	0–125,000	0	—
	125,001–250,000	2	—
	250,001–925,000	5	—
	925,001–1,500,000	10	—
	1,500,001 and over	12	—
	Over 500,000	15[1][2]	—

Rate on entire property value

Period	Band £	Rate %
20 March 2014 to 3 December 2014	0–125,000	0
	125,001–250,000	1
	250,001–500,000	3
	500,001–1,000,000	4
	1,000,001–2,000,000	5
	Over 2,000,000	7
	Over 500,000	15[1][2]
22 March 2012 to 19 March 2014	0–125,000	0
	125,001–250,000	1
	250,001–500,000	3
	500,001–1,000,000	4
	1,000,001–2,000,000	5
	Over 2,000,000	7
	Over 2,000,000	15[1][2]
6 April 2011 to 21 March 2012	0–125,000	0
	125,001–250,000	1
	250,001–500,000	3
	500,001–1,000,000	4
	Over 1,000,000	5

Notes

[1] The 15% rate applies if the property is acquired by certain non-natural persons (e.g. companies, partnerships with corporate members and collective investment schemes) with effect from 21 March 2012.

[2] *Finance Act* 2013 introduced a number of reliefs to reduce the 15% rate to 7% with effect in relation to transactions with an effective date on or after 17 July 2013 (Royal Assent). The reliefs broadly match those where there is relief against the annual tax on enveloped dwellings. However, the SDLT reliefs will apply only if the property continues to satisfy the qualifying conditions throughout the following three years, otherwise, additional SDLT will become payable.

[3] Reliefs available from the 15% higher rate of SDLT extended to equity release schemes (home reversion plans), property development activities and properties occupied by employees from 1 April 2016 (FA 2003, Sch. 4A, as amended by FA 2016, s. 129–131).

[4] From 1 April 2016, higher rates of stamp duty land tax apply to purchases of additional residential properties, such as second homes and buy-to-let properties in England, Wales and Northern Ireland. Purchasers have 36 months to claim a refund of the higher rates if they buy a new main residence before disposing of their previous main residence. Purchasers also have 36 months between selling a main residence and replacing it with another without having to pay the higher rates. A share (of up to 50%) in a property which has been inherited within the 36 months prior to a transaction will not be considered as an additional property when applying the higher rates (FA 2003, s. 55 and Sch. 4ZA).

[5] First time buyers relief to be introduced with effect in relation to transactions with an effective date on or after 22 November 2017 by legislation in Finance Bill 2017–18. Those claiming the relief will pay no SDLT on the first £300,000 of the consideration and 5% on any remainder. No relief will be available where the total consideration is more than £500,000. (Autumn Budget 2017).

[¶16-020]   SDLT: non-residential or mixed property rates

(FA 2003, s. 55)

(SDLT Reporter: ¶50-110)

Rate on portion of value above threshold

Period	Portion of value £	Rate %
On or after 17 March 2016[(1)]	0–150,000	0
	150,001–250,000	2
	Over 250,000	5

Note

[(1)] Where contracts were exchanged but transactions have not completed before 17 March 2016 purchasers had a choice of whether the old or new structure and rates apply (FA 2016, s. 127(13)–(14)).

Rate on entire property value

Period	Band £	Rate %
6 April 2011 to 16 March 2016	0–150,000	0
	150,001–250,000	1
	250,001–500,000	3
	Over 500,000	4

[¶16-030]   SDLT: lease rental rates

(FA 2003, Sch. 5)

(SDLT Reporter: ¶60-405)

Residential

Period	Rate %	Net present value of rent £
From 1 January 2010	0	0–125,000
	1	Over 125,000

Non-residential (on portion of value above threshold)

Period	Rate %	Net present value of rent £
On or after 17 March 2016	0	0–150,000
	1	150,001–5,000,000
	2	Over 5,000,000
From 1 January 2010	0	0–150,000
	1	150,001–5,000,000

Note:

Duty on premium is the same as for transfers of land (except special rules apply for premium where rent exceeds £1,000 annually.

[¶16-100]   Stamp duty land tax returns and payment dates

(FA 2003, s. 76 and 86)

(SDLT Reporter: ¶50-500)

Event	Deadline[2]
Delivery of land transaction return	30 days of the effective date[1]
Payment of tax	Not later than the filing date for the land transaction return

Notes

[1] Where the transaction is completed by a conveyance, the effective dates of the transaction is the date of completion or, if earlier, the date the contract is substantially performed (FA 2003, s. 44).

[2] As announced at Autumn Statement 2015, the Government consulted in 2016 on changes to the SDLT filing and payment process, including a reduction in the filing and payment window from 30 days to 14 days. Spring Budget 2017 announced that the reduction in the filing and payment window will be delayed until after April 2018.

[¶16-200]   Stamp duty land tax penalties

(SLDT Reporter: ¶100-400)

Failure to deliver a land transaction return by the filing date (FA 2003, Sch. 10, para. 3 and 4)	£100 if return delivered within three months of filing date, otherwise £200. If not delivered within 12 months, maximum penalty of amount of tax chargeable		
Failure to comply with a notice to deliver return within specified period (FA 2003, Sch. 10, para. 5)	Maximum of £60 for each day on which the failure continues after notification		
Failure to keep or preserve records under FA 2003, Sch. 10, para. 9 or Sch. 11, para. 4	Maximum of £3,000 unless other documentary evidence provided		
Errors in returns[1] (FA 2007, Sch. 24) Errors in returns for periods starting 1 April 2009 where return is filed on or after 1 April 2010, or where liability arises on or after 1 April 2010:	**Percentage of potential lost revenue Category 1**		
• careless action • deliberate but not concealed action • deliberate and concealed action	30% 70% 100%		
Reductions for disclosure: maximum reduction weighted according to quality of disclosure determined as:	**Standard penalty**	**Prompted disclosure minimum**	**Unprompted disclosure minimum**
• 30% for telling	30%	15%	0%
• 40% for helping	70%	35%	20%
• 30% for giving access	100%	50%	30%

Error in taxpayer's document attributable to another person[(1)] (FA 2007, Sch. 24)	100% potential lost revenue Subject to reductions for disclosure as above
Failure to notify HMRC of an under-assessment within 30 days[(1)] (FA 2007, Sch. 24)	30% of potential lost revenue Subject to reductions for disclosure as above
Failure to comply with an information notice (FA 2008, Sch. 36)	Initial penalty £300 Up to £60 per day for each day for continued failure Tax-related penalty determined by tribunal where significant tax at stake
Inaccurate information/documents in complying with an information notice (FA 2008, Sch. 36) Inaccuracy careless or deliberate	Up to £3,000 for each inaccuracy

Note
[(1)] No penalties for errors that occur despite taking reasonable care.

[¶16-250]   Stamp duty land tax interest

(SLDT Reporter: ¶100-000ff.)

The rates are as follows:

	Rate %	
Period of application	**Underpayments**	**Repayments**
From 23 August 2016	2.75	0.50
29 September 2009 to 22 August 2016	3.00	0.50

Finance Act 2009, s. 101–104 and Sch. 53 and 54 contain provisions to harmonise interest regimes across all HMRC taxes and duties.

Stamp duty

[¶17-000]   Stamp duty rates

Conveyance or transfer on sale of shares and securities

(FA 1986, s. 67(3); FA 1999, Sch. 13, para. 3)

Instrument[1][2][3][4][5]	Rate of tax %
Stock transfer	0.5
Conversion of shares into depositary receipts	1.5
Take overs and mergers	0.5
Purchase by company of own shares	0.5
Letters of allotment	0.5

Notes
[1] Stamp duty is rounded up to the nearest multiple of £5 (FA 1999, s. 112).
[2] Loan capital is generally exempt from transfer on sale duty subject to specific exclusions (designed to prevent exemption applying to quasi-equity securities) (FA 1986, s. 79).
[3] Stamp duty is not chargeable on a transfer of stock or marketable securities where the amount or value of the consideration for the sale is £1,000 or under, and the instrument is certified at £1,000 (with effect in relation to instruments executed on or after 13 March 2008 and not stamped before 19 March 2008) (FA 1999, Sch. 13, para. 1(3A)).
[4] From 28 April 2014, transfers of securities admitted to trading on recognised growth markets are exempt from stamp duty (FA 2014, Sch. 24). See ¶15-200 for a list of recognised growth markets.
[5] Shares transferred to a clearance service or depositary receipt issuer as a result of the exercise of an option are now charged the 1.5% higher rate of stamp duty based on either their market value or the option strike price, whichever is higher. Share transfers made other than to a clearance service or depositary receipt system as a result of exercising an option are unaffected. The change applies to options exercised on or after 23 March 2016 which were entered into on or after 25 November 2015 (FA 1986, s. 67 and 70, as amended by FA 2016, s. 138).

[¶17-200]   Stamp duty penalties

Type of document	Penalties applicable if document presented for stamping more than
Document executed in UK	30 days after execution
Document executed abroad relating to UK land and buildings	30 days after execution
Document executed abroad	30 days after document first received in UK[1]

Note
[1] Free standing penalty (see table further below) may apply if written information confirming date of receipt in UK is incorrect.

The maximum penalties are:

*   £300 or the amount of duty, whichever is less; on documents submitted up to one year late; and

*   £300 or the amount of duty, whichever is greater; on documents submitted more than one year late.

Mitigated penalties due on late stamping

The Stamp Office publishes tables of mitigated penalty levels that will be applied in straightforward cases at www.hmrc.gov.uk/sd/pay-penalties/penalties.htm#1.

From 1 October 2014

Length of delay	Penalty
Documents late by up to 12 months	10% of the duty, capped at £300
Documents late by 12 to 24 months	20% of the duty
Documents late by more than 24 months	30% of the duty

Before 1 October 2014

Months late	Up to £300	£305–£700	£705–£1,350	£1,355–£2,500	£2,505–£5,000	Over £5,000
Under 3	Nil	£20	£40	£60	£80	£100
Under 6	£20[1]	£40	£60	£80	£100	£150
Under 9	£40[1]	£60	£80	£100	£150	£200
Under 12	£60[1]	£80	£100	£150	£200	£300
Under 15	15% of the duty or £100 if greater					20% of the duty
Under 18	25% of the duty or £150 if greater					40% of the duty
Under 21	35% of the duty or £200 if greater					60% of the duty
Under 24	45% of the duty or £250 if greater					80% of the duty

Note

[1] Or the amount of the duty if that is less.

If a document is over 24 months late, the penalty is the higher of:

– the amount of stamp duty that's due;

– £300.

Reasonable excuse

In all cases above, the penalties will not apply if the person responsible for stamping can show a 'reasonable excuse' for the failure to submit the document(s) within the time limit. Interest is due on any unpaid penalty.

[¶17-250] Stamp duty interest

In respect of instruments executed on or after 1 October 1999, interest is chargeable on stamp duty that is not paid within 30 days of execution of a stampable document, wherever execution takes place (SA 1891, s. 15A). Interest is payable on repayments of overpaid duty, calculated from the later of 30 days from the date of execution of the instrument, or lodgement with the Stamp Office of the duty repayable (FA 1999, s. 110). Interest is rounded down (if necessary) to the nearest multiple of £5. No interest is payable if that amount is under £25. The applicable interest rate is as prescribed under FA 1989, s. 178.

For interest periods from 1 October 1999 onwards, the rate of interest charged on underpaid or late paid stamp duty and SDRT exceeds that on repayments:

	Rate %	
Period of application	**Underpayments**	**Repayments**
From 23 August 2016	2.75	0.50
29 September 2009 to 22 August 2016	3.00	0.50

Finance Act 2009, s. 101–104 and Sch. 53 and 54 contain provisions to harmonise interest regimes across all HMRC taxes and duties.

Stamp duty reserve tax

[¶18-000]   Stamp duty reserve tax rates
(FA 1986, s. 87, 93 and 96)

Principal charge

Subject matter of charge	Rate of tax %
Agreements to transfer chargeable securities[1] for money or money's worth	0.5
Renounceable letters of allotment	0.5
Shares converted into depositary receipts[2][4]	1.5
Chargeable securities[1] put into clearance system[2][4]	1.5

Notes

[1] Chargeable securities = stocks, shares, loan capital, units under unit trust scheme (FA 1986, s. 99(3)). From 28 April 2014, the definition of chargeable securities for SDRT purposes excludes securities admitted to trading on a recognised growth market (FA 1986, s. 99(4A) and 99A). See ¶15-200 for a list of recognised growth markets.

[2] Following the European Court of Justice judgment in *HSBC Holdings plc & Vidacos Nominees Ltd v R & C Commrs* (Case C-569/07) [2010] BTC 13, HMRC accept that no duty such as the charge to SDRT imposed by FA 1986, s. 96 may be levied the issue of shares to a depositary receipt issuer or a clearance service located within the European Union.

[3] From 30 March 2014, the stamp duty reserve tax charge for which fund managers are liable when investors surrender their units in UK unit trust schemes or shares in UK OEICs is abolished. Previously, the charge was at the 0.5% rate. Non-pro rata in specie redemptions remain subject to the principle SDRT charge (FA 2014, s. 114).

[4] Shares transferred to a clearance service or depositary receipt issuer as a result of the exercise of an option are now charged the 1.5% higher rate of stamp duty based on either their market value or the option strike price, whichever is higher. Share transfers made other than to a clearance service or depositary receipt system as a result of exercising an option are unaffected. The change applies to options exercised on or after 23 March 2016 which were entered into on or after 25 November 2015 (FA 1986, s. 93 and 96, as amended by FA 2016, s. 139).

[¶18-100]   Stamp duty reserve tax notification and payment deadlines
(SI 1986/1711, reg. 2 and 3)

Transfer type	Deadline
Share transfers involving CREST (where notification and payment to HMRC is automatic) and any transfer that could have been made through CREST but was not	14 calendar days after the date when the trade took place
Off-market share transfers (when shares are transferred off-market using a system other than CREST and the transfer could not have been made through CREST)	Seventh day of the month following the month when the trade took place

[¶18-200] Stamp duty reserve tax penalties

Errors in returns[1] (FA 2007, Sch. 24)	Percentage of potential lost revenue		
Errors in returns for periods starting 1 April 2009 where return is filed on or after 1 April 2010, or where liability arises on or after 1 April 2010:	Category 1		
• careless action	30%		
• deliberate but not concealed action	70%		
• deliberate and concealed action	100%		
Reductions for disclosure: maximum reduction weighted according to quality of disclosure determined as:	Standard penalty	Prompted disclosure minimum	Unprompted disclosure minimum
• 30% for telling	30%	15%	0%
• 40% for helping	70%	35%	20%
• 30% for giving access	100%	50%	30%
Failure to comply with an information notice (FA 2008, Sch. 36)	Initial penalty £300 Up to £60 per day for each day continued failure Tax-related penalty determined by tribunal where significant tax at stake		
Inaccurate information/documents in complying with an information notice (FA 2008, Sch. 36) Inaccuracy careless or deliberate	Up to £3,000 for each inaccuracy		
Failure to make return[2] (FA 2009, Sch. 55) **From 1 January 2015** in relation to a charge to stamp duty reserve tax under regulations under FA 1986, s. 98			
Failure to submit return	£100		
Continued failure – three months from penalty date	£10 per day for a period up to 90 days beginning with date specified in notice (maximum £900)		
Continued failure – six months from penalty date	The greater of £300 or 5% of the liability to tax shown by the return		

Failure still continues after 12 months after the penalty date	Greater of relevant percentage of liability shown by the return and £300		
	Relevant percentage		
• withholding information deliberate and concealed	100%		
• withholding information deliberate but not concealed	70%		
• any other case	5%		
Reductions for disclosure: maximum reduction weighted according to quality of disclosure determined as:	**Standard penalty**	**Prompted disclosure minimum**	**Unprompted disclosure minimum**
• 30% for telling	70%	35%	20%
• 40% for helping	100%	50%	30%
• 30% for giving access			
Failure to notify HMRC and pay tax (TMA 1970, s. 93; SI 1986/1711) **Before 1 January 2015**			
Failure to give notice	£100		
Failure continues after 12 months	Penalty of amount of tax due		

Notes
[1] No penalties for errors that occur despite taking reasonable care.
[2] Defences of 'reasonable excuse' or 'special circumstances' may be available.

Penalties for late payment of stamp duty reserve tax

(FA 2009, Sch. 56)

From 1 January 2015

Tax overdue	Penalty
30 days	5% of unpaid tax
6 months	Further 5% of unpaid tax
12 months	Further 5% of unpaid tax

Stamp Taxes

[¶18-250]   Stamp duty reserve tax interest

(TMA 1970, s. 86; FA 1986, s. 92; FA 1989, s. 178; FA 2009, s. 101 and 102; SI 1986/1711)

Late payment interest is charged on unpaid stamp duty reserve tax from the due date for payment (see ¶18-100) to the actual date of payment. Repayment interest is paid on amounts of overpaid stamp duty reserve tax of £25 or more and runs from the date of payment to the date of repayment.

Period	Rate %	
	Late payment	Repayment
From 23 August 2016	2.75	0.5
29 September 2009 to 22 August 2016[(1)]	3.00	0.5

Note
[(1)] From 1 January 2015, FA 2009, s. 101 and 102 apply for the purposes of stamp duty reserve tax (including any penalties in relation to that tax) but only to a charge with a due and payable date falling after 31 December 2014. Late payment and repayment rates prior to 1 January 2015 were prescribed under FA 1989, as 3% and 0.5% respectively from 29 September 2009.

VALUE ADDED TAX

[¶19-000] Rates
(VATA 1994, s. 2)

(Indirect Tax Reporter: ¶18-014)

Period of application	Standard rate[1] %	VAT fraction %	Reduced rate[1][2][3] %	VAT fraction %
From 4 January 2011	20	1/6	5.0	1/21
1 January 2010 to 3 January 2011	17.5	7/47	5.0	1/21

Notes

[1] VAT lock: F(No. 2)A 2015, s. 2 sets a ceiling on the standard and reduced rates of VAT at 20% and 5% respectively, for the period beginning with 18 November 2015 and ending immediately before the date of the first Parliamentary general election after that day (the 'VAT lock period').

[2] Supplies of fuel and power for domestic, residential and charity non-business use and certain other supplies are charged at 5% (VATA 1994, Sch. 7A).

[3] Imports of certain works of art, antiques and collectors' items are charged at an effective rate of 5% from 27 July 1999 (VATA 1994, s. 21(4)–(6)).

The zero rate has applied from 1 April 1973 to date.

[¶19-040] Flat-rate scheme
(VATA 1994, s. 26B; SI 1995/2518, reg. 55A–55V; Notice 733; HMRC 'Flat-rate scheme' manual)

(Indirect Tax Reporter: ¶55-350)

Limited cost businesses

From 1 April 2017, a flat rate of 16.5% applies to all limited cost businesses. A limited cost business is a business where the amount spent on 'relevant goods' including VAT is either:

- less than 2% of the business's VAT flat rate turnover; or

- greater than 2% of the business's VAT flat rate turnover but less than £1,000 per year (£250 per quarterly return period).

> **Relevant goods** are goods that are used exclusively for the purposes of the business, but **do not include:**
> - vehicle costs including fuel, unless the business is operating in the transport sector using its own, or a leased vehicle
> - food or drink for the business or its staff
> - capital expenditure goods of any value

• goods for resale, leasing, letting or hiring out if the main business activity does not ordinarily consist of selling, leasing, letting or hiring out such goods
• goods that are intended for re-sell or hire out, unless selling or hiring is the main business activity
• any services

Examples of relevant goods
This is not an exhaustive list:
- stationery and other office supplies to be used exclusively for the business
- gas and electricity used exclusively for the business
- fuel for a taxi owned by a taxi firm
- stock for a shop
- cleaning products to be used exclusively for the business
- hair products to use to provide hairdressing services
- standard software, provided on a disk

Examples of supplies that are not relevant goods
This is not an exhaustive list:
- accountancy fees, these are services
- advertising costs, these are services
- an item leased/hired to the business, this counts as services, as ownership will never transfer to the business
- food and drink for the business or its staff, these are excluded goods
- fuel for a car this is excluded unless operating in the transport sector using owned, or a leased vehicle
- laptop or mobile phone for use by the business, this is excluded as it is capital expenditure
- anything provided electronically, for example a downloaded magazine, these are services
- rent, this is a service
- software you download, this is a service
- software designed specifically (bespoke software), this is a service even if it is not supplied electronically

Flat-rate percentages applying from 4 January 2011

Generally, the percentage that applies to the flat-rate scheme (FRS) for small firms is cut by 1% for the first year of VAT registration.

Category of business	Appropriate percentage	
	From 4 Jan. 2011	1 Jan. 2010 to 3 Jan. 2011
Accountancy or book-keeping	14.5	13
Advertising	11	10
Agricultural services	11	10
Any other activity not listed elsewhere	12	10.5
Architect, civil and structural engineer or surveyor	14.5	13
Boarding or care of animals	12	10.5

	Appropriate percentage	
Category of business	From 4 Jan. 2011	1 Jan. 2010 to 3 Jan. 2011
Business services that are not listed elsewhere	12	10.5
Catering services including restaurants and takeaways	12.5	11
Computer and IT consultancy or data processing	14.5	13
Computer repair services	10.5	9.5
Entertainment or journalism	12.5	11
Estate agency or property management services	12	10.5
Farming or agriculture that is not listed elsewhere	6.5	6
Film, radio, television or video production	13	11.5
Financial services	13.5	12
Forestry or fishing	10.5	9.5
General building or construction services[(1)]	9.5	8.5
Hairdressing or other beauty treatment services	13	11.5
Hiring or renting goods	9.5	8.5
Hotel or accommodation	10.5	9.5
Investigation or security	12	10.5
Labour-only building or construction services[(1)]	14.5	13
Laundry or dry-cleaning services	12	10.5
Lawyer or legal services	14.5	13
Library, archive, museum or other cultural activity	9.5	8.5
Management consultancy	14	12.5
Manufacturing fabricated metal products	10.5	9.5
Manufacturing food	9	8
Manufacturing that is not listed elsewhere	9.5	8.5
Manufacturing yarn, textiles or clothing	9	8
Membership organisation	8	7
Mining or quarrying	10	9
Packaging	9	8
Photography	11	10
Post offices	5	4.5
Printing	8.5	7.5
Publishing	11	10
Pubs	6.5	6
Real estate activity not listed elsewhere	14	12.5
Repairing personal or household goods	10	9
Repairing vehicles	8.5	7.5

Value Added Tax

	Appropriate percentage	
Category of business	From 4 Jan. 2011	1 Jan. 2010 to 3 Jan. 2011
Retailing food, confectionary, tobacco, newspapers or children's clothing	4	3.5
Retailing pharmaceuticals, medical goods, cosmetics or toiletries	8	7
Retailing that is not listed elsewhere	7.5	6.5
Retailing vehicles or fuel	6.5	6
Secretarial services	13	11.5
Social work	11	10
Sport or recreation	8.5	7.5
Transport or storage, including couriers, freight, removals and taxis	10	9
Travel agency	10.5	9.5
Veterinary medicine	11	10
Wholesaling agricultural products	8	7
Wholesaling food	7.5	6.5
Wholesaling that is not listed elsewhere	8.5	7.5

Note
[1] 'Labour-only building or construction services' means building or construction services where the value of materials suppls than 10% of relevant turnover from such services; any other building or construction services are 'general building or construction services'.

[¶19-060]   Farmer's flat-rate scheme
(VATA 1994, s. 54; SI 1992/3220; SI 1992/3221; SI 1995/2518, reg. 202 ff.; Notice 700/46; HMRC 'VAT – Agricultural flat-rate scheme' manual)

(Indirect Tax Reporter: ¶53-500)

The rate which applies to the farmers' flat-rate scheme is 4%.

[¶19-080]   Registration limits

(1) Taxable supplies in the UK

(VATA 1994, Sch. 1; Notice 700/1)

(Indirect Tax Reporter: ¶43-025)

Period of application	Past turnover 1 year £	Future turnover 30 days £	Unless turnover for next year will not exceed £
From 1/4/17[1]	85,000	85,000	83,000
1/4/16–31/3/17	83,000	83,000	81,000
1/4/15–31/3/16	82,000	82,000	80,000
1/4/14–31/3/15	81,000	81,000	79,000
1/4/13–31/3/14	79,000	79,000	77,000

Notes

[1] The VAT registration and deregistration thresholds will not be uprated for a period of two years (Autumn Budget 2017).

Taxable supplies at both the zero rate and positive rates are included in the above limits.

All of a person's taxable supplies are considered, because it is 'persons' not 'businesses' who can or must register. If a person took over a business as a 'going concern', he is deemed to have made the vendor's supplies for the purposes of registration.

These limits are exclusive of VAT, as VAT is not chargeable unless a person is registered or liable to be registered.

The limit which applies for a particular past period is that which is in force at the end of the period.

The following are excluded from the supplies for the purpose of applying the registration limits:

(1)   the value of capital supplies (other than of land); and

(2)   any taxable supplies which would not be taxable supplies apart from VATA 1994, s. 7(4), which concerns removal of goods to the UK.

Any supplies made at a previous time when the person was registered are disregarded if all necessary information was given to HMRC when the earlier registration was cancelled.

(2) Supplies from other member states (distance selling into the UK)

(VATA 1994, Sch. 2; Notice 700/1)

(Indirect Tax Reporter: ¶43-030)

Period of application	Cumulative relevant supplies from 1 January in year to any day in same year £
From 1/1/93 (VATA 1994, Sch. 2; Notice 700/1)	70,000

Generally, the value of relevant supplies is of those made by persons in other member states to non-taxable persons in the UK.

If certain goods, which are subject to excise duty, are removed to the UK, the person who removes the goods is liable to register in the UK because all such goods must be taxed in the country of destination. There is no de minimis limit.

Value Added Tax

(3) Acquisitions from other member states

(VATA 1994, Sch. 3; Notice 700/1)

(Indirect Tax Reporter: ¶43-035)

Period of application	Cumulative relevant supplies from 1 January in year to any day in same year £
From 1/4/17[(1)]	85,000
1/4/16–31/3/17	83,000
1/4/15–31/3/16	82,000
1/4/14–31/3/15	81,000
1/4/13–31/3/14	79,000

Note

[(1)] The VAT registration and deregistration thresholds will not be uprated for a period of two years (Autumn Budget 2017).

Future prospects rule: a person is also liable to register at any time if there are reasonable grounds for believing that the value of his relevant acquisitions in the period of 30 days then beginning will exceed the given limit. This limit is the same as that for the period starting on 1 January above.

(4) Assets supplied in the UK by overseas persons

(VATA 1994, Sch. 3A; Notice 700/1)

(Indirect Tax Reporter: ¶43-045)

From 21 March 2000, any person without an establishment in the UK making or intending to make 'relevant supplies' must VAT register, regardless of the value of those supplies.

'Relevant supplies' are taxable supplies of goods, including capital assets, in the UK where the supplier has recovered UK VAT under:

- Directive 2008/9 for a person in a member state as regards VAT incurred in another member state; or
- Directive 86/560 (the thirteenth VAT directive) for claimants established outside the member states.

This applies where:

- the supplier (or his predecessor in business) was charged VAT on the purchase of the goods, or on anything incorporated in them, and has either claimed it back or intends to do so; or
- the VAT being claimed back was VAT paid on the import of goods into the UK.

(5) Electronic, telecommunication and broadcasting services

(VATA 1994, Sch. 3B and 3BA; Notice 700/1)

(Indirect Tax Reporter: ¶43-047)

A person can register if he makes or intends to make qualifying supplies, i.e. electronically supplied services to a person who belongs in the UK or another member state and who receives such services otherwise than for business purposes. The person who registers must have neither a business establishment nor a fixed establishment in the UK or in another member state in relation to any supply. Generally, the person must also be neither registered nor required to be registered for VAT in the UK or the Isle of Man or, under equivalent legislation, in another member state.

The place of supply rules for telecommunication services supplied to a person other than a 'relevant business person' (i.e. to a private consumer) with effect in relation to supplies of services made on or after 1 November 2017 (see VATA 1994, Sch. 4A, para. 9E, as inserted by SI 2017/778).

Digital services in the EU from 1 January 2015 (VAT MOSS)

From 1 January 2015, there are new place of supply rules for VAT on the supply of digital services by businesses to consumers in the EU. VAT on digital services will be paid in the consumer's country, not the supplier's country. It will be charged at the rate that applies in the consumer's country. Suppliers of digital services to EU consumers can either:

- register for VAT in each EU country; or
- register to use the VAT Mini One Stop Shop (VAT MOSS) online service.

VAT MOSS enables businesses to account for the VAT due on business-to-consumer (B2C) sales in other EU countries by submitting a single quarterly return and payment to HMRC. HMRC will send an electronic copy of the appropriate part of the return, and any payment, to each relevant country's tax authority.

(6) Non-established taxable persons

(VATA 1994, Sch. 1A; Notice 700/1)

(Indirect Tax Reporter: ¶43-049)

From 1 December 2012, if a person makes taxable supplies in the UK but has no establishment there, he must register for VAT regardless of the value of such supplies. Thus, non-UK established taxable persons (NETPs) no longer benefit from the UK VAT registration threshold.

A NETP is any person not normally resident in the UK, does not have a UK establishment and, in the case of a company, is not incorporated here.

[¶19-100]   Deregistration limits

(1) Taxable supplies in the UK

(VATA 1994, Sch. 1; Notice 700/11)

(Indirect Tax Reporter: ¶43-925)

Period of application	Future turnover £
From 1/4/17[(1)]	83,000
1/4/16–31/3/17	81,000
1/4/15–31/3/16	80,000
1/4/14–31/3/15	79,000
1/4/13–31/3/14	77,000

Notes
(1) The VAT registration and deregistration thresholds will not be uprated for a period of two years (Autumn Budget 2017).
A registered person ceases to be liable to be registered if, at any time, HMRC are satisfied that the value of his taxable supplies in the period of one year, then beginning will not exceed the limit.
The value of supplies of capital assets is excluded from the supplies for the purpose of applying the deregistration limits.
The deregistration limits exclude VAT.
Taxable supplies at both the zero rate and positive rates are included in the above limits.

Value Added Tax

(2) Supplies from other member states (distance selling into the UK)

(VATA 1994, Sch. 2; Notice 700/11)

(Indirect Tax Reporter: ¶43-930)

Period of application	Past relevant supplies in last year to 31 December £	Future relevant supplies in immediately following year £
From 1/1/93	70,000	70,000

Generally, the value of supplies is of those made by persons in other member states to non-taxable persons in the UK.

(3) Acquisitions from other member states

(VATA 1994, Sch. 3; Notice 700/11)

(Indirect Tax Reporter: ¶43-940)

Period of application	Past relevant acquisitions in last year to 31 December £	Future relevant acquisitions in immediately following year £
From 1/4/17[1]	85,000	85,000
1/4/16–31/3/17	83,000	83,000
1/4/15–31/3/16	82,000	82,000
1/4/14–31/3/15	81,000	81,000
1/4/13–31/3/14	79,000	79,000

Note

[1] The VAT registration and deregistration thresholds will not be uprated for a period of two years (Autumn Budget 2017).

(4) Assets supplied in the UK by overseas persons

(VATA 1994, Sch. 3A; Notice 700/11)

(Indirect Tax Reporter: ¶43-945)

If HMRC are satisfied that a person registered under VATA 1994, Sch. 3A has ceased to make relevant supplies, HMRC can deregister the person from the date on which he so ceased or from an agreed later date. However, HMRC must not deregister a person unless they are satisfied that he is not liable to be registered under another provision in VATA 1994.

(5) Electronic services

(VATA 1994, Sch. 3B and 3BA; Notice 700/11)

(Indirect Tax Reporter: ¶43-946)

HMRC cancel a person's registration under VATA 1994, Sch. 3B if he notifies them, or they determine, that he ceased to make, or have the intention to make, qualifying supplies.

(6) Non-established taxable persons

(VATA 1994, Sch. 1A; Notice 700/11)

(Indirect Tax Reporter: ¶43-920)

HMRC may cancel the registration of a non-UK established taxable person (NETP) under VATA 1994, Sch. 1A if they are satisfied that:

(1)   the person has ceased to make taxable supplies in the course or furtherance of a business; or

(2)   the person is no longer a person in relation to whom condition C in Sch. 1A, para. 1 is met, i.e. the person has a business establishment, or another fixed establishment, in the UK in relation to any business carried on by him.

[¶19-120]   Special accounting limits

Cash accounting scheme

(SI 1995/2518, reg. 56–65; Notice 731; HMRC 'VAT – Cash accounting scheme' manual)

(Indirect Tax Reporter: ¶55-450)

Period of application	Joining threshold (next 12 months supplies)[1] £	Leaving threshold (last 12 months supplies) £
From 1/4/07	1,350,000	1,600,000

Note

[1] Includes zero-rated supplies, but excludes any capital assets previously used in the business. Exempt supplies are also excluded.

Outstanding VAT on supplies made and received while using the cash accounting scheme may be brought into account on a cash basis for a further six months after withdrawal from the scheme, but only where withdrawal was voluntary or because the turnover threshold was exceeded.

Annual accounting scheme

(SI 1995/2518, reg. 49–55; Notice 732; HMRC 'VAT – Annual accounting scheme' manual)

(Indirect Tax Reporter: ¶55-300)

Period of application	Joining threshold (next 12 months supplies)[1] £	Leaving threshold (last 12 months supplies) £
From 1/4/06	1,350,000	1,600,000

Note

[1] Positive and zero-rated supplies excluding any supplies of capital assets and any exempt supplies.

Persons with a taxable turnover of up to (from 10 April 2003) £150,000 may join the annual accounting scheme immediately, i.e. without having to be registered for at least 12 months.

Value Added Tax

Flat-rate scheme for small businesses scheme

(SI 1995/2518, reg. 55A–55V; Notice 733; HMRC 'Flat-rate scheme' manual)

(Indirect Tax Reporter: ¶55-350)

Period of application	Joining threshold (next 12 months taxable supplies)[1] £	Leaving threshold (flat-rate turnover at anniversary or next 30 days) £
From 1/4/09	150,000	230,000

Note

[1] Zero-rated and positive-rated supplies excluding VAT. Exempt supplies are excluded.

Net VAT liability is calculated by applying a flat-rate percentage to the VAT-inclusive turnover. The flat-rate percentage depends on the trader sector. However from 1 January 2004, in the first year of VAT registration, the flat-rate percentage can be reduced by 1%, i.e. if the normal rate is 10%, then 9% applies.

If a user of the flat-rate scheme exceeds the annual exit threshold as a result of a one-off transaction, but in the subsequent year he expects his VAT-inclusive annual flat-rate turnover to be under £191,500 (before 4 January 2011: £187,500), he may remain in the scheme with HMRC's agreement (SI 1995/2518, Pt. VIIA; Notice 733).

[¶19-140]   Zero-rated supplies

(VATA 1994, Sch. 8)

(Indirect Tax Reporter: ¶20-000)

A zero-rated supply is a taxable supply, but the tax rate is nil.

VAT lock: F(No. 2)A 2015, s. 2 provides that no goods, services or supply specified in VATA 1994, Sch. 8, at the beginning of the VAT lock period (period beginning with 18 November 2015 and ending immediately before the date of the first parliamentary general election after that day) may be removed from it under VATA 1994, s. 30(4) during that period.

Group	
1.	Food (this includes most food for human and animal consumption – the exceptions are mainly food supplied in the course of catering, confectionary, pet foods and hot take-away food)
2.	Sewerage services and water (except distilled and bottled water) but not if supplied to industry
3.	Books, pamphlets, newspapers, journals, maps, music, etc. (but not stationery and posters)
4.	Talking books for the blind and handicapped and wireless sets for the blind
5.	Construction of buildings, etc.
6.	Protected buildings[1]
7.	International services
8.	Transport
9.	Caravans and houseboats[2]
10.	Gold
11.	Bank notes
12.	Drugs, medicines, aids for the handicapped, etc.

Group	
13.	Imports, exports, etc.
14.	(repealed for supplies made after 30 June 1999) Tax-free shops
15.	Charities, etc.
16.	Clothing and footwear
17.	(for supplies made after 30 July 2009, but repealed for supplies made after 31 October 2010 when the reverse charge applies) Emissions allowances
18.	European Research Infrastructure Consortia (ERIC; from 1 January 2013)
[19.]	[Women's sanitary products[3]]

Notes

Except for exported goods and certain transactions in commodities, generally a supply is not zero-rated *unless* it is specified in the zero-rated schedule (VATA 1994, Sch. 8). A supply which can be classified as zero-rated overrides exemption. A supply which is not outside the scope of VAT is standard-rated *unless* it falls within one of the categories of exempt or zero-rated or reduced-rate supplies.

[1] From 1 October 2015, alterations of listed buildings are omitted from the list bringing their VAT treatment in line with other non-listed buildings and repairs and maintenance for all buildings which are standard-rated.

[2] From 6 April 2013, criteria for zero-rating is amended to ensure 'holiday' caravans are consistently either standard-rated (tourers) or subject to the reduced rate of VAT (static, non-residential).

[3] VATA 1994, Sch. 8, Grp. 19 prospectively inserted by FA 2016, s. 126, with effect from the later of 1 April 2017 and the earliest date that may be appointed consistently with the UK's EU obligations.

Note: The UK's discretion in determining the structure of VAT is limited by European VAT law and the introduction of a new zero rate would contravene the current agreement on VAT rates which entitles member states to charge a reduced rate of VAT (between 5% and 15%), but not a zero rate, on this supply. In 2016, European Finance Ministers called on the European Commission to publish legislation to provide an option to member states of VAT reduced or zero rating for women's sanitary products at the earliest opportunity but to date the Commission has not done this.

[¶19-160] Exempt supplies

(VATA 1994, Sch. 9)

(Indirect Tax Reporter: ¶27-000)

No VAT is chargeable on an exempt supply, but input tax cannot be reclaimed except as computed under the provisions on partial exemption.

Group	
1.	Land
2.	Insurance
3.	Postal services (restricted after 30 January 2011 to supplies of public postal services and incidental goods made by the universal service provider)
4.	Betting, gaming, dutiable machine games and lotteries
5.	Finance
6.	Education
7.	Health and welfare
8.	Burial and cremation
9.	Subscriptions to trade unions, professional bodies and other public interest bodies

Group	
10.	Sport, sports competitions and physical education
11.	Works of art, etc.
12.	Fund-raising events by charities and other qualifying bodies
13.	Cultural services, etc.
14.	Supplies of goods where input tax cannot be recovered (from 1 March 2000)
15.	Investment gold (from 1 January 2000)
16.	Supplies of services by groups involving cost sharing (from 17 July 2012)

Note

The descriptions of the zero-rated and exempt groups are for ease of reference only and do not affect the interpretation of the groups (VATA 1994, s. 96(10)). Some suppliers can unilaterally opt to tax certain land and buildings (VATA 1994, Sch. 10, para. 2–4).

[¶19-180]   Reduced-rate supplies

(VATA 1994, Sch. 7A)

(Indirect Tax Reporter: ¶32-000)

VAT is chargeable at 5% on a reduced-rated supply

VAT lock: F(No. 2)A 2015, s. 2 provides that no goods, services or supply specified in VATA 1994, Sch. 7A, at the beginning of the VAT lock period (period beginning with 18 November 2015 and ending immediately before the date of the first parliamentary general election after that day) may be removed from it under VATA 1994, s. 30(4) during that period.

Group	
1.	Domestic fuel and power
2.	Installation of energy-saving materials
3.	Grant-funded installation of heating equipment or security goods or connection of gas supply
4.	Women's sanitary products[3]
5.	Children's car seats
6.	Residential conversions
7.	Residential renovations and alterations
8.	Contraceptive products (from 1 July 2006)
9.	Welfare advice or information (from 1 July 2006)
10.	Installation of mobility aids for the elderly (from 1 July 2007)
11.	Smoking cessation products (from 1 July 2007)
12.	Caravans (from 6 April 2013)
13.	Cable-suspended passenger transport systems (from 1 April 2013)

Notes

(1) The 'Listed Places of Worship Grants Scheme', which is administered by the Department for Culture, Media and Sport (DCMS), effectively leaves a listed place of worship bearing VAT at 5% on repairs by funding the difference between VAT at 5% and at the standard rate. This runs along with the scheme for UK charities which refunds the VAT charged on qualifying supplies made after 15 March 2005 in the construction, renovation and maintenance of certain memorials.

(2) From 6 April 2013, Group 12 'Caravans' is added to the list in VATA 1994, Sch. 7A by way of recategorisation of 'holiday' (static, non-residential) caravans previously treated as zero-rated.

(3) VATA 1994, Sch. 7A, Grp. 4 prospectively omitted by FA 2016, s. 126, with effect from the later of 1 April 2017 and the earliest date that may be appointed consistently with the UK's EU obligations.
Note: The UK's discretion in determining the structure of VAT is limited by European VAT law and the introduction of a new zero rate would contravene the current agreement on VAT rates which entitles member states to charge a reduced rate of VAT (between 5% and 15%), but not a zero rate, on this supply. In 2016, European Finance Ministers called on the European Commission to publish legislation to provide an option to member states of VAT reduced or zero rating for women's sanitary products at the earliest opportunity but to date the Commission has not done this.

[¶19-200]   Partial exemption

(SI 1995/2518, reg. 99–111; Notice 706; HMRC 'Partial exemption' manual)

(Indirect Tax Reporter: ¶19-400)

The law on partial exemption may restrict the amount of deductible input tax.

Where input tax cannot be attributed directly to taxable or exempt supplies (residual input tax), the standard method apportions the residual input tax according to the values of taxable and exempt supplies made in a period. In relation to input tax incurred after 17 April 2002, persons must adjust the input tax deductible under the standard method at the end of their tax year if that amount is substantially different from an attribution based on the use of purchases. 'Substantially' means in excess of:

● £50,000; or

● 50% or more of the value of the residual input tax and £25,000.

Where the residual input tax is less than £50,000 per year, the standard method can be used, unless the person is defined as a group undertaking under the Companies Acts and the residual input tax is greater than £25,000 per year.

Generally, the established de minimis limit for applying the partial exemption rules is as follows:

Period	Exempt input tax not exceeding
Tax years beginning after 30/11/94	● £625 per month on average; and ● 50% of total input tax for prescribed accounting period

In order to establish whether the de minimis limit has been breached, for partial exemption years starting after 31 March 2010, some taxable persons need only carry out simplified tests, rather than carry out detailed partial exemption calculations. The simplest test is whether total input tax incurred by a taxable person is less than £625 per month on average. If so, as long as 50% or less of the turnover is exempt, the de minimis test is passed. If that test is failed, the next simplified test is to strip out all input tax that is directly and solely attributable to taxable supplies. If the remainder is less than £625 per month on average then, as long as the value of exempt supplies does not exceed one-half of the value of all supplies, the de minimis test is passed.

Value Added Tax

For accounting periods commencing after 31 March 2005, rounding up the recovery rate under the standard method to the next whole number is only allowed for persons incurring no more than £400,000 residual input tax per month on average. Other persons round to two decimal places.

HMRC's approval of a partial exemption special method from 1 April 2007 is subject to a declaration by the taxable person that to the best of his knowledge and belief the intended method is fair and reasonable.

[¶19-220]   Capital goods scheme
(SI 1995/2518, reg. 112–116; Notice 706/2)

(Indirect Tax Reporter: ¶19-800)

The capital goods scheme affects the acquisition, etc. by a partially exempt person for use in a business of certain items as follows:

Item	Value	Adjustment period
Computers and computer equipment	£50,000 or more	Five years
Land and buildings	£250,000 or more	Ten years (five years where interest had less than ten years to run on acquisition)
Aircraft, ships, boats and other vessels (from 1 January 2011)	£50,000 or more	Five years

Where the capital goods scheme applies, any initial deduction of input tax is made in the ordinary way, but must then be reviewed over the adjustment period by reference to the use of the asset concerned.

[¶19-240]   Particulars to be shown on a valid VAT invoice
(SI 1995/2518, reg. 14; Notice 700, para. 16.3ff. (August 2013))

(Indirect Tax Reporter: ¶55-800)

VAT invoices generally where supplied to a person who is also in the UK

VAT invoices must show:
- a sequential number based on one or more series which uniquely identifies the document;
- the time of supply (tax point);
- date of issue of the document (where different to the time of supply);
- trader's name, address and VAT registration number;
- customer's name and address;
- a description which identifies the goods or services supplied;
- for each **description**, the quantity of the goods or the extent of the services, and the rate of VAT and the amount payable, excluding VAT, expressed in any currency;

- the gross total amount payable, excluding VAT, expressed in any currency;
- the rate of any cash discount offered;
- the total amount of VAT chargeable, expressed in sterling;
- the unit price; and
- the reason for any zero rate or exemption.

The final bullet point refers to the following types of supply:

- supplies subject to a second-hand margin scheme;
- supplies subject to the Tour Operators Margin Scheme (TOMS);
- intra-EC exempt supplies;
- intra-EC reverse charge supplies; and
- intra-EC zero-rated supplies.

Generally, VAT officers adopt a 'light touch' for about one year after any change to the requirements for a valid VAT invoice in order to give reasonable time to change procedures and help minimise the cost of change.

Persons providing VAT invoices for leasing certain motor cars must state on the invoice whether the car is a qualifying vehicle. This enables the lessee to claim the correct proportion of the VAT charged by the lessor.

The requirements for invoices concerning supplies intra-EU member states are in the *Value Added Tax Regulations* 1995 (SI 1995/2518, reg. 14(2)).

Also, a VAT invoice must be provided for an exempt supply made to a person in another member state for the purposes of that person's business.

Less detailed VAT and modified VAT invoices

For retail sales, a VAT invoice must be provided if the customer asks for one. However, it may be possible to issue a less detailed or modified VAT invoice as follows, otherwise a full VAT invoice must be issued:

Value of charge made for individual sale	Less detailed invoice requirements
is **£250 or less** (including VAT)	<ul><li>name of supplier, address and VAT registration number;</li><li>the time of supply (tax point);</li><li>a description which identifies the goods or services supplied;</li><li>and for each VAT rate applicable, the total amount payable, including VAT and the VAT rate charged.</li></ul> Exempt supplies must not be included in this type of VAT invoice. To work out the amount of VAT in a VAT-inclusive price, multiply the sale price by the VAT fraction.
exceeds £250 and you are asked for a VAT invoice	must issue either a:<ul><li>full VAT invoice; or</li><li>modified VAT invoice (see below).</li></ul>

Value Added Tax (side text)

Credit card sales

Where credit cards, such as Visa/Mastercard or Barclaycard, are accepted, the sales voucher given to the cardholder at the time of the sale may be adapted to serve as a less detailed VAT invoice.

Requirements
The credit card voucher should show: •   retailer's name and address; •   the charge made, including VAT; and •   the date of sale. Additional requirements: •   VAT registration number; •   rate of VAT; and •   a description of the goods or services supplied.

Modified VAT invoice

Can be issued provided the customer agrees.

Requirements
•   the VAT-inclusive value of each standard-rated or reduced-rated supply (instead of the VAT-exclusive values). At the foot of the invoice, separate totals must be shown of: •   VAT-inclusive value of the standard-rated or reduced rate supplies; •   VAT payable on those supplies shown in sterling; •   value, excluding VAT, of those supplies; •   value of any zero-rated supplies included on the invoice; and •   value of any exempt supplies included on the invoice. In all other respects the invoice should show the details required for a full VAT invoice.

See Notice 700, for the rules on invoices concerning:
•   petrol, derv, paraffin, and heating oil;
•   credit cards;
•   another form of modified VAT invoice for retailers;
•   cash and carry wholesalers;
•   computer invoicing; and
•   calculation of VAT on invoices.

Continuous supplies of services

Certain additional particulars are required to be shown on a VAT invoice for a supply of continuous services, if the supplier chooses to use the advance invoicing facility (SI 1995/2518, reg. 90). Similar provisions apply for advance invoicing in respect of long leases (reg. 85) and in respect of supplies of water, gas, power, heat, refrigeration and ventilation (reg. 86).

[¶19-260] 'Blocked' input tax

(VATA 1994, s. 24)

(Indirect Tax Reporter: ¶19-004)

Any input tax charged on the following items is generally 'blocked', i.e. non-recoverable:

- motor cars, but:
  - any person can recover input tax on motor cars used exclusively for business; and
  - only 50% of VAT on car leasing charges is recoverable if lessee makes any private use of the car and if lessor recovered the VAT on buying the car.

  A list of particular makes and models of car derived vans and combi vans for the purposes of determining whether VAT can be reclaimed as input tax is available at www.gov.uk/government/publications/hm-revenue-and-customs-car-derived-vans-and-combi-vans;

- entertainment, except of employees. However, if there is a strict business purpose and if it is necessary for the business to make supplies, input tax is recoverable as regards entertaining overseas customers (HMRC Brief 44/2010 (2 November 2010));

- in the case of claims by builders, articles of a kind not ordinarily installed by builders as fixtures in new houses;

- goods supplied under the second-hand scheme;

- goods imported for private purposes;

- non-business element of supplies to be used only partly for business purposes. VAT incurred on supplies not intended for business use generally does not rank as input tax, so cannot be recovered. *Lennartz* accounting starting before 1 January 2011 should run its course. Generally, *Lennartz* accounting does not apply to VAT incurred after 31 December 2010; and

- goods and services acquired by a tour operator for re-supply as a designated travel service.

'Exempt input tax' is generally not recoverable by a partially exempt person.

[¶19-280] Input tax and mileage allowances (advisory fuel rates)

(SI 2005/3290)

(Indirect Tax Reporter: ¶19-071)

An employer can reclaim the VAT incurred by employees on fuel costs that are reimbursed by the employer on the basis of cost or via a mileage allowance. VAT can only be reclaimed by an employer on fuel which is used in the course of the business to make taxable supplies and employers must obtain and retain a valid VAT invoice to support the reclaim.

HMRC publish 'advisory fuel rates' to determine the business fuel cost, but rates set by recognised motoring agencies, such as the RAC and the AA, are usually acceptable.

Value Added Tax

Transition to revised 'advisory fuel rate': one-month rule

For one month from the date of change, employers may use either the previous or new current rates, as they choose.

Engine size	Rate per mile		
	Petrol	Diesel	LPG
For journeys from 1 December 2017			
1400cc or less	11p	9p	7p
1401cc to 1600cc	14p	9p	9p
1601cc to 2000cc	14p	11p	9p
Over 2000cc	21p	13p	14p
For journeys from 1 September 2017			
1400cc or less	11p	9p	7p
1401cc to 1600cc	13p	9p	8p
1601cc to 2000cc	13p	11p	8p
Over 2000cc	21p	12p	13p
For journeys from 1 June 2017			
1400cc or less	11p	9p	7p
1401cc to 1600cc	14p	9p	9p
1601cc to 2000cc	14p	11p	9p
Over 2000cc	21p	13p	14p
For journeys from 1 March 2017			
1400cc or less	11p	9p	7p
1401cc to 1600cc	14p	9p	9p
1601cc to 2000cc	14p	11p	9p
Over 2000cc	22p	13p	14p
For journeys from 1 December 2016			
1400cc or less	11p	9p	7p
1401cc to 1600cc	14p	9p	9p
1601cc to 2000cc	14p	11p	9p
Over 2000cc	21p	13p	13p
For journeys from 1 September 2016			
1400cc or less	11p	9p	7p
1401cc to 1600cc	13p	9p	9p
1601cc to 2000cc	13p	11p	9p
Over 2000cc	20p	13p	13p

Engine size	Rate per mile		
	Petrol	**Diesel**	**LPG**
For journeys from 1 June 2016			
1400cc or less	10p	9p	7p
1401cc to 1600cc	13p	9p	9p
1601cc to 2000cc	13p	10p	9p
Over 2000cc	20p	12p	13p
For journeys from 1 March 2016			
1400cc or less	10p	8p	7p
1401cc to 1600cc	12p	8p	8p
1601cc to 2000cc	12p	10p	8p
Over 2000cc	19p	11p	13p

[¶19-300]   VAT on private fuel (scale charges)

(VATA 1994, Sch. 6, para. B1; SI 2013/2911; Notice 700/64)

(Indirect Tax Reporter: ¶18-320ff.)

From 1 May 2017

Fuel scale charges for 12-month period

CO_2 band	VAT fuel scale charge, 12-month period £	VAT on 12-month charge £	VAT exclusive 12-month charge £
120 or less	563.00	93.83	469.17
125	842.00	140.33	701.67
130	901.00	150.17	750.83
135	955.00	159.17	795.83
140	1,013.00	168.83	844.17
145	1,068.00	178.00	890.00
150	1,126.00	187.67	938.33
155	1,180.00	196.67	983.33
160	1,239.00	206.50	1,032.50
165	1,293.00	215.50	1,077.50
170	1,351.00	225.17	1,125.83
175	1,405.00	234.17	1,170.83
180	1,464.00	244.00	1,220.00

Value Added Tax

CO$_2$ band	VAT fuel scale charge, 12-month period £	VAT on 12-month charge £	VAT exclusive 12-month charge £
185	1,518.00	253.00	1,265.00
190	1,577.00	262.83	1,314.17
195	1,631.00	271.83	1,359.17
200	1,689.00	281.50	1,407.50
205	1,743.00	290.50	1,452.50
210	1,802.00	300.33	1,501.67
215	1,856.00	309.33	1,546.67
220	1,914.00	319.00	1,595.00
225 or more	1,969.00	328.17	1,640.83

Fuel scale charges for 3-month period

CO$_2$ band	VAT fuel scale charge, 3-month period £	VAT on 3-month charge £	VAT exclusive 3-month charge £
120 or less	140.00	23.33	116.67
125	211.00	35.17	175.83
130	224.00	37.33	186.67
135	238.00	39.67	198.33
140	252.00	42.00	210.00
145	267.00	44.50	222.50
150	281.00	46.83	234.17
155	295.00	49.17	245.83
160	309.00	51.50	257.50
165	323.00	53.83	269.17
170	337.00	56.17	280.83
175	351.00	58.50	292.50
180	365.00	60.83	304.17
185	379.00	63.17	315.83
190	393.00	65.50	327.50
195	408.00	68.00	340.00
200	422.00	70.33	351.67

CO$_2$ band	VAT fuel scale charge, 3-month period £	VAT on 3-month charge £	VAT exclusive 3-month charge £
205	436.00	72.67	363.33
210	449.00	74.83	374.17
215	463.00	77.17	385.83
220	478.00	79.67	398.33
225 or more	492.00	82.00	410.00

Fuel scale charges for 1-month period

CO$_2$ band	VAT fuel scale charge, 1-month period £	VAT on 1-month charge £	VAT exclusive 1-month charge £
120 or less	46.00	7.67	38.33
125	70.00	11.67	58.33
130	74.00	12.33	61.67
135	79.00	13.17	65.83
140	84.00	14.00	70.00
145	88.00	14.67	73.33
150	93.00	15.50	77.50
155	98.00	16.33	81.67
160	102.00	17.00	85.00
165	107.00	17.83	89.17
170	111.00	18.50	92.50
175	116.00	19.33	96.67
180	121.00	20.17	100.83
185	125.00	20.83	104.17
190	131.00	21.83	109.17
195	136.00	22.67	113.33
200	140.00	23.33	116.67
205	145.00	24.17	120.83
210	149.00	24.83	124.17
215	154.00	25.67	128.33
220	159.00	26.50	132.50
225 or more	163.00	27.17	135.83

Value Added Tax

From 1 May 2016 to 30 April 2017

Fuel scale charges for 12-month period

CO$_2$ band	VAT fuel scale charge, 12-month period £	VAT on 12-month charge £	VAT exclusive 12-month charge £
120 or less	467.00	77.83	389.17
125	699.00	116.50	582.50
130	747.00	124.50	622.50
135	792.00	132.00	660.00
140	841.00	140.17	700.83
145	886.00	147.67	738.33
150	934.00	155.67	778.33
155	979.00	163.17	815.83
160	1,028.00	171.33	856.67
165	1,073.00	178.83	894.17
170	1,121.00	186.83	934.17
175	1,166.00	194.33	971.67
180	1,214.00	202.33	1,011.67
185	1,259.00	209.83	1,049.17
190	1,308.00	218.00	1,090.00
195	1,353.00	225.50	1,127.50
200	1,401.00	233.50	1,167.50
205	1,446.00	241.00	1,205.00
210	1,495.00	249.17	1,245.83
215	1,540.00	256.67	1,283.33
220	1,588.00	264.67	1,323.33
225 or more	1,633.00	272.17	1,360.83

Fuel scale charges for 3-month period

CO$_2$ band	VAT fuel scale charge, 3-month period £	VAT on 3-month charge £	VAT exclusive 3-month charge £
120 or less	116.00	19.33	96.67
125	175.00	29.17	145.83
130	186.00	31.00	155.00
135	197.00	32.83	164.17
140	209.00	34.83	174.17

CO$_2$ band	VAT fuel scale charge, 3-month period £	VAT on 3-month charge £	VAT exclusive 3-month charge £
145	221.00	36.83	184.17
150	233.00	38.83	194.17
155	245.00	40.83	204.17
160	256.00	42.67	213.33
165	268.00	44.67	223.33
170	279.00	46.50	232.50
175	291.00	48.50	242.50
180	303.00	50.50	252.50
185	314.00	52.33	261.67
190	326.00	54.33	271.67
195	338.00	56.33	281.67
200	350.00	58.33	291.67
205	362.00	60.33	301.67
210	373.00	62.17	310.83
215	384.00	64.00	320.00
220	396.00	66.00	330.00
225 or more	408.00	68.00	340.00

Fuel scale charges for 1-month period

CO$_2$ band	VAT fuel scale charge, 1-month period £	VAT on 1-month charge £	VAT exclusive 1-month charge £
120 or less	38.00	6.33	31.67
125	58.00	9.67	48.33
130	61.00	10.17	50.83
135	65.00	10.83	54.17
140	69.00	11.50	57.50
145	73.00	12.17	60.83
150	77.00	12.83	64.17
155	81.00	13.50	67.50
160	85.00	14.17	70.83
165	89.00	14.83	74.17
170	92.00	15.33	76.67
175	96.00	16.00	80.00

Value Added Tax

CO$_2$ band	VAT fuel scale charge, 1-month period £	VAT on 1-month charge £	VAT exclusive 1-month charge £
180	101.00	16.83	84.17
185	104.00	17.33	86.67
190	108.00	18.00	90.00
195	112.00	18.67	93.33
200	116.00	19.33	96.67
205	120.00	20.00	100.00
210	123.00	20.50	102.50
215	128.00	21.33	106.67
220	132.00	22.00	110.00
225 or more	135.00	22.50	112.50

[¶19-320]   VAT publications having legal force

(Indirect Tax Reporter: ¶4-200)

Certain VAT publications that have legal force in whole or part are listed in Notice 747.

[¶19-340]   VAT registration numbers: country code prefix

(SI 1995/2518, reg. 2(1); Notice 725, para. 16.19 (October 2012))

(Indirect Tax Reporter: ¶63-160)

Certain invoices should show the invoicer's registration number prefixed by the country code (also known as the alphabetical code).

Member state	Country code
Austria	AT
Belgium	BE
Bulgaria[2]	BG
Croatia[3]	HR
Cyprus[1]	CY
Czech Republic[1]	CZ
Denmark	DK
Estonia[1]	EE
Finland	FI

Member state	Country code
France	FR
Germany	DE
Greece	EL
Hungary[1]	HU
Ireland	IE
Italy	IT
Latvia[1]	LV
Lithuania[1]	LT
Luxembourg	LU
Malta[1]	MT
Netherlands	NL
Poland[1]	PL
Portugal	PT
Romania[2]	RO
Slovakia[1]	SK
Slovenia[1]	SI
Spain	ES
Sweden	SE
United Kingdom	GB

Notes

[1] This country joined the European Union on 1 May 2004.

[2] Bulgaria and Romania joined the EU on 1 January 2007.

[3] Croatia joined the EU on 1 July 2013.

[¶19-344] Territory of the EU

(Directive 2006/112, art. 5; Notice 60, para. 2.5; Notice 725, para. 2.4; Notice 741A, para. 21)

Comprehensive tables of VAT rates applied in the EU member states as at 1 September 2015 are available at http://ec.europa.eu/taxation_customs/resources/documents/taxation/vat/how_vat_works/rates/vat_rates_en.pdf.

Member states
The territory of the EU for VAT purposes consists of the following member states:
(1)   Austria (including Jungholtz and Mittelberg);
(2)   Belgium;
(3)   Bulgaria (from 1 January 2007);
(4)   Croatia (from 1 July 2013);

Value Added Tax

Member states
(5) Cyprus (from 1 May 2004, including the British Sovereign Base Areas of Akrotiri and Dhekelia);
(6) Czech Republic (from 1 May 2004);
(7) Denmark;
(8) Estonia (from 1 May 2004);
(9) Finland;
(10) France (including Monaco);
(11) Germany;
(12) Greece;
(13) Hungary (from 1 May 2004);
(14) Ireland (the Republic of) (also known as Eire);
(15) Italy;
(16) Latvia (from 1 May 2004);
(17) Lithuania (from 1 May 2004);
(18) Luxembourg;
(19) Malta (from 1 May 2004);
(20) Netherlands (also known as Holland);
(21) Poland (from 1 May 2004);
(22) Portugal (including the Azores and Madeira);
(23) Romania (from 1 January 2007);
(24) Slovakia (from 1 May 2004);
(25) Slovenia (from 1 May 2004);
(26) Spain (including the Balearic Islands);
(27) Sweden; and
(28) UK (including the Isle of Man).

Excluded territories
The following territories of member states are excluded from the 'territory of the country':
(1) re Cyprus: the United Nations buffer zone and the part of Cyprus to the north of the buffer zone where the Republic of Cyprus does not exercise effective control;
(2) re Denmark: the Faroe Islands and Greenland;
(3) re Finland: the Åland Islands;
(4) re France: Guadeloupe, French Guiana, Martinique, Mayotte, Réunion and Saint-Martin (French Republic);
(5) re Germany:
(a) the Island of Heligoland; and
(b) Büsingen,

Excluded territories
(6)   re Greece: Mount Athos (also known as Agion Oros);
(7)   re Italy:
(a)   Campione d'Italia; and
(b)   the Italian waters of Lake Lugano and Livigno;
(8)   re Netherlands: Antilles.
(9)   re Spain:
(a)   the Canary Islands
(b)   Ceuta; and
(c)   Melilla; and
(10)   re UK:
(a)   the Channel Islands; and
(b)   Gibraltar.

Included areas: Monaco and the Isle of Man

Monaco and the Isle of Man are not treated as 'third territories'. They are part of France and the UK respectively. Thus, transactions originating in or intended for:

(1)   Monaco are treated as transactions originating in or intended for France; and

(2)   the Isle of Man are treated as transactions originating in or intended for the UK.

Areas not within the EU

Andorra, San Marino, the Vatican City and Liechtenstein are not within the EU for VAT purposes.

[¶19-400]   EC Sales List (ESL)

(SI 1995/2518, reg. 21–23)

(Indirect Tax Reporter: ¶64-800ff.)

VAT-registered businesses in the UK supplying goods and services to VAT-registered customers in another EU country must tell HMRC about those supplies using an EC Sales list. An EC sales list reports:

* details of each EU customer;

* the sterling value of supplies made to them; and

* the customer's country code.

Value Added Tax

Reporting of supplies to VAT-registered customers in other EU countries

Supplies of:	Value	Frequency
Goods	Over £35,000 threshold in current or four previous quarters	Monthly
Goods	Under £35,000 threshold in the current or previous four quarters	Quarterly
Services subject to reverse charge in customer's country	N/A	Quarterly (but monthly returns optional)
Goods and services where required to send monthly lists for goods	N/A	Monthly for all supplies or monthly for goods, and quarterly for services
Goods or services by traders submitting annual VAT returns	• taxable turnover does not exceed £145,000 • annual value of supplies to other EU countries is not more than £11,000 • sales do not include New Means of Transport	Annually (subject to application and approval by HMRC)
Goods only (not services)	• taxable turnover does not exceed £93,500 • supplies £11,000 or less • supplies exclude New Means of transport	Annually (subject to application and approval by HMRC)

ESL deadlines

Submission	Due date (following end of period)
Paper	Within 14 days
Electronic	Within 21 days

[¶19-450]   Intrastat

(SI 1992/2790)

(Indirect Tax Reporter: ¶64-600)

All VAT-registered businesses show the total value of goods dispatched to other EU member states in box 8 and the total arrivals of goods acquired from other EU member states in box 9 of their VAT Return. In addition, those who trade in the EU above the Intrastat exemption threshold in force during the year must also complete a monthly Supplementary Declaration (SD). Larger businesses that trade above the Intrastat delivery terms threshold must also specify delivery terms information on their SD. The table below shows recent thresholds:

Period	Acquisitions (Arrivals) £	Supplies (Dispatches) £	Delivery terms £
From 1 January 2015	1,500,000	250,000	24,000,000
From 1 January 2014	1,200,000	250,000	24,000,000

Intrastat deadlines

Monthly submission	Due date (following end of period)
Online (only)	by 21st day following

Administration

[¶19-500]   Civil penalties

(Notices 700/41 (Late registration penalty) and 700/50 (Default surcharge); HMRC 'Compliance handbook' manual; HMRC 'VAT – Civil penalties' manual)

(Indirect Tax Reporter: ¶59-600ff.)

Offence	Civil penalty
• **Dishonest conduct by a tax agent** (FA 2012, Sch. 38 from 1 April 2013)	• no less than £5,000; • no more than £50,000; • but the penalty may be reduced below £5,000 if there are special circumstances; • also HMRC may publish certain information about the tax agent if the penalty is more than £5,000.
• Failure of a data-holder to comply with a notice requiring **data to be provided to HMRC** (FA 2011, Sch. 23, Pt. 4 from 1 April 2012) • Inaccurate data provided	• a fixed penalty of £300 for the failure; • if the assessment of the £300 penalty has been notified, a further penalty of £60 for each subsequent day of default. If HMRC apply, the tribunal may increase the daily default penalty to £1,000 for each applicable day; • £3,000 if inaccurate data is provided.
• Failure of a company to notify HMRC of the name of its **senior accounting officer** for a financial year beginning after 20 July 2009 (FA 2009, s. 93 and Sch. 46, para. 7)	Penalty of £5,000

Value Added Tax

Offence	Civil penalty
• Failure of a senior accounting officer (1) to take reasonable steps to ensure that the company establishes and maintains **appropriate tax accounting arrangements** or (2) to provide an accurate **certificate** to HMRC (FA 2009, s. 93 and Sch. 46, para. 4 and 5 in relation to financial years beginning after 20 July 2009)	Penalty of £5,000
• Failure of a third party to comply with a notice from HMRC requiring **contact details for a debtor** for the purpose of collecting VAT (FA 2009, Sch. 49, para. 5)	Penalty of £300
• Failure to make **quarterly returns** on time (FA 2009, Sch. 55 from a date **to be appointed** to replace the default surcharge)	• a fixed £100 penalty that escalates by £100 for each subsequent failure up to a maximum of £400 per failure; • a penalty of 5% of tax or £300 if greater at six and 12 months from the date of the failure; • a penalty of up to 100% of tax or £300 if greater if, by failing to make the return, the taxpayer is deliberately withholding information to stop HMRC correctly assessing.
• Failure to make **quarterly payments on time** (FA 2009, Sch. 56 from a date **to be appointed** to replace the default surcharge)	• a penalty of 2% of the unpaid tax for a second failure during a penalty period; • a penalty of 3% of the unpaid tax for a third failure during a penalty period with further failures attracting a maximum penalty of 4%; • if any of the failures are prolonged, additional penalties of 5% of the unpaid tax are charged at six and 12 months from the date of the failure.
• Deliberately **obstructing an officer** in the course of an inspection that has been pre-approved by the tribunal	• a fixed £300 penalty (FA 2008, Sch. 36, para. 39); and • daily penalties of up to £60 for continuing default (Sch. 36, para. 40).

Offence	Civil penalty	
• Failure to notify liability for **registration** or change in nature of supplies by person exempted from registration or certain acquisitions of goods in the UK from another member state (FA 2008, Sch. 41, para. 1, in relation to an obligation arising after 31 March 2010)[(4)]	**Type of failure**	**Percentage of the tax unpaid**
	Non-deliberate failure	30%
	Deliberate but not concealed	70%
	Deliberate and concealed	100%
• Unauthorised issue of VAT **invoice** (FA 2008, Sch. 41, para. 2, in relation to an unauthorised issue of an invoice taking place after 31 March 2010)[(4)]	Penalty is the same as for the late notification penalty under Sch. 41, para. 1	
• **Error** in taxpayer's document sent to HMRC (FA 2007, Sch. 24, para. 1)[(1)(2)(4)]	Maximum penalty, i.e. without disclosure, • for careless action, 30% of the 'potential lost revenue' (PLR); • for deliberate but not concealed action, 70% of the PLR; and • for deliberate and concealed action, 100% of the PLR.	
• **Failure to notify** HMRC within 30 days of an **underassessment** (FA 2007, Sch. 24, para. 2)[(1)]	30% of the potential lost revenue[(2)]	
• Inaccuracy **delays tax** (FA 2007, Sch. 24, para. 8)	5% of the delayed tax for each year or a percentage of the delayed tax, for each separate period of delay of less than one year, equating to 5% p.a.[(2)]	
• Evasion of VAT due on **imports** (FA 2003, s. 25)	Amount of import VAT evaded	
• Contravention of HMRC rules relating to **exports** (FA 2003, s. 26; *Customs (Contravention of a Relevant Rule) Regulations* 2003 (SI 2003/3113))	Penalty of up to £2,500	

Value Added Tax

Offence	Civil penalty	
• Default **surcharge** (VATA 1994, s. 59 but from a date **to be appointed** to be replaced by the penalty in FA 2009, Sch. 55 and 56)	1st default in surcharge period	2%
	2nd	5%
	3rd	10%
	4th or later	15%
	If a return is late, but either no VAT is due or the VAT is paid on time, although a default is recorded, no surcharge is assessed.	
	HMRC generally only issue a surcharge assessment at the 2% or 5% rate if the assessment is at least £400. The surcharge may be suspended while there is an agreement for deferred payment (FA 2009, s. 108).	
	There is no automatic default surcharge for persons with an annual turnover of up to £150,000. Generally, by concession, such persons are first offered help and advice when they are late with a VAT payment. Small businesses are often allowed two defaults before a default surcharge is assessed: a first default should trigger a letter and a second default should trigger a surcharge liability notice.	
	The penalty regime in FA 2009, Sch. 55 and 56 is due to replace the default surcharge and apply to taxpayers who fail (1) to file their VAT returns on time or (2) to pay their VAT liabilities in full and on time. The revised penalties will treat late payment of VAT and late-filed returns separately and try to encourage filing and payment by the correct dates by imposing an escalating series of penalties, depending on the number of failures within a penalty period. Further penalties arise if there is a prolonged delay in filing returns or paying the VAT due. A late payment penalty may be avoided where the taxpayer has agreed a 'time to pay' arrangement with HMRC.	

Offence	Civil penalty		
• Incorrect **certificates** as to zero-rating and reduced-rate certificates re fuel and power, etc. (VATA 1994, s. 62)	VAT chargeable if certificate had been correct minus any VAT actually charged.		
• Inaccurate **EU sales statement** or **reverse charge sales statement** (VATA 1994, s. 65)	£100 for a material inaccuracy on a statement submitted within two years of a penalty notice (itself issued after a second materially inaccurate statement)		
• **Failure to submit** EU sales statement or reverse charge sales statement (VATA 1994, s. 66)	1st default including that to which the default notice relates	£5 per day	
	2nd	£10 per day	
	3rd	£15 per day	
	(Maximum: 100 days – minimum: £50)		
• Breach of **walking possession agreement** (VATA 1994, s. 68)	50% of the VAT due or amount recoverable		
• Breach of **regulatory provision** (VATA 1994, s. 69) (The penalty cannot be imposed without a prior written warning (VATA 1994, s. 76(2)))	Failure to preserve records: £500		
	• **Submission of return or payment is late**		
	Number of relevant failures in two years before the failure	**Greater of:**	
	0	£5 or 1/6 of 1% of VAT due	
	1	£10 or 1/3 of 1% of VAT due	
	2 or more	£15 or 1/2 of 1% of VAT due	
	• **Other breaches**		
	Number of relevant failures in two years before the failure	**Prescribed daily rate**	
	0	£5	
	1	£10	
	2 or more	£15	
	Penalty: the number of days of failure (100 maximum) multiplied by above prescribed daily rate (minimum penalty £50)		
• Failure to comply with requirements of scheme for **investment gold** (VATA 1994, s. 69A)	20% of the value of the transaction concerned		

Value Added Tax

Offence	Civil penalty		
• Breach of **record-keeping requirements** imposed by a direction (VATA 1994, s. 69B)	Penalty: the number of days of failure (30 maximum) multiplied by £200 daily rate		
• Failure to notify acquisition of **excise duty goods** or **new means of transport** (VATA 1994, s. 75)	**Period of failure**	**Percentage of relevant VAT**	
	Three months or less	5%	
	Over three months but not over six months	10%	
	Over six months	15%	
• **Failure to pay** on time correct amount of a relevant tax (such as VAT) (SI 2013/1894; formerly SI 1997/1431)	Taking control of goods (from 6 April 2014; formerly distress)		
• Failure of certain persons to use an **electronic return system** to make a VAT return (SI 1995/2518, reg. 25A)	**Annual VAT-exclusive turnover**	**Penalty**	
	£22,800,001 or more	£400	
	£5,600,001 to £22,800,000	£300	
	£100,001 to £5,600,000	£200	
	£100,000 and under	£100	

Notes
[1] The penalty under FA 2007, Sch. 24, para. 1 and 2 is calculated on the '**potential lost revenue**' (PLR) by reference to:
(a) the amount of VAT understated;
(b) the nature of the behaviour giving rise to the understatement; and
(c) the extent of the taxpayer's disclosure.

Penalised behaviour	Maximum penalty, without disclosure, based on PLR	Minimum penalty, with prompted disclosure, based on PLR	Minimum penalty, with unprompted disclosure, based on PLR
Careless	30%	15%	Nil
Deliberate but not concealed	70%	35%	20%
Deliberate and concealed	100%	50%	30%

If HMRC think it right, because of special circumstances, they may reduce a penalty. 'Special circumstances' excludes:
(a) ability to pay; or
(b) the fact that the PLR from one taxpayer is balanced by a potential over-payment by another.

The penalty regime includes the concept of suspended penalties for careless (not deliberate) action for up to two years where the taxpayer shows that his compliance has improved. In due course, any such suspended penalty is cancelled or becomes payable. Apparently, suspension will only be used for weaknesses in the system for accounting for VAT and not for a one-off error.

The 'potential lost revenue' (PLR) in respect of an inaccuracy in a VAT return is the additional amount due or payable in respect of VAT as a result of correcting the inaccuracy or assessment. If an inaccuracy resulted in VAT being declared later than it should have been ('the delayed tax'), the PLR is:

(a) 5% of the delayed tax for each year of the delay; or

(b) a percentage of the delayed tax, for each separate period of delay of less than a year, equating to 5% per year, i.e. the 5% is calculated pro rata for part-years.

[2] The penalty under FA 2007, Sch. 24 for incorrect returns, etc. applies from the **appointed date** which, subject to the transitional provisions in SI 2008/568 (C. 20), art. 3, is:

- 1 April 2008 in relation to relevant documents relating to tax periods commencing on or after 1 April 2008;

- 1 April 2008 in relation to assessments falling within FA 2007, Sch. 24, para. 2 for tax periods commencing on or after 1 April 2008;

- 1 July 2008 in relation to relevant documents relating to claims under the 13th VAT directive for years commencing on or after 1 July 2008;

- 1 January 2009 in relation to relevant documents relating to claims under the eighth VAT directive for years commencing on or after 1 January 2009;

- 1 April 2009 in relation to documents relating to all other claims for repayments of relevant tax made on or after 1 April 2009 which are not related to a tax period;

- 1 April 2009 in relation to documents given where a person's liability to pay relevant tax arises on or after 1 April 2009.

The penalty for under-assessment by HMRC applies from 1 April 2008 in relation to assessments under FA 2007, Sch. 24, para. 2 for tax periods commencing on or after that date, but no person is liable to the penalty in respect of a tax period for which a return is required to be made before 1 April 2009.

[3] HMRC may waive certain interest and surcharges on VAT that was paid late and was payable by those who were adversely affected by designated **national disasters**, e.g. certain severe flooding (FA 2008, s. 135).

[4] HMRC may publish certain details of **deliberate tax defaulters** as regards return periods starting after 31 March 2010 and for failing to meet obligations that arise after 31 March 2010 (FA 2009, s. 94).

However, there is no publication of the details of an offender who made a full disclosure, either unprompted or prompted in a time considered appropriate by HMRC.

Criminal offences relating to VAT

(1) Knowingly engaged in fraudulent evasion

If a person is knowingly concerned in, or in the taking of steps with a view to, the fraudulent evasion of VAT by him or another person, he is liable:

- on summary conviction, to a penalty of the statutory maximum (£5,000) or of three times the amount of the VAT, whichever is the greater, or to imprisonment for a term not exceeding six months or to both; or

- on conviction on indictment, to a penalty of any amount or to imprisonment for a term not exceeding seven years or to both

(VATA 1994, s. 72).

HMRC must prove fraud to criminal standards of proof, i.e. beyond reasonable doubt, rather than on a balance of probabilities.

The circumstances in which HMRC consider prosecution under the criminal law are described in Notice 700.

A tax evader may be charged with 'false accounting' or the common law offence of cheating the Public Revenue (*Theft Act* 1968, s. 32(1)).

Finance (No. 2) Act 2017 introduces a new and more effective penalty for participating in VAT fraud to be applied to businesses and company officers when they knew or should have known that their transactions were connected with VAT fraud. The penalty will improve the application of penalties to those facilitating orchestrated VAT fraud. The new penalty will be a fixed rate penalty of 30% for participants in VAT fraud. This will be implemented following Royal Assent 2017 (VATA 1994, s. 69C, as inserted by F(No. 2)A 2017, s. 68).

(2) Supplementary declarations (Intrastats)

As regards supplementary declarations, a failure to submit a declaration under the Intrastat system can result on summary conviction in a fine up to £2,500 (level 4 on the standard scale) (SI 1992/2790, reg. 6).

(3) Impersonating an officer

It is a criminal offence to impersonate an HMRC officer with a view to obtaining:

* admission to premises;
* information; or
* any other benefit.

On summary conviction the penalty is imprisonment for up to 51 weeks, a fine not exceeding level 5 on the standard scale (£5,000), or both (CRCA 2005, s. 30).

[¶19-530] Reckonable dates

(VATA 1994, s. 74; FA 2009, s. 101; Notice 700/43)

(Indirect Tax Reporter: ¶60-630)

The reckonable dates for VAT are:

* *interest on overdue VAT*: due date for submission of return (usually last day of month following end of return period);
* *interest on VAT incorrectly repaid*: seven days after issue of instruction directing payment of amount incorrectly repaid.

From 1 September 2008, HMRC may charge interest on a voluntary disclosure of underdeclared VAT even if the underdeclaration error is below the disclosure threshold. However, underdeclaration errors properly corrected on a return still avoid an interest charge.

Proposed harmonisation of interest charged by HMRC

From a date to be appointed, interest charged on late paid VAT and certain other taxes is to be harmonised (FA 2009, s. 101 and Sch. 53).

[¶19-560] Interest on underpaid VAT (default interest)

(VATA 1994, s. 74; Notice 700/43; HMRC 'VAT default interest' manual)

(Indirect Tax Reporter: ¶60-630)

Period of application	Days in period	Interest %
From 23/08/16	—	2.75
29/09/09 to 22/08/16	2520	3.00

Proposed harmonisation of interest charged by HMRC

From a date to be appointed, interest charged on late paid VAT and certain other taxes is to be harmonised (FA 2009, s. 101 and Sch. 53).

[¶19-590]   Interest on overpaid VAT (statutory interest)

(VATA 1994, s. 78)

(Indirect Tax Reporter: ¶60-680)

Interest on overpaid VAT (statutory interest) arises in certain cases of official error.

Such interest is not free of income or corporation tax.

Period of application	Interest rate %
From 29/9/09	0.5

Proposed harmonisation of interest on overpaid VAT

From a date to be appointed, interest on overpaid VAT and certain other taxes is to be harmonised (FA 2009, s. 102 and Sch. 54).

Value Added Tax

INSURANCE PREMIUM TAX

[¶20-000]   Rates

(FA 1994, Pt. III; Notice IPT 1; HMRC 'Insurance premium tax' manual)

Insurance premium tax (IPT) is imposed on certain insurance premiums where the risk is located in the UK.

Period of application	Standard rate[1] %	Higher rate %
From 1 June 2017	12.0	20.0
From 1 October 2016	10.0	20.0
From 1 November 2015	9.5	20.0

Note
[1] Standard rate of IPT increased from 9.5% to 10% with effect from 1 October 2016, with an exception for those insurers who use a special accounting scheme rather than the cash receipt method. The exception operates to require the new standard rate to be applied by them only to premiums received on or after 1 February 2017, where the premium relates to risks covered by the terms of a contract entered into before 1 October 2016 (FA 2016, s. 141).

[¶20-100]   Error correction

(SI 1994/1774, reg. 13)

If the underdeclarations or overdeclarations on previous returns do not exceed a limit, such errors may be corrected on the return for the period in which the errors are discovered.

The limit is the greater of £10,000 and 1% of the net IPT turnover as per box 10 on the IPT return. However, this is subject to an upper limit of £50,000.

LANDFILL TAX

Note: See ¶26-300 for rates applicable in Scotland from 1 April 2015.

[¶21-000]   Rates

(FA 1996, s. 42; Notices LFT 1; HMRC 'Landfill tax' manual)

Landfill tax was introduced on 1 October 1996 and is collected from landfill site operators. Landfill tax aims to encourage diversion of waste disposal from landfill sites.

Type of waste	Rate (per tonne) £
Inactive waste liable to lower rate	
From 1 April 2019	2.90[2]
From 1 April 2018	2.80[1]
From 1 April 2017	2.70
From 1 April 2016 to 31 March 2017	2.65
1 April 2015 to 31 March 2016	2.60
1 April 2008 to 31 March 2015	2.50
Active waste liable to standard rate	
From 1 April 2019	91.35[2]
From 1 April 2018	88.95[1]
From 1 April 2017	86.10
From 1 April 2016 to 31 March 2017	84.40
1 April 2015 to 31 March 2016	82.60
1 April 2014 to 31 March 2015	80.00
1 April 2013 to 31 March 2014	72.00

Note
[1] Rates set by FA 2016, s. 143.
[2] Rates per Autumn Budget 2017.

[¶21-100]   Landfill communities fund: tax credit

(SI 1996/1527, reg. 31(3))

The Landfill Communities Fund Scheme encourages landfill site operators to fund local community environmental projects. Under the scheme, a landfill site operator can claim a tax credit worth 90% of any qualifying contributions made to approved environmental bodies (bodies enrolled by ENTRUST) for spending on an approved object, subject to a maximum percentage of the landfill tax liability during a contribution year as set out in the table below.

Maximum percentage credit

Date	Maximum credit %
From 1 April 2017	5.3
1 April 2016 to 31 March 2017	4.2
1 April 2015 to 31 March 2016	5.7
1 April 2014 to 31 March 2015	5.1
1 April 2013 to 31 March 2014	6.8

[¶21-150]   Error correction

(SI 1996/1527, reg. 13)

If the underdeclarations on previous returns do not exceed a limit, such errors may be corrected on the return for the period in which the errors are discovered.

The limit is the greater of £10,000 and 1% of net VAT turnover as per Box 6 on the VAT return for the return period. However, this is subject to an upper limit of £50,000. If the person is not required to be VAT registered, there is a single limit of £10,000.

AGGREGATES LEVY

[¶22-000]   Rates

(FA 2001, s. 16; Notices AGL 1 and AGL 2; HMRC 'Aggregates levy' manual)

Aggregates levy seeks to incorporate the environmental costs imposed by aggregates extraction into the price of virgin aggregate, and to encourage the use of alternative materials such as wastes from construction and demolition.

Generally, 'aggregate' is rock, gravel or sand and whatever occurs or is mixed with it as well as, in certain circumstances, spoil, offcuts and by-products.

Period of application	Rate (per tonne) £
From 1 April 2017[1]	2.00
1 April 2009 to 31 March 2017	2.00

Note
[1] The aggregates levy rate for 2018–19 will be frozen at £2 per tonne, continuing the freeze that has been in place since 2009 (Autumn Budget 2017).

[¶22-100]   Error correction

(SI 2002/761)

If the undercalculations or overcalculations on previous returns do not exceed a limit, such errors may be corrected on the return for the period in which the errors are discovered.

The limit is the greater of £10,000 and 1% of net VAT turnover as per box 6 on the VAT return for the return period. However, this is subject to an upper limit of £50,000. If the person is not required to be VAT registered, there is a single limit of £10,000.

Aggregates Levy

CLIMATE CHANGE LEVY

[¶23-000]   Rates: climate change levy
(FA 2000, Sch. 6)

CCL is a tax on the taxable supply of specified energy products ('taxable commodities') for use as fuels (that is for lighting, heating and power) by business consumers including consumers in industry, commerce, agriculture, public administration and other services. CCL does not apply to taxable commodities supplied for use by domestic consumers or to charities for non-business use. There are four groups of taxable commodities, as follows:

• electricity;

• natural gas when supplied by a gas utility;

• liquid petroleum gas (LPG) and other gaseous hydrocarbons in a liquid state; and

• coal and lignite; coke, and semi-coke of coal or lignite; and petroleum coke.

CCL is charged at a specific rate per unit of energy. There is a separate rate for each of the four categories of taxable commodity. The rates are based on the energy content of each commodity and are expressed in kilowatt-hours (kWh) for gas and electricity, and in kilograms for all other taxable commodities. The rates, including the reduced rate for participants of the climate change agreement scheme and for gas in Northern Ireland where a lower rate for gas applies, are set out in the following tables.

[¶23-070]   Main rates from 1 April 2017, 2018 and 2019
(FA 2000, Sch. 6, para. 42, as prospectively amended by FA 2016, s. 144–148)

Commodity	1 April 2017		1 April 2018		1 April 2019	
	Rate £	Reduced rate	Rate £	Reduced rate	Rate £	Reduced rate
Electricity (per kilowatt hour)	0.00568	10%	0.00583	10%	0.00847	7%
Natural gas (per kilowatt hour)	0.00198	35%	0.00203	35%	0.00339	22%
Liquefied petroleum gas[2] (per kilogram)	0.01272	35%	0.01304	35%	0.02175	22%
Any other taxable commodity (per kilogram)	0.01551	35%	0.01591	35%	0.02653	22%

Notes
[1] Transitional period for claims for the exemption for renewable electricity that was generated before 1 August 2015 ends 31 March 2018 (FA 2000, Sch. 6, para. 19(1), as amended and prospectively repealed by FA 2016, s. 144).
[2] Rate from 1 April 2020 will be £0.02175 per kilogram (Autumn Budget 2017).

[¶23-080]   Main rates from 1 April 2016

(FA 2000, Sch. 6, para. 42)

Commodity	Rates from 1 April 2016	Reduced rate for holders of a CCA
Electricity	£0.00559 per kilowatt hour	10%
Natural gas	£0.00195 per kilowatt hour	35%
Liquefied petroleum gas	£0.01251 per kilogram	35%
Any other taxable commodity	£0.01526 per kilogram	35%

Note
(1) Climate change levy (CCL) exemption for renewably sourced electricity abolished from 1 August 2015 (FA 2000, Sch. 6, para. 19(3)(za)), subject to a transitional period for suppliers to claim the CCL exemption on any renewable electricity that was generated before that date. *Finance Act* 2016 legislates for an end date to the transitional period of 31 March 2018 (FA 2000, Sch. 6, para. 19(1), as amended and prospectively repealed by FA 2016, s. 144).

[¶23-090]   Main rates from 1 April 2015

(FA 2000, Sch. 6, para. 42)

Commodity	Rates from 1 April 2015	Reduced rate for holders of a CCA
Electricity[(1)]	£0.00554 per kilowatt hour	10%
Natural gas	£0.00193 per kilowatt hour	35%
Liquefied petroleum gas	£0.01240 per kilogram	35%
Any other taxable commodity	£0.01512 per kilogram	35%

Note
(1) Climate change levy (CCL) exemption for renewably sourced electricity abolished from 1 August 2015 (FA 2000, Sch. 6, para. 19(3)(za)), subject to a transitional period for suppliers to claim the CCL exemption on any renewable electricity that was generated before that date.

[¶23-100]   Rates from 1 April 2014

(FA 2000, Sch. 6, para. 42)

Taxable commodity supplied	Unit	Rate from 1 April 2014		
		Rate	Reduction on main commodity rate for holders of a CCA	Lower rate when used in approved metal recycling process
Electricity	per kWh	£0.00541	10%	20% of full electricity rate
Natural gas	per kWh	£0.00188	35%	20% of main gas rate
Liquefied petroleum gas and other gaseous hydrocarbons in a liquid state	per kilogram[(1)]	£0.01210	35%	20% of main LPG, etc. rate
Any other taxable commodity	per kilogram	£0.01476	35%	20% of rate for other taxable commodities

Note
(1) For CCL purposes, the conversion rate of 2,000 litres per tonne is to be used when converting litres of butane and propane to kilograms.

[¶23-200]   Rates from 1 April 2013

(FA 2000, Sch. 6, para. 42)

Taxable commodity supplied	Unit	Rate from 1 April 2013		
		Rate	Reduction on main commodity rate for holders of a CCA	Lower rate when used in approved metal recycling process
Electricity	per kWh	£0.00524	10%	20% of main electricity rate
Natural gas (in GB)	per kWh	£0.00182	35%	20% of main gas rate
Natural gas (in Northern Ireland)	per kWh	0.00064 until 31 October 2013 (then GB rate applies)	n/a up to 31 October 2013 then 35%	n/a up to 31 October 2013 then 20% of main gas rate for GB
Liquefied petroleum gas and other gaseous hydrocarbons in a liquid state	per kilogram(1)	£0.01172	35%	20% of main LPG, etc. rate
Any other taxable commodity	per kilogram	£0.01429	35%	20% of rate for other taxable commodities

Note
(1) For CCL purposes, the conversion rate of 2,000 litres per tonne is to be used when converting litres of butane and propane to kilograms.

[¶23-500]   Carbon price floor

(FA 2000, Sch. 6)

From 1 April 2013, supplies of solid fossil fuels, gas and liquefied petroleum gas (LPG) used in most forms of electricity generation are liable to newly created carbon price support (CPS) rates of climate change levy. The commodities liable to the CPS rates of CCL when they become the subject of a deemed supply for use in electricity generation on or after 1 April 2013 are:

• gas of a kind supplied by a gas utility;

• LPG; and

• coal and other solid fossil fuels (petroleum coke; lignite; coke and semi-coke of coal or lignite).

Electricity is not a CPS rate commodity and does not become the subject of a deemed supply if used in electricity generation. The CPS rates of CCL do not apply to offshore (outside the UK's 12-mile territorial limit) electricity generation.

Climate Change Levy

[¶23-600]   Carbon price support (CPS) rates of CCL from 1 April 2013

(FA 2000, Sch. 6; FA 2014, s. 98)

CPS rates of CCL	2016–17 [until 31 March 2020][1]	2015–16	2014–15	2013–14
Natural gas (£ per kilowatt hour)	0.00331	0.00334	0.00175	0.00091
LPG (£ per kilogram)	0.05280	0.05307	0.02822	0.01460
Coal and other taxable solid fossil fuels (£ per gross gigajoule)	1.54790	1.56860	0.81906	0.44264

Note

[1] Rates per *Finance Act* 2014. At Spring Budget 2017, the Government confirmed the continued cap on CPS rates until 31 March 2020. Indicative rates from 1 April 2020 to 31 March 2021 announced at Autumn Budget 2017 as follows: Natural gas – £0.00341; LPG – 0.05432; Coal and other taxable solid fossil fuels – £1.59259.

AIR PASSENGER DUTY

[¶24-000]   Rates

(FA 1994, s. 30)

Air passenger duty (APD) is an excise duty which is due on chargeable passengers being carried from a UK airport on chargeable aircraft.

The rate of APD depends on the passengers' final destination which are allocated into bands based on the distance between London and the capital city of the destination country/territory. Each destination band has three rates of duty depending on the class of travel and the type of aircraft used.

Air passenger duty rates from 1 April 2015[1][4]												
Band (approximate distance in miles from London)	Reduced rate (lowest class of travel) from 1 April				Standard rate (other than lowest class of travel)[2] from 1 April				Higher rate[3] from 1 April			
	2015 £	2016 £	2017 £	2018[5] £	2015 £	2016 £	2017 £	2018[5] £	2015 £	2016 £	2017 £	2018[5] £
Band A (0–2,000 miles)	13	13	13	13	26	26	26	26	78	78	78	78
Band B (Over 2,000 miles)	71	73	75	78	142	146	150	156	426	438	450	468

Notes

[1] From 1 April 2015, the number of destination bands was reduced from four to two by merging the former bands B, C and D and the higher rates that apply to aircraft with an authorised take off weight of 20 tonnes or more and with fewer than 19 seats was increased to six times the reduced rate (previously twice the standard rate).

[2] If any class of travel provides a seat pitch in excess of 1.016 metres (40 inches) the standard rate is the minimum rate that applies.

[3] The higher rate applies to flights aboard aircraft of 20 tonnes and above with fewer than 19 seats.

[4] From 1 May 2015, economy tickets for children under 12 are exempt from the reduced rate of APD. The exemption was extended to include children under 16 from 1 March 2016 (FA 1994, s. 31, as amended by FA 2015, s. 57).

[5] Legislation in Finance Bill 2017–18 will increase the APD long-haul (band B) standard rate to £172 and the long-haul higher rate to £515 on and after 1 April 2019. Short haul (Band A) rates, and the long haul reduced rate for economy passengers will be frozen at the tax year 2018–19 levels (Autumn Budget 2017).

Air passenger duty rates[1][2]						
Bands (approximate distance in miles from the UK)	Reduced rate (lowest class of travel)		Standard rate (other that the lowest class of travel)[3]		Higher rate[4]	
From	1 April 2013 £	1 April 2014 £	1 April 2013 £	1 April 2014 £	1 April 2013 £	1 April 2014 £
Band A (0–2,000 miles)	13	13	26	26	52	52
Band B (2,001–4,000 miles)	67	69	134	138	268	276
Band C (4,001–6,000 miles)	83	85	166	170	332	340
Band D (over 6,000 miles)	94	97	188	194	376	388

Notes

[1] From 1 April 2013, APD has applied to all flights aboard aircraft 5.7 tonnes and above.

[2] From 1 January 2013, the rates for direct long-haul flights from NI were devolved to the Northern Ireland Executive, and set at £0. Direct long haul journeys from NI are those where the first part of the journey is to a destination outside Band A.

[3] If any class of travel provides a seat pitch in excess of 1.016 metres (40 inches), the standard rate is the minimum rate that applies.

[4] The higher rate applies to flights aboard aircraft of 20 tonnes and above with fewer than 19 seats.

[¶24-100]   Destinations by band

(FA 1994, Sch. 5A)

Band A			
Country/Territory	**Capital City**	**Country/Territory**	**Capital City**
Albania	Tirana	Malta	Valletta
Algeria	Algiers	Moldova	Chisinau
Andorra	Andorra la Vella	Monaco	Monaco
Austria	Vienna	Montenegro	Podgorica
Belarus	Minsk	Morocco	Rabat
Belgium	Brussels	Netherlands	Amsterdam
Bosnia & Herzegovina	Sarajevo	Norway	Oslo
Bulgaria	Sofia	Poland	Warsaw
Corsica	Ajaccio	Portugal	Lisbon
Croatia	Zagreb	Romania	Bucharest
Cyprus	Nicosia	Russian Federation (West of the Urals)	Moscow
Czech Republic	Prague		
Denmark	Copenhagen	San Marino	San Marino
Estonia	Tallinn	Sardinia	Cagliari
Faroe Islands	Torshavn	Serbia	Belgrade
Finland	Helsinki	Sicily	Palermo
France	Paris	Slovakia	Bratislava
Germany	Berlin	Slovenia	Ljubljana
Gibraltar	Gibraltar	Spain	Madrid
Greece	Athens	Svalbard	Longyearbyen
Greenland	Nuuk	Sweden	Stockholm
Hungary	Budapest	Switzerland	Bern
Iceland	Reykjavik	The Azores	Ponta Delgada
Ireland	Dublin	The Balearic Islands	Palma
Isle of Man	Douglas	The Canary Islands	Santa Cruz de Tenerife
Italy	Rome	The Channel Islands	Encompassing the Bailiwick of Guernsey and the Bailiwick of Jersey
Kosovo	Pristina		
Latvia	Riga		
Libya	Tripoli		
Liechtenstein	Vaduz	Tunisia	Tunis
Lithuania	Vilnius	Turkey	Ankara
Luxembourg	Luxembourg	Ukraine	Kiev
Macedonia	Skopje	United Kingdom	London
Madeira	Funchal	Vatican City	Vatican City

Band B: From 1 April 2015 destinations from bands B, C and D were merged into a single band B			
Country/Territory	Capital City	Country/Territory	Capital City
Afghanistan	Kabul	Kazakhstan	Astana
Armenia	Yerevan	Kuwait	Kuwait City
Azerbaijan	Baku	Kyrgyzstan	Bishkek
Bahrain	Manama	Lebanon	Beirut
Benin	Porto-Novo	Liberia	Monrovia
Bermuda	Hamilton	Mali	Mali
Burkina Faso	Ouagadougou	Mauritania	Nouakchott
Cameroon	Yaounde	Niger	Niamey
Canada	Ottawa	Nigeria	Abuja
Cape Verde	Praia	Oman	Muscat
Central African Republic	Bangui	Pakistan	Islamabad
Chad	N'Djamena	Qatar	Doha
Congo, Democratic Republic of	Kinshasa	Russian Federation (East of the Urals)	
Congo, Republic of	Brazzaville		
Djibouti	Djibouti	Saint Pierre & Miquelon	Saint-Pierre
Egypt	Cairo	Sao Tome and Principe	Sao Tome
Equatorial Guinea	Malabo	Saudi Arabia	Riyadh
Eritrea	Asmara	Senegal	Dakar
Ethiopia	Addis Ababa	Sierra Leone	Freetown
Gabon	Libreville	Republic of South Sudan	Juba
Gambia	Banjul	Sudan	Khartoum
Georgia	Tblisi	Syria	Damascus
Ghana	Accra	Tajikistan	Dushanbe
Guinea	Conakry	Togo	Lome
Guinea-Bissau	Bissau	Turkmenistan	Ashgabat
Iran	Tehran	Uganda	Kampala
Iraq	Baghdad	United Arab Emirates	Abu Dhabi
Israel	Jerusalem	United States	Washington D.C.
Ivory Coast	Yamoussoukro	Uzbekistan	Tashkent
Jordan	Amman	Yemen	Sanaa

Band B (former band C): From 1 April 2015 destinations from bands B, C and D were merged into a single band B			
Country/Territory	Capital City	Country/Territory	Capital City
Angola	Luanda	Lesotho	Maseru
Anguilla	The Valley	Macao SAR	–
Antigua & Barbuda	Saint John's	Madagascar	Antananarivo
Aruba	Oranjestad	Malawi	Lilongwe
Bahamas	Nassau	Maldives	Male
Bangladesh	Dhaka	Martinique	Fort de France
Barbados	Bridgetown	Mauritius	Port Louis
Belize	Belmopan	Mayotte	Mamoudzou
Bhutan	Thimphu	Mexico	Mexico City
Bonaire	Kralendijk	Mongolia	Ulaanbaatar
Botswana	Gabarone	Montserrat	Plymouth
Brazil	Brasilia	Mozambique	Maputo
British Indian Ocean Territories		Namibia	Windhoek
		Nepal	Kathmandu
British Virgin Islands	Road Town	Nicaragua	Managua
Burma	Rangoon	Panama	Panama City
Burundi	Bujumbura	Puerto Rico	San Juan
Cayman Islands	George Town	Reunion	Saint Denis
China	Beijing	Rwanda	Kigali
Colombia	Bogota	Saba	The Bottom
Comoros	Moroni	Saint Barthelemy	Gustavia
Costa Rica	San Jose	Saint Helena, Ascension and Tristan da Cunha	Jamestown
Cuba	Havana	Saint Kitts & Nevis	Basseterre
Curacao	Willemstad	Saint Lucia	Castries
Dominica	Roseau	Saint Martin	Marigot
Dominican Republic	Santo Domingo	Saint Vincent Grenadines	Kingstown
Ecuador	Quito	Seychelles	Victoria
El Salvador	San Salvador	Sint Eustatius	Oranjestad
French Guiana	Cayenne	Sint Maarten	Philipsburg
Grenada	Saint George's	Somalia	Mogadishu
Guadeloupe	Basse Terre	South Africa	Pretoria

Band B (former band C): From 1 April 2015 destinations from bands B, C and D were merged into a single band B			
Country/Territory	Capital City	Country/Territory	Capital City
Guatemala	Guatemala	Sri Lanka	Colombo
Guyana	Georgetown	Suriname	Paramaribo
Haiti	Port-au-Prince	Swaziland	Mbabane
Honduras	Tegucigalpa	Tanzania	Dar es Salaam
Hong Kong SAR	–	Thailand	Bangkok
India	New Delhi	Trinidad & Tobago	Port of Spain
Jamaica	Kingston	Turks & Caicos Islands	Grand Turk
Japan	Tokyo	Venezuela	Caracas
Kenya	Nairobi	Vietnam	Hanoi
Korea, North	Pyongyang	Virgin Islands	Charlotte Amalie
Korea, South	Seoul	Zambia	Lusaka
Laos	Vientiane	Zimbabwe	Harare

VEHICLE EXCISE DUTY

[¶25-000] Rates: general
(VERA 1994, Sch. 1, Pt. I)

VED bands and rates for cars and vans registered before 1 March 2001 (pre-graduated VED)					
Engine size	2017–18 £	2016–17 £	2015–16 £	2014–15 £	2013–14 £
1549cc and below	150	145	145	145	140
Above 1549cc	245	235	230	230	225

[¶25-050] Rates: light passenger vehicles registered on or after 1 April 2017
(VERA 1994, Sch. 1, Pt. 1AA)

VED bands and rates for cars first registered on or after 1 April 2017				
CO_2 emissions (g/km)	2017–18	2018–19[2]		
	First year rate £	Std rate[1] £	First year rate £	First year diesel rate £
0	0	0	0	0
1–50	10	140	10	25
51–75	25	140	25	105
76–90	100	140	105	125
91–100	120	140	125	145
101–110	140	140	145	165
111–130	160	140	165	205
131–150	200	140	205	515
151–170	500	140	515	830
171–190	800	140	830	1,240
191–225	1,200	140	1,240	1,760
226–255	1,700	140	1,760	2,070
Over 255	2,000	140	2,070	2,070

Notes
[1] Cars with a list price of over £40,000 when new pay a supplement of £310 per year on top of the standard rate, for five years (VERA 1994, Sch. 1, para. 1GE).
[2] Rates per Autumn Budget 2017.

Vehicle Excise Duty

[¶25-100] Rates: light passenger vehicles: graduated rates of duty

(VERA 1994, Sch. 1, Pt. IA)

VED bands and rates for cars registered on or after 1 March 2001 but before 1 April 2017 (graduated VED)

VED band	CO₂ emissions (g/km)	2018–19[3] Std rate[1] £	2017–18 Std rate[1] £	2016–17 Std rate[1] £	2016–17 First year rate[1] £	2015–16 Std rate[1] £	2015–16 First year rate[1] £	2014–15 Std rate[1] £	2014–15 First year rate[1] £
A	Up to 100	0	0	0	0	0	0	0	0
B	101–110	20	20	20	0	20	0	20	0
C	111–120	30	30	30	0	30	0	30	0
D	121–130	120	115	110	0	110	0	110	0
E	131–140	140	135	130	130	130	130	130	130
F	141–150	155	150	145	145	145	145	145	145
G	151–165	195	190	185	185	180	180	180	180
H	166–175	230	220	210	300	205	295	205	290
I	176–185	250	240	230	355	225	350	225	345
J	186–200	290	280	270	500	265	490	265	485
K[2]	201–225	315	305	295	650	290	640	285	635
L	226–255	540	520	500	885	490	870	485	860
M	Over 255	555	535	515	1,120	505	1,100	500	1,090

Notes
(1) Alternative fuel discount 2010–11 onwards: £10 for all cars.
(2) Includes cars emitting over 225g/km registered before 23 March 2006.
(3) Rates per Autumn Budget 2017.

[¶25-200] Rates: light goods vehicles

(VERA 1994, Sch. 1, Pt. IB)

VED bands and rates for vans registered on or after 1 March 2001

Vehicle registration date	2018–19[1] £	2017–18 £	2016–17 £	2015–16 £	2014–15 £
Early Euro 4 and Euro 5 compliant vans	140	140	140	140	140
All other vans	250	240	230	225	225

Note
(1) Rates per Autumn Budget 2017.

[¶25-300] Rates: motorcycles
(VERA 1994, Sch. 1, Pt. II)

VED bands and rates for motorcycles					
Engine size	2018–19[1] £	2017–18 £	2016–17 £	2015–16 £	2014–15 £
Not over 150cc	19	18	17	17	17
151cc and 400cc	42	41	39	38	38
401cc to 600c	64	62	60	59	58
Over 600cc	88	85	82	81	80

VED bands and rates for motor tricycles					
Engine size	2018–19[1] £	2017–18 £	2016–17 £	2015–16 £	2014–15 £
Not over 150cc	19	18	17	17	17
All other tricycles	88	85	82	81	80

Note
[1] Rates per Autumn Budget 2017.

[¶25-400] Rates: trade licences
(VERA 1994, s. 13)

VED bands and rates for trade licences					
Vehicle type	2018–19[1] £	2017–18 £	2016–17 £	2015–16 £	2014–15 £
Available for all vehicles	165	165	165	165	165
Available only for bicycles and tricycles (weighing no more than 450kg without a sidecar)	88	85	82	81	80

Note
[1] Rates per Autumn Budget 2017.

[¶25-500] Rates: haulage and goods vehicles
(VERA 1994, Sch. 1, Pt. VII and VIII)

From 2014–15[1]						
VED and levy bands and rates for articulated vehicles and rigid vehicles without trailers						
VED band (letter) and rate (number)	Total VED and levy		VED rates		Levy rates	
	12 months	6 months	12 months	6 months	Levy bands	12 months	6 months
	£	£	£	£	£	£	£
A0	165.00	90.75	165.00	90.75	n/a	0	0
B0	200.00	110.00	200.00	110.00			

VED band (letter) and rate (number)	Total VED and levy		VED rates		Levy rates		
	12 months	6 months	12 months	6 months	Levy bands	12 months	6 months
	£	£	£	£	£	£	£
A1	165.00	91.00	80.00	40.00	A	85	51
A2	169.00	93.00	84.00	42.00			
A3	185.00	101.00	100.00	50.00			
A4	231.00	124.00	146.00	73.00			
A5	236.00	126.50	151.00	75.50			
B1	200.00	110.50	95.00	47.50	B	105	63
B2	210.00	115.50	105.00	52.50			
B3	230.00	125.50	125.00	62.50			
C1	450.00	249.00	210.00	105.00	C	240	144
C2	505.00	276.50	265.00	132.50			
C3	529.00	288.50	289.00	144.50			
D1	650.00	360.00	300.00	150.00	D	350	210
E1	1,200.00	664.00	560.00	280.00	E	640	384
E2	1,249.00	688.50	609.00	304.50			
F	1,500.00	831.00	690.00	345.00	F	810	486
G	1,850.00	1,025.00	850.00	425.00	G	1000	600

Note
[1] Rates from April 2018 will remain unchanged (continuing the freeze that has been in place since 1 April 2015) (Autumn Budget 2017).

From 2014–15[1]

VED and levy amounts payable for rigid vehicles with trailers (vehicles WITH Road Friendly Suspension)

HGV axles	Levy band	Trailer weight category	Total weight of HGV and trailer, not over	VED band (letter) and rate (number)	VED rates		Levy rates	
					12 months	6 months	12 months	6 months
					£	£	£	£
Two	B(T)	4,001–12,000kg	27,000kg	B(T)1	230.00	115.00	135	81
		Over 12,000kg	33,000kg	B(T)3	295.00	147.50		
			36,000kg	B(T)6	401.00	200.50		
			38,000kg	B(T)4	319.00	159.50		
			—	B(T)7	444.00	222.00		
	D(T)	4,001–12,000kg	30,000kg	D(T)1	365.00	182.50	450	270
		Over 12,000kg	38,000kg	D(T)4	430.00	215.00		
			—	D(T)5	444.00	222.00		
Three	B(T)	4,001–12,000kg	33,000kg	B(T)1	230.00	115.00	135	81
		Over 12,000kg	38,000kg	B(T)3	295.00	147.50		
			40,000kg	B(T)5	392.00	196.00		
			—	B(T)3	295.00	147.50		

HGV axles	Levy band	Trailer weight category	Total weight of HGV and trailer, not over	VED band (letter) and rate (number)	VED rates 12 months £	VED rates 6 months £	Levy rates 12 months £	Levy rates 6 months £
	C(T)	4,001–12,000kg	35,000kg	C(T)1	305.00	152.50	310	186
		Over 12,000kg	38,000kg	C(T)2	370.00	185.00		
			40,000kg	C(T)3	392.00	196.00		
			–	C(T)2	370.00	185.00		
	D(T)	4,001–10,000kg	33,000kg	D(T)1	365.00	182.50	450	270
			36,000kg	D(T)3	401.00	200.50		
		10,001–12,000kg	38,000kg	D(T)1	365.00	182.50		
		Over 12,000kg	–	D(T)4	430.00	215.00		
Four	B(T)	4,001–12,000kg	35,000kg	B(T)1	230.00	115.00	135	81
		Over 12,000kg	–	B(T)3	295.00	147.50		
	C(T)	4,001–12,000kg	37,000kg	C(T)1	305.00	152.50	310	186
		Over 12,000kg	–	C(T)2	370.00	185.00		
	D(T)	4,001–12,000kg	39,000kg	D(T)1	365.00	182.50	450	270
		Over 12,000kg	–	D(T)4	430.00	215.00		
	E(T)	4,001–12,000kg	44,000kg	E(T)1	535.00	267.50	830	498
		Over 12,000kg	–	E(T)2	600.00	300.00		

Note
(1) Rates from April 2018 will remain unchanged (continuing the freeze that has been in place since 1 April 2015) (Autumn Budget 2017).

From 2014–15[1]

VED and levy amounts payable for rigid vehicles with trailers (vehicles WITHOUT Road Friendly Suspension)

HGV axles	Levy band	Trailer weight category	Total weight of HGV and trailer, not over	VED band (letter) and rate (number)	VED rates 12 months £	VED rates 6 months £	Levy rates 12 months £	Levy rates 6 months £
Two	B(T)	4,001–12,000kg	27,000kg	B(T)1	230.00	115.00	135	81
		Over 12,000kg	31,000kg	B(T)3	295.00	147.50		
			33,000kg	B(T)6	401.00	200.50		
			36,000kg	B(T)10	609.00	304.50		
			38,000kg	B(T)7	444.00	222.00		
			–	B(T)9	604.00	302.00		
	D(T)	4,001–12,000kg	30,000kg	D(T)1	365.00	182.50	450	270
		Over 12,000kg	33,000kg	D(T)4	430.00	215.00		
			36,000kg	D(T)8	609.00	304.50		
			38,000kg	D(T)5	444.00	222.00		
			–	D(T)7	604.00	302.00		

HGV axles	Levy band	Trailer weight category	Total weight of HGV and trailer, not over	VED band (letter) and rate (number)	VED rates 12 months £	VED rates 6 months £	Levy rates 12 months £	Levy rates 6 months £
Three	B(T)	4,001–10,000kg	29,000kg	B(T)1	230.00	115.00	135	81
			31,000kg	B(T)2	289.00	144.50		
		10,001–12,000kg	33,000kg	B(T)1	230.00	115.00		
		Over 12,000kg	36,000kg	B(T)3	295.00	147.50		
			38,000kg	B(T)5	392.00	196.00		
			–	B(T)8	542.00	271.00		
	C(T)	4,001–10,000kg	31,000kg	C(T)1	305.00	152.50	310	186
			33,000kg	C(T)4	401.00	200.50		
		10,001–12,000kg	35,000kg	C(T)1	305.00	152.50		
		Over 12,000kg	36,000kg	C(T)2	370.00	185.00		
			38,000kg	C(T)3	392.00	196.00		
			–	C(T)5	542.00	271.00		
	D(T)	4,001–10,000kg	31,000kg	D(T)1	365.00	182.50	450	270
			33,000kg	D(T)3	401.00	200.50		
			35,000kg	D(T)8	609.00	304.50		
		10,001–12,000kg	36,000kg	D(T)1	365.00	182.50		
			37,000kg	D(T)2	392.00	196.00		
		Over 12,000kg	38,000kg	D(T)4	430.00	215.00		
			–	D(T)6	542.00	271.00		
Four	B(T)	4,001–12,000kg	35,000kg	B(T)1	230.00	115.00	135	81
		Over 12,000kg	–	B(T)3	295.00	147.50		
	C(T)	4,001–12,000kg	37,000kg	C(T)1	305.00	152.50	310	186
		Over 12,000kg	–	C(T)2	370.00	185.00		
	D(T)	4,001–10,000kg	36,000kg	D(T)1	365.00	182.50	450	270
			37,000kg	D(T)5	444.00	222.00		
		10,001–12,000kg	39,000kg	D(T)1	365.00	182.50		
		Over 12,000kg	–	D(T)4	430.00	215.00		
	E(T)	4,001–10,000kg	38,000kg	E(T)1	535.00	267.50	830	498
			–	E(T)3	604.00	302.00		
		10,001–12,000kg	–	E(T)1	535.00	267.50		

Note
[1] Rates from April 2018 will remain unchanged (continuing the freeze that has been in place since 1 April 2015) (Autumn Budget 2017).

From 2014–15[1]				
Rigid goods vehicle – WITHOUT trailer				
Revenue weight of vehicle, kg		**2 axles**	**3 axles**	**4 or more axles**
Over	Not over			
3,500	7,500	A0	A0	A0
7,500	11,999	B0	B0	B0
11,999	14,000	B1	B1	B1
14,000	15,000	B2		
15,000	19,000	D1		
19,000	21,000		B3	
21,000	23,000		C1	
23,000	25,000		D1	C1
25,000	27,000			D1
27,000	44,000			E1

Note
[1] Rates from April 2018 will remain unchanged (continuing the freeze that has been in place since 1 April 2015) (Autumn Budget 2017).

From 2014–15[1]				
Rigid vehicles – WITH trailer				
Weight of rigid (not trailer), kg		**Two-axled rigid**	**Three-axled rigid**	**Four-axled rigid**
Over	Not over			
11,999	15,000	B(T)	B(T)	B(T)
15,000	21,000	D(T)		
21,000	23,000	E(T)	C(T)	
23,000	25,000		D(T)	C(T)
25,000	27,000			D(T)
27,000	44,000		E(T)	E(T)

Note
[1] Rates from April 2018 will remain unchanged (continuing the freeze that has been in place since 1 April 2015) (Autumn Budget 2017).

Vehicle Excise Duty

From 2014–15[1]

Articulated vehicles – tractive unit with three or more axles

Revenue weight of vehicle, kg		One or more semi-trailer axles	Two or more semi-trailer axles	Three or more semi-trailer axles
Over	Not over			
3,500	11,999	A0	A0	A0
11,999	25,000	A1	A1	A1
25,000	26,000	A3		
26,000	28,000	A4		
28,000	29,000	C1		
29,000	31,000	C3		
31,000	33,000	E1	C1	
33,000	34,000	E2	D1	
34,000	36,000			C1
36,000	38,000	F	E1	D1
38,000	44,000	G	G	E1

Note
[1] Rates from April 2018 will remain unchanged (continuing the freeze that has been in place since 1 April 2015) (Autumn Budget 2017).

From 2014–15[1]

Articulated vehicles – tractive unit with two axles

Revenue weight of vehicle, kg		One or more semi-trailer axles	Two or more semi-trailer axles	Three or more semi-trailer axles
Over	Not over			
3,500	11,999	A0	A0	A0
11,999	22,000	A1	A1	A1
22,000	23,000	A2		
23,000	25,000	A5		
25,000	26,000	C2	A3	
26,000	28,000		A4	
28,000	31,000	D1	D1	
31,000	33,000	E1	E1	C1
33,000	34,000		E2	
34,000	38,000	F	F	E1
38,000	44,000	G	G	G

Note
[1] Rates from April 2018 will remain unchanged (continuing the freeze that has been in place since 1 April 2015) (Autumn Budget 2017).

SCOTTISH TAXES

[¶26-000]   Scottish taxes

(*Scotland Act* 1998; *Scotland Act* 2012)

(Tax Reporter: ¶102-930)

The establishment of the Scottish Parliament and the Scottish Government was provided for in the *Scotland Act* 1998 (as amended by the *Scotland Act* 2012). The Scottish Parliament was officially convened on 1 July 1999.

The *Scotland Act* 1998 does not specify which matters are devolved to the Scottish Parliament, rather it specifies those matters that are reserved to the UK Parliament and those matters not reserved are devolved to the Scottish Parliament. Schedule 5 to the Act (as amended) sets out those matters which are reserved to the UK Parliament and all other issues are deemed to be devolved. The Scottish Parliament has primary legislative powers, i.e. the power to pass Acts.

The *Scotland Act* 2012 amended the *Scotland Act* 1998 to introduce a new power to set a Sottish rate of income tax, which took effect from 2016–17 (see below) and to fully devolve the power to raise taxes on land transactions and on waste disposal to landfill which took effect from 1 April 2015 and since then, the existing stamp duty land tax and landfill tax do not apply in Scotland. The Act also provides powers for new taxes to be created in Scotland and for additional taxes to be devolved.

Further devolution

The *Scotland Act* 2016 received Royal Assent on 23 March 2016 and is an enabling Act setting out further powers that are being transferred to the Scottish Parliament and or the Scottish Ministers. In particular, the Act provides the structure within which the Scottish Parliament may legislate to set the rates of income tax and the limits at which these are paid for the non-savings and non-dividend income of Scottish taxpayers, replacing the power of the Scottish Parliament to set, by resolution, a single Scottish rate of income tax, enabling it to instead set a basic rate and any other rates of income tax; makes provision for Scotland to control the first ten percentage points of the standard rate of VAT receipts and first two and a half percentage points of the reduced rate of VAT receipts; and provides that air passenger duty and aggregates levy will be fully devolved taxes.

Administration of devolved taxes

The devolved taxes are collected by Revenue Scotland, Scotland's new tax authority which started accepting returns and collecting taxes from 1 April 2015. Revenue Scotland was established by the *Revenue Scotland and Tax Powers Act* 2014 which received Royal Assent on 24 September 2014 and came into force on 1 April 2015 (to the extent not already in force). The RSTPA 2014:

*   establishes Revenue Scotland and provides for its general functions and responsibilities (Pt. 2);

*   makes provision about the use and protection of taxpayer and other information (Pt. 3);

*   establishes the Scottish Tax Tribunals (the First-tier Tribunal for Scotland and the Upper Tribunal for Scotland) to exercise functions in relation to devolved taxes (Pt. 4);

- puts in place a general anti-avoidance rule (Pt. 5);
- contains provisions on the self-assessment system, the checking of tax returns by Revenue Scotland and claims for repayment of tax (Pt. 6);
- makes provision for Revenue Scotland's investigatory powers (Pt. 7);
- sets out the matters in relation to which penalties may be imposed (Pt. 8);
- makes provision about the interest payable on unpaid tax, on penalties and on tax repayments (Pt. 9);
- contains provisions on debt enforcement by Revenue Scotland (Pt. 10); and
- sets out the system for the review, mediation and appeal of Revenue Scotland decisions (Pt. 11).

Scottish Tribunals

The *Tribunals (Scotland) Act* 2014, which received Royal Assent on 15 April 2014 (and came into force on 1 April 2015 (so far as not already in force)), established the First-tier Tribunal for Scotland and the Upper Tribunal for Scotland. However, functions in relation to devolved taxes were initially exercised by the Scottish Tax Tribunals, as established under the RSTPA 2014, which were constituted on 1 April 2015. Functions of the First-tier Tax Tribunal and Upper Tax Tribunal for Scotland were subsequently transferred to the First-tier Tribunal for Scotland and Upper Tribunal for Scotland from 24 April 2017 and the earlier tax tribunals were abolished from the same date.

Opinions

In order to allow taxpayers to file with certainty, Revenue Scotland will, in certain circumstances, provide its opinion on the tax consequences of specific transactions.

Applications should be sent to:

Revenue Scotland Opinions

PO Box 24068

Victoria Quay

Edinburgh

EH6 9BR

For further information, see www.revenue.scot/help/revenue-scotland-opinions.

[¶26-100]   Scottish income tax

(*Scotland Act* 1998; ITA 2007, s. 6A and 11A)

(Tax Reporter: ¶148-160)

Scottish income tax: 2017–18

Scottish rates	Rate[1] %	Taxable income band[1] £	Tax on band £
Scottish basic rate	20	1–31,500	6,300
Scottish higher rate	40	31,501–150,000	47,400
Scottish additional rate	45	Over 150,000	

Note
[1] On 21 February 2017, the Scottish Parliament voted to freeze the basic rate of income tax of 20%, also freeze the higher and additional rates at 40% and 45% respectively, and maintain the higher rate of income tax threshold at £43,000 in 2017–18.

Scottish income tax: 2016–17

UK rate for England, Wales and Northern Ireland	Taxable income band £	UK rate paid in Scotland %	Scottish rate[1] %	Total rate for Scottish taxpayers %
Basic rate 20%	1–32,000	10	10	20
Higher rate 40%	32,001–150,000	30	10	40
Additional rate 45%	Over £150,000	35	10	45

Note
[1] Rate agreed by the Scottish Parliament on 11 February 2016.

Under the *Scotland Act* 2016 provisions, where the Scottish Parliament sets more than one rate of income tax, it must, by resolution, set out the limits at which those rates apply or make provision to determine which rates apply in relation to a Scottish taxpayer, however, a Scottish rate resolution may not provide for different rates to apply in relation to different types of income.

The Scottish basic, higher and additional rates of income tax will only apply to non-savings, non-dividend income of those defined as 'Scottish taxpayers' (ITA 2007, s. 11A, 13).

A 'Scottish taxpayer' is defined as an individual who in any tax year is treated as resident in the UK for income tax purposes for that year and who either:

• has a close connection with Scotland;

• does not have a close connection with England, Wales or Northern Ireland, and spends more days of that year in Scotland than in any other part of the UK; or

• is a member of Parliament for a constituency in Scotland, a member of the European Parliament for Scotland, or a member of the Scottish Parliament.

A close connection is defined by reference to where the individual has their only or main residence. If an individual has one residence and it is in Scotland, they are a Scottish taxpayer. Where an individual has more than one residence, they will need to determine which has been their main residence for the longest period in the tax year and if this is in Scotland, they are a Scottish taxpayer. Individuals who cannot identify a main place of residence will need to count the days spent in Scotland and elsewhere in the UK and if they spend more days in Scotland, they are a Scottish taxpayer. Scottish taxpayer status applies for a whole year and split year treatment is not available (it is not possible to be a Scottish taxpayer for part of a tax year). HMRC's detailed technical guidance on who, from 6 April 2016, will be a Scottish taxpayer is available at www.gov.uk/government/publications/scottish-taxpayer-technical-guidance.

Administration

Scottish income tax is administered by HMRC as part of the UK income tax system.

For employees and pensioners, the income tax change will be applied through PAYE. Scottish taxpayers have an 'S' prefix to their PAYE tax code.

Scottish Taxes

DEVOLVED TAXES

Land and Buildings Transaction Tax (LBTT)

[¶26-200]   LBTT rates from 1 April 2015

(*Land and Buildings Transaction Tax (Scotland) Act* 2013; SSI 2015/126)

(SLDT Reporter: ¶200-000ff.)

Scottish LBTT applies to transactions consisting of or including interests in land situated in Scotland from 1 April 2015, replacing stamp duty land tax which no longer applies in Scotland. The Scottish LBTT has a progressive rate structure, which means that the rates shown in the table below are marginal rates, payable on the portion of the total value which falls within each band. Tax bands and percentage tax rates are set by order of the Scottish Ministers.

Residential transactions		Non-residential transactions		Non-residential leases	
	Rate %		Rate %		Rate %
Up to £145,000	nil	Up to £150,000	nil	Up to £150,000	nil
£145,001 to £250,000	2.0	£150,001 to £350,000	3.0	Over £150,000	1.0
£250,001 to £325,000	5.0	Over £350,000	4.5		
£325,001 to £750,000	10.0				
Over £750,000	12.0				

Note
A 3% supplement is charged on additional residential properties such as buy to let or second homes where the relevant consideration exceeds £40,000 (LBTTSA 2013, Sch. 2A).

Scottish Landfill Tax

[¶26-300]   SLT rates from 1 April 2015

(*Landfill Tax (Scotland) Act* 2014; SSI 2016/93 and SSI 2016/94)

Rates are specified by order of the Scottish Ministers.

	Standard rate (per tonne) £	Lower rate (per tonne) £	Scottish Landfill Communities Fund Credit rate %
From 1 April 2016	84.40	2.65	5.6
From 1 April 2015	82.60	2.60	5.6

SCOTTISH LAW

[¶26-500] Succession Scotland

Prior rights of surviving spouse, on intestacy, in dwelling house and furniture

(*Succession (Scotland) Act* 1964, s. 8–9; SSI 2011/436)

Prior rights apply where the deceased dies intestate leaving a spouse or civil partner. The surviving spouse or civil partner takes as follows:

Period	House £	Furniture £	Cash (children survive) £	Cash (no children) £
From 1/2/2012	473,000	29,000	50,000	89,000
1/6/2005–31/1/2012	300,000	24,000	42,000	75,000
1/4/1999–31/5/2005	130,000	22,000	35,000	58,000

Legal rights

(HMRC manuals: IHTM12221)

Legal rights vest in beneficiaries by force of law and apply whether the deceased dies testate or intestate. Accordingly, rights by any provision in the deceased's will or rules of intestacy can only take effect once legal rights have been met. Prior rights may reduce or extinguish the estate that would otherwise be available to settle legal rights. Legal rights apply to the deceased's moveable estate only (which includes money, shares, cars, furniture, jewellery but excludes heritable property (land and buildings)).

Surviving family	Right of surviving spouse or civil partner	Right of children	Deceased's part[1]
Spouse or civil partner and children	One-third	One-third	One-third
Spouse or civil partner but no children	One-half	N/A	One-half
Children but no spouse or civil partner	N/A	One-half	One-half
Neither spouse, civil partner or children	N/A	N/A	Whole moveable estate

Note
[1] The balance of the estate is the part which the deceased was free to dispose of by will, or which passes under the rules of intestacy.

Distributions under intestacy

(*Succession (Scotland) Act* 1964, s. 2)

After prior and legal rights have been satisfied, the remainder of the estate, both heritable and moveable devolves in the following order:

Surviving family	Beneficiaries take:
Children	Whole estate
Parents and brothers/sisters Either of, or both, parents and also by brothers or sisters, but not by any prior relative	Surviving parent(s) take half; Surviving brothers and sisters take half
Brother and sisters Brothers or sisters, but not any prior relative	Surviving brothers and sisters take whole estate
Parents Either of, or both, parents, but not survived by any prior relative	Surviving parent(s) take whole estate
Spouse Husband or a wife, but not any prior relative	Spouse takes whole estate
Uncles or aunts Uncles or aunts (being brothers or sisters of either parent of the intestate), but not any prior relative	Surviving uncles and aunts take whole estate
Grandparents A grandparent or grandparents (being a parent or parents of either parent of the intestate), but not any prior relative	Surviving grandparent(s) take whole estate
Great uncles or aunts Brothers or sisters of any of his grandparents (being a parent or parents of either parent of the intestate), but not by any prior relative	Surviving brothers and sisters (or grandparents) take whole estate
Other ancestors Where not survived by any prior relative, the ancestors of the intestate (being remoter than grandparents) generation by generation successively, without distinction between the paternal and maternal lines, shall have right to the whole of the intestate estate; so however that, failing ancestors of any generation, the brothers and sisters of any of those ancestors shall have right thereto before ancestors of the next more remote generation.	

WELSH TAXES

[¶27-000] Welsh taxes

(GoWA 2006, Pt. 4A; WA 2014, Pt. 2)

(Tax Reporter: ¶102-950)

The *Government of Wales Act* 1998 provided for the establishment of the National Assembly for Wales and for the transfer of all the powers of the Secretary of State for Wales to the new Assembly. The Assembly was established in 1999.

The *Government of Wales Act* (GoWA) 2006 led to the creation of a separate legislature (the National Assembly for Wales) and executive (the Welsh Government). The Assembly's enhanced legislative competence is set out in GoWA 2006, Sch. 7, Pt. 4 collectively known as the 'Assembly Act provisions'. These provisions enable the Assembly to legislate in relation to the subjects listed under the 20 headings in Sch. 7, as qualified by the exceptions and restrictions in that Schedule and in GoWA, s. 108.

The *Wales Act* 2014, which received Royal Assent on 19 December 2014, makes provision about the devolution of taxation powers to the Assembly and, in particular, makes provision about:

*   elections to and membership of the National Assembly for Wales;
*   the Welsh Assembly Government;
*   the setting by the Assembly of rates of income tax to be paid by Welsh taxpayer; and
*   borrowing by the Welsh Ministers.

The *Wales Act* 2017 received Royal Assent on 31 January 2017 and is an enabling Act with the majority of provisions setting out the powers that are being transferred to the National Assembly for Wales and or the Welsh Ministers. In particular, the Act:

*   amends the *Government of Wales Act* 2006 by moving to a reserved powers model for Wales (the same model as underpins the devolution settlement in Scotland);
*   includes a declaration that the Assembly and the Welsh Ministers are considered permanent parts of the UK's constitutional arrangements and will not be abolished without a decision of the people of Wales, and that the UK Parliament will not normally legislate in devolved areas without the consent of the Assembly, whilst retaining sovereignty to do so.
*   devolves further powers to the Assembly and in areas where there was a political consensus in support of devolution, including greater responsibility to run its own affairs (including deciding its name), responsibility for ports policy, speed limits, bus registration, taxi regulation, local government elections, sewerage and energy consenting (up to 350MW), marine licensing and conservation and energy consents in the Welsh offshore region, building regulations (including excepted energy building), power over all elements of Assembly elections and powers of the licensing of onshore oil and gas extraction.

The *Land Transaction Tax and Anti-avoidance of Devolved Taxes (Wales) Act* 2017 received Royal Assent on 24 May 2017 and makes provision about the taxation of land transactions in Wales, amends the *Tax Collection and Management (Wales) Act* 2016 and makes provision about counteracting avoidance of devolved taxes. From April 2018, land transaction tax (LTT) will replace UK stamp duty land tax (SDLT) in Wales.

Administration of devolved taxes

On 25 April 2016, the *Tax Collection and Management (Wales) Act* 2016 received Royal Assent. The purpose of this Act is to put in place the legal framework necessary for the future collection and management of devolved taxes in Wales. In particular, the Act:

- establishes the Welsh Revenue Authority and makes provision about its organisation and main functions (which will be the collection and management of devolved taxes) (Pt. 2);
- makes provision about the assessment of devolved taxes (Pt. 3);
- makes provision about the Welsh Revenue Authority's investigatory powers, including provision about notices requiring information and the inspection of premises (Pt. 4);
- makes provision for and in connection with the imposition of penalties in relation to devolved taxes (Pt. 5);
- makes provision for interest to be payable on late payments to the Welsh Revenue Authority and on repayments by the Welsh Revenue Authority (Pt. 6);
- makes provision about payments to the Welsh Revenue Authority and the recovery of unpaid amounts (Pt. 7);
- makes provision for and in connection with reviews of and appeals against decisions of the Welsh Revenue Authority (Pt. 8);
- confers powers to make subordinate legislation about the investigation of criminal offences relating to devolved taxes (Pt. 9);
- contains provision that applies generally for the purposes of the Act (Pt. 10).

[¶27-100]   Welsh rates of income tax

(WA 2014, s. 8–10; ITA 2007, s. 6B, 11B)

(Tax Reporter: ¶148-165)

The *Wales Act* 2014, which received Royal Assent on 17 December 2014, legislates for new Welsh rates of income tax by conferring on the Assembly a power to set, by resolution, a Welsh basic, higher and additional rate of income tax, for 'Welsh taxpayers'.

The Welsh basic rate, the Welsh higher rate and the Welsh additional rate for a tax year will be calculated under ITA 2007, s. 6B, as follows:

Step 1:

Take the basic rate, higher rate or additional rate.

Step 2:

Deduct ten percentage points.

Step 3:

Add the Welsh rate (if any) set by the National Assembly for Wales for that year for the purpose of calculating the Welsh basic rate, the Welsh higher rate or the Welsh additional rate (as the case may be).

The Welsh tax rates will only apply to non-saving, non-dividend income and applies for one tax year only, for the whole of that year.

A Welsh taxpayer is defined as an individual who is UK resident for income tax purposes for the tax year and who either:

- has a close connection with Wales;
- does not have a close connection with England, Scotland or Northern Ireland, and spends more days of that year in Wales than in any other part of the UK; or
- for the whole or any part of the year, is a member of Parliament for a constituency in Wales, a member of the European Parliament for Wales, or an Assembly member.

(GoWA 2006, s. 116E, as inserted by WA 2014, s. 8)

As with Scotland, the overall administration of Welsh income tax will remain with HMRC.

Welsh Taxes

NORTHERN IRISH TAXES

[¶28-000]   Northern Irish taxes

(*Northern Ireland Act* 1998)

(Tax Reporter: ¶102-910)

The Agreement reached on Good Friday 1998, often referred to as the Belfast or Good Friday Agreement, and the subsequent *Northern Ireland Act* 1998 (as amended a number of times since 1998, particularly following the 2006 St Andrews Agreement) continue to form the basis of the constitutional structure in Northern Ireland with the devolved institutions in Northern Ireland being constituted under the *Northern Ireland Act* 1998.

The Northern Ireland devolution settlement gives legislative control over certain matters (known as 'transferred matters') to the Northern Ireland Assembly. In the main, these are in the economic and social field. The NI Assembly may also, in principle, legislate in respect of 'reserved' category matters subject to various consents, but has not yet done so to any significant degree.

Matters of national importance which, in the normal course of events, it is expected will remain the responsibility of HM Government and Westminster, are known as 'excepted matters', and the NI Assembly does not have competence to legislate on these. The *Northern Ireland Act* 1998, Sch. 2 sets out these areas.

Many UK-wide issues such as broadcasting and genetic research are known as 'reserved matters'. The *Northern Ireland Act* 1998, Sch. 3 sets out which matters fall into the 'reserved' category.

Anything that is not explicitly reserved or excepted in Sch. 2 or 3 is deemed to be devolved and the Assembly has full legislative competence. It does not require consent from Westminster or HM Government to legislate.

Further details on devolution, including a full list of transferred, excepted and reserved matters can be found at www.gov.uk/devolution-settlement-northern-ireland.

[¶28-100]   Northern Irish corporation tax

(*Corporation Tax (Northern Ireland) Act* 2015)

On 26 March 2015, the *Corporation Tax (Northern Ireland) Act* 2015 received Royal Assent. The Act makes provision for devolution of tax powers to the NI Assembly which should allow Northern Ireland to set its own rate of corporation tax for certain trading profits only from April 2017.

The Northern Ireland Assembly has the power to set the rate (including a nil rate) for one or more future financial years by way of a resolution. Corporation tax will then be charged at the Northern Ireland rate on Northern Ireland profits as distinct from mainstream profits. Once set, the Northern Ireland Assembly may cancel that rate by resolution, which will have effect provided the cancelling resolution is passed before the beginning of the financial year to which the rate applies. If a rate is not set by resolution for a financial year, the rate for that year will be the rate set for the previous financial year. Until the Northern Ireland

Assembly exercises the power to set a rate for the first time, the Northern Ireland rate will be the UK main rate.

The rate, in general, will apply to all of the trading profits of a company if that company is a micro, small or medium-sized enterprise (SME), and the company's employee time and costs fall largely in Northern Ireland. It will also apply to a corporate partner's share of the profits of a partnership trade if that company and partnership are both SMEs and the partnership's employee time and costs fall largely in Northern Ireland. The rate will also apply to the profits of large companies, and (in the case of a corporate partner not covered by the SME rules referred to above) to a corporate partner's share of the profits of a partnership that are attributable to a Northern Ireland trading presence, that presence being termed as a 'Northern Ireland regional establishment' (NIRE).

HMRC's draft guidance on the operation of the Northern Ireland corporation tax legislation is available at www.gov.uk/government/uploads/system/uploads/attachment_data/file/554921/160922_Draft_guidance_Northern_Ireland_rate_of_Corporation_Tax.pdf.

Rate from 2018

The Northern Ireland Executive has committed to setting a rate of 12.5% in April 2018.

INDEX

References are to paragraph numbers.

Index

Index

336

Index

Index

Index

Index

Index